VBSCRIPT

IN A NUTSHELL

VBSCRIPT

IN A NUTSHELL

Second Edition

Paul Lomax, Matt Childs, and Ron Petrusha

Beijing • Cambridge • Farnham • Köln • Sebastopol • Tokyo

VBScript in a Nutshell, Second Edition

by Paul Lomax, Matt Childs, and Ron Petrusha

Published by O'Reilly Media, Inc., 1005 Gravenstein Highway North, Sebastopol, CA 95472.

O'Reilly Media, Inc. books may be purchased for educational, business, or sales promotional use. Online editions are also available for most titles (*safari.oreilly.com*). For more information, contact our corporate/institutional sales department: 800-998-9938 or *corporate@oreilly.com*.

Editor:	Ron Petrusha
Production Editor:	Mary Brady
Cover Designer:	Ellie Volckhausen
Interior Designer:	Bret Kerr

Printing History:

May 2000:	First Edition.
March 2003:	Second Edition.

ISBN: 978-0-596-00488-0
[LSI]   [2010-09-30]

Table of Contents

Part II. Reference

Part III. Appendixes

Foreword

The evolution of VBScript has been an interesting and somewhat unpredictable ride for everyone involved, from the product team here at Microsoft to, more importantly, the VBScript scripting community. We started VBScript back in 1994 as a lightweight scripting language that could be integrated into a set of technologies then known as Sweeper, which eventually saw the light of day as Internet Explorer 3. The intent was to provide a small, fast, and safe subset of Visual Basic that would allow for scripting of HTML and ActiveX Controls (actually they were still OLE Controls back then) in HTML pages. Since this seemed like a pretty simple task, a couple of developers set out on a Friday evening to implement it over a weekend, and sure enough, on Monday there was a working version of the language, albeit a very small subset of the language. We spent the next six months polishing the rough edges, resulting in the release of VBScript 1.0 with Internet Explorer 3.0. VBScript then was a pretty good language, including many of the features of VB—many more than were first imagined in that first weekend.

The plan for VBScript was always to let the language grow to make it usable to develop not just client-side web browser code, but also to script server-side pages. VBScript 2.0 was shipped with the first release of Active Server Pages just eight months after the release of Version 1.0—ah, the halcyon days of Internet time. Active Server Pages proved to be wildly successful, and VBScript usage and interest skyrocketed. The next big step for VBScript was the introduction of Windows Script Host, which added administrative capabilities to the VBScripter's toolkit. This proved to be very successful, since it finally provided a modern alternative to batch files that could take advantage of the rich COM components available in Windows.

The success of VBScript led to requests to expand the language to meet the expanded expectations of VBScript programmers. Some of the key design tenets for VBScript were to keep it small, simple to understand, flexible to grow with the programmer, and, most of all, fun to use. The last releases of VBScript Versions 5, 5.5 and 5.6 saw major additions to the language, including the long sought after with block, classes, function references for better Internet Explorer integration, and regular expressions. VBScript is now a much more capable and powerful language than we ever imagined it would be, and having a reference guide to all the language features becomes even more important. VBScript in a Nutshell is a great reference to the language, and I hope it makes your scripting even more enjoyable and productive.

Script Happens.

—Andrew Clinick

Preface

Visual Basic Scripting Edition, or VBScript, as it's commonly called, began its life amid a certain amount of fanfare as a client-side scripting language for web browsers. Its appeal was that it was a subset of *Visual Basic for Applications* (VBA), the most widely used programming language in the world, and hence promised to make Internet programming easy not only for the huge installed base of VB/VBA programmers, but also for new programmers.

But for the most part, VBScript failed to deliver on its promise as a client-side scripting language. The problem wasn't the language or its capabilities; rather, VBScript suffered because it was the second language to arrive in the arena of client-side scripting and was never able to supplant its rival, JavaScript. In fact, Netscape Navigator, the browser with the largest market share at the time, completely failed to support VBScript, leaving it a language that could be used exclusively for client-side scripting on corporate intranets (or for content providers on the public Internet who didn't care that their content was incompatible with most browsers).

But while VBScript's success as a client-side scripting language has been marginal, it has become one of the three major scripting languages (along with JavaScript and Perl) in use today. With the release of Internet Information Server (IIS) 2.0 in 1997, VBScript rapidly became the primary scripting language used in developing Active Server Pages (ASP), Microsoft's server-side scripting technology for IIS. Also in 1997, Microsoft released the first version of Outlook, which was programmable and customizable only by using VBScript. Finally, in 1998, Microsoft released the first version of Windows Script Host (WSH), the long awaited "batch language" for Windows. Here again, VBScript rapidly emerged as the predominant choice for writing WSH scripts.

Why This Book?

The major source of documentation for VBScript is the Visual Basic Scripting HTML Help file, the official documentation that is included with VBScript itself.

While VBScript's online help is an indispensable resource that most VBScript programmers turn to first, it has a number of limitations:

- It offers a rather bare-bones approach to the language. There isn't a level of detail that allows one to move beyond the basics or to make the documentation useful in troubleshooting and diagnosing sources of error.
- The examples rarely, if ever, move beyond the self-evident and obvious.
- In a very small number of cases, it incorrectly documents a feature that turns out not to work in VBScript, but that is implemented in VBA. This leads one to suspect that the documentation was originally written for VBA and then was quickly adapted to VBScript.
- Since one of the strengths of VBScript is that it allows VBA programmers to leverage their existing skills in learning a new technology, it is peculiar that the documentation totally disregards differences between VBA and VBScript.

In other words, the documentation included with VBScript just doesn't have the depth of information that you need when you need it. Most of us can get by day-to-day without even opening VBScript Help. But when you need to open the Help file, it's probably because you've either hit an unexpected problem or need to know what the consequences of coding a particular procedure in a particular way will be. However, Help tends only to show you how a function should be included in your code. This is understandable; after all, the help information for any language must be created before that language goes into general use, but it is only general everyday use in real-life situations that highlight how the language can best be used and its problems and pitfalls. Therefore, online help confines itself to the main facts: what the syntax is and, in a general way, how you should implement the particular function or statement.

This book takes up where the Help file leaves off. Contained within these pages are the experiences of professional VB and VBScript developers who have used these languages all day, every day, over many years, to create complex applications. It is these experiences from which you can benefit. Whether you have come to VBScript recently or have been using it since its introduction, there are always new tricks to learn. And it's always important to find out about the gotchas that'll getcha!

Who Should Read This Book?

This book is aimed at experienced VBScript developers or experienced developers coming to VBScript for the first time from another programming or scripting language (including, of course, VB/VBA programmers).

This book is a reference work and not a tutorial—for example, we won't explain the concept of a For...Next loop; as an experienced developer, you already know this, so you don't want someone like us insulting your intelligence. But we will explain in detail how a For...Next loop works in VBScript, how it works in practice, what the alternatives to it are, how it can be used to your best advantage, and what pitfalls it has and how to get around them.

Although this book is not intended as a tutorial, we have provided in Part I, *The Basics*, a concise introduction to the language that focuses not only on the general structure of the VBScript language, but on also its application in the four major environments in which it is used. If you're learning VBScript as a second language, the introduction combined with the reference is probably all that you'll need to get started.

How This Book Should Be Used

VBScript in a Nutshell focuses on the needs of three different audiences: programmers and script developers who are new to VBScript, VB/VBA programmers who are new to VBScript, and VBScript programmers.

If You're New to VBScript

This book is based upon the assumption that if you're new to VBScript, you know one or more other programming languages. The first half of the book leads you through the important areas of VBScript programming, which, while very different from most other languages, are straightforward and easily mastered. We suggest therefore that you read these chapters in order while referring to the Language Reference when necessary.

If You're a VBScript Programmer

As an experienced VBScript programmer, you will be able to dip into the book to get the lowdown on the language element that interests you. Appendix A lists all the functions, statements, and object models by category to help you find the relevant section in the Language Reference more easily.

If You're a VB or VBA Developer New to VBScript

If you know VBA, you know VBScript, since the latter is a subset of the former. On the whole, you'll find that VBScript is a much "cleaner" language than VBA—many of the archaic elements of VBA (elements that survived as Basic and QBasic evolved into VBA and as statement-based programming evolved into function-based programming and then object-based programming) have been removed from the language. But you'll also find some incompatibilities, as particular language features that you're accustomed to in VBA work differently in VBScript. We've tried to document those differences in this book.

How This Book Is Structured

This book is divided into three parts. The first part of the book, *The Basics*, is an introduction to the main features and concepts of VBScript programming, as well as an examination of how VBScript is used in its four major scripted environments: Active Server Pages, Windows Script Host, Outlook forms programming, and client-side scripting for Microsoft Internet Explorer (IE).

Even seasoned VB professionals should find items of interest here. If you're new to VB, this part of the book is essential reading. It is divided into the following chapters:

Chapter 1, *Introduction*
> In this chapter, you'll find information on the VBScript language and how it fits in to the family of VB products. We'll also discuss the notion that a scripting language is a kind of "glue" meant to hold together and control various objects. Finally, there's also a short discussion of the history of VBA.

Chapter 2, *Program Structure*
> This chapter details how to create the basic program structures in VBScript; how to implement classes, procedures, functions, and properties and how a program follows proceeds in a VBScript program.

Chapter 3, *Data Types and Variables*
> VBScript actually only has a single data type, the variant. This chapter looks at the variant and all its data types and shows how to use them.

Chapter 4, *Error Handling and Debugging*
> On the assumption that we all strive to create robust applications, this chapter covers error handling in your VBScript application and discusses the process of debugging in order to identify and remove program bugs.

Chapter 5, *VBScript with Active Server Pages*
> This chapter shows how to incorporate VBScript code into an Active Server Page and discusses the IIS object model that you access when creating an ASP application.

Chapter 6, *Programming Outlook Forms*
> Outlook 97 and 98 used VBScript as their only programming language and Outlook forms as their only programmable feature. Outlook 2000 includes two programming languages: VBA for application-level development, and VBScript for forms-based development. In this chapter, we focus on the latter topic by examining the VBScript development environment, discussing how to structure and run Outlook code, and listing some of the basic objects in the Outlook object model.

Chapter 7, *Windows Script Host 5.6*
> Programmers, administrators, and power users have long clamored for a "batch language" that would offer the power of the old DOS batch language in a graphical environment. Microsoft's answer is Windows Script Host (WSH) and a scripting language of your choice. In this chapter, we look at VBScript as the "Windows batch language" by examining program flow and how to launch a WSH script, discussing the WSH object model, and focusing on the XML language elements that you can use to better structure your scripts.

Chapter 8, *VBScript with Internet Explorer*
> VBScript was first introduced as a scripting language for Internet Explorer, which remains an important, although secondary, area of application for VBScript. In this chapter, we provide a quick overview of how to add script to HTML pages and focus on some of the functionality available through the Internet Explorer object model.

Chapter 9,
Windows Script Components (WSC) is a technology that allows you to create what appear to be reusable binary COM components with script. Chapter 9 documents WSC and shows how you can use it to create your own binary COM components.

The second part of the book, *The Reference*, consists of one large chapter. Chapter 10, *The Language Reference* thoroughly details all the functions, statements, and object models that make up the VBScript language. The emphasis here is on the language elements found in VBScript 5 and 5.5 (which is currently in public beta). See the following section for a detailed explanation of how to use the Language Reference.

The third and final section consists of the following appendixes:

Appendix A, *Language Elements by Category*
This lists all VBScript functions, statements, and major keywords by category.

Appendix B, *VBScript Constants*
This lists the constants built into the VBScript language that are available at all times.

Appendix C, *Operators*
This lists the operators supported by VBScript, along with a slightly more detailed treatment of Boolean and bitwise operators.

Appendix D, *Locale IDs*
This lists the locale IDs by the *GetLocale* and *SetLocale* functions.

Appendix E, *The Script Encoder*
This documents Script Encoder (a command-line utility that hides source code) and shows how to use it for encoding all VBScript scripts except for those in Outlook forms.

The Format of the Language Reference

The following template has been used for all functions and statements that appear in Chapter 10:

Syntax
This section uses standard conventions (detailed in the following section) to give a synopsis of the syntax used for the language item.

Description (of parameters and replaceable items)
Where applicable, this section details whether the item is optional, the data type of the item, and a brief description of the item.

Return Value
Where applicable, this section provides a very brief description of the value or data type returned by the function or property.

Description
This section provides a short description of what the language element does and when, and why it should be used.

Rules at a Glance

This section describes the main points of how to use the function, presented in the form of a bulleted list to enable you to quickly scan through the list of rules. In the vast majority of cases, this section goes well beyond the basic details found in the VB documentation.

Example

It's not uncommon for documentation to excel at providing bad examples. How often do we encounter code fragments like the following:

```
' Illustrate conversion from Integer to Long!
Dim iVar1 As Integer
Dim lVar2 as Long
iVar1 = 3
lVar2 = CLng(iVar1)
Response.Write "The value of lVar2 is: " & lVar2
```

So you won't find the gratuitous use of examples in this book. We see little point in including a one- or two-line code snippet that basically reiterates the syntax section. Therefore, we've tried to include examples only where they enhance the understanding of the use of a language element or demonstrate a poorly documented feature of a language element.

VBA/VBScript Differences

If you're programming in the Professional or Enterprise Editions of Visual Basic, or in one of the hosted environments (like Microsoft Word or AutoCAD) using Visual Basic for Applications, this section shows you how a particular VBScript language element differs from its VB/VBA counterpart. If no differences are noted, the element functions identically in both environments. This helps you get up to speed with unfamiliar language elements quickly, as well as to get VBA code running under VBScript or VBScript code running under VBA.

Programming Tips and Gotchas

This is the most valuable section of the Language Reference, gained from years of experience using the VBA language in many different circumstances. The information included in here will save you countless hours of head-scratching and experimentation. This is the stuff Microsoft doesn't tell you!

See Also

A simple cross-reference list of related or complimentary functions.

Conventions in This Book

Throughout this book, we've used the following typographic conventions:

Constant width

Constant width in body text indicates a language construct such as a VBA statement (like For or Set), an intrinsic or user-defined constant, a user-defined type, or an expression (like dElapTime = Timer( ) - dStartTime). Code fragments and code examples appear exclusively in constant-width text. In syntax statements and prototypes, text in constant width indicates such language elements as the function's or procedure's name, and any invariable elements required by the syntax.

Constant width italic
> Constant width italic in body text indicates parameter and variable names. In syntax statements or prototypes, it indicates replaceable parameters.

Constant width bold
> Constant width bold in code listings and examples is used to emphasize particular lines of code.

Italic
> Italicized words in the text indicate intrinsic or user-defined functions and procedure names. Many system elements like paths and filenames are also italicized, as are new terms where they are defined.

 This symbol indicates a note.

 This symbol indicates a warning.

How To Contact Us

Please address comments and questions concerning this book to the publisher:

O'Reilly & Associates, Inc.
1005 Gravenstein Highway North
Sebastopol, CA 95472
(800) 998-9938 (in the United States or Canada)
(707) 829-0515 (international or local)
(707) 829-0104 (fax)

We have a web page for this book, where we list errata, examples, or any additional information. You can access this page at:

http://www.oreilly.com/catalog/vbscriptian2

To comment or ask technical questions about this book, send email to:

bookquestions@oreilly.com

For more information about our books, conferences, Resource Centers, and the O'Reilly Network, see our web site at:

http://www.oreilly.com and *http://vb.oreilly.com*

Acknowledgments

We'd like to thank Eric Lippert of Microsoft for his careful and thorough review of the manuscript. Eric went far beyond the call of duty in working to make this a better book.

The Basics

This section serves as a general introduction to VBScript, the scripting language that is commonly used in Active Server Pages, Outlook Forms, Windows Script Host scripts, and client-side scripts for Internet Explorer. Taken together, these chapters form an extremely fast-paced introduction to the most critical VBScript programming topics. If you're an experienced programmer learning VBScript as a second (or additional) programming or scripting language, this material should help to familiarize you with VBScript in as short a time as possible.

In addition to its role as a tutorial, Chapter 3 is an essential reference to the data subtypes supported by VBScript.

Part I consists of the following chapters:

- Chapter 1, *Introduction*
- Chapter 2, *Program Structure*
- Chapter 3, *Data Types and Variables*
- Chapter 4, *Error Handling and Debugging*
- Chapter 5, *VBScript with Active Server Pages*
- Chapter 6, *Programming Outlook Forms*
- Chapter 7, *Windows Script Host 5.6*
- Chapter 8, *VBScript with Internet Explorer*
- Chapter 9, *Windows Script Components*

1

Introduction

Microsoft Visual Basic Scripting Edition, commonly known as VBScript, is a relative of the Visual Basic family, which includes the Microsoft Visual Basic Development System (the retail version of Visual Basic in its Enterprise, Professional, and Learning Editions) and Visual Basic for Applications (the language component of Visual Basic, which is included in the individual applications within Microsoft Office and Microsoft Project, as well as in a host of third-party applications).

VBScript is, for the most part, a subset of the Visual Basic for Applications programming language. It was developed so that the millions of Visual Basic developers could leverage their knowledge of VB/VBA in Internet scripting. One of the strengths of VBScript is that it uses the same familiar and easy syntax that has made VBA so popular as a programming language, making it very easy to learn for those who have some Visual Basic background. In addition, VBScript is fairly easy to learn for those without any programming experience.

Ironically, VBScript started as a client-side scripting language to create interactive web pages, but it had a major liability: it was and is not supported by Netscape Navigator. Instead, the two major web browsers on the market, Navigator and Microsoft Internet Explorer, both supported a common scripting language, ECMAScript, that became the *de facto* standard and is now the *de jure* standard for client-side scripting. (Netscape's implementation of ECMAScript is named JavaScript, while Microsoft's implementation is named JScript.) Despite its failure in this area, however, VBScript rapidly became the major scripting language in three other areas:

- Active Server Pages (ASP) applications
- Outlook forms
- Windows Script Host (WSH) scripts

VBScript's History and Uses

Version 1.0 of VBScript was initially introduced in Microsoft Internet Explorer (IE) 3.0, which was released in 1996. Its intended use at that point was to allow web page developers to enhance their pages through client-side scripting. In contrast to plain HTML, which supported the creation of static web pages only, the combination of HTML and client-side script allows the creation of web pages that are both interactive and responsive to the user. For instance, a script could allow the web page to display extended information about hyperlinks as the user's mouse passes over them, or it could be used to validate data entered by the user without submitting it to the server. A script could even be used to generate a web page on the fly, without using any "hardcoded" HTML. The only limitation to VBScript as a language for client-side scripting was that VBScript could be used inside of Internet Explorer only (the only browser to support it) and thus was suitable only for use on corporate intranets that had standardized on Internet Explorer. Using VBScript for client-side scripting on Internet Explorer is discussed in Chapter 8.

Version 2.0 of VBScript was introduced in Internet Information Server (IIS) 3.0 in 1997. The most notable additions to the language were "web-friendly" language elements (such as lightweight *Format...* functions and the *Filter*, *InStrRev*, *Reverse*, and *Join* functions) that in most cases were incorporated into the VBA language only with the release of VBA 6.0. In addition, VBScript 2.0 added support for a number of intrinsic constants to make code more readable and also implemented the Const statement to allow user-defined constants. Finally, the *CreateObject* and *GetObject* functions were added to instantiate external COM objects; these functions, which are inoperative in a client-side scripting environment, are essential for supporting components that are capable of extending a scripted server-side application.

This new version of VBScript was released with IIS to support server-side scripting using ASP. ASP is itself the object model exposed by IIS that allows your script to access information about the client's request and to write to the server's output stream. An *ASP application* consists of conventional web pages (that is, HTML and possibly client-side script written in any language) along with script that executes on the server. The output of an ASP script most commonly is HTML, which is simply inserted into the output stream returned by the server in response to a client request. This makes ASP important for several reasons. First, it can be used to produce output that is customized for the browser on which it's displayed. Secondly, it provides a very strong web application environment, particularly one that takes advantage of backend processing. Along with ASP, Microsoft introduced *ActiveX Data Objects* (ADO) as its primary data access technology. Developing ASP applications with VBScript is discussed in Chapter 5.

Although IIS itself is language-independent and supports a number of available scripting languages, it is precisely in this realm—scripting for ASP—that VBScript quickly found its major application.

Version 3.0 of VBScript, released in 1998, had no new language features. Nevertheless, it was significant for marking the spread of VBScript beyond a scripted web environment. Besides IIS Version 4.0 and Internet Explorer Version 4.0, VBScript was now incorporated into Outlook 98 (an interim release of Outlook that was developed out of sync from the other applications in Microsoft Office) and Windows Script Host 1.0.

Windows Script Host (WSH), which first appeared in the Windows NT 4 Option Pack, exposes some core system resources (like the registry, the network, printers, and the filesystem) and allows system administrators to write scripts that access or control them using VBScript, JavaScript, or any of a number of other scripting languages. Using WSH, administrators can write sophisticated scripts that run either locally or remotely to handle typical administrative tasks. WSH is considerably more powerful than typical Windows Shell scripting, and is also available in Windows 98. Microsoft has built the WSH to help companies address the growing concern of the total cost of administration. In addition, WSH appeals to power users who prefer writing a simple script rather than performing a repetitive task multiple times. Scripting for WSH is discussed in Chapter 7.

Microsoft Outlook was originally released in Office 97 as Microsoft's entry into the personal information manager/workgroup messaging market. Outlook featured a number of forms to handle standard MAPI message types (such as messages, contacts, tasks, notes, and appointments) out of the box. However, VBScript made it possible to design new forms and customize their behavior. Although Outlook's latest release, Outlook 2002, includes support for VBA, VBScript remains the programming language for Outlook 2002 forms. Developing Outlook forms with VBScript is covered in Chapter 6.

Version 4.0 of VBScript was also released as part of Visual Studio 6.0 in 1998. As in Version 3.0, no new language features were present. The difference was in the Microsoft Scripting Runtime Library (*scrrun.dll*), which now included a File System object model as well as the Dictionary object introduced with VBScript 2.0. The addition of the object model made the library an essential component in any scripted environment.

Version 5.0, which shipped with Internet Explorer 5.0 and IIS 5.0 (which shipped with Windows 2000), added a number of new language enhancements, including support for scripted classes using the Class...End Class construct, support for regular expression searches through the RegExp object, and the ability to dynamically build expressions to be evaluated using the *Eval* function or executed using the Execute method.

As you can see, even though VBScript's advent as a client-side scripting language was largely unsuccessful, Microsoft remained committed to VBScript as a "lightweight" form of VBA and continued to move the language forward. As a result, it came to be used in a number of environments other than client-side scripts, and in fact, has become one of the major scripting languages in use today.

What VBScript Is Used For: Gluing Together Objects

We've outlined the four major areas in which VBScript is used, but if we were to look at how scripts are written in each of these environments, we'd quickly note far more differences than similarities. (Because of this, we've devoted a separate chapter to each area in which VBScript is commonly used.) Yet this is misleading.

If we take a more high-level view, we can see that the role of VBScript and the role of the environment in which its scripts are run are broadly similar, regardless of the environment's unique features.

Typically, scripting languages are described as "glue" languages. That is, they are used to glue things together. That means that the glue itself does relatively little—it simply binds the rest of the script together. The "things" that the scripting language binds together are *components* or *objects*—that is, the objects exposed by the environment for which the script is being written (like ASP, Internet Explorer, Outlook, or WSH), as well as objects that are exposed by external applications, environments, or components (such as ActiveX Data Objects, Collaboration Data Objects, Microsoft Word, Microsoft Excel, or custom components created in Visual Basic). A map of a single high-level object (such as the Microsoft Word application, for instance, which is represented by the Application object) along with its child objects is known as an *object model*.

One type of object model that's particularly suitable for scripting is shown in Figure 1-1. In this particular case, the figure shows the ASP object model. Two features that are particularly noteworthy are its flatness and its lack of interdependence. (Contrast it, for example, with the Microsoft Word object model, a portion of which is shown in Figure 1-2.) In particular, a flatter object model and/or one whose objects have a fair degree of independence has a number of advantages:

Ease of navigation
    Since the object model is flat, you don't have to be concerned with navigating upward and downward through the object hierarchy. This makes coding easier, reduces the time spent debugging, and improves performance.

Ease of instantiating objects
    Since objects are independent of one another, you can easily create them or retrieve a reference to them, instead of having to figure out which portion of the object model you must navigate to in order to instantiate that object, or which property or method you must call that returns that object.

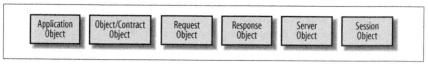

Figure 1-1. The Active Server Pages object model

Individual objects within an object model expose properties, methods, and events. We'll discuss each of these in turn.

Properties

Properties are attributes or values of an object that can be read and set. (In other words, properties are variables that belong to an object.) As long as the value returned by the property is not an object, setting and retrieving property values requires a simple assignment statement. For example, the following line of code stores the value of the ASP Session object's TimeOut property to a variable named *lTimeOut*:

```
lTimeOut = Session.TimeOut    ' Retrieve property value
```

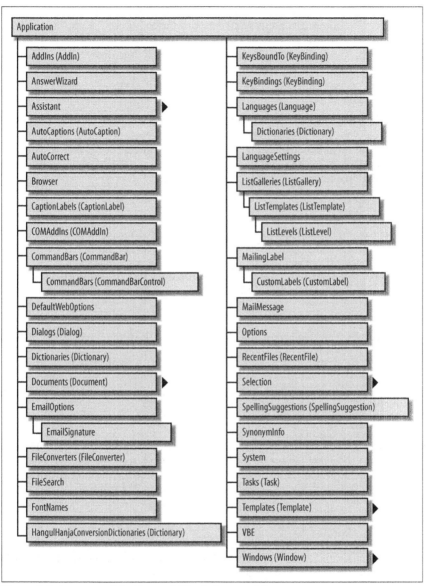

Figure 1-2. A portion of the Microsoft Word object model

Storing a new value to the property is just as easy. For instance, the following line of code changes the value of the Session object's TimeOut property to 10 minutes:

```
Session.TimeOut = 10        ' Set property value
```

Some properties are read-only; that is, while you can retrieve a property's value, attempting to set it is not permitted and generates an error. For example, the code:

```
lSVars = Request.ServerVariables.Count     ' Read-only property
```

assigns the count of the number of variables in the Request object's Server-Variables collection to a variable named *ISVars*. Attempting to set the value of the Count property, however, generates an error, since the property (as well as the ServerVariables collection itself) is read-only. Rarely, you may also encounter properties that are write-only, or that are write-only under certain conditions; you can set the property's value, but you can't retrieve it. Typically, this is done for security reasons.

Many properties return either individual objects or collections. (A collection is an object that serves as a container for other data items or objects.) These also require assignment statements that use the Set statement. For example, you can retrieve a reference to the root folder of the C: drive on a local system with a code fragment like the following:

```
Set oFS = CreateObject("Scripting.FileSystemObject")
Set oFolder = oFS.Drives.Item("C").RootFolder
```

Note that in the second line of code, we navigate the File System object model from its top-level object, the FileSystemObject object, to the Drives collection object. We use the collection's Item property to retrieve a reference to the Drive object representing Drive C:, and then retrieve the value of its RootFolder property to get a reference to an object representing the drive's root folder.

Methods

Methods are simply public functions or subroutines exposed by an object. You call them in the same way that you call any function or subroutine, except that you must preface the method name with a reference to the object whose method you are calling. If you are calling a subroutine or a function whose return value does not interest you, you can use syntax like:

```
Response.Write "<HTML><HEAD>"
```

which calls the ASP Response object's Write method to write the beginning of a web page to the server's output buffer in response to a client request. To call a method that returns an object, use an assignment statement along with the Set statement and enclose the argument list in parentheses. For example:

```
Set oShell = WScript.CreateObject("WScript.Shell")
Set oShortcut = oShell.CreateShortcut("My First Script.lnk")
```

is a fragment from a WSH script that creates a shortcut and returns the WshShortcut object representing that shortcut. If the method returns an ordinary value, the Set statement must not be used. For instance, the second line of the code:

```
Set oFS = CreateObject("Scripting.FileSystemObject")
strTempFile = oFS.GetTempName( )
```

calls the FileSystemObject object's GetTempName method to retrieve a temporary filename, which is stored to the variable *strTempFile*. The opening and closing parentheses after the method name are optional, since the method in this case takes no arguments.

Events

Methods are routines belonging to an object that we call in code. *Event handlers*, on the other hand, are functions or subroutines that we write that are called by the VBScript engine in response to some *event* that occurs to the object. For instance, when an ASP application is accessed for the first time, its OnStart event is fired. If we have included code like the following in our *global.asa* file:

```
Sub Application_OnStart
' application startup code goes here
End Sub
```

then that code is executed automatically.

Differences Between VBScript and VBA

VBScript is a subset of the Visual Basic for Applications language. There are several features that VB and VBA programmers have become accustomed to that are not present in VBScript. This does not lessen the usability of VBScript: it only serves to reinforce that VBScript is meant for scripting and not full-blown client/ server application development or COM component development. Let's take a look at a few of the larger differences between VBScript and VBA:

VBScript is a weakly typed language.
Unlike Visual Basic and Visual Basic for Applications, in which the developer can define the data type of a variable in advance, all variables in VBScript are variants. There are types to handle different types of data; you can use these as you would the traditional data types in Visual Basic. For more information, see Chapter 3.

VBScript does not support early binding.
Because variables are untyped and code is not compiled, all external objects instantiated in VBScript code are necessarily late-bound. This has a number of implications. First, late binding typically entails a substantial performance penalty in comparison to early binding. Second, while the properties and methods of early-bound objects can be examined in Visual Basic or hosted VBA environments using the Object Browser, this is not the case with late-bound objects. Finally, the help facilities available for early-bound objects in VB and VBA (like Auto List Members and Auto Quick Info) are not available, making syntax errors more likely and ready access to good documentation all the more necessary.

VBScript does not support named arguments.
VBA supports both positional and named arguments for most functions and procedures. For example, the VBA *MsgBox* function can be called using positional arguments as follows:

```
lResult = MsgBox("Delete this file?", _
          vbYesNo Or vbQuestion Or vbDefaultButton2, _
          "Confirm File Deletion")
```

A method call using named arguments takes the following form:

```
lResult = MsgBox(Prompt:="Delete this file?", _
          Title:="Confirm File Deletion", _
          Buttons:=vbYesNo Or vbQuestion Or vbDefaultButton2)
```

Note that while positional arguments must occur in a predefined sequence, named arguments need not. At least in our experience, more advanced programmers tend to prefer positional syntax, while more novice programmers tend to prefer named arguments.

Given all of this, it is unfortunate that VBScript supports only positional arguments.

VBScript does not have an IDE.

There is no integrated development environment for VBScript that parallels the IDE for Visual Basic and Visual Basic for Applications. Development tools are available for all of the environments in which VBScript is used, but all fall short of the power, simplicity, elegance, and ease of use of the VB/VBA IDE. Typically, web developers have had their own environments for writing their code. VBScript for the Web, whether it is client-side or server-side, is embedded inside of a <SCRIPT> tag. This allows web developers to continue to use their tool of choice even when using VBScript; a wide array of tools for web script development are available. Scripts for WSH can be created with the use of a simple text editor like Windows Notepad. Outlook comes with its rudimentary IDE (a glorified version of Notepad) for attaching code to Outlook forms.

We should also mention one difference between VBScript and VB/VBA that developers and commentators often emphasize—namely, that VBScript is slower than VB/VBA. This contention, though, raises more questions than it answers. First, if VBScript is used as "glue code," as it typically is, then the limiting factor in a VBScript program's performance will be the components it consumes, rather than the performance of the script itself. Second, performance cannot be measured in a vacuum. Rather than asking whether VBScript is faster or slower in the abstract, we have to consider the particular tasks for which it is being used.

But practically speaking, "Which is faster?" is usually the wrong question. The right question to ask is, "Which is fast enough?", which is a very different question. "Which is faster?" is a bad metric to use when choosing or comparing programming languages. Many factors influence performance, and not all are obvious. Code reliability, maintainability, robustness, and cost of development are all important factors to be considered along with performance.

Performance ("faster" and "slower") is also inherently hard to measure, since the terms themselves are more subjective than objective. Do they refer to "UI snappiness," "time to first byte," "throughput," or "page faults per second," or to something else?

As a programming language, VBScript offers acceptable performance along with an elegance and simplicity that make it a valuable tool for the range of scripted applications for which it was developed.

2

Program Structure

In order to write VBScript programs, you have to know how to structure your code so that your scripts and programs execute properly. Each of the different runtime environments for which you write VBScript code has different rules regarding program structure. We'll look at each of these in turn. We'll also examine the ways in which your host environment allows you to import VBScript code libraries, thus allowing you to create reusable code. Finally, we'll end the chapter with a discussion of VBScript usage to write class modules. First, though, it's important to cover the basic structures of VBScript that are relevant to all of the different script types: that global code calls code in individual functions or procedures.

Functions and Procedures

Functions and procedures (or subroutines) are central to modern programming. Dividing our script into subroutines helps us to maintain and write programs by segregating related code into smaller, manageable sections. It also helps to reduce the number of lines of code we have to write by allowing us to reuse the same subroutine or function many times in different situations and from different parts of the program. In this section, we'll examine the different types of subroutines, how and why they are used, and how using subroutines helps to optimize code.

Defining Subroutines: The Sub . . . End Sub Construct

The Sub...End Sub construct is used to define a *subroutine*; that is, a procedure that performs some operation but does not return a value to its calling program. Blocks of code defined as subroutines with the Sub...End Sub construct can be called in three ways:

Automatically

Some subroutines provide the means by which an object interfaces with the script. For instance, when a class defined with the Class...End Class construct is initialized, its Initialize event, if one has been defined, is executed automatically. For subroutines of this type, the routine's name can be constructed in only one way, as follows:

Sub *objectname_event*

For example, Sub Class_Initialize is a valid name of a subroutine. This type of subroutine is known as an *event handler* or an *event procedure*.

Defining it as an event handler

A subroutine can be executed automatically if it is defined as an event handler—as a routine that is executed whenever some event occurs. For the most part, the functionality to wire events and their event handlers is defined by the application environment rather than by the VBScript language itself. An exception, however, is the *GetRef* function, which allows you to define event handlers for Dynamic HTML pages in Internet Explorer.

Referring to it by name

A subroutine can be executed at any time by referring to it by name in another part of the script. (For additional details, including the syntax required to call subroutines, see "Calling a Subroutine" later in this chapter.) While it is possible to execute event procedures in this way, this method is most commonly used to execute *custom subroutines*. Custom subroutines are constructed to perform particular tasks within a program and can be assigned virtually any name that you like. They allow you to place code that's commonly used or that is shared by more than one part of a program in a single place, so that you don't have to duplicate the same code throughout your application.

Example 2-1 illustrates the use of a custom subroutine in a client-side script to contain code that is common to more than one part of an application. It provides a simple example of some common code that is placed in a custom subroutine. The web page in Example 2-1 contains three intrinsic HTML command buttons. But rather than handling the user's click of a particular button separately, each button's OnClick event procedure simply calls the *ShowAlertBox* routine. Had we not included the *ShowAlertBox* subroutine, which contains code common to all three event handlers in our web page, we would have had to create a script several times longer than the one shown in Example 2-1.

Along with showing how to use a custom subroutine to share code, Example 2-1 also demonstrates how to pass variables from one procedure to another, a topic discussed in greater depth in the section "Passing Variables into a Subroutine" later in this chapter. In particular, the *ShowAlertBox* routine is passed the caption of the button on which the user has clicked so that it can display it in an alert box.

Subroutine Names

Subroutine names follow the same rules as all identifiers, like classes, variables, and properties. This means that there are several very straightforward rules to remember when giving names to your subroutines:

- The name can contain any alphabetical or numeric characters and the underscore character.
- The name must start with a letter, not a numeric character or underscore, and it cannot contain embedded spaces.
- The name cannot contain any spaces. Use the underscore character to separate words to make them easier to read.
- The name cannot be a VBScript reserved word, such as a VBScript statement.

For example, in the following:

```
Sub 123MySub( )          ' Illegal
Sub My Sub Routine( )    ' Illegal
```

both names contain illegal subroutine names. However:

```
Sub MySub123( )      ' Legal
Sub MySubRoutine( )  ' Legal
```

are legal subroutine names.

Most of these rules can be broken by enclosing the subroutine name in brackets. The following VBScript code for WSH, for instance, defines valid subroutines whose names begin with an underscore and a numeric string character, include an embedded space, and conflict with a VBScript reserved word:

```
[_Main]

Public Sub [_Main]
    MsgBox "In_Main"
    [1Routine]
    [2 Routine]
    [Dim]
End Sub

Public Sub [1Routine]
    MsgBox "In 1Routine"
EndSub

Public Sub [2 Routine]
    MsgBox "In 2 Routine"
    End Sub

    Public Sub [Dim]
    MsgBox "In Dim"
End Sub
```

Example 2-1. Using a custom subroutine to share code

```
Sub cmdButton1_OnClick
  Call ShowAlertBox(cmdButton1.Value)
End Sub

Sub cmdButton2_OnClick
  ShowAlertBox cmdButton2.Value
End Sub

Sub cmdButton3_OnClick
  ShowAlertBox cmdButton3.Value
End Sub

Sub ShowAlertBox(strButtonValue)
  dim strMessage
  strMessage = "This is to let you know" & vbCrLf
  strMessage = strMessage & "you just pressed the button" & vbCrLf
  strMessage = strMessage & "marked " & strButtonValue
  Alert strMessage
End Sub
```

Calling a Subroutine

In Example 2-1, you may have noticed that the cmdButton1_OnClick event procedure uses a different syntax to invoke the *ShowAlertBox* routine than the cmdButton2_OnClick and cmdButton3_OnClick procedures. The second form of the call to the *ShowAlertBox* function:

```
showAlertBox cmdButton2.Value
```

is currently the preferred method. Note that it is unclear that this is actually a call to a subroutine named *ShowAlertBox*. Presumably, *ShowAlertBox* could be a variable. In fact, in order to identify *ShowAlertBox* as a subroutine, we have to rely on a visual clue: it is followed by another variable on the same line of code. This assumes, of course, that the code is correct, and that we haven't inadvertently omitted an equal sign between two variables.

In contrast, invoking a procedure by using a Call statement like the following:

```
Call showAlertBox(Top.cmdButton1.Value)
```

makes the code much more readable. You may prefer using it for this reason.

The rules for calling procedures are quite simple. If you use the Call statement, you must enclose the argument list in parentheses. If you do not use Call, you cannot use parentheses unless you're passing a single variable. In this case, though, parentheses also cause the variable to be passed by value rather than by reference to the subroutine (for the meanings of "by value" and "by reference," see the section "Passing Variables into a Subroutine" later in this chapter), a behavior that may have undesirable consequences.

Defining Functions: The Function . . . End Function Construct

As we've seen, subroutines created by the Sub...End Sub construct are used to manipulate data that is passed to them (assuming that the subroutine accepts

---

parameters) or to perform some useful operation. However, subroutines have one major shortcoming: they don't return data, such as the results of their manipulations or information on whether they were able to execute successfully.

It is possible for a subroutine to "return" a value by passing it an argument by reference (a topic discussed in the later section "Passing Variables into a Subroutine"). However, that has one major disadvantage: it requires that you declare a variable to pass to the subroutine, even if you're not concerned with that variable's value or with the value "returned" by the subroutine.

There's also an additional way that a subroutine can return a value: you can pass the subroutine the value of a global variable that is visible throughout your routine. For instance, we could use the following code fragment to create a subroutine that cubes any value that is passed to it as a parameter:

```
<SCRIPT LANGUAGE="vbscript" RUNAT="Server">
  dim cube       ' global variable

  Sub CubeIt(x)
     cube = x^3
  end sub
</SCRIPT>
```

Another routine can then access the result with a code fragment like the following:

```
<%
Dim intVar
intVar = 3
CubeIt intVar
Response.Write cube
%>
```

This approach, though, suffers from two limitations. First, it means that the global variable must remain in memory for the entire life of our script, even though the variable itself may be used only briefly, if at all. In most cases, this is a very minor concern, unless that variable is a large string or it's used on a particularly busy web server. Second, and much more important, it creates a variable that can be accessed and modified from anywhere within our script. This makes it very easy for a routine to accidentally modify the value of a variable that is used elsewhere in the script. The availability or unavailability of a variable within a particular procedure is called its *scope*. And in general, the variables in a well-designed application should have the most restrictive scope possible.

Through its support for functions, VBScript supports a much safer way of retrieving some value from a routine. Functions share many of the same characteristics as subroutines defined with the Sub...End Sub construct:

- Through their optional argument list, they can be used to manipulate data that is passed to them.
- Since they can be called from anywhere in a script, they can be used to contain code that is shared by more than one part of the application.

However, unlike subroutines, functions return some value to the calling procedure. This makes functions ideal for such uses as storing the code for frequently used calculations and conversions.

Functions are defined by using the `Function...End Function` construct, and by placing the function's code between these two statements. The full form of the `Function...End Function` statements is:

```
Function functionname(argumentlist)
End Function
```

Defining a Function's Return Value

If you've used VB or VBA to create functions, you probably have used the `As` keyword to define the data type of the value returned by a function, as in the following statement:

```
Function CubeIt(ByVal x As Long) As Long
```

Since VBScript supports only the variant data type, though, the `As` keyword is not supported, and you don't have to worry about the data type returned by your custom function. All functions defined by the `Function` statement return data of type variant.

A function's argument list is defined in exactly the same way as a subroutine's: the list of arguments is separated by commas and is enclosed in parentheses.

So how do we have our function return a value to the calling procedure? Within the body of our function, we assign the value that we want our function to return to a variable whose name is the same as the name of the function, as illustrated by the following code fragment:

```
Function functionname(argumentlist)
   ... some calculation or manipulation
     functionname = result of calculation or manipulation
End Function
```

This variable is automatically initialized through the use of the `Function` statement. This means that if you're accustomed to defining your variables before using them, and especially if you've included the `Option Explicit` statement in your script, you should *not* use the `Dim` statement to explicitly initialize the variable for the function's return value.

To implement our earlier *CubeIt* procedure as a function rather than a subroutine, we dispense with the need to define a global variable to hold the cube of the argument passed to the function and enormously simplify our code, as the following code fragment shows:

```
<SCRIPT LANGUAGE="vbscript" RUNAT="Server">
   Function CubeIt(x)
      CubeIt = x^3
   End Function
</SCRIPT>

<%
Dim intVar
```

```
    intVar = 3
    Response.Write CubeIt(intVar)
    %>
```

Once a custom function is correctly defined using the `Function...End Function` statement, it can be called just as if it were an intrinsic function that is built into the VBScript language. The function call itself can take either of two forms. The most common form involves using the function name and its argument list on the right side of an expression, and assigning its return value to a variable on the left side of the expression. For example, the most common way to call the *CubeIt* function is:

```
    y = CubeIt(x)
```

This assigns the value returned by the *CubeIt* function to the variable *y*. Unlike a call to a subroutine, though, this means that the argument list, if one is present, must always be surrounded by parentheses. (If the function accepts no parameters, though, the opening and closing parentheses are typically still used, although they're not required.)

In some cases, you may not actually be concerned with a function's return value. This doesn't happen very often—usually, you call a function precisely in order to have it return some value, so ignoring its return value renders the function useless. Nevertheless, if you do want to discard a function's return value, you can call a function just like you would call a subroutine. For example:

```
    Call CubeIt(x)
```

or:

```
    CubeIt x
```

Example 2-2 provides a real-world example—a client-side script that converts inches to either millimeters or meters—that shows how functions are defined and called. Along with two event procedures, it contains a function, *sngMetric*, that has a single argument, *strInches*, which is a string containing the number of inches that the user has input into the form's text box. The function converts this value to a single precision number, multiplies by 25.4, and, by storing it to the variable *sngMetric*, returns the result. The cmdButton1_OnClick and cmdButton2_OnClick event handlers call the function as necessary and pass the appropriate values to it. As you can see, the result returned by the *sngMetric* function is immediately displayed in a message box.

Example 2-2. Calling a function and returning a result

```
<HTML>
 <HEAD>
  <SCRIPT LANGUAGE="vbscript">
  <!--
    Sub cmdButton1_OnClick
     Dim strImperial
     strImperial = txtText1.Value
     Alert CStr(sngMetric(strImperial)) & " mm"
    End Sub
```

Example 2-2. Calling a function and returning a result (continued)

```
Sub cmdButton2_OnClick
 Dim strImperial
 strImperial = txtText1.Value
 Alert CStr(sngMetric(strImperial)/1000) & " m"
End Sub

Function sngMetric(strInches)
 Dim sngInches
 sngInches = CSng(StrInches)
 sngMetric = sngInches * 25.4
End Function
-->
</SCRIPT>
</HEAD>

<BODY BGCOLOR="white">
 Input Inches: <INPUT TYPE="text" NAME="txtText1">
 <INPUT TYPE="button" NAME="cmdButton1" VALUE="Show Millimeters">
 <INPUT TYPE="button" NAME="cmdButton2" VALUE="Show Meters">
</BODY>
</HTML>
```

Passing Variables into a Subroutine

The ability to pass variables from one procedure to another is an important part of using custom procedures. It allows us to write custom "black box" routines that can behave differently depending on where the routine has been called from and also on the particular data values that the routine receives from the calling program.

The data is passed from a calling routine to a subroutine by an *argument list*. The argument list is delimited with commas and can contain any data types, including objects and arrays. For instance, the following *mySubRoutine* procedure expects three arguments: *intDataIn1*, *strDataIn2*, and *lngDataIn3*:

```
Sub AnotherSubRoutine( )
 some code. . . .
   mySubRoutine intvar1, strvar2, lngvar3
 more code that executes after mySubRoutine
End Sub

Sub mySubRoutine(intDataIn1, strDataIn2, lngDataIn3)
 code which uses incoming data
End Sub
```

When *mySubRoutine* is called from *AnotherSubRoutine*, it is passed three variables as arguments: *intvar1*, *strvar2*, and *lngvar3*. So as you can see, the names of variables passed in the calling routine's argument list do not need to match the names in the custom procedure's argument list. However, the number of variables in the two argument lists does need to match or a runtime error results.

Passing Parameters by Reference

If you're accustomed to programming in VB or VBA, you'll recognize the way that you pass arguments in VBScript. However, in Versions 1 and 2 of VBScript, this wasn't the case. Parameters could be passed only by value, and there was no support for passing parameters by reference.

In addition, because VBScript is so flexible in its use of data types, you must take care when building subroutines that use data passed into them. The variables designated in the custom subroutine's argument list are automatically assigned the data types of the calling program's argument list. If a custom subroutine attempts to perform some inappropriate operation on the data passed to it, an error results, as the following code fragment illustrates:

```
Sub AnotherSubRoutine( )
 some code. . .
   intVar1 = "Hello World"
   Call mySubRoutine (intvar1, strvar2, lngvar3)
 more code that executes after mySubRoutine
End Sub

Sub mySubRoutine(intDataIn1, strDataIn2, lngDataIn3)
 code that uses incoming data
   intResult = intDataIn1 * 10 'this will generate an error
End Sub
```

The custom subroutine *mySubRoutine* assumed that *intDataIn1* would be an integer, but instead the calling program passed it a string variable, *intVar1*. Therefore, VBScript automatically casts *intDataIn1* as a string. The subroutine then produces a runtime error when it attempts to perform multiplication on a nonnumeric variable. As you can see, while weakly typed languages like VBScript have many advantages, one of their major drawbacks is the fact that you must be on your guard for rogue data at all times.

You can pass an argument to a procedure either by reference or by value. By default, arguments are passed *by reference*, which means that the calling routine passes the called function or subroutine the actual variable (that is, its actual address in memory). As a result, any modifications made to the variable are reflected once control returns to the calling routine. The ASP code in Example 2-3 illustrates passing a variable by reference. The variable *x* is initially assigned a value of 10 in the *DoSubroutine* procedure. This value is then changed to 100 in the *CallAnotherSub* procedure. When control returns to the *DoSubroutine* procedure, the value of *x* remains 100 because the variable was passed by reference to *CallAnotherSub*.

Example 2-3. Passing a variable by reference

```
<SCRIPT LANGUAGE="VBScript" RUNAT="Server">
Sub DoSubroutine( )
   Dim x
```

Example 2-3. Passing a variable by reference (continued)

```
   x = 10
   Response.Write "In DoSubroutine, x is " & x & "<P>"
   CallAnotherSub x
   Response.Write "Back in DoSubroutine, x is " & x & "<P>"
End Sub

Sub CallAnotherSub(ByRef var1)
   var1 = var1^2
   Response.Write "In CallAnotherSub, var1 is " & var1 & "<P>"
End Sub
</SCRIPT>

About to call DoSubroutine <P>
<%
   DoSubroutine
%>
```

The Sub statement for *CallAnotherSub* explicitly indicates that its single parameter, *var1*, is to be passed by reference because of the ByRef keyword. Since this is the default method of passing parameters, however, the keyword could have been omitted. The statement:

```
   Sub CallAnotherSub(ByRef var1)
```

is identical to:

```
   Sub CallAnotherSub(var1)
```

On the other hand, *by value* means that the calling routine passes the called function or subroutine a copy of the variable. This means that any changes to the variable's value are lost when control returns to the calling program. The ASP code in Example 2-4 illustrates passing a variable by value. As was also true in Example 2-3, the variable *x* is initially assigned a value of 10 in the *DoSubroutine* procedure. This value is then changed to 100 in the *CallAnotherSub* procedure. When control returns to the *DoSubroutine* procedure, the value of *x* remains 10 because the variable *x* was passed by value to *CallAnotherSub*.

Example 2-4. Passing a variable by value

```
<SCRIPT LANGUAGE="VBScript" RUNAT="Server">
Sub DoSubroutine( )
   Dim x
   x = 10
   Response.Write "In DoSubroutine, x is " & x & "<P>"
   CallAnotherSub x
   Response.Write "Back in DoSubroutine, x is " & x & "<P>"
End Sub

Sub CallAnotherSub(ByVal var1)
   var1 = var1^2
   Response.Write "In CallAnotherSub, var1 is " & var1 & "<P>"
End Sub
</SCRIPT>
```

Example 2-4. Passing a variable by value (continued)

```
About to call DoSubroutine <P>
<%
    DoSubroutine
%>
```

Note that the Sub statement for *CallAnotherSub* explicitly indicates that its single parameter, *var1*, is to be passed by value because of the ByVal keyword. This is necessary, since otherwise the variable would have been passed by reference.

To call a subroutine and pass it one or more arguments, you would use syntax like the following:

```
DoSomeSub x, y, z
```

where each argument in the argument list is separated from the other arguments by a comma, and the argument list is separated from the subroutine by a space. You cannot use parentheses to surround the argument list of a subroutine unless it has only a single argument.

To call a function, you can use the same syntax as you would use for a subroutine if you intend to discard the function's return value. For example:

```
DoSomeFunc x, y, z
```

passes three arguments to a function and ignores its return value. If the function has only a single argument, you can also call it and ignore its return value as follows:

```
DoSomeFunc(x)
```

More commonly, however, you are interested in the return value of a function. In that case, the argument list should be enclosed in parentheses, and each argument should be separated from other arguments by a comma. For example:

```
retval = DoSomeFunc(x, y, z)
```

Although the called routine defines whether an argument is to be passed to it by value or by reference, there is actually no way to *force* the caller to call a routine and pass it an argument by reference. This is because there is one additional way to pass an argument to a procedure that overrides the explicit or default ByRef keyword: you can enclose the argument in parentheses. This is a subtle difference that you should be aware of when passing parameters to procedures, since it can have unintended consequences. Imagine, for example, that we have the following subroutine, which accepts two arguments by reference:

```
Sub DoSomething(x1, x2)
```

The caller can pass the first argument to the subroutine by value by using the following syntax:

```
DoSomething (x1), x2
```

Similarly, the caller can pass the second argument to the subroutine by value by using the following syntax:

```
DoSomething x1, (x2)
```

If a subroutine has only a single parameter, then calling it with a syntax like the following:

```
DoSomething(x)
```

also passes the argument *x* to it by value.

 The converse does not work: parentheses do not cause an argument to be passed by reference to a routine that is expecting to receive an argument passed by value.

Overriding a by reference parameter when calling a function works similarly; arguments enclosed in parentheses are always passed by value rather than by reference. If the caller wishes to discard the function's return value, then a function is called exactly as if it were a subroutine, and by reference parameters are overridden in the same way as in calls to subroutines. If the caller retrieves the function's return value, then the function name must be followed by parentheses, as must the argument to be passed by value rather than by reference. For example, given a function with the signature:

```
Function CallFunction(var1, var2)
```

the code:

```
retVal = CallFunction(x1, (x2))
```

passes the *x2* argument to the function by value rather than by reference. If a function has a single parameter, an argument can be passed to it by value rather than by reference using the following syntax:

```
retVal = CallFunction((x1))
```

Note the double parentheses around the single argument.

Exiting a Routine with the Exit Statement

Ordinarily, when you call a function or a subroutine, all code between the initial Function or Sub statement and the concluding End Function or End Sub statement is executed. In some cases, though, you may not want all of a routine's code to be executed.

For example, imagine a situation in which you only want to execute a subroutine if a particular condition is met. One way of implementing this in your code is to test for the condition before calling the subroutine, as follows:

```
... some code
If condition Then
  Call MySubRoutine( )
End if
... more code
```

However, if you call the routine from multiple locations in your code, and you want to apply this test to each call, you'll have to include this control structure at every place in the script in which you call the subroutine. To avoid this redundant code, it's better to call the subroutine regardless of the condition, and to place the test within the subroutine. One way of doing this is as follows:

```
Sub MySubRoutine( )
   If condition then
      . . . all our subroutine code
   End if
End Sub
```

This is all well and good, and quite legal. However, in a large and complex subroutine, the End If statement becomes visually lost, especially if there are several conditions to be met. The preferred alternative is the Exit Sub and the Exit Function statements, which are used with the Sub . . . End Sub and Function . . . End Function constructs, respectively. Our conditional test at the beginning of a subroutine then appears as follows if we use the Exit Sub statement:

```
Sub MySubRoutine( )
 If Not condition Then Exit Sub
 . . . all our subroutine code
End Sub
```

Exit Sub and Exit Function immediately pass execution of the program back to the calling procedure; the code after the Exit statement is never executed. As you can see from the previous code fragment, the code is clean and clearly understandable. If the particular condition is not met, the remainder of the subroutine is not executed. Like the Exit Do and Exit For statements, any number of Exit Sub or Exit Function statements can be placed anywhere within a procedure, as the following code fragment demonstrates:

```
Function functionname(argumentlist)

   . . . some calculation or manipulation

   If condition1 Then
      functionname = result of calculation or manipulation
      Exit Function
   End If

   . . . perhaps some more code

   If condition2 Then
      functionname = result of calculation or manipulation
      Exit Function
   End If

End Function
```

Classes

Since VBScript 5.0, developers have been able to create classes to use in their scripts—a definite step along the road of object-oriented programming in VBScript. Writing classes with VBScript is very similar to writing COM objects with VB. Before we look at writing an actual class, let's go over some of the terminology so we are clear on what we are doing and what we are referring to.

A *class* is simply the template for an object. When you *instantiate an object* (that is, create an instance of a class) in code, VBScript makes a copy of the class for your use. All objects come from a class. Writing the class is simply a matter of creating a design for the objects that you want to use.

So naturally, it follows that an *object* is simply a copy of the class that you are making available to your program. You can make as many copies as you like for your use. The copies are temporary structures for holding information or creating interactions. When you are done with the objects, you can release them. If you need another one, you can instantiate another copy.

In VBScript, classes must be created in the scripts where you want to use them or they must be included in the scripts that use them. Since VBScript isn't compiled, unless you use Windows Script Components, you don't have the advantage of being able to write a set of VBScript COM classes that are reusable outside of the scripts in which they're defined or that can be easily accessed by programs and scripts written in other languages.

The Class Construct

You declare a class using the Class...End Class construct. The syntax of the Class statement is:

```
Class classname
```

where *classname* is the name you want to assign to the class. It must follow standard VBScript variable naming conventions.

Classes can contain variables, properties, methods, and events. How many of these and of what types is completely up to you. It is possible to have an object that has no properties or methods and supports only the two default events, but it won't be a very useful class.

To instantiate an object—that is, to create an instance of your class that you can use in your code—use the following syntax:

```
Set oObj = New classname
```

where *oObj* is the name you want to assign to your object variable (it again must follow standard VBScript variable naming conventions), and *classname* is the name of the class. The statement creates an *object reference*—that is, the variable *oObj* contains the address of your object in memory, rather than the object itself.

Class Variables

In addition to properties, methods (which are either functions or subroutines), and events (which are subroutines), the code inside a Class structure can include variable definitions (but not variable assignments). The variable definition can take any of the following forms:

```
Dim varName1 [, varName2...]
Private varName1 [, varName2...]
Public varName1 [, varName2...]
```

The variable name must once again follow standard VBScript variable naming conventions.

The Dim, Private, and Public keywords indicate whether the variable is accessible outside of the class. By default, variables are public—that is, they are visible outside of the Class...End Class structure. This means that the Dim and Public keywords both declare public variables, while the Private keyword declares a variable that's not visible outside of the class.

In general, it is poor programming practice to make a class variable visible outside of the class. There are numerous reasons for this, the most important of which is that you have no control over the value assigned to the variable (which is especially a problem when dealing with a weakly typed language like VBScript) and no ability to detect when the value of the variable has been changed. As a rule, then, all variables declared within your classes should be private.

Class Properties

Typically, class properties are used to "wrap" the private variables of a class. That is, to change the value of a private variable, the user of your class changes the value of a property; the property assignment procedure (called a *Property Let* procedure) handles the process of data validation and assigning the new value to the private variable. If the private variable is an object, use an object property assignment procedure (called a *Property Set* procedure) to assign the new property value to the private object variable. Similarly, to retrieve the value of a private variable, the user of your class retrieves the value of a property; the property retrieval procedure (called a *Property Get* procedure) handles the process of returning the value of the private variable.

Read-only properties (which wrap read-only private variables) have only a *Property Get* procedure, while write-only properties (which are rare) have only a *Property Let* or a *Property Set* procedure. Otherwise, properties have a Property Get procedure and either a *Property Let* or a *Property Set* procedure and are read-write.

The use of public properties that are available outside of the class to wrap private variables is illustrated in Example 2-5, which shows a simple class that defines a private variable, *modStrType*, and two read-write properties, ComputerType and OperatingSystem, the latter of which is an object property. Normally, you would validate the incoming data in the Property Let and Property Set procedures before assigning it to private variables, although that hasn't been done here to keep the example as simple as possible.

Example 2-5. Using properties to wrap private variables

```
Class Computer

    Private modStrType
    Private oOS

    Public Property Let ComputerType(strType)
        modStrType = strType
    End Property

    Public Property Get ComputerType( )
        ComputerType = modStrType
    End Property
```

Example 2-5. Using properties to wrap private variables (continued)

```
    Public Property Set OperatingSystem(oObj)
        Set oOS = oObj
    End Property

    Public Property Get OperatingSystem( )
        Set OperatingSystem = oOS
    End Property

End Class
```

Class Methods

Methods allow the class to do something. There is no magic to methods—they are simply subroutines or functions that do whatever it is you wish for the object to do. For example, if we created an object to represent a laptop computer in a company's inventory, then we would like to have a method that reports the laptop's owner. Example 2-6 shows a class with such a method.

Example 2-6. Creating a class method

```
Class LaptopComputer
Private modOwner

Public Property Let CompOwner(strOwner)
    modOwner = strOwner
End Property

Public Property Get CompOwner( )
    CompOwner = modOwner
End Property

Public Function GetOwner( )
    GetOwner = modOwner
End Function

End Class
```

As with properties, you can use the Public and Private keywords to make methods available inside or outside of the class. In the previous example, the method and both properties are available outside of the class because they are declared as Public.

Note that in Example 2-6, the *Property Get* procedure performs the same functionality as the *GetOwner* method. This is quite common: you often can choose whether you want to implement a feature as a property or as a method. In this case, you could define both property procedures to be private; then the only way for anyone to get the owner information from the object would be to invoke the *GetOwner* method.

The *GetOwner* method is declared as a function because it returns a value to the calling code. You can write methods as subroutines as well. You would do this when the method that you are calling does not need to pass back a return value to the caller.

Class Events

Two events are automatically associated with every class you create: Class_ Initialize and Class_Terminate. Class_Initialize is fired whenever you instantiate an object based on this class. Executing the statement:

```
Set objectname = New classname
```

causes the event to fire. You can use this event to set class variables, to create database connections, or to check to see if conditions necessary for the creation of the object exist. You can make this event handler either public or private, but usually event handlers are private—this keeps the interface from being fired from outside code. The general format of the Class_Initialize event is:

```
Private Sub Class_Initialize( )
Initalization code goes here
End Sub
```

The Class_Terminate event handler is called when the script engine determines that there are no remaining references on an object. That might happen when an object variable goes out of scope or when an object variable is set equal to Nothing, but it also might not happen at either of these times if other variables continue to refer to the object. You can use this handler to clean up any other objects that might be opened or to shut down resources that are no longer necessary. Consider it a housekeeping event. This is a good place to make sure that you have returned all memory and cleaned up any objects no longer needed. The format of the Class_Terminate event is:

```
Private Sub Class_Terminate( )
Termination code goes here
End Sub
```

Once again, the event handler can either be public or private, though ordinarily it's defined as private to prevent termination code from being executed from outside of the class.

Global Code

We've seen that code can be organized into functions, subroutines, and classes, and that some subroutines (and an occasional function) can be executed automatically if they are event handlers and the event they handle fires. However, that seems to offer a relatively limited "hook" for a script to run, and it doesn't seem to make it possible for a script to perform whatever initialization might be required in order for its event handlers to function successfully.

Global code—that is, code outside functions and subroutines—is the answer to this dilemma. It is executed automatically when the script loads or as the HTML on the page is parsed. The precise meaning of global code and the exact way in which it is executed depends on the host environment for which the script is written. We'll examine these in turn.

Active Server Pages

In ASP, global code is synonymous with code in direct ASP commands—it is script that is preceded by the <% or <%= tags and terminated by the %> tag. (For details on how script is embedded within in ASP page, see Chapter 5.) This code is executed automatically as the page's HTML is parsed.

It is also possible to include global code in <SCRIPT>...</SCRIPT> tags in an ASP. However, this is not genuine global code; aside from variable declarations, the order in which this code is executed is undefined.

Figure 2-1 shows the web page produced by Example 2-7, which illustrates global code in an Active Server Page. Note that although the variable x is defined and assigned a value in global code within the <SCRIPT> tag, the variable declaration is recognized but the variable assignment isn't. We can determine this because we've used the Option Explicit statement to require variable declaration, and the VBScript language engine did not raise an error when it first encountered the use of x on the second line after the <BODY> tag. But our assignment of 10 to x is not recognized, since the second line of our web page strongly suggests that x is uninitialized.

Example 2-7. Global code in an Active Server Page

```
<% Option Explicit %>
<HEAD>
<TITLE>Global code in ASP</TITLE>
<SCRIPT LANGUAGE="VBScript" RUNAT="Server">

Dim x
x = 10

Function Increment(lVar)
   lVar = lVar + 1
   Increment = lVar
End Function

Function Decrement(lVar)
   lVar = lVar - 1
   Decrement = lVar
End Function

</SCRIPT>
</HEAD>
<BODY>
<H2><CENTER>An Active Server Page</CENTER></H2>
The current value of x is <%= x %> <BR>
<%
   Dim y
   y = 20
   If x = 0 Then x = 10
%>
Value returned by Increment function: <%= Increment(x) %> <BR>
Value returned by Increment function: <%= Increment(x) %> <BR>
Value returned by Decrement function: <%= Decrement(x) %> <BR>
The value of <I>x</I> is now <%= x %>.
The value of <I>y</I> is <%= y %>.
</BODY>
</HTML>
```

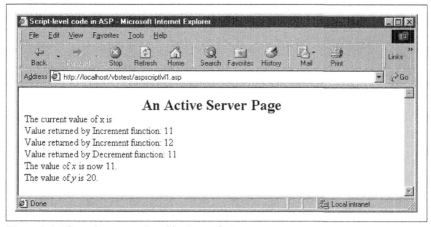

Figure 2-1. The web page produced by Example 2-7

We can draw the following conclusions from Example 2-7:

- Variable declarations placed at script level within the <SCRIPT> tag are recognized by ASP.
- Aside from variable declarations, no global code should be placed within the <SCRIPT> tag. The remaining code located within a <SCRIPT> tag should consist solely of function, subroutine, and class definitions.
- Direct commands can contain any global code.
- All direct commands are executed as the web server is parsing the HTML and generating a response to the client. In other words, along with handlers for the events supported by ASP (Application_OnStart, Application_OnEnd, Session_OnStart, Session_OnEnd, OnTransactionAbort, and OnTransaction-Commit), direct commands are basic "hooks" that allow your code to run.

Windows Script Host

In a standard VBScript file for WSH, global code is any code that's not located in function, subroutine, or class definitions. This code is executed sequentially regardless of where it is located in the file. This produces some interesting possibilities for spaghetti code, as illustrated in Example 2-8, which provides a WSH equivalent of the ASP script in Example 2-7. This script produces the dialog shown in Figure 2-2. Although its program structure should not be duplicated in your own code, Example 2-8 illustrates that all global code is executed from the beginning of a VBScript file to the end.

Example 2-8. Global code in WSH

```
Option Explicit

Dim x
x = 10
```

Example 2-8. Global code in WSH (continued)

```
Function Increment(lVar)
    lVar = lVar + 1
    Increment = lVar
End Function

Function Decrement(lVar)
    lVar = lVar - 1
    Decrement = lVar
End Function

Dim sMsg
sMsg = "The current value of x is " & x & vbCrLf

Dim y
y = 20
If x = 0 Then x = 10

sMsg = sMsg & "Value returned by Increment: " & Increment(x) & vbCrLf
sMsg = sMsg & "Value returned by Increment: " & Increment(x) & vbCrLf
sMsg = sMsg & "Value returned by Decrement: " & Decrement(x) & vbCrLf
sMsg = sMsg & "The value of x is now " & x & vbCrLf
sMsg = sMsg & "The value of y is " & y & vbCrLf

MsgBox sMsg
```

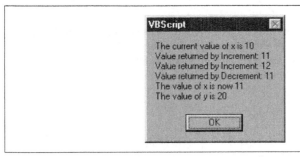

Figure 2-2. The dialog produced by the script in Example 2-8

If you're using a *.wsf* file with XML elements rather than a simple VBScript file, the same principles apply to code within the XML ‹job› and ‹/job› tags. All code must be assigned to a particular job, and code assigned to a job is independent of and unrelated to code assigned to any other job. Within the ‹job› tag, all global code is executed sequentially, regardless of how many ‹script› tags are used to contain it.

Client-Side Scripts for Internet Explorer

Global code in client-side scripts is found inside ‹SCRIPT› . . . ‹/SCRIPT› tags but not inside of functions, subroutines, and classes. All global code is executed by Internet Explorer, as Example 2-9 and Figure 2-3 show. In fact, global code can be used as a replacement for the Window_OnLoad event.

Example 2-9. Global code for Internet Explorer

```
<SCRIPT LANGUAGE="VBScript">
Option Explicit

Dim x
x = 10

Function Increment(lVar)
   lVar = lVar + 1
   Increment = lVar
End Function

Function Decrement(lVar)
   lVar = lVar - 1
   Decrement = lVar
End Function

</SCRIPT>
<CENTER><H2>Welcome to our web page!</H2></CENTER>
<SCRIPT LANGUAGE="VBScript">

Document.Write "The current value of x is " & x & "<BR>"

Dim y
y = 20
If x = 0 Then
   Document.Write "Initializing <I>x</I> in the second script block" & "<BR>"
   x = 10
End If

Document.Write "Value returned by Increment: " & Increment(x) & "<BR>"
Document.Write "Value returned by Increment: " & Increment(x) & "<BR>"
Document.Write "Value returned by Decrement: " & Decrement(x) & "<BR>"
Document.Write "The value of x is now " & x & "<BR>"
Document.Write "The value of y is " & y & "<BR>"

</SCRIPT>
```

Outlook Forms

Like Windows Script Host, Outlook executes all global code—not just variable declarations—when a form is loaded. In this case, global code corresponds closely to the Outlook form's Item_Open event procedure, which is fired when the form is opened.

Although you can use global code for executable statements, in most cases it is preferable that you do not. Most Outlook form programming is event-driven; you should use events, including the Item_Open event, to handle variable initialization, and confine yourself to using global code to declare public and private variables.

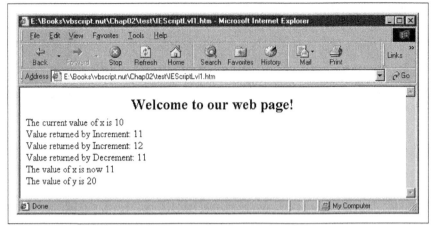

Figure 2-3. The document produced by Example 2-9

Reusable Code Libraries

We've now discussed all of the basic principles of structuring VBScript programs, of constructing subroutines that can be used by various parts of your program, of building functions that perform calculations and other manipulations and pass the result back to the calling part of the program, and of creating classes that allow you to encapsulate real-world processes and objects. The emphasis on subroutines, functions, and classes, though, raises another issue—that of code reuse. Typically, classes are defined so that they can be used in a variety of applications. Similarly, many subroutines and functions are intended not only to reduce code in a single application, but also to be "black boxes" that can provide some service to multiple applications.

Although it generally hasn't been emphasized and is dependent on the host platform, VBScript code can be reused on three of the four host platforms discussed here. The only platform that doesn't support code reuse is Outlook forms. That means that if you're scripting for WSH, ASP, or Internet Explorer, you can develop code libraries that you import into your script.

Active Server Pages

You can import HTML, client-side script, or server-side script into an ASP file by using the #include server-side directive. Its syntax is:

```
<!-- #include PathType = sFileName -->
```

where *PathType* is one of the following keywords:

File
   Indicates that *sFileName* is relative path from the current directory

Virtual
   Indicates that *sFileName* is a full virtual path from the web server's root folder to the file to be included

and *sFileName* is the name of the file whose contents are to be included. Note that the #include directive must be surrounded by an HTML comment. The included file can consist of any combination of client-side script, server-side script, and HTML, as long as it is syntactically correct and consistent with the script or HTML source at the point in the ASP page at which it is inserted.

Examples 2-10 and 2-11 illustrate one possible use of the #include directive. Example 2-10 shows the contents of *classes.inc*, an include file that contains a class definition to be used by the ASP application. Example 2-11 shows the ASP page that includes the file. Note that the include file consists entirely of script and is delimited with the HTML <SCRIPT> and </SCRIPT> tags (or the ASP <% and %> symbols). The ASP page in Example 2-11 inserts the contents of the include file in the HTML header, immediately after the </TITLE> tag.

Example 2-10. classes.inc, an include file

```
<SCRIPT RUNAT="Server" LANGUAGE="VBScript">

Class CServer

    Private sName, sProtocol, sSoftware, sURL, lPort

    Public Property Get Name( )
        Name = sName
    End Property

    Public Property Get Port( )
        Port = lPort
    End Property

    Public Property Get Protocol( )
        Protocol = sProtocol
    End Property

    Public Property Get URL( )
        URL = sURL
    End Property

    Public Property Get Software( )
        Software = sSoftware
    End Property

    Private Sub Class_Initialize( )
        sName = Request.ServerVariables("SERVER_NAME")
        lPort = Request.ServerVariables("SERVER_PORT")
        sProtocol = Request.ServerVariables("SERVER_PROTOCOL")
        sSoftware = Request.ServerVariables("SERVER_SOFTWARE")
        sURL = Request.ServerVariables("URL")
        sSoftware = Request.ServerVariables("SERVER_SOFTWARE")
    End Sub

End Class

</SCRIPT>
```

Example 2-11. An ASP page that uses an include file

```
<% Option Explicit %>
<HTML>
<HEAD>
<TITLE>Including a Library File</TITLE>
<!-- #include File="Classes.inc" -->
</HEAD>
<BODY>
<H2>Welcome to our web site!</H2>
Here is information about our server: <P>
<%
    Dim oServer
    Set oServer = New CServer
%>
Name: <%= oServer.Name %> <BR>
Software: <%= oServer.Software %> <BR>
Port: <%= oServer.Port %> <BR>
Protocol <%= oServer.Protocol %> <BR>
Resource: <%= oServer.URL %> <BR>
</BODY>
</HTML>
```

The advantage of this approach is obvious: you can store common code in a separate file, making it available to all the ASP pages and all the ASP applications that require it. When that code requires modification, you need do so only once since there is only a single copy in a single location, rather than having to search through all of your web pages to discover which ones incorporate the code.

While reusable code libraries can be useful in ASP development, you should only include the code you actually need in your library. This is because there's a *runtime* cost associated with declaring a function for ASP. Including massive libraries in an ASP application tends to produce noticeable slowdowns in throughput.

Windows Script Host

Although standard Windows Script host files (i.e., *.vbs* files) do not allow you to import other files, WSH files with XML elements (i.e., *.wsf* files) do. Include another file by using the <SCRIPT SRC> tag. The syntax is:

```
<SCRIPT LANGUAGE="sLanguage" SRC="sFilename" />
```

where *sLanguage* is "VBScript" (or any other valid scripting language) and *sFileName* is either an absolute or a relative path to the file to be excluded. Note that using the <SCRIPT> tag requires that the *.wsf* file be structurally correct—that is, that the <PACKAGE> and <JOB> tags should be present.

The included file must be a standard WSH script file. It can contain only script, without any XML elements or tags. The include file is simply inserted into the *.wsf* file as if it were an intrinsic part of it.

Examples 2-12 and 2-13 illustrate the use of an include file. In this case, the code in Example 2-13 imports *Lib.vbs*, the include file shown in Example 2-12.

Example 2-12 simply displays a message box displaying drives and their free space. To retrieve this information, it calls the *GetFreeSpace* function, which is located in the include file. This function returns a Dictionary object whose keys are drive names and whose values are the amount of free space available on the respective drive.

Example 2-12. Lib.vbs, an include file

```
Public Function GetFreeSpace( )

Dim oDict, oFS, oDrives, oDrive

Set oDict = WScript.CreateObject("Scripting.Dictionary")
Set oFS = WScript.CreateObject("Scripting.FileSystemObject")
Set oDrives = oFS.Drives
For Each oDrive in oDrives
    If oDrive.IsReady Then
        oDict.Add oDrive.DriveLetter, oDrive.FreeSpace
    End If
Next

Set GetFreeSpace = oDict

End Function
```

Example 2-13. A WSH script that uses an include file

```
<package>
<job id=GetFreeSpace>
<script language="VBScript" src="Lib.vbs" />
<script>
Option Explicit

Dim oSpace, aDrives
Dim sMsg, sDrive
Dim iCtr

Set oSpace = GetFreeSpace( )
aDrives = oSpace.Keys
For iCtr = 0 To UBound(aDrives)
    sDrive = aDrives(iCtr)
    sMsg = sMsg & sDrive & ": " & oSpace(sDrive) & vbCrLf
Next

MsgBox sMsg
</script>
</job>
</package>
```

Note that files must be included on a per-job basis. In other words, if a *.wsf* file contains multiple jobs, you must have a separate <SCRIPT SRC> tag for each job in which you want to include a particular file. An include file applies only to the job in which it's been included.

Client-Side Scripts for Internet Explorer

Like Windows Script Host, Internet Explorer supports the <SCRIPT SRC> tag, which allows you to include script files. The syntax of the tag is:

```
<SCRIPT SRC="sURL " LANGUAGE="sLanguage"> </SCRIPT>
```

where *sURL* is the URL of the include file and *sLanguage* is the language in which the file designated by *sURL* is written. *sLanguage* can be "VBScript" or any other valid scripting language.

The include file is simply inserted into the text stream on the client at the point that the <SCRIPT SRC> tag is encountered, and both it and the original document are viewed by the VBScript language engine as a single document. The inserted file can contain only script, without any HTML tags.

Example 2-14 contains an include file and Example 2-15 contains an HTML document that includes a client-side script to validate data. Note that the *IsBlank* routine is visible to the web page, since the included script is considered part of the original document. Note also that *Validate.inc* contains only script, without any HTML tags, and that the source document contains a <SCRIPT SRC> tag immediately followed by a </SCRIPT> tag.

Example 2-14. Validate.inc, an include file

```
Private Function IsBlank(sValue)
    If Trim(sValue) = "" Then
        IsBlank = True
    Else
        IsBlank = False
    End If
End Function
```

Example 2-15. A web page that uses an include file

```
<HTML>
<HEAD>
<TITLE>The SRC Attribute</TITLE>
<SCRIPT SRC="Validate.inc" LANGUAGE="VBScript" > </SCRIPT>
</HEAD>
<BODY>
<SCRIPT LANGUAGE="VBScript">
Private Function frmInfo_OnSubmit( )
 With Document.frmInfo
   If IsBlank(.txtName.Value) Or _
      IsBlank(.txtAddress.Value) Or _
      IsBlank(.txtCity.Value) Or _
      IsBlank(.txtState.Value) Then
         frmInfo_OnSubmit = False
         Alert "Please make sure the Name, Address, City, " & _
                "State fields are not blank."
   End If
 End With
End Function
</SCRIPT>
```

Example 2-15. A web page that uses an include file (continued)

```
<H3>Please enter the following data</H3>
<FORM METHOD=POST ACTION="Submission.asp" NAME="frmInfo">
Name: <INPUT TYPE="Text" NAME="txtName"> <P>
Address: <INPUT TYPE="Text" NAME="txtAddress"> <P>
City: <INPUT TYPE="Text" NAME="txtCity">
State <INPUT TYPE="Text" NAME="txtState">
Zip Code <INPUT TYPE="Text" NAME="txtZip"><P>
<INPUT TYPE="submit">
</BODY>
</HTML>
```

3

Data Types and Variables

In this chapter, we'll discuss VBScript's rather unusual support for a single data type before turning to variables and constants in VBScript.

VBScript Data Types: The Many Faces of the Variant

Unlike Visual Basic and Visual Basic for Applications, VBScript has only a single data type, called a *variant*. A variant is a very special data type, since it can contain many different types of data and can automatically select the most appropriate data type for the particular context in which it is being used. A simplified view of a variant is that it can hold both string data (characters) and numerical data as well as other data, such as dates, Booleans, and objects. Internally it is much more complex, which permits it to hold a wide range of different numeric types.

Variant Data Types

While the only data type recognized by VBScript is the variant, any item of variant data belongs to a particular type. Let's look at the range of *types*—or the different types of data—that a variant can hold:

Empty

Empty is a type that consists of a single value, also called Empty, that is automatically assigned to new variables when you declare them, but before you explicitly assign a value to them. For instance, in the code fragment:

```
Dim var1, var2
var2 = 0
```

the type of *var1* is Empty, whereas *var2* is only Empty for the brief period of time between the execution of the Dim statement on the first line (which declares a variable; it is discussed later in this chapter in "Declaring Variables and Constants") and the assignment statement on the second line. In addition, a variable's type is Empty if it has been explicitly assigned a value of Empty, as in the following code fragment:

```
Dim var1
var1 = Empty
```

Null

Null is a special type that consists of a single value, also called Null, that is used to indicate that a variable does not contain any valid data. Typically, a Null is used to represent missing data. For instance, a variable called JanSales might be assigned a value of Null if the total of January's sales is unknown or unavailable. This must be done by explicit assignment, as in the statement:

```
JanSales = Null
```

Because it represents missing data, once a Null value is assigned to a variable, it propagates to any variable whose value results from the value of the original variable. For instance, in the code

```
Dim JanSales, FebSales, MarSales, Q1Sales
' At this stage, all four variables are Empty

JanSales = 1276000
FebSales = 1000000
MarSales = Null
' We now have made MarSales Null

Q1Sales = JanSales + FebSales + MarSales
' Because MarSales is Null, Q1Sales will also be Null
```

the value of Q1Sales will be Null, since its value results from an expression that also includes a Null value. Because the Null type represents missing or unknown data, this makes sense: if March's sales data is unknown, then any value that wholly or partially results from it, such as the total sales for the first quarter, must also be unknown.

Boolean

The Boolean type can contain either of two values, True or False. The keywords True and False are constants (if you're not sure what a constant is; see "Variables and Constants" later in this chapter) that are predefined in VBScript, so you can make use of them in your code when you want to assign a Boolean value to a variable, as the following code fragment shows:

```
var1 = True
var2 = False
```

Many object properties have possible values of True or False, such as the Drive object's IsReady property. In addition, Boolean variables within programs often serve as flags to control program flow, as the following code fragment shows:

```
If Not myBool Then
  myVar = 4
  myBool = True
Else
  myVar = 5
  myBool = False
End If
```

Note that this example toggles (or reverses) the value of *myBool* within the If...Else...End If construct.

Byte

A Byte is the smallest numeric type available in VBScript. One byte (8 binary bits) can represent 256 integer numbers, ranging from 0 to 255 in decimal or 00 to FF in hexadecimal. Because the Byte is an unsigned data type, only zero or positive integers are valid Byte values. Attempting to convert a value outside this range to a Byte results in a runtime error.

Integer

An Integer is a whole number that VBscript uses two bytes (or 16 bits) to store in memory. Since one bit is used to represent the sign (either positive or negative), the value of Integer data can range from −32,768 to 32,767. Attempting to convert a value outside this range to an Integer results in a runtime error.

Long

A Long is a signed integer that VBscript stores in four bytes (or 32 bits) of memory. This allows it to hold a far greater range of negative or positive numbers than the Integer type; the value of a Long can range from −2,147,483,648 to 2,147,483,647.

Single

The three numeric data types that we've examined so far (Byte, Integer, and Long) are all integers; they're unable to represent fractional numbers. Fractions can be handled by a floating-point data type, two of which are available in VBScript. The first is Single, which is an abbreviation for single precision; it represents numbers with about seven digits of precision. Because of the large and small numbers involved, we are forced to specify the ranges as exponential numbers. There are two ranges, one for negative values and one for positive values. A negative single precision value can range from −3.402823E38 to −1.401298E−45, while the range of a positive single precision value is 1.401298E−45 to 3.402823E38. A Single can also have a value of zero.

If you need to use a floating-point number in VBScript, there is no reason to use a Single; use a Double instead. Generally, Singles are used because they offer better performance than Doubles, but this is not true in VBScript. Not only are Singles not smaller than Doubles in the VBScript implementation, but the processor also converts Singles to Doubles, performs any numeric operations, and then converts Doubles back to Singles.

Double

The Double type stores a double precision floating-point number; basically, it's the industrial-strength version of the Single data type. Its value can range from −1.79769313486232E308 to −4.94065645841247E−324 for negative values and from 4.94065645841247E-324 to 1.79769313486232E308 for positive values. A Double can also have a value of zero.

Date/Time

The Date type represents the date or time. If the number holds a date value, the earliest date that can be represented is January 1, 100, and, taking the view that our web sites will be around for a long time, the furthest into the future that we can go is December 31, 9999.

A literal date can be defined by surrounding the date with the # symbol. For example:

```
Dim myvacationDay
myVacationDay = #01/10/03#
```

Currency

The Currency type provides a special numeric format for storing monetary values that eliminates floating-point error. Because of this, it, rather than the floating-point types, should be used when working with monetary values. Its value can range from 922,337,203,685,477.5808 to 922,337,203,685,477.5807.

String

The most commonly used VBScript data type is String, which can contain virtually an unlimited number of characters—the theoretical limit is the size of the address space, which is two billion bytes on Win32 systems. In practice, though, strings in scripted applications should never be longer than a few thousand bytes at most. The String type used in VBScript is a variable length data type, so you don't have to worry about specifying how much memory to allocate to the variable, as you do in some programming languages.

Object

This data type contains a reference to an object. The Object type includes the intrinsic VBScript Err object, as well as objects defined by the Class ... End Class construct. It also represents references to external COM objects instantiated with the *CreateObject* or *GetObject* methods. If we view script as the "glue" that binds the services provided by components together, then the Object is the most important data type supported by VBScript.

Error

The Error type contains an error number and is typically used to signal a missing argument or other condition resulting from missing data. Typically, Error variants are returned by calls to Visual Basic component methods. VBScript itself does not allow direct creation or manipulation of Error variants.

So what does all this mean to the VBScript programmer? Above all, it means simplicity: as with any well-designed system, the variant is complex, but not complicated. That is to say, the interface—the part that you deal with—is straightforward, yet behind the scenes the variant data type does some incredibly complex things, which means you don't have to concern yourself with juggling code to ensure that data types are not mismatched, as Example 3-1 shows.

Example 3-1. The power of the variant data type

```
<HTML>
<HEAD>
<TITLE>The Variant #1</TITLE>
</HEAD>
<BODY>
<H2>
<CENTER>VBScript's Automatic Data Type Conversion</CENTER>
</H2>
<P>
<% Dim vVar1, vVar2, vResult
```

Example 3-1. The power of the variant data type (continued)

```
    vVar1 = 1
    vResult = 1
    vVar2 = 50000000.2658
    vResult = vVar1 + vVar2
%>
The result of adding <%=vVar1 %> and <%=vVar2 %> is <%=vResult %>.
</BODY>
</HTML>
```

When the user requests the ASP page, its script executes. It begins by using the Dim statement to declare three variables. Next, it assigns the integer value 1 to the first variable, *vVar1*, and to the third variable, *vResult*. Just to make things interesting, it assigns a large, double-precision number, 50,000,000.2658, to the second variable, *vVar2*. Then the routine adds the two variables together and stores their result to the integer variable *vResult*. As you may recall from the overview of data types, the value assigned to an integer cannot exceed 32,767, nor can it include any digits to the left of the decimal. Yet our script does not generate a compiler error because of this. So in the process of performing the calculation, the VBScript engine converts *vVar1* to a double-precision number. In most other programming languages, this task would have to be performed by the programmer.

If you modify the VBScript code in Example 3-1 to try different values for *Var1* and *Var2*, you'll find that the only time that the variant cannot handle the conversion occurs when one of the expressions is a String—i.e., you can't add 100 to "Hello" and expect a valid result. When this happens, the VBScript engine displays a "Type mismatch" error, which indicates that one of the items of data was of the wrong type and the engine was unable to convert it. This raises a good point, though: in a numeric operation, it is possible—especially if the data is input by the user into an HTML form or a dialog produced by the *InputBox* function—that one or more of the variables is a string data type. How would you be able to know this in advance, before VBScript stops executing your script and displays an error message?

Determining the Variant Type

Having the variant data type take care of all your data typing is all well and good, but what happens when you need to know exactly what type of data is stored to a variable? VBScript provides two easy-to-use functions, *VarType*, which returns an integer that indicates the type of data stored to a variable; and *TypeName*, which returns the name of the data type.

VarType

The syntax of *VarType* is:

```
VarType(expression)
```

where *expression* is an expression whose type you want to determine; you can provide the name of only a single variable at a time. Table 3-1 lists the possible values returned by *VarType* and the data types that they represent. For purposes of reference, Table 3-1 also lists the VBScript constants that you can use in your code to compare with the values returned by the *VarType* function; for details, see "Intrinsic Constants" later in this chapter.

Table 3-1. The values returned by the VarType function

Value	Data type	Constant
0	Empty	vbEmpty
1	Null	vbNull
2	Integer	vbInteger
3	Long	vbLong
4	Single	vbSingle
5	Double	vbDouble
6	Currency	vbCurrency
7	Date	vbDate
8	String	vbString
9	Object	vbObject
10	Error	vbError
11	Boolean	vbBoolean
12	Array of Variant	vbVariant
17	Byte	vbByte
8192	Array	vbArray

Before we see how you use *VarType* within a script, we should quickly note the value returned by *VarType* if it detects an array. Actually, the function never returns 8192 or vbArray, as shown in Table 3-1. 8192 is only a base figure that indicates the presence of an array. When passed an array, *VarType* returns 8192 plus the value of the array type. For a VBScript array, it returns 8192 (or vbArray) plus 12 (or vbVariant), or 8204. For a string array returned by a COM object, for instance, it returns 8200 (vbArray + vbString).

Example 3-2 provides a simple WSH script that uses the *VarType* function. It assigns a value of 9 to the *MyVal* variable and calls the *VarType* function, passing to it *MyVal* as a parameter. The value returned by the function, 2, is then displayed in a message box; this indicates that *MyVal* is an Integer.

Example 3-2. The VarType function

```
Dim MyVal
MyVal = 9
MsgBox VarType(MyVal)
```

Try modifying this code by assigning various numbers and strings to *MyVal*. You'll find that you can enter a very large integer for *MyVal* and the code will return 3 for Long, or you can enter a word or string (enclosed in quotation marks) and the code will return 8. You can even enter a number in quotation marks and it will return 8, indicating a String.

TypeName

The *TypeName* function returns the actual variant type rather than a number representing the data type. The syntax for *TypeName* is:

```
result = TypeName(expression)
```

Like its older brother, *TypeName* is read-only, which means that you can use it to determine the type of a variable, but you can't use it to explicitly set the type of a variable; to do this, you must use the conversion functions discussed in the next section. Table 3-2 shows the string that the *TypeName* function returns for each data type.

Table 3-2. Strings returned by the TypeName function

Return value	Description
`<object type>`	Actual type name of an object
Boolean	Boolean value: True or False
Byte	Byte value
Currency	Currency value
Date	Date or time value
Decimal	Decimal (single-precision) value
Double	Double-precision floating-point value
Empty	Uninitialized
Error	Error
Integer	Integer value
Long	Long integer value
Nothing	Object variable that doesn't refer to an object instance
Null	No valid data
Object	Generic object
Single	Single-precision floating-point value
String	Character string value
Variant( )	Variant array
Unknown	Unknown object type

Of interest in Table 3-2 is the variant array type, which is not listed in the VBScript official documentation. Whenever you pass the name of an array to *TypeName*, even an array that you have forced to be a certain data type by using the conversion functions, the return value is always "Variant()". Unfortunately, because VBScript does not support strong typing, there's no clear answer as to what data type lurks within your array; you can determine the data type of only one element at a time.

As for making your code easier to maintain, just look at this snippet:

```
If TypeName(x) = "Double" Then
```

Now you've no excuse for getting those nasty "type mismatch" errors!

Example 3-3 illustrates the use of *TypeName*. When you type something into the text box and press the OK button, a message box indicates whether you entered a string, a date, or a number. You may notice, though, that it always identifies (or perhaps misidentifies) numbers as data of type double. That's because our script uses the *CDbl* function to arbitrarily convert a numeric string entered into the text box to a variable of type double; for details on converting data from one type to another, see the following section.

Example 3-3. The TypeName function

```
Dim sInput, vResult
Do

    sInput = InputBox("Enter a data value:" , " TypeNameFunction", " ")
    If sInput = " " Then Exit Do

    If IsDate (sInput) Then
        vResult = CDate (sInput)
    ElseIf IsNumeric (sInput) Then
        vResult = CDbl (sInput)
    Else
      vResult = Trim (sInput)
    End If

    MsgBox TypeName(vResult)
Loop While Not sInput =      " "
```

Converting from One Data Type to Another

VBScript provides us with a range of built-in conversion functions that are simple and quick to use. The syntax for each is basically the same. For example:

```
CBool(expression)
```

where *expression* is either the name of a variable, a constant, or an expression (like x – y). The conversion functions supported by VBScript are:

CBool
> Converts *expression* to a Boolean. *expression* can contain any numeric data type or any string capable of being converted into a number.

CByte
> Converts *expression* to a Byte. *expression* can contain any numeric data or string data capable of conversion into a number that is greater than or equal to 0 and less than or equal to 255. If *expression* is out of range, VBScript displays an Overflow error message. If *expression* is a floating-point number, it is rounded to the nearest integer before being converted to byte data.

CDate
> Converts *expression* to a Date/Time. *CDate* accepts numeric data and string data that appears to be a date, converting it to the correct format for the machine. The date is returned in the format specified by the locale information on the client computer. On a machine set to the American date format mm/dd/yy, if you enter the British date format dd/mm/yy in a text box and then use the *CDate* function on the contents of the text box, *CDate* will convert it to the American mm/dd/yy format.

CCur

> Converts *expression* to a Currency. *CCur* accepts any numeric or string data that can be expressed as a currency value. The function recognizes the decimal and thousands separators based on locale information on the client computer.

CDbl

> Converts *expression* to a Double. The function accepts any numeric data within the limits of the Double or any string data that can be converted to a number within the range of the double data type.

CInt

> Converts *expression* to an Integer. *CInt* accepts any numeric data within the limits of the Integer or any string data that can be converted to a number within the limits of the integer data type.

CLng

> Converts *expression* to a Long. The function accepts any numeric data within the limits of the long integer data type or any string data that can be converted to a number whose value lies within the range of a long integer.

CSng

> Converts *expression* to a Single. The function accepts any numeric data within the limits of the Single or any string data that can be converted to a number within the range of the single data type.

CStr

> Converts *expression* to a String. *CStr* accepts any kind of data.

So now you know what data types VBScript can handle and how to convert from one type to another. You know how to find out how the variant is handling your data, and you can convert from one type to another. Let's now look at how you're going to use these data types and data within your scripts.

Variables and Constants

A variable is a name for an abstract concept (such as an object, a string value, or a numeric value) in a computer program. Using variables allows us to refer to the variable by its name, rather than to focus on its implementation details. Think of the nightmare you'd have trying to keep track of just which memory location your particular piece of data was occupying (completely ignoring the possibility that its memory location might change while the program executes). Those nice people who write the software we use to create our programs and scripts solved this problem a long time ago by giving us variables and constants.

What Is a Variable?

A variable is a placeholder or recognizable name for a memory location. This location is of no consequence to us; all we have to do is remember the name. When we use the name, the script engine will go to the correct memory location and either retrieve the data stored there or change the data, depending upon our instructions. It is important therefore to learn the rules for naming variables. (These in fact are the rules for naming any identifier in VBScript, including variables, functions, subs, classes, and constants.)

- Variable names can be no more than 255 characters in length. Variable names tend to become pretty unreadable after about 20 characters anyhow, which defeats the purpose of having longer variable names.

- The name must be unique within the scope it is being used. Don't worry too much about scope right now; we'll discuss it a little later. For now, remember not to use the same name for more than one variable in the same procedure—it makes sense, really.

- The variable name must start with an alphabetic character. *2myVar* is illegal, but *myVar2* is good.

- Variable names must be composed only of letters, numbers, and underscore characters. If you need to split up the variable name in some way to improve its readability, use the underscore character, like this: *This_Is_My_First_Variable*.

- You cannot use *reserved words*—which include some VBScript keywords; these language elements, which include statement names and intrinsic constant names, are part of the VBScript language.

- You can override most of these rules by enclosing the name in brackets. You can, for instance, use names that include embedded spaces, that start with numeric characters, or that are reserved words.

Variable names within VBScript are not case-sensitive, so *myvar* is the same as *MyVar*. You may have noticed in the examples so far (and if you haven't, go back and take a look) that we've used a combination of lower- and uppercase, with the first few letters usually in lowercase, for variable names like *myVar*. This is called *camel casing*. It improves readability, but is also a good habit to form; you'll see why when we discuss naming conventions.

So variables can either be a simple single character:

```
x = 10
y = "Hello World"
```

or they can be more descriptive:

```
tableRows = 10
greetingString = "Hello World"
```

Variables are so called because their value can change throughout their lifetime in your script. But you may have a requirement for a variable that isn't variable at all, whose value remains the same throughout your script. Guess what they're called?

What Is a Constant?

Constants perform a similar function to variables: they allow you to replace a value with a more descriptive and intuitive string. The difference is that a constant keeps the same value throughout its lifetime.

Values are assigned to constants using the same method used for variables, and can contain most of the same data types. (Constants cannot be of type Single or Object, for instance.) In most respects, therefore, a constant is the same as a variable. In fact, it could be described as a variable whose value doesn't vary!

VBScript uses the Const declaration to define a constant. A constant, which is declared as follows:

```
Const  myConstant = 10
```

cannot have its value changed throughout the life of the program. If your script mistakenly attempts to modify its value, VBScript raises an "Illegal Assignment" error. You'll know therefore—using the previous example—that whenever you use myConstant in your script, you are sure to be using the value 10.

> Like the constant declaration in VB, Const in VBScript cannot be used to assign nonconstant values or the values returned by VBScript functions. This means that a statement like the following:
>
> ```
> Const numConstant = myVar        ' Invalid
> ```
>
> is invalid, since it attempts to assign the value of a variable to a constant. It also means that a statement like:
>
> ```
> Const long_Int_Len = Len(lNum)  ' Invalid
> ```
>
> is invalid, since it relies on the value returned by the VBScript *Len* function. Finally, unlike VB or VBA, you are not allowed to use any value that includes an operator in defining a constant. For example, the following declaration, which is valid in VB, generates a syntax error in VBScript:
>
> ```
> Const added_Const = 4 + 1        ' Invalid
> ```

Intrinsic Constants

In addition to allowing you to define your own constants using the Const keyword, VBScript includes a number of built-in or intrinsic constants whose values are predefined by VBScript. Along with saving you from having to define these values as constants, the major advantage of using intrinsic constants is that they enhance the readability of your code. So, for instance, instead of having to write code like this:

```
If myObject.ForeColor = &hFFFF Then
```

you can write:

```
If myObject.ForeColor = vbYellow Then
```

Intrinsic constants are available for the following:

- Color
- Comparison
- Date/Time
- Date Format
- Message Box
- Miscellaneous
- Object Error
- String
- Tristate
- VarType

Appendix B contains a complete listing of the built-in constants, along with their meanings and values.

Constants in Type Libraries

Type library files provide definitions of enumerated constants as well as of COM classes and their members (that is, of their properties, methods, and events). If you're developing either ASP or WSH scripts, you can make type library definitions accessible to your script. In that case, they are treated just as if they were intrinsic VBScript constants, and you don't have to define them yourself by using innumerable Const statements.

In ASP, you can make constants in type libraries available to all of the pages of your ASP application by including a METDATA tag in *Global.asa*. This offers significantly improved performance over a common alternative—using the ASP #include preprocessor directive on a page-by-page basis. Its syntax is:

```
<!-METADATA TYPE="TypeLibrary" FILE="FileName"
    UUID="TypeLibraryUUID"
    VERSION="MajorVersionNumber.MinorVersionNumber"
    LCIS="LocaleID"  →
```

where its parameters are as follows:

FileName
> Optional. The physical path and name of the type library file. (Type libraries are often stored with the *.DLLs* that they describe, and can also be housed in separate files with an extension of *.tlb* or *.olb*.) While optional, either *FileName* or *TypeLibraryUUID* must be specified to identify the type library.

TypeLibraryUUID
> Optional. The universally unique identifier of the type library, as defined in the HKEY_CLASSES_ROOT\TypeLib key of the registry. While optional, either *FileName* or *TypeLibraryUUID* must be specified in order to identify the type library.

MajorVersionNumber
> Optional. The major version number of the type library. If you include a *MajorVersionNumber*, you must also include a *MinorVersionNumber*. If version number information is specified and ASP cannot find the library with that version, a runtime error occurs.

MinorVersionNumber
> Optional. The minor number of the type library. If you include a MinorVersionNumber, you must also include a MajorVersionNumber. If version information is specified and ASP cannot find the library with that version, a runtime error occurs.

LocaleID
> Optional. The locale to use for this type library if the library supports multiple locales. If a *LocaleID* is specified that cannot be found in the type library, a runtime error occurs.

For example, the following code from *Global.asa* makes the enumerated constants in the ADO 2.5 type library accessible to an ASP application:

```
<!--METADATA
      TYPE="typelib"
      FILE="D:\Program Files\CommonFiles\System\ADO\msado21.tlb"
-->
```

In WSH, you can make constants in a type library available to your script by including the `<reference />` tag in a script in a *.wsf* file. The constants are available only to the script within a single `<job>` tag. The syntax of `<reference />` is:

```
<reference [object="progID"|guid="typelibGUID"
           [version="version"] />
```

with the following parameters:

progID

> Optional. The version-independent or version-dependent programmatic identifier of the type library, as defined in the system registry. You must specify either *ProgID* or *typeLibGUID*.

typelibGUID

> The globally unique identifier (GUID) of the type library, as defined in the system registry. This is the most common way to reference and access a type library from WSH. You must specify either *ProgID* or *typelibGUID*.

version

> The version number of the type library your script needs to access.

For example, the following code makes the constants defined in Data Access Objects Version 5.0 available to a WSH script:

```
<reference guid="{00025E01-0000-0000-C000-000000000046}"
           version="5.0" />
```

Declaring Variables and Constants

Unlike many other programming languages, VBScript allows the implicit declaration of variables. This means that as soon as you use a variable within your script, VBScript does all the necessary work of allocating memory, etc., and the variable is considered to be declared. However, it is good programming practice to explicitly declare any variables you want to use at the start of the procedure or script by using the Dim statement. Its syntax is:

```
Dim Variable_Name
```

If you have a number of variables to declare, you can do this on the same line by separating them with commas, as in the following Dim statement:

```
Dim intRefNo, intAnyVar
```

As you start to write more and more complex scripts, you can reduce the number of bugs by referring back to the Dim statements to check the spelling of the variables you are using. Many bugs have been found to be simple typos of a variable name. Try the simple WSH script in Example 3-4 exactly as it's written (including the deliberate mistake). Enter a value into the input box and check the result.

Example 3-4. A typo in a variable name

```
Dim tstVar1

tstVar1 = InputBox("Enter a value")

MsgBox testVar1
```

Interesting result, isn't it? No matter what you type into the input box, the message box is always blank. Now in this small script, it's pretty noticeable that we misspelled the name of the variable, and that VBScript treats *tstVar1* and *testVar1* as two different variables altogether. However, more complicated scripts won't bear out this error so easily. We know many frustrated programmers who have tracked down significant logic errors to misspelled variable names. Don't despair, though—VBScript has a tool for helping us to eliminate this problem.

Option Explicit

Make a very slight amendment to the script shown in Example 3-4: add the statement Option Explicit on a line directly before the Dim statement. Run the script again, with the mistake still there. Now, instead of getting a useless empty text box that gives us no clue why our script didn't work, we get the error message, "Variable is undefined." We now know what we are looking for: the message tells us that we haven't declared a variable, and gives us the line number on which the error occurred. Even in a complex script, it usually takes only a couple of seconds to find and correct the bug.

Using Option Explicit is good programming practice. It forces us to declare all variables with Dim, and, should we make an error in the script, makes it easier to find.

Array Variables

The variables we have dealt with so far have contained single values, or, to give them their correct title, are *scalar variables*. But there are many occasions when you need to assign a range of values to a single variable. This type of variable is called an *array*. Arrays allow us to store a range of values in memory, each of which can be accessed quickly and efficiently by referring to its position within the array. You can think of an array as a very simple database of values. Arrays can hold all data types supported by VBScript.

Before examining arrays in VBScript in detail, let's quickly cover some of the terminology used when talking about arrays. Creating an array is called *dimensioning* (i.e., defining its size). The individual data items within the array are known as *elements*, and the reference number we use to access these elements is known as an *index*. The lowest and highest index numbers are known as *bounds* or *boundaries*. There are four main types of arrays; arrays can be either fixed or dynamic; arrays can also be either one-dimensional or multidimensional.

Fixed arrays

Most of the time, we know how many values we need to store in an array in advance. We can therefore dimension it to the appropriate size, or number of elements, prior to accessing it by using a Dim statement like the following:

```
Dim myArray(5)
```

This line of code creates an array, named *myArray*, with six elements. Why six? All VBScript arrays start with location 0, so this Dim statement creates an array whose locations range from *myArray(0)* to *myArray(5)*.

Example 3-5 contains a simple WSH script that illustrates a fixed array. The script begins by instructing the VBScript engine to check that all our variables are correctly declared, then uses the Dim statement to dimension *iArray* as an array containing six elements, with indexes ranging from 0 to 5, as well as to dimension three other variables. The next six lines of code populate the array with values by explicitly assigning a value to each array element. This entire process of declaring and populating the array is done outside of a defined subroutine, which means that *iArray* is available to all subroutines and functions on the page (if there were any). This is known as scope, which we cover in depth later in this chapter.

Example 3-5. Using a fixed array

```
Option Explicit

Dim sNumber, iNumber, iElement
Dim iArray(5)

iArray(0) = 12
iArray(1) = 3
iArray(2) = 13
iArray(3) = 64
iArray(4) = 245
iArray(5) = 75

sNumber = InputBox("Enter a number between 0 and 5", _
                   "Fixed Array", "0")
If Not IsNumeric(sNumber) Then
    MsgBox "Invalid string entry"
Else
    iElement = iArray(sNumber)
    MsgBox iElement
End If
```

When we enter a number into the text box and click the button, the routine makes sure that our entry can be converted to a number; if not, it displays an error dialog. Otherwise, a message box containing the value of the array element whose index we entered is displayed. Note that, in this case, VBScript is able to automatically convert the string that we entered using the *InputBox* function into an integer used as the array index. If it hadn't been able to do this, or if we had chosen to handle the conversion ourselves, we could have used the *CInt* function.

Being the inquisitive type, you've probably already entered a number greater than 5 or less than 0 just to see what happens, right? You get an error message, "Subscript out of range." The subscript is the index number, and in a real application, we'd have checked that the number entered was within the limits—or bounds—of the array prior to using the number. We'll see how this is done in the section "Determining array boundaries: UBound and LBound" later in this chapter.

Fixed arrays are fine when we know in advance how many values or elements we need. But there are many cases where we do not have prior knowledge of this, and we need a way to expand our array should we have to. We can do this by declaring and using a dynamic array.

Dynamic arrays

The most convenient uses of an array are to store input from the user and to allow the user to input as many items of data as they like. Our application therefore has no way of knowing how to dimension the array beforehand. This type of problem calls for a *dynamic array*. Dynamic arrays allow you to expand the number of array elements by using the ReDim statement to redimension the array while the program is running.

A dynamic array is declared by leaving out the number of elements, like this:

```
Dim myDynamicArray( )
```

When you need to resize the array, use the ReDim keyword:

```
ReDim myDynamicArray(10)
```

You can also declare a dynamic array, and specify the initial number of elements at the same time, using ReDim:

```
ReDim anyDynamicArray(4)
```

To populate an array with a series of values, you can use the intrinsic *Array* function. The function allows you to quickly assign a range of comma-delimited values to an array. For instance, assigning values to the array in Example 3-6 with the *Array* function would be quite easy.

```
Dim myArray
myArray = Array(12,3,13,64,245,75)
```

To use the *Array* function, simply declare a variable, then assign the values of the array to the variable using the *Array* function. Any data type (even mixed data types) can be used with the *Array* function, as the ASP page in Example 3-5 shows.

There is no limit to the number of times you can redimension a dynamic array, but obviously messing around with variables in this way carries an element of risk. As soon as you redimension an array, the data contained within it is lost. Don't panic. If you need to keep the data, use the Preserve keyword:

```
ReDim Preserve myDynamicArray(10)
```

In fact, ReDim creates a new array (hence its emptiness). Preserve copies the data from the old array into the new array. This means that redimensioning arrays using the Preserve keyword results in poor performance for large arrays or for arrays with elements that have long strings. Another important point to note is that if you resize an array by contracting it, you lose the data in the deleted array elements.

Example 3-6. Using the array function

```
<HTML>
<HEAD>
<TITLE>Using the Array Function</TITLE>
</HEAD>
<BODY>
```

Example 3-6. Using the array function (continued)

```
<SCRIPT LANGUAGE="VBScript" RUNAT="Server">

Sub ShowArray( )

Dim myArray

myArray = Array("Hello", "World", 2, 1)

Response.Write "Element 0: " & myArray(0) & "<BR>"
Response.Write "Element 1: " & myArray(1) & "<BR>"
Response.Write "Element 2: " & myArray(2) & "<BR>"
Response.Write "Element 3: " & myArray(3) & "<BR>"

End Sub

</SCRIPT>

<% ShowArray %>

</BODY>
</HTML>
```

Example 3-7 contains a client-side script that shows how to use a dynamic array to save multiple inputs from the user. When the user clicks the "Add to array" button, the contents of the text box are added to *myArray*, an array that is dynamically resized beforehand. When the user clicks the Show Array Contents button, a dialog box like the one shown in Figure 3-1 displays the data stored to the array.

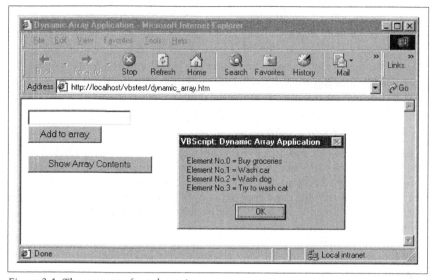

Figure 3-1. The contents of our dynamic array

Example 3-7. Using dynamic arrays

```
<HTML>
<HEAD>
<TITLE>Dynamic Array Application</TITLE>
<SCRIPT LANGUAGE="vbscript">

Option Explicit     'require all variables to be declared

ReDim myArray(0)    'create a dynamic array with 1 element
Dim intIndex        'variable to track the array index

intIndex = 0        'assign the first index number to counter

Sub cmdButton1_OnClick

    ' Store the user input in the array
    myArray(intIndex) = Document.frmForm1.txtText1.Value
    intIndex = intIndex + 1           'increment the array counter by one
    ReDim Preserve myArray(intIndex)  'increase the size of the array
    Document.frmForm1.txtText1.Value = ""      'Empty the text box again
End Sub

Sub cmdButton2_OnClick
    Dim x, y, strArrayContents         'declare some variables we'll need

    'repeat this process as many times as there are array elements
    'note: the last element will always be empty because we've
    'incremented the counter *after* the assignment.
    'try changing the above sub so that we always fill every element
    For x = 0 to intIndex - 1
        'assign a short description and the element no to the variable
        strArrayContents = strArrayContents & "Element No." & _
                        CStr(x) & " = "
        'add to this the contents of the element
        strArrayContents = strArrayContents & myArray(x) & vbCRLF
        'go back and do it again for the next value of x
    Next
    'when we're done show the result in a message box
    y = MsgBox(strArrayContents,0,"Dynamic Array Application")
End Sub

</SCRIPT>
</HEAD>
<BODY BGCOLOR="white">
  <FORM NAME="frmForm1">
   <INPUT TYPE="text" NAME="txtText1"><BR>
   <INPUT TYPE="button" NAME="cmdButton1" VALUE="Add to array"><P>
   <INPUT TYPE="button" NAME="cmdButton2" VALUE="Show Array Contents">
  </FORM>
</BODY>
</HTML>
```

Because the HTML text box controls return string data, you can save any type of data in your array, but they will automatically be saved as strings. This means that you must remember to convert the data saved in arrays before using them in calculations. This in turn requires that you check to make sure that data is actually numeric before accepting it or using it.

The previous example is fine as it stands, except that, as you can see from the source code, we have to keep track of the size of the array by using the *intIndex* variable. But VBScript allows a much cleaner approach to the problem of finding out how many elements there are in the array.

Determining array boundaries: UBound and LBound

The *UBound* and *LBound* functions can be used to find the lower index and the upper index, respectively, of an array. *UBound* can be put to good use: to find the current size of a dynamic array.

VBScript and the Option Base Statement

In VB and VBA, you can use the Option Base statement to define the initial position of an array. The Option Base statement, however, is not supported by VBScript. All VBScript arrays begin at position zero. But note that an ActiveX component created with Visual Basic can return an array with a nonzero lower bound to a VBScript script.

The syntax for *UBound* is:

```
x = UBound(arrayname)
```

UBound returns the highest index number of an array. This is always one less than the actual number of elements in the array, unless the array was returned to the script by a Visual Basic component and has had its lower bound set to a non-zero value. For example, if *myArray* has ten elements, *Ubound(myArray)* returns the number nine. So we determine the total number of elements in an array as follows:

```
myArraySize = UBound(array) + 1
```

To illustrate the use of *UBound*, let's rewrite parts of the dynamic array program in Example 3-7, as shown in Example 3-8. Instead of using an integer variable like *intIndex* in Example 3-7 to continually track the size of the dynamic array, Example 3-8 uses the *UBound* function.

Example 3-8. The UBound function

```
<HTML>
<HEAD>
<TITLE>Dynamic Array Application No.2</TITLE>
<SCRIPT LANGUAGE="vbscript">
```

Example 3-8. The UBound function (continued)

```
Option Explicit          'require all variables to be declared
ReDim myArray(0)              'create a dynamic array with 1 element

Sub cmdButton1_OnClick
    'Store the value enter by the user in the array
    myArray(UBound(myArray)) = Document.frmForm1.txtText1.Value
    'grow the array to be one element greater than its current size
    'Preserve its contents
    ReDim Preserve myArray(UBound(myArray) + 1)
    'Empty the text box for the user
    Document.frmForm1.txtText1.Value = ""
End Sub

Sub cmdButton2_OnClick
    'declare some variables we're going to need
    Dim x, y, strArrayContents
    'repeat this process as many times as there are array elements
    For x = 0 to UBound(myArray) - 1
        'add a short description and the element number to the variable,
        'along with the contents of the element and a carriage return
        strArrayContents =  strArrayContents & "Element No." & CStr(x) & _
                        " = " & myArray(x) & vbCrLf
    'go back and do it again for the next value of x
    Next
    'when we're done, show the result in a message box
    y = MsgBox(strArrayContents,0,"Dynamic Array Application #2")
End Sub

</SCRIPT>
</HEAD>
<BODY BGCOLOR="white">
  <FORM NAME="frmForm1">
  <INPUT TYPE="text" NAME="txtText1"><BR>
  <INPUT TYPE="button" NAME="cmdButton1" VALUE="Add to array"><P>
  <INPUT TYPE="button" NAME="cmdButton2" VALUE="Show Array Contents">
  </FORM>
</BODY>
</HTML>
```

The arrays that we have looked at so far are termed *single-dimension arrays*. They hold one element of data in each index location, which is fine for most needs. However there are times when you need to hold a full set of data for each element. These are called *multidimensional arrays*.

Multidimensional arrays

To get a sense of when using multidimensional arrays is appropriate, let's look at two situations in which our scripts benefit from using arrays. First, there's the simple case of the single-dimension array. Let's say we're an importer putting together an application that will display to a user the country of origin of our company's products when they click a button. We can use a single-dimension array to hold the data—in this case, a string containing the country of origin. We have one piece of data for each element, as follows:

Element number	Data
0	Product 1 Country of Origin
1	Product 2 Country of Origin
2	Product 3 Country of Origin

Then the marketing department suggests that the application be "improved." Instead of just showing the country of origin of each product, they also want to show its weight and any potential shipping hazard. If we continue to use a single dimension array, this poses something of a problem, as we can see from the following table.

Element number	Data
0	Product 1 Country of Origin
1	Product 1 Weight
2	Product 1 Hazards
3	Product 2 Country of Origin
4	Product 2 Weight
5	Product 2 Hazards
6	Product 3 Country of Origin
7	Product 3 Weight
8	Product 3 Hazards
etc.	

As you can see, there is no structure to this data; it's all held sequentially, and as a result, can be very difficult to access. The solution is to use a multidimensional array. A multidimensional array allows you to have a separate array of data for each element of your array. Therefore, each element of the array in turn contains an array. To continue our product importer example, let's say that we have four products, and for each product we want to store three items of data. We define the multidimensional array as follows:

```
Dim ourProductData(3,2)
```

VBScript and User-Defined Structures

If you're an experienced VB or VBA programmer, you might prefer another solution—an array of user-defined structures—to a multidimensional array. However, this solution is not available with VBScript. VBScript does not support the Type...End Type construct, and therefore does not allow you to define a structured data type.

This is the equivalent of the following data table, which consists of four rows and three columns. Each data cell of the table can therefore be viewed as a coordinate, with the first cell (the one containing product 1's country of origin) starting at 0,0. The row number defines the first value of the coordinate, while the column number defines the second:

	Country of origin	Weight	Hazards
Product 1	Element (0,0)		Element (0,2)
Product 2			
Product 3			
Product 4	Element (3,0)		Element (3,2)

 Multidimensional arrays can contain up to 60 dimensions, though it is extremely rare to use more than two or three dimensions.

Figures 3-2 and 3-3 illustrate the difference between a one-dimensional array and a multidimensional array—in this case, with a two-dimensional array. Notice how the two-dimensional array can be thought of as a one-dimensional array (the top row) with each element having its own individual array dropping down from it to form a column.

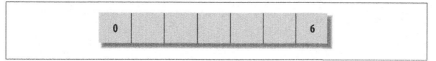

Figure 3-2. A one-dimensional array

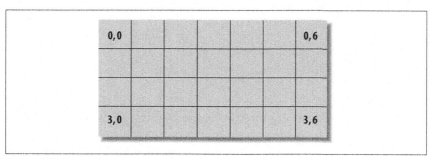

Figure 3-3. A two-dimensional array

If in our sample ASP application, which is shown in Example 3-9, we set ourselves a rule that the country of origin will always be in element 0, the weight in element 1, etc., then we have a method by which we can quickly access each individual element of data. So if we need to access the weight for product 3, we use the following line of code:

```
strDataString = strShippingData(2,1) ' row #3 column #2
```

Because we know that the weight will always be in column two, we can use a constant to help the readability of the code—something known as *self-commenting code*. This is an ideal job for a constant, as the following code fragment shows:

```
Const weight = 1
strDataString = strShippingData(2, weight)
```

In this case, the most important part of creating our ASP application occurs before we actually begin writing our script, when we decide how we want to structure our multidimensional array.

Once that is done, implementing the goal for which the ASP page is created—to display shipping information about a selected product—is fairly straightforward, as shown in Example 3-9. The ASP page can display a simple list of products, or it can display a list of products along with information about one product whose hyperlink the user has clicked. Since the user clicks any of four hyperlinks to display shipping information about a particular product, a single routine can handle the display of information, as long as it knows which "row" of the multidimensional array contains that product's information; that routine is named *ProductInfo*. The HREF attribute of each product's <A> tag includes a query string consisting of the Product element and its value, which is the index of the product's information in the *strShippingData* array. This index value is then passed as an argument to the *ProductInfo* routine if the user has clicked on a product hyperlink. The *ProductInfo* routine then simply retrieves the value of each element in the subarray belonging to the designated row and displays it to the web page. The result resembles Figure 3-4.

Example 3-9. Using a multidimensional array

```
<HTML>
<HEAD>
<TITLE>Product Shipping Data</TITLE>
<SCRIPT LANGUAGE="vbscript" RUNAT="Server">

'declare a subroutine to display product info
Sub ProductInfo(Index)
    'declare variable to be used in this sub
    Dim iCtr
    ' Show product caption
    Response.Write "<B>Shipping Data for Product" & CStr(Index + 1) & "</B><P>"

    'we want a line for each data item - use the constants
    For iCtr = country To hazards
        Response.Write strShippingData(Index,iCtr) & "<BR>"
    Next
End Sub

</SCRIPT>
</HEAD>
<BODY BGCOLOR="white">
<%
    'declare the constants
```

Example 3-9. Using a multidimensional array (continued)

```
    Const country = 0
    Const weight = 1
    Const hazards = 2

    Dim strShippingData(3,2)        ' declare a multidimensional array

    'assign values to the array
    strShippingData(0, country) = "Made in Finland"
    strShippingData(1, country) = "Made in Malawi"
    strShippingData(2, country) = "Made in USA"
    strShippingData(3, country) = "Made in Outer Mongolia"
    strShippingData(0,weight) = "Weight = 34 Kilos"
    strShippingData(1,weight) = "Weight = 17 Kilos"
    strShippingData(2,weight) = "Weight = 10 Kilos"
    strShippingData(3,weight) = "Weight = 15 Kilos"
    strShippingData(0,weight) = "No Hazard"
    strShippingData(1,hazards) = "Highly Inflammable"
    strShippingData(2,hazards) = "No Hazard"
    strShippingData(3,hazards) = "Highly Inflammable"
%>

<FONT FACE="ARIAL" SIZE=3>
    <%
        Dim iCtr
        For iCtr = 0 to 3
    %>
    <A HREF=MultiDim.asp?Product=<%=iCtr %> >
                    Product <%=iCtr + 1 %></A><P>
    <%
        If Request.QueryString.Count > 0 Then
            If CInt(Request.QueryString("Product")) = iCtr Then
                ProductInfo CInt(Request.QueryString("Product"))
            End If
        End If
        Response.Write "<P>"
    Next
    %>

</FONT>
</BODY>
</HTML>
```

You can use a multidimensional array as a rudimentary database that is located within the client machine's memory. When you access a particular element of a multidimensional array, the value of the first dimension indicates a particular record of your database, while the value of the second dimension designates a particular field belonging to that record.

Dynamic multidimensional arrays

Earlier, you saw how a one-dimensional dynamic array can be resized while your program is executing. Multidimensional arrays can be dynamic, too (as shown in

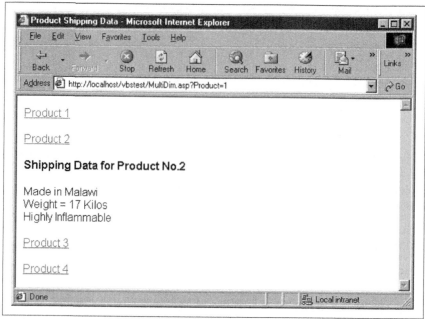

Figure 3-4. Sample output from Example 3-9

Example 3-10), and the rules for redimensioning them are similar, but since you have more than one dimension to think about, you have to take care how you use and redimension them. The rules for using a dynamic multidimensional array are:

- You can ReDim a multidimensional array to change both the number of dimensions and the size of each dimension. This is illustrated by the WSH script in Figure 3-4, where the *myArray* dynamic array is originally defined as a dynamic array and the user can choose between redimensioning it as a two-dimensional array with 11 elements in the first dimension and six in the second, or as a three-dimensional array with five elements in the first dimension, 11 in the second, and three in the third.

- If you use the Preserve keyword, you can resize only the last array dimension, and you can't change the number of dimensions at all. For example:

```
   ...
   ReDim myArray(10,5,2)
   ...
   ReDim Preserve myArray(10,5,4)
   ...
```

Example 3-10. Redimensioning a two-dimensional array

```
Dim myArray( ), nDims, iSelection

iSelection = vbYes
Do While iSelection <> vbCancel

   iSelection = MsgBox("Create 2 dimension array?", _
```

Example 3-10. Redimensioning a two-dimensional array (continued)

```
                vbQuestion Or vbYesNoCancel, "Dynamic Arrays")

    If iSelection = vbYes Then
        ReDim myArray(10,5)
        nDims = 2
    ElseIf iSelection = vbNo Then
        ReDim myArray(4,10,2)
        nDims = 3
    End If

    If iSelection <> vbCancel Then
        MsgBox "The upper bound of dimension " & nDims & _
            " is " & UBound(myArray, nDims)
    End If
Loop
```

Using UBound with multidimensional arrays

As you saw earlier, the *UBound* function returns the highest subscript (element number) in an array—that is, its **Upper Bound**ary. You can also use *UBound* with a multidimensional array, except to find the largest element of a multidimensional array, you need to also specify a dimension:

```
largestElement = UBound(arrayname, dimensionNo)
```

To sum up, use fixed arrays to hold predetermined blocks of data in memory. If you don't know the precise size of an array prior to defining it, use a dynamic array. Finally, if you need to reference more than one data field per data item, use a multidimensional array.

We have now covered the basics of variables and constants, apart from one major issue. You may have noticed in some of the previous examples that some variables and constants were declared at the very beginning of the script, outside of any subroutines, while some were declared within particular subroutines. Precisely where in a program or script you declare a variable or constant determines its scope and its lifetime.

Scope and Visibility

A variable's scope determines where within a script you are able to access that particular variable and whether that variable is *visible* within a particular routine. In a nutshell, variables declared outside of subroutines and functions can be accessed by the whole script, while those declared within a subroutine or function can be accessed only in the procedure in which they've been declared.

Global scope

Example 3-11 demonstrates the use of global variables and constants in a WSH script. Since *lngMyVar* is defined outside of any of the script's procedures, it is a global variable that is visible to all routines. This is apparent from the *GetUserInput* procedure, which prompts the user to assign a value to *lngMyVar*

Global Scope

A variable has global scope when it can be accessed by all the subroutines and functions contained in a particular script. Variables and constants that have global scope also reside in memory for the lifetime of the script. That is to say, as long as the script remains in memory, its global variables and constants also remain in memory. To create a variable with global scope, you must declare it outside of any subroutine or function.

and then calls the *MySecondProcedure* subroutine. *MySecondProcedure* displays a message box showing the value of *lngMyVar*, even though *lngMyVar* was not passed as a formal parameter to the procedure. (For a discussion of passing parameters, see Chapter 2.) If *lngMyVar* were not visible throughout the script, *GetUserInput* would not have been able to assign a value to *lngMyVar*, and the *MySecondProcedure* routine would not have been able to access that value.

The *IncrementValue* procedure illustrates the use of a global constant. Because MY_CONST is defined and assigned a value outside of a function or procedure, it is visible to *IncrementValue*, which adds it to the value that the user entered in the input box and assigns the result back to *lngMyVar*.

Example 3-11. Global scope

```
Option Explicit

'any variable or constant declared here will be available to
'all scripts in the document
Dim lngMyVar
Const my_Const=5

GetUserInput( )
'use lngMyVar in unrelated procedures just to check whether it's global
MySecondProcedure
IncrementValue
MySecondProcedure
MultiplyConstant
MySecondProcedure

Sub GetUserInput( )

    'lngMyVar does not need to be declared here - it's global
    lngMyVar = InputBox("Enter a Number: ", "Script-Level", 0)


End Sub

Sub MySecondProcedure( )
    'display the value of lngMyVar
    MsgBox "lngMyVar: " & lngMyVar
End Sub
```

Example 3-11. Global scope (continued)

```
Sub IncrementValue

   'let's add the value of the global constant to lngMyVar
   lngMyVar = lngMyVar + my_Const

End Sub

Sub MultiplyConstant

   lngMyVar = lngMyVar + (my_Const * 2)

End Sub
```

One peculiarity of this script is worth noting: in addition to including global constant and variable declarations in this WSH script, we have also included global executable code. In WSH, Outlook forms, and Internet Explorer, assignments and other executable code statements that are stored globally are executed. In Internet Explorer, you can include multiple <SCRIPT> tags, and all constants and variables declared in them but outside of functions and subroutines have global scope. In addition, all global code is executed.

ASP is an exception to this. Although global code does not generate an error, code generally will not execute. This means that you should only declare global variables and constants in ASP; you should never make assignments or other executable code global in scope.

Local scope

A variable that is declared within an individual procedure (that is, within a subroutine or a function) can only be used within that procedure, and is therefore said to have *procedure-level scope*. As soon as the procedure is complete, references to the variables defined within that procedure are erased from the computer's memory. You can therefore define different variables in different procedures that use the same name, as in the case of the simple *x* variable commonly used in the For...Next loop. Procedure-level variables are ideal for temporary, localized storage of information.

To prove that when variables are declared (either implicitly by simply using their name or explicitly using the Dim statement) within a procedure they do not have scope outside that procedure, take a look at the Example 3-12. Here we have a variable named *MyTestVar*. The variable is declared globally and again within a subroutine. However, the scope is local only to the level where the variable was declared. In this example, the *DemonstrateScope* subroutine is called first and displays the value of *MyTestVar* as "Vacaville, CA", then the subroutine exits back to the main program and the variable's value is shown as "Anchorage, AK". This clearly demonstrates that the variables are not one and the same, and hold values only at the scope where they were declared. (Incidentally, this "hiding" of variables with global scope by assigning identical names to local variables is called *shadowing* and is generally regarded as a poor programming practice.)

Example 3-12. Procedure-level scope

```
Option Explicit

Sub DemonstrateScope
Dim MyTestVar
MyTestVar= "Vacaville, CA"
Msgbox MyTestVar
End sub

Dim MyTestVar
myTestVar = "Anchorage, AK"
DemonstrateScope
Msgbox MyTestVar
```

Public visibility

Used outside of a procedure in place of the Dim statement, Public allows a variable to be seen not only by all procedures in all scripts in the current document, but also by all scripts in all procedures in all currently loaded documents.

Private

The Private declaration allows you to protect a variable by restricting its visibility to the document in which it has been declared. As with the Public declaration, the Private keyword can only be used outside a procedure; its use within a procedure generates an error. The Public and Private keywords are useful primarily in client-side Internet Explorer applications, where it is important to make variables either accessible or inaccessible between frames and documents.

4

Error Handling and Debugging

Errors, bugs, and therefore, debugging, are a part of life for a programmer. As the saying goes, if you haven't found any mistakes, then you aren't trying hard enough.

Dealing with errors actually involves two very different processes: error handling and debugging. *Error handling* is a combination of coding and methodology that allows your program to anticipate user and other errors. It allows you to create a robust program. Error handling does not involve weeding out bugs and glitches in your source code, although some of the error-handling techniques covered in this chapter can be used to great advantage at the debugging stage. In general, error handling should be part of your overall program plan, so that when you have an error-free script, nothing is going to bring it to a screeching halt. With some sturdy error handling in place, your program should be able to keep running despite all the misuse that your users can—and certainly will—throw at it.

The following ASP page illustrates some simple error handling:

```
<HTML>
<HEAD><TITLE>Error Checking</TITLE>
<BODY>
<SCRIPT LANGUAGE="VBSCRIPT" RUNAT="SERVER">

Dim n, x

n = 10
x = Request.Form.Item("txtNumber")

If x = 0 Or Not IsNumeric(x) Then
  Response.Write "x is an invalid entry"
Else
  y = n / x
  Response.Write y
End If

</SCRIPT>
```

```
</BODY>
</HTML>
```

The error handling in this example is the best kind—it stops an error before it can occur. Suppose you hadn't used the conditional If...Else statement and had allowed any value to be assigned to *x*. Sooner or later, some user will fail to enter a value or will enter a zero. In the former case, it would generate a type mismatch error, while in the latter, it would generate divide by zero error. So error handling, as this code fragment illustrates, is as much about careful data validation as it is about handling actual errors.

While preventing an error before it can occur is one approach to handling errors, the second is to handle the error after it occurs. For example, the following code fragment is a "real" error handler that we'll examine later in this chapter, so don't worry about the syntax at this stage. Like the previous code fragment, it aims at handling the "cannot divide by zero" runtime error—in this case, only after it occurs:

```
<HTML>
<HEAD><TITLE>Error Checking</TITLE>
<BODY>
<SCRIPT LANGUAGE="VBSCRIPT" RUNAT="SERVER">

On Error Resume Next

Dim n, x, y

n = 10
x = Server.HTMLEncode(Request.Form.Item("txtNumber"))
y = n / x

If Err.Number <> 0 Then
  y = "Oops! " & Err.Description
End If

Response.Write y

</SCRIPT>

</BODY>
</HTML>
```

As both of the previous examples show, the code itself is error-free and doesn't contain any bugs, but without either the data validation code or the error handling code, this program would be brought to its knees the first time a user enters a zero in the text box. Error handling therefore is a way to prevent a potentially disastrous error from halting program execution. Instead, if an error does occur, your program can inform the user in a much more user-friendly manner, and you can still retain control over the program.

Debugging, on the other hand, involves finding errors and removing them from your program. There are many types of errors that you can unwittingly build into your scripts, and finding them provides hours of fun for all the family. Errors can result from:

- Including language features or syntax that the scripting engine does not support within the script.
- Failing to correctly implement the intent of the program or some particular algorithm. This occurs when code produces behavior or results other than those you intend, although it is syntactically correct and does not generate any errors.
- Including components that contain bugs themselves. In this case, the problem lies with a particular component, rather than with your script, which "glues" the components together.

The single most important thing you need when debugging is patience: you have to think the problem through in a structured logical fashion in order to determine why you are experiencing a particular behavior. The one thing that you do have on your side is that programs will never do anything of their own free will (although they sometimes seem to). Let's begin by looking more closely at this structured, logical approach to debugging your scripts.

Debugging

You've designed your solution and written the code. You start to load it into the browser with high hopes and excitement, only to be faced with an big ugly gray box telling you that the VBScript engine doesn't like what you've done. So where do you start?

When confronted with a problem, you first need to know the type of error you're looking for. Bugs come in two main flavors:

Syntax errors
> You may have spelled something incorrectly or made some other typographical or syntactical error. When this happens, usually the program won't run at all.

Logical errors
> Although syntactically correct, your program either doesn't function as you expect or it generates an error message.

Bugs appear at different times, too:

At compile time
> If a compile-time error is encountered, an error message appears as the page is loading. This usually is the result of a syntax error.

At runtime
> The script loads OK, but the program runs with unexpected results or fails when executing a particular function or subroutine. This can be the result of a syntax error that goes undetected at compile time (such as an undefined variable) or of a logical error.

Let's look at each type of bug individually. We'll begin by looking at syntax errors—first at compile time and then at runtime—before looking at logical errors.

Syntax Errors

Ordinarily, objects containing script are compiled as they are loaded, and are then immediately executed. Errors can occur at either stage of the process. Although the distinction between compile-time and runtime errors is rapidly losing its importance, it is sometimes helpful to know that the entire script compiled successfully and that the error was encountered at a particular point in the script.

Syntax errors at compile time

Syntax errors at compile time are usually the easiest to trace and rectify. When the script loads, the host calls the scripting engine to compile the code. If the VBScript engine encounters a syntax error, it cannot compile the program and instead displays an error message.

For instance, an attempt to run the client-side script shown in Example 4-1 produces the error message shown in Figure 4-1. In this case, it's very easy to identify the source of the error: in the call to the *LCase* function, the closing parenthesis is omitted.

Example 4-1. Client-side script with a syntax error

```
<HTML>
<HEAD>
<TITLE>Syntax Error</TITLE>
<SCRIPT LANGUAGE="vbscript">
Sub cmdButton1_OnClick
  Alert LCase("Hello World"
End Sub
</SCRIPT>
</HEAD>
<BODY BGCOLOR="white">
<INPUT TYPE="button" NAME="cmdButton1" VALUE="OK">
</BODY>
</HTML>
```

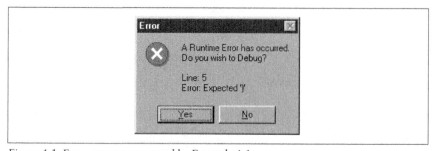

Figure 4-1. Error message generated by Example 4-1

When using ASP, diagnosing and fixing compile-time errors is a bit more difficult, since errors appear on the client browser, rather than in a dialog displayed on the server. For example, the simple ASP page shown in Example 4-2 displays the error message shown in Figure 4-2. This is a fairly standard ASP message display.

The error code (which is expressed as a hexadecimal number in this case) appears to be meaningless. The line number causing the error, however, is correctly identified, and the description informs us of the exact cause of the error. So we can quickly see that we've omitted a closing quotation mark around the argument we passed to the ServerVariables property of the Request object.

Example 4-2. ASP page with a syntax error

```
<HTML>
<HEAD>
<TITLE>ASP Syntax Error</TITLE>
</HEAD>
<BODY>
<SCRIPT LANGUAGE="VBScript" RUNAT="Server">
    Function BrowserName()
        BrowserName = Request.ServerVariables("HTTP_USER-AGENT)
    End Function
</SCRIPT>
<H2><CENTER>Welcome to Our Web Page!</CENTER></H2>
We are always happy to welcome surfers using <%= BrowserName %>.
</BODY>
</HTML>
```

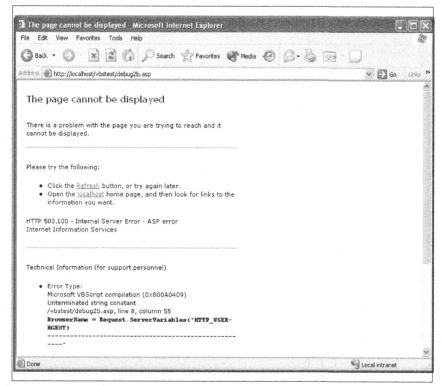

Figure 4-2. ASP error information

Syntax errors at runtime

Very often, a syntax error in VBScript appears only at runtime. Although the VBScript engine can successfully compile the code, it cannot actually execute it. (Note, though, that you may not actually be able to tell the difference between compile-time and runtime behavior in a relatively short script, since these two behaviors occur one after the other.) Example 4-3 shows a part of an ASP page that, among other things, tries to determine whether an ISBN number is correct. But attempting to access this page generates a runtime error, which is shown in Figure 4-3.

Example 4-3. Excerpt from an ASP page that generates an error

```
<HTML>
<HEAD>
<TITLE>Verifying an ISBN</TITLE>
</HEAD>
<BODY>
<SCRIPT LANGUAGE="VBScript" RUNAT="Server">

Function VerifyISBN(sISBN)

Dim sCheckSumDigit, sCheckSum

Dim iPos, iCtr, iCheckSum
Dim lSum
Dim sDigit

iPos = 1
sCheckSumDigit = Right(Trim(sISBN), 1)

' Make sure checksum is a valid alphanumeric
If Instr(1,"0123456789X", sCheckSumDigit) = 0 Then
   VerifyISBN = False
   Exit Function
End If

' Calculate checksum
For iCtr = 1 to Len(sISBN) - 1
   sDigit = Mid(sISBN, iCtr, 1)
   If IsNumeric(sDigit) Then
      lSum = lSum + (11 - iPos) * CInt(sDigit)
      iPos = iPos + 1
   End If
Next
iCheckSum = 11 - (lSum Mod 11)
Select Case iCheckSum
   case 11
      sCheckSum = "0"
   case 10
      sCheckSum = "X"
   case else
      sCheckSum = CStr(iCheckSum)
End Select
```

Example 4-3. Excerpt from an ASP page that generates an error (continued)

```
' Compare with last digit
If sCheckSum = sCheckSumDigit Then
   VerifyISBN = True
Else
    VerifyISBN = False
End If

End Function

</SCRIPT>

<H2><CENTER>Title Information</CENTER></H2>
Title: <%=Server.HTMLEncode(Request.Form("txtTitle")) %> <P>
ISBN:
<%
    sISBN = Server.HTMLEncode(Request.Form("txtISBN"))
    If Not VerifyIBN(sISBN) Then
        Response.Write "The ISBN you've entered is incorrect."
    Else
        Response.Write sISBN
    End If
%>

</BODY>
</HTML>
```

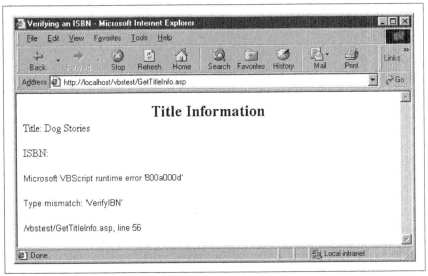

Figure 4-3. Error message generated by Example 4-3

In this example, all code has successfully compiled, since the server was able to begin returning output from the page. At compile time, even though the *Veri-fyIBN* (instead of *VerifyISBN*) function does not exist, the line of code appears to the compiler to identify a valid function, since it contains the correct syntax for a function call: *functioname* is followed by *argumentlist*. The VBScript engine can therefore compile the code into a runtime program, and an error is generated only when the engine tries to pass *argumentlist* to the nonexistent function *VerifyIBN*.

Logical Errors

Logical errors are caused by code that is syntactically correct—that is to say, the code itself is legal—but the logic used for the task at hand is flawed in some way. There are two categories of logical errors. One category of errors produces the wrong program results; the other category of errors is more serious, and generates an error message that brings the program to a halt.

Logical errors that affect program results

This type of logical error can be quite hard to track down, because your program will execute from start to finish without failing, only to produce an incorrect result. There are an infinite number of reasons why this kind of problem can occur, but the cause can be as simple as adding two numbers together when you meant to subtract them. Because this is syntactically correct (how does the scripting engine know that you wanted "−" instead of "+"?), the script executes perfectly.

Logical errors that generate error messages

The fact that an error message is generated helps you pinpoint where an error has occurred. However, there are times when the syntax of the code that generates the error is not the problem.

For instance, Example 4-4 shows a web page that invokes an ASP page shown in Example 4-5. The ASP page in turn generates a runtime error, which is shown in Figure 4-4.

Example 4-4. Division.htm, a web page for developing division skills

```
<HTML>
<HEAD>
<TITLE>A Test of Division</TITLE>
</HEAD>
<BODY>
<FORM METHOD="POST" ACTION="GetQuotient.asp">
    Enter Number: <INPUT TYPE="Text" NAME="txtNum1"> <P>
    Enter Divisor: <INPUT TYPE="Text" NAME="txtNum2"> <P>
    Enter Quotient: <INPUT TYPE="Text" NAME="txtQuotient"> <P>
    <INPUT TYPE="Submit">
</FORM>
</HEAD>
</HTML>
```

Example 4-5. GetQuotient.asp, the ASP page invoked by division.htm

```
<HTML>
<HEAD>
<TITLE>Checking your division...</TITLE>
</HEAD>
<BODY>
```

Example 4-5. GetQuotient.asp, the ASP page invoked by division.htm (continued)

```
<SCRIPT LANGUAGE="VBScript" RUNAT="Server">

Dim nNum1, nNum2, nQuot

Public Function IsCorrect( )

   nNum1 = CDbl(Server.HTMLEncode(Request.Form("txtNum1")))
   nNum2 = CDbl(Server.HTMLEncode(Request.Form("txtNum2")))
   nQuot = CDbl(Server.HTMLEncode(Request.Form("txtQuotient")))

   If (nNum1 / nNum2 = nQuot) Then
      IsCorrect = True
   Else
      nQuot = nNum1 / nNum2
   End If

End Function

</SCRIPT>

<%
   If IsCorrect( ) Then
      Response.Write "<H2><CENTER>Correct!</H2></CENTER>"
      Response.Write "Your answer is correct.<P>"
   Else
      Response.Write "<H2><CENTER>Incorrect!</H2></CENTER>"
      Response.Write "Your answer is wrong.<P>"
   End If
%>

<%=nNum1 %> divided by <%=nNum2 %> is <%=nQuot %> <P>

Answer <A HREF="Division.htm">another division problem</A>.

</BODY>
</HTML>
```

Errors,
Debugging

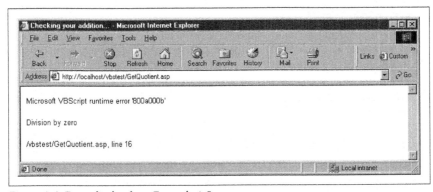

Figure 4-4. Error display from Example 4-5

The problem here is not one of syntax. Line 16 (the line with the If statement in the *IsCorrect* function) is syntactically correct. We won't get this error every time that we display the HTML page and it invokes the ASP page in Example 4-5. However, the values of variables can change (after all, that's why they're called variables), and here, the values of the variables in the ASP page are defined by the values that the user enters into the web page's text boxes—in this case, by the user entering a 0 into the *txtNum2* text box in Example 4-4. It could be said that this type of logical error produces a syntax error because the following syntax:

```
If (nNum1 / 0 = nQuot) Then
```

entails a division by zero and is therefore illegal.

In this case, we should have checked the value of the divisor to make sure that it was nonzero before calling the function. But more generally, this scenario—in which the value of a variable is incorrect either all of the time or, more commonly, only under certain conditions—is the essence of the logical error.

The Microsoft Script Debugger

The Script Debugger has been designed to allow you to debug your scripts while they are running in the browser. You can trace the execution of your script and determine the value of variables during execution. The Script Debugger is freely downloadable from the Microsoft web site. (For details, see the Microsoft Scripting home page at *http://msdn.microsoft.com/scripting/*.) It arrives in a single self-extracting, self-installing archive file, so that you can be up and running with the debugger in minutes.

 You can also use Visual Interdev or Visual Studio .NET to debug scripts.

Launching the Script Debugger

The Script Debugger is not a standalone application in the sense that you cannot launch it on its own. Instead, the Script Debugger runs in the context of the browser or of WSH. When you are running Internet Explorer, there are two ways to access the debugger:

Select the Script Debugger option from the View menu
A submenu is displayed that allows you to open the debugger to cause a break at the next statement.

Automatically when a script fails for any reason
This launches the debugger and displays the source code for the current page at the point where the script failed.

When you are running a WSH script, you can launch the debugger if an error occurs by supplying the //D switch, or you can run a script in the context of the debugger by supplying the //X switch. Figure 4-5 shows the Script Debugger.

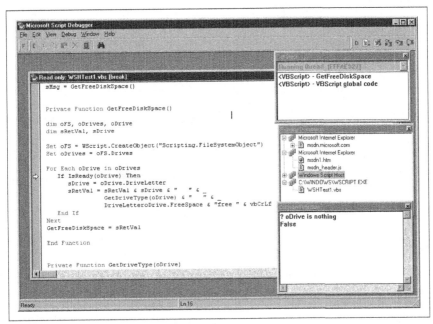

Figure 4-5. The Microsoft Script Debugger

The Script Debugger interface

When you launch the Script Debugger, you're faced with a number of different windows, each with its own special function:

The Script window
This contains the code for the current HTML page just as if you'd selected the View Source option to launch Notepad. It is from the script window that you control how the debugger steps through program execution and that you watch the execution of the script. The script in this window is read-only.

The Running Documents window
This displays a graphical view of the applications that support debugging and the documents that are active in them. To open a particular document, simply double-click its name in the Running Documents window.

The Call Stack window
This displays the current hierarchy of calls made by the program. If the Call Stack window is hidden, you can display it by selecting the Call Stack option from the View menu. The Call Stack window allows you to trace the path that program execution has followed to reach the current routine (and, implicitly, that it must also follow in reverse to "back out" of these routines). For example, let's say you have a client-side script attached to the OnClick event of a button called cmdButton1, which in turn calls a function named *sMyFunction*. When *sMyfunction* is executing, the call stack will be:

```
cmdButton1_OnClick
sMyFunction
```

This allows you to see how program flow has reached the routine it's currently in. It is all too easy when you have a breakpoint set in a particular function to lose track of how the script reached the function. A quick glance at the Call Stack window will tell you.

The Command window

This is the most important part of the debugger. If you have experience in Visual Basic, you can now breath a sigh of relief! The Command window allows you to interrogate the script engine and find the value of variables, expressions, and built-in functions. If the Command window is not visible, you can open it by selecting the Command Window option from the View menu. To use the Command window, type a question mark (?) followed by the name of the variable or value you wish to see, then press Enter. For example:

```
? sMyString
"Hello World"
```

Tracing execution with the Script Debugger

The goal of tracing program execution is to discover, in a logical sequence, how your program is operating. If your program runs but generates an error message— or produces results that are inconsistent with what you expected—it is obviously not operating according to plan. You therefore need to follow the flow of your program as it executes, and at various stages, test the value of key variables and build up an overall "picture" of what is really happening inside of your program. This should enable you to discover where and why your program is being derailed.

To trace the execution of your script, you need a way to "break into" the script while it is running, and then to step through each line of code to determine what execution path is being followed or perhaps where the script is failing. The Script Debugger gives you two ways to halt execution and pass control over to the debugging environment:

Break at Next Statement

The simplest option is to select the Break at Next Statement option from the Script Debugger's Debug menu (or from the Script Debugger submenu of the Internet Explorer View menu). Then run your script in the normal way in the browser. As soon as the first line of scripting code is encountered by the browser, execution is suspended, and you have control over the script in the debugger. However, the part of the script you want to concentrate upon may be many lines of code further on from the first, in which case you will waste time stepping through to the portion that interests you.

Set Breakpoint

You will mostly have a good idea where your code is either failing or not producing the desired results. In this case, you can set a breakpoint by placing your cursor on the line of code at which to halt execution, and then either pressing F9 or selecting Toggle Breakpoint from the Script Editor's Debug menu. A line's breakpoint set is highlighted in red. Run your script from the browser. When the code containing the breakpoint is reached, execution is suspended; you have control over the script in the Debugger.

When the code has been suspended, it must be executed manually from the debugger. There are three methods you can use for stepping through a script one line at a time. For each method, you can either select an option from the debugger's Debug menu or press a keyboard combination. The options are:

Step Into (F8)
> This executes the next line of code. Using Step Into, you can follow every line of execution even if the next line to be executed is within another subroutine or function.

Step Over (Shift-F8)
> This executes the next line of code only within the current subroutine or function. If a call is made to another subroutine or function, the procedure executes in the background before control is passed back to you in the current subroutine.

Step Out (Ctrl-Shift-F8)
> This is required only if you have chosen Step Into and your script has called a function or subroutine. In some cases, you may realize that this is a lengthy procedure that has no consequence to your debugging. In this case, you can select Step Out to automatically execute the rest of the function and break again when control returns to the original subroutine or function.

Determining the value of a variable, expression, or function at runtime

One of the main functions of the Immediate window is to allow you to check the value of a particular variable while the script is running. The most frustrating part about debugging a script prior to the release of the Script Debugger was that you could see the results of your script only after it had run (or failed). Most debugging requires you to get inside the script and wander around while it's in the middle of execution.

In the absence of a debugger, many programmers and content providers inserted calls to the *Window.Alert* method (for client-side scripting), to the *Response.Write* method (for server-side scripting), or to the *MsgBox* function (for WSH scripts and Outlook forms) to serve as breakpoints in various places in a script. The dialog would then display the values of particular variables or expressions selected by the programmer. Although this can still be the most efficient method of debugging when you have a very good idea of what's going wrong with your code, it becomes very cumbersome to continually move these calls and to change the information the dialogs display when you don't really have a very good idea of where or why your script is failing.

In contrast, using the Command window to display the value of any non-object variable is easy. Simply type a question mark (?) followed by a space and the variable name, then press Enter. The Script Debugger will then evaluate the variable and display its value in the Immediate window. Note, though, that if your script requires variable declaration because you've included the Option Explicit statement, you must have declared the variable and it must be in scope for the debugger to successfully retrieve its value; otherwise, an error dialog is displayed. The debugger cannot evaluate the result of user-defined functions; it can evaluate only *intrinsic functions* (functions that are a built-in part of the scripting language).

But you aren't limited to using the Command window to view the values of variables; you can also use it to inspect the values of expressions, of VBScript intrinsic functions, and of the properties and methods of particular objects. To see how this works, and also to get some experience using the Script Debugger, let's try out the web page and client-side script in Example 4-6. Basically, the user should be able to enter a number and, if it is actually between zero and two, be shown the element of the array at that ordinal position. Somewhere in this code is a sneaky little bug causing problems. The script always tells the user that the number entered into the text box is too large, which indicates that it is greater than the upper boundary of the array. But this isn't the case; the user can enter the numbers 0 or 2 and still be told that the number is too large.

Example 4-6. A badly behaving web page

```
<HTML>
<HEAD><TITLE>Testing the Script Debugger</TITLE></HEAD>
<BODY>
<SCRIPT LANGUAGE="VBSCRIPT">

Dim sTest
sTest = Array("Hello World", "Some Data", "AnyData")

Sub cmdButton1_OnClick
    Dim iTest
    iTest = Document.frmForm1.txtText1.Value
    Alert sGetValue(iTest)
End Sub

Function sGetValue(iVal)
    If iVal > UBound(sTest) Then
        sGetValue = "Number too big"
    Elseif iVal < 0 Then
        sGetValue = "Number too small"
    Else
        sGetValue = sTest(iVal)
    End If
End Function

</SCRIPT>

<FORM NAME="frmForm1">
    Input a Number (0-2): <INPUT TYPE="text" NAME="txtText1"> <P>
    <INPUT TYPE="button" NAME="cmdButton1" VALUE="OK">
</FORM>

</BODY>
</HTML>
```

To debug the script in Example 4-6, you can place a breakpoint on the first line of the *sGetValue* function, since this is probably where the problem lies. Then run the script and enter the number 2 into the text box txtText1. When execution is suspended, you can investigate the values of the program's variables. As you can see, the call to the *sGetValue* function has a single argument, *iTest*, which is passed to the function as the *iVal* parameter. So our first step is to determine the value of *iVal* at runtime by entering the following into the Command window:

```
? iVal
```

Press Enter, and the debugger displays the result:

```
2
```

Next, find out what the script thinks the upper boundary of the array is by entering the following in the immediate window and pressing Enter:

```
? UBound(sTest)
```

Note that here you're not simply asking for the value of a variable; you're actually asking the debugger to evaluate the *UBound* function on the *sTest* array and return the result, which is:

```
2
```

So *iVal* is not greater than UBound(sTest). Next, go back to the script window and press F8 to follow the flow of program control. Execution is suspended on the following line, where the string "Number too big" is assigned to the variable *sGetValue*. That indicates that the scripting engine has evaluated the expression incorrectly and has decided that *iVal* is greater then UBound(sTest). So go back to the Command window, and this time try to evaluate the complete expression:

```
? iVal > UBound(sTest)
```

As you might expect from the appearance of the "Number too big" dialog when the script is run, the result of the expression is True, even though the expression that is evaluated (once we replace the variable and expression with their values) is 2 > 2, which is clearly False. Given this apparent incongruity, it seems likely that our problem may be centered in the data types used in the comparison. So try the following:

```
? TypeName(UBound(sTest))
```

Here, you're asking the debugger to evaluate the *UBound* function on the *sTest* array, and, by calling the *TypeName* function, to indicate the data type of the value returned by the *UBound* function. The result is:

```
Long
```

Now find out what data type *iVal* is:

```
? TypeName(iVal):
```

The debugger returns:

```
String
```

Aha! The Script Debugger shows that, in reality, you're performing the following comparison:

```
If "2" > 2 Then
```

which of course is nonsense! Remember that *iVal* is the name within the *sGetValue* function of the *iTest* variable in the button's OnClick event procedure. And *iTest* in turn represents the value retrieved from the textbox, which of course must be string data, as typing the following into the Command window establishes:

```
? TypeName(iTest)
String
```

Try this in the debugger:

```
? CLng(iVal) > UBound(sTest)
```

Success! The Command window shows:

```
False
```

You can see from this debugging exercise that the Command window is a powerful tool allowing you to perform function calls, evaluate complete expressions, and try out different ways of writing your code.

Changing variable values at runtime

Another use for the Command window is to assign a new value to a variable. For example, if you open the web page and client-side script shown in Example 4-7 and click the button, you'll find that an error halts execution on line 10 with the message "Invalid procedure call or argument". If you use the Command window to determine the value of *myNum*, which specifies the starting position of the *InStr* search, you'll find that it was erroneously set to −1, an invalid value that generated the runtime error.

Example 4-7. Runtime error caused by an invalid argument

```
<HTML>
<HEAD><TITLE>Logical Error</TITLE>
<SCRIPT LANGUAGE="vbscript">

Sub cmdButton1_OnClick
    Dim myNum
    Dim sPhrase

    sPhrase = "This is some error"
    myNum = GetaNumber(CInt(Document.frmForm1.txtText1.Value))
    If Instr(myNum, sPhrase, "is") > 0 Then
        Alert "Found it!"
    End If
End Sub

Function GetaNumber(iNum)
    iNum = iNum - 1
    GetaNumber = iNum
End Function

</SCRIPT>
</HEAD>
<BODY BGCOLOR="white">
<FORM NAME="frmForm1">
<INPUT TYPE="hidden" NAME="txtText1" VALUE=0>
<INPUT TYPE="button" NAME="cmdButton1" VALUE="Click Me">
```

Example 4-7. Runtime error caused by an invalid argument (continued)

```
<FORM>
</BODY>
</HTML>
```

You can, however, correct the error and continue executing the script. Just place a breakpoint on the offending line and click on the button when the browser displays it so that the script executes. When program execution halts, you can check the value of *myNum*:

```
? myNum
-1
```

How the VB Debugger and the Script Debugger Differ

If you have experience with Visual Basic, the debugging concepts covered in this section will be familiar to you. However, there are a few features that aren't available to you in the Script Debugger:

No "on the fly" editing
Because the scripting window is read-only, you cannot edit the code during execution, as you can most of the time with VB.

No Instant Watch (Shift-F9)
The VB debugger's instant watch facility, which allows you to high-light a variable in your code, press Shift-F9, and see the value of the variable, is not available in the Script Debugger.

Cannot set watches
Watches do not exist in the Script Debugger.

Cannot set the next statement
Using the VB Debugger, you can place the cursor on a line of code and, by clicking CTRL-F9, have program execution resume at that line. This is particularly useful to backtrack or to re-execute a section of code. Unfortunately, this feature is not available in the Script Debugger.

Error Handling

Error handling does not involve finding errors in your scripts. Instead, use error-handling techniques to allow your program to continue executing even though a potentially fatal error has occurred. Ordinarily, all runtime errors that are generated by the VBScript engine are fatal, since execution of the current script is halted when the error occurs. Error handling allows you to inform the user of the problem and either halt execution of the program or, if it is prudent, continue executing the program.

The On Error Resume Next Statement

There are two main elements to error handling in VBScript. The first is the On Error statement, which informs the VBScript engine of your intention to handle

---

errors yourself, rather than to allow the VBScript engine to display a typically uninformative error message and halt the program. This is done by inserting a statement like the following at the start of a procedure:

```
On Error Resume Next
```

This tells the VBScript engine that, should an error occur, you want it to continue executing the program starting with the line of code that directly follows the line in which the error occurred. For example, in the simple WSH script:

```
On Error Resume Next
x = 10
y = 0
z = x / y
Alert z
```

a "Cannot divide by Zero" error is generated on the fourth line of code because the value of *y* is 0. But because you've placed the On Error statement in line 1, program execution continues with line 5. The problem with this is that when an error is generated, the user is unaware of it; the only indication that an error has occurred is the blank Alert box (from line 5) that's displayed for the user.

 A particular On Error statement is valid until another On Error statement in the line of execution is encountered, or an On Error Goto 0 statement (which turns off error handling) is executed. This means that if Function A contains an On Error statement, and Function A calls Function B, but Function B does not contain an On Error statement, the error handling from Function A is still valid. Therefore, if an error occurs in Function B, it is the On Error statement in Function A that handles the error; in other words, when an error is encountered in Function B, program flow will immediately jump to the line of code that followed the call to Function B in Function A. When Function A completes execution, the On Error statement it contains also goes out of scope. This means that, if the routine that called Function A did not include an On Error statement, no error handling is in place.

This is where the second element of VBScript's error handling comes in. VBScript includes an error object, named Err, which, when used in conjunction with On Error Resume Next, adds much more functionality to error handling, allowing you to build robust programs and relatively sophisticated error-handling routines.

The Err Object

The Err object is part of the VBScript language and contains information about the last error to occur. By checking the properties of the Err object after a particular piece of code has executed, you can determine whether an error has occurred and, if so, which one. You can then decide what to do about the error—you can, for instance, continue execution regardless of the error, or you can halt execution of the program. The main point is that error handling using On Error and the Err object puts you in control of errors, rather than allowing an error to take control of the program (and bring it to a grinding halt). To see how the Err object works and how you can use it within an error-handling regimen within your program, let's begin by taking a look at its properties and methods.

Exception Handling in ASP

ASP 3.0/IIS 5.0 (unlike previous versions of ASP) supports built-in exception handling. Errors in ASP scripts are handled automatically by the web server in one of three ways: by sending a default message to the client, by sending the client the contents of a particular file, or by redirecting the client to an error-handling web page, depending on how the IIS has been configured. Within the error-handling page, the ASPError object can be examined to determine the cause of the error. In ASP 3.0, using the VBScript On Error Resume Next statement circumvents ASP's built-in exception handling and replaces it with VBScript's less flexible error-handling system.

Err object properties

Like all object properties, the properties of the Err object can be accessed by using the name of the object, Err, the dot (or period) delimiter, and the property name. The Err object supports the following properties:

Number

The Number property is a Long value that contains an error code value between -2,147,483,648 and 2,147,483,647. (The possibility of a negative error code value seems incongruous but results from the fact that error codes are unsigned long integers, a data type not supported by VBScript.) VBScript itself provides error code values that range from 0 to 65,535. COM components, however, often provide values outside of this range. If the value of *Err. Number* is 0, no error has occurred. A line of code like the following, then, can be used to determine if an error has occurred:

```
If Err.Number <> 0 Then
```

Although the properties of the Err object provide information on the last error to occur in a script, they do not do so permanently. All the Err object properties, including the Number property, are set either to zero or to zero-length strings after an End Sub, End Function, Exit Sub, or Exit Function statement. In addition, you can explicitly reset *Err.Number* to zero after an error by calling the Err object's Clear method. The WSH script in Example 4-8 illustrates the importance of resetting the Err object after an error occurs.

Example 4-8. Failing to reset the Err object

```
Dim x, y ,z

On Error Resume Next

x = 10
y = 0
z = x / y
If Err.Number <> 0 Then
    MsgBox "There's been an error #1"
```

Example 4-8. Failing to reset the Err object (continued)

```
Else
  MsgBox z
End IF


z = x * y
If Err.Number <> 0 Then
    MsgBox "There's been an error #2"
Else
    MsgBox z
End If


End Sub
```

The division by zero on the fifth line of the script in Example 4-8 generates an error. Therefore, the conditional statement on line 6 evaluates to True and an error dialog is displayed. Program flow then continues at line 12. Line 12 is a perfectly valid assignment statement that always executes without error, but the Err.Number property still contains the error number from the previous error in line 5. As a result, the conditional statement on line 13 evaluates to True, and a second error dialog is displayed. Despite the two error messages, there's only been a single error in the script.

Description

The Description property contains a string that describes the last error that occurred. You can use the Description property to build your own message box alerting the user to an error, as the WSH script in Example 4-9 shows.

Example 4-9. Using the Description property to display error information

```
Dim x, y ,z
On Error Resume Next

x = 10
y = 0
z = x / y
If Err.Number <> 0 Then
    MsgBox "Error number " & Err.Number & ", " & _
          Err.Description & ", has occurred"
    Err.Clear
Else
    MsgBox z
End If


z = x * y
If Err.Number <> 0 Then
    MsgBox "Error No:" & Err.Number & " - " & _
          Err.Description & " has occurred"
    Err.Clear
Else
    Alert z
End If
```

Source

The Source property contains a string that indicates the class name of the object or application that generated the error. You can use the Source property to provide users with additional information about an error—in particular, about where an error occurred.

The value of the Source property for all errors generated within scripted code is simply "Microsoft VBScript runtime error." This is true of all VBScript scripts, whether they're written for Active Server Pages, Windows Script Host, Internet Explorer, or Outlook forms. Obviously, this makes the Source property less than useful in many cases. However, you can assign a value to the Source property in your own error-handling routines to indicate the name of the function or procedure in which an error occurred. In addition, the primary use of the Source property is to signal an error that is generated by some other object, like an OLE automation server (such as Microsoft Excel or Microsoft Word).

Err object methods

The two methods of the Err object allow you to raise or clear an error, while simultaneously changing the values of one or more Err object properties. The two methods are:

Raise

The *Err.Raise* method allows you to generate a runtime error. Its syntax is:[*]

```
Err.Raise(ErrorNumber)
```

where *ErrorNumber* is the numeric code for the error you'd like to generate. At first glance, generating an error within your script may seem like a very odd thing to want to do! However, there are times, particularly when you are creating large, complex scripts, that you need to test the effect a particular error will have on your script. The easiest way to do this is to generate the error by using the *Err.Raise* method and providing the error code to the *ErrorNumber* parameter, then sit back and note how your error-handling routine copes with the error, what the consequences of the error are, and what side effects the error has, if any. The client-side script in Example 4-10, for instance, allows the user to enter a number into a text box, which is passed as the error code value to the *Err.Raise* method. If the value of the error code is non-zero, an Alert box opens that displays the error code and its corresponding description. Figure 4-6, for instance, shows the Alert box that is displayed when the user enters a value of 13 into the text box.

---

[*] A more complete version of the syntax of the Raise method is:

```
Err.Raise(number, source, description)
```

where *source* is the name of the module that generates the error, and *description* is a string describing the error. The latter parameter is useful in particular when handling an application-defined error. This topic—and therefore the complete syntax of the Raise method—is beyond the scope of this chapter.

Example 4-10. Calling the Err.Raise method

```
<HTML>
<HEAD>
<TITLE>Using the Err Object</TITLE>
<SCRIPT LANGUAGE="vbscript">

Sub cmdButton1_OnClick
On Error Resume Next
errN = Document.frm1.errcode.value
Err.Raise(errN)

If Err.Number <> 0 Then
 Alert "Error No:" & Err.Number & " - " & Err.Description
 Err.Number = 0
End If

End Sub

</SCRIPT>
</HEAD>
<BODY BGCOLOR="white">
<CENTER>
<H2>Generating an Error</H2>
<P>
<FORM NAME="frm1">
Enter an Error Code  
<INPUT TYPE="text" NAME="errcode">
<INPUT TYPE="button" NAME="cmdButton1" VALUE="Generate Error">
</CENTER>
</BODY>
</HTML>
```

 An Error Code Generator (*ERRCODES1.HTML*, *ERRCODES1. ASP*, and *ERRCODES1.VBS*), which allows you to generate a complete list of current VBScript error codes, can be found on the O'Reilly Visual Basic web site at *http://vb.oreilly.com*.

Figure 4-6. Generating a Type mismatch error at runtime

Table 4-1 lists a few of the most common runtime errors.

Table 4-1. Some common VBScript error codes

Error number	Description
5	Invalid procedure call
6	Overflow
7	Out of memory
9	Subscript out of range
11	Division by zero
13	Type mismatch

Clear

The Clear method clears the information that the Err object is storing about the previous error; it takes no parameters. It sets the values of *Err.Number* to 0 and the Err object's Source and Description properties to a null string.

Common Problem Areas and How to Avoid Them

There is much to be said for the old maxim, "The best way to learn is by making mistakes." Once you have made a mistake, understood what you did wrong, and rectified the error, you will—in general—have a much better understanding of the concepts involved and of what is needed to build a successful application. But to save you from having to experience this painful process of trial and error in its entirety, we'd like to share with you some of the most common errors that ourselves and other programmers we've worked with have made over the years. These types of errors are actually not unique to VBScript, nor in fact to VB, but to programming in general. In approximate order of frequency, they are:

1. Syntax errors generated by typing errors. This is a tough one. Typing errors— the misspelled function call or variable name—are always going to creep into code somewhere. They can be difficult to detect, particularly because they are typing errors; we frequently train our eyes to see what *should* be there, rather than what is there. When the effect of the typing error is subtle, it becomes even more difficult to detect. For instance, in a client-side script, we had spelled LANGUAGE as LANGAUGE in coding the <SCRIPT> tag. The result was that Internet Explorer immediately began reporting JavaScript syntax errors. This isn't surprising, given that in the absence of a valid LANGUAGE attribute, Internet Explorer used its default scripting language, JScript. But when confronted with this situation, it takes a while to recognize the obvious—that the LANGUAGE attribute for some reason is improperly defined; instead, it seems that Internet Explorer and VBScript are somehow mysteriously "broken." One way to reduce the time spent scratching your head is to build code in small executable stages, testing them as you go. Another good tip is to use individual small sample scripts if you are using a function or set of functions for the first time and aren't sure how they'll work. That allows you to concentrate on just the new functions rather than on the rest of the script as well. And perhaps the most effective technique for reducing troublesome misspelling of variables is to include the Option Explicit directive under the first <SCRIPT> tag in ASP, Internet Explorer, and WSH/XML scripts, and at the top of the page of WSH and Outlook form scripts. This way, any undefined variable—which includes misspelled variables—is caught at runtime.

2. Type mismatches by everyone's favorite data type, the variant. Type mismatches occur when the VBScript engine is expecting data of one variant type—like a string—but is actually passed another data type—like an integer.) Type mismatch errors are fairly uncommon in VBScript, since most of the time the variant data type itself takes care of converting data from one type to another. That tends, though, to make type mismatch errors all the more frustrating. For instance, in Example 4-5, if we hadn't used the statements:

```
nNum1 = CDbl(Server.HTMLEncode(Request.Form("txtNum1")))
nNum2 = CDbl(Server.HTMLEncode(Request.Form("txtNum2")))
nQuot = CDbl(Server.HTMLEncode(Request.Form("txtQuotient")))
```

to convert the form data submitted by the user to numeric data, our application would not have functioned as expected. The best way to reduce or eliminate type mismatch errors is to adhere as closely as possible to a uniform set of VBScript coding conventions. (For a review of coding conventions and their significance, see Chapter 2.) For instance, when you know that a variable is going to hold a string, use a variable name like *strMyVar* to indicate its type, etc. Code becomes easier to use if you can tell instantly that some operation (like strMyString = intMyInt * dteMyDate) doesn't make sense, but you're none the wiser if your line of code reads a = b * c.

3. Subscript Out Of Range is an error that occurs frequently when using arrays. It actually doesn't take much to eliminate this error for good. All you have to do is check the variable value you're about to use to access the array element against the value of the *UBound* function, which lets you know exactly what the maximum subscript of an array is.

4. The next most common error is division by zero. If you try to divide any number by zero, you'll kill your script stone dead. While it's very easy to generate a division by zero error in a script, it's also not at all difficult to prevent it. A division by zero error is easy to diagnose: whenever a variable has a value of zero, it's likely to cause a problem. So all your script has to do is check its value and, if it turns out to be zero, not perform the division. There's no rocket science here! Simply use an If x = 0 Then conditional statement, where *x* is the variable representing the divisor.

5

VBScript with Active Server Pages

At root, web servers are pieces of software: they receive an incoming client request and handle it by transmitting a stream of bytes back to the client. Getting the web server to do something else—for instance, to respond to user interaction by sending back one byte stream rather than another, to save user state information from page to page, to add data from a database to the byte stream returned to the client, or to perform backend processing on the client request—requires a web server *extension*. Traditionally, web server extensions for Windows were developed using two technologies: Common Gateway Interface (CGI) and Common Gateway Interface for Windows (WinCGI). These are out-of-process extensions that communicate with the web server through standard input and output (in the case of CGI) or initialization files (WinCGI), which are both very inefficient methods that do not scale well. Microsoft Internet Information Server 1.0 added a new technology, Internet Server Application Programming Interface (ISAPI), that allowed developers to create applications or filters that ran in the same process as the web server, thus achieving better performance and greater scalability. Unfortunately, developing ISAPI applications and filters required an experienced C or C++ programmer, and thus was out of the reach of the vast majority of web content providers.

Active Server Pages was first introduced in Microsoft Internet Information Server 3.0 and allows web server extensions to be developed using *scripts* that can be written in any language that supports Microsoft's Component Object Model (COM)—although the most common language for developing ASP scripts is VBScript. This makes ASP application development accessible to more web content providers than any previous technology for creating shell extensions.

In addition, Active Server Pages allows for the use of server-side components (that is, of COM components written in any of a number of programming languages, most notably Visual Basic) to enhance and better control web applications. The reasons for developing an ASP component rather than a simple script include the items shown in the following list.

- The functionality that an application requires is not available from VBScript or other scripted languages.

- The functionality is to be implemented in multiple web pages or web applications, rather than for just one web page or web application.

- The component offers significantly better performance than its scripted counterpart. That is, the scripted equivalent of the component is a performance bottleneck.

For a book that shows how to develop ASP components using Visual C++, Visual Basic, and Visual J++, see *Developing ASP Components*, by Shelley Powers (O'Reilly & Associates).

How ASP Works

Active Server Pages is implemented as an IIS component—in fact, as an ISAPI filter—that resides in a dynamic link library named *ASP.DLL*. (ISAPI filters are custom web server extensions that are called for every HTTP request received by the web server.) If the file extension of the resource requested by the client is *.asp*, Active Server Pages is used to parse the file and handle the client request; otherwise, it is bypassed.

ASP does not view pages purely on a one-by-one basis. Instead, it organizes its pages into *applications*. An ASP application is the entire set of files that can be accessed in a virtual directory and its subdirectories. This notion of an ASP application allows you to define global variables whose values are shared across all users of your ASP application, as well as to have ASP save state information from a particular client's session.

When ASP is used to parse a web page, it first checks to see whether the request has originated from a new client. If the client is new, ASP checks the *global.asa* file (which is stored in the application's virtual root directory) to determine whether any session-level data is to be initialized. If the client's is the first request for the ASP application, ASP also checks *global.asa* for any application-level data as well. ASP then parses the HTML page, executes any script contained on the page, and includes any output from scripts into the HTML stream. Note that the output of ASP is HTML with or without client-side script; no server-side script contained in the ASP page is passed on to the client.

The global.asa File

As we've noted, when ASP receives a request from a new user, it checks the *global.asa* file, which must be located in the ASP application's virtual root directory. If the request from the new user is the first request for the ASP application, the Application_OnStart event procedure, if it is present, is executed before the Session_OnStart event. When a user session ends, usually because the session has timed out, ASP checks *global.asa* for a Session_OnEnd event. When the application's last user session ends, ASP also checks whether code for the Applictaion_OnEnd event is present as well.

In addition, *global.asa* can use the <OBJECT> tag to define application-level and session-level objects. All objects declared to have application scope with the <OBJECT> tag are available throughout the application and can be accessed through the Application object's StaticObjects collection. <OBJECT> tagged objects that have session scope are available in a single client session and can be accessed through the Session object's StaticObjects collection. The syntax of the <OBJECT> tag is:

```
<OBJECT RUNAT=SERVER SCOPE=scope ID=name PROGID=progid>
```

where scope is either Application or Session, name is the name by which the object variable will be referenced in code, and progid is the object's programmatic identifier, as defined in the registry.

Example 5-1 shows the shell of a simple *global.asa* file. This file is fully customizable, so it can be changed to cater to your specific application needs. Of course, event handlers that you don't intend to use need not be present in the file. If you choose not to take advantage of any application-level or session-level variables, initialization, and cleanup, you need not create a *global.asa* file.

Example 5-1. The structure of a global.asa file

```
<OBJECT RUNAT=Server SCOPE=Session ID=strName PROGID="progid">
</OBJECT>

<OBJECT RUNAT=Server SCOPE=Application ID=strName
        PROGID="progid">
</OBJECT>

<Script Language=VBScript Runat=Server>

Sub Application_OnStart
    'Code for handling startup events goes here
End Sub

Sub Application_OnEnd
    'Code for terminating events goes here
End Sub

Sub Session_OnStart
    ' Code for handling session startup goes here
End Sub

Sub Session_OnEnd
    'Code for handling session termination goes here
End Sub

</Script>
```

Including Server-Side Script in Web Pages

ASP offers two methods for incorporating server-side script into a web page: server-side includes and the HTML <SCRIPT> tag.

The <SCRIPT>...</SCRIPT> tags define a single code block. The <SCRIPT> tag has the following format if you're developing your ASP applications with VBScript:

```
<SCRIPT LANGUAGE="VBScript" RUNAT="Server">
    VBScript code goes here
</SCRIPT>
```

RUNAT="Server"

A common source of error for those writing their own ASP code is the omission of the RUNAT attribute. This causes the code to execute on the client rather than on the server, which invariably produces numerous syntax and other errors.

A single web page can include any number of <SCRIPT>...</SCRIPT> tags. The tags can be located anywhere within the <HEAD>...</HEAD> or the <BODY>...</BODY> tags of an ASP document. A single script block must contain code written in a single language to run at a single location (i.e., either the server or the client). If you want to run code on both the server and the client, separate script blocks are required. In the latter case, you can omit the RUNAT attribute from the <SCRIPT> clause. If you want to write script in multiple languages, separate code blocks are required for each language. Just supply a string that identifies the language to the LANGUAGE attribute for each scripting block.

Within the script tags, the order of execution of any page-level code (that is, code not located within functions or procedures) is undefined. In other words, you can't rely on it having been executed at the point in your script when values of its variables may be needed. As a result, it's best to limit the code contained within the <SCRIPT>...</SCRIPT> tags to complete functions and procedures, as well as to variable declarations (but not assignments) using the Dim, Public, and Private statements.

The second way to include script in an HTML page is to use the <%...%> or <%= %> delimiters, or the *primary script commands*. All code within the delimiters must be written in the primary scripting language defined for the application or for the ASP page, whichever has the least restrictive scope. The default application scripting language is defined by the Default ASP Language property on the App Options tab in the snap-in for IIS 5.0. It can be overridden for an individual page by including the <@ LANGUAGE=*ScriptingEngine*%> directive at the beginning of an ASP page, where *ScriptingEngine* is the name of the language.

Both types of primary script commands contain code that is executed sequentially as the portion of the HTML page that contains them is parsed. The difference between the <%...%> and the <%=...%> delimiters is that the former can contain executable code but does not automatically send output to the HTML response stream, while the latter contains a variable or expression whose value is output into the HTML response stream. In practice, this is not a restriction for the former tag, since you can use the *Response.Write* method from the ASP object model to write to the HTML output stream.

Example 5-2 shows a simple ASP page that contains both a script block and primary script commands. The first primary script command calls the user-defined *Greeting* function and writes the string it returns to the HTML response stream. The *Greeting* function itself is defined in the script block. It retrieves the time on the server and returns a string indicating whether it is morning, afternoon, or evening. The second primary script command simply calls the VBScript

Now function to insert the date and time into the HTML response stream. Notice from the HTML source shown in Figure 5-1 that the HTML page produced by the ASP page in Example 5-2 contains HTML only; the server-side script has been either discarded or replaced with the text that it has output.

Example 5-2. A simple ASP page

```
<HTML>
<HEAD><TITLE>A Simple ASP Page</TITLE></HEAD>
<BODY>
<SCRIPT LANGUAGE="VBScript" RUNAT="Server">
Private Function Greeting( )
    Dim timNow
    timNow = Time
    If timNow <= CDate("12:00:00") Then
        Greeting = "Good Morning"
    ElseIf timNow <= CDate("18:00:00") Then
        Greeting = "Good Afternoon"
    Else
        Greeting = "Good Evening"
    End If
End Function
</SCRIPT>

<%=Greeting( ) %>, the time is <%= Now %> on the server.<P>

</BODY>
</HTML>
```

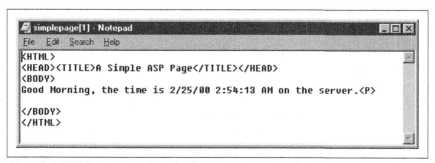

Figure 5-1. HTML source produced by the ASP page in Example 5-2

Note that ASP allows you to import script or HTML from external files by using the #include server-side directive. It is discussed in Chapter 3.

Active Server Pages Object Model

Although VBScript is a powerful, flexible scripting language when used to develop ASP applications, you can do relatively little with VBScript by itself. That is, most of the power and efficiency of ASP becomes available only when you use VBScript to access the Active Server Pages object model. In an ASP application, each of the objects in the ASP object model is globally available throughout your script; you don't have to do anything special to instantiate ASP objects.

ASP includes six intrinsic objects, each of which are detailed in the following:

Application

An object whose collections and property values are shared across all instances of the application. (An *ASP application*, once again, is the entire set of files that can be accessed in a virtual directory and its subdirectories.) The Application object supports the members listing in Table 5-1.

Table 5-1. Members of the Application object

Name	Description
Contents Collection	Contains all application-scoped variables and objects added by script.
Lock Method	Locks the Contents collection, preventing other instances from accessing it until it is unlocked. Its syntax is `Application.Lock( )`.
OnEnd Event	Fired when the last user session ends.
OnStart Event	Fired when the first user session starts.
StaticObjects Collection	Contains all application-scoped variables added by the `<OBJECT>` tag.
Unlock Method	Unlocks the Contents collection so that other instances can access it. Its syntax is `Application.Unlock( )`.

The Contents and StaticObjects collections have the members shown in Table 5-2.

Table 5-2. Members of the Application object's Contents collections

Name	Description
Count Property	Indicates the number of members in the collection.
Item Property	Retrieves a member by its ordinal position in the collection or its name. Its syntax is `oCollec.Item(index)` where *index* is the one-based position of the member in the collection or its name.
Key Property	Returns the name of a particular element in the collection that's found at a specified ordinal position. Its syntax is `oCollec.Key(index)` where *index* is the one-based position of the member in the collection.
Remove Method	Removes a designated member from the Contents collection; it is not supported for the StaticObjects collection. Its syntax is `oCollec.Key(index)` where *index* is the one-based position of the member in the collection or its name. Available in IIS 5.0 only.
RemoveAll Method	Removes all the members from the Contents collection; it is not supported for the StaticObjects collection. Available in IIS 5.0 only.

ObjectContext

An object that provides transactional support to scripts. The ObjectContext object supports the members listed in Table 5-3 from a scripted page.

Table 5-3. Members of the ObjectContext object

Name	Description
OnTransactionAbort Event	Fired when a transaction is aborted.
OnTransactionCommit Event	Fired when a transaction is committed.

Table 5-3. Members of the ObjectContext object (continued)

Name	Description
SetAbort Method	Indicates the transaction cannot complete and changes should be rolled back. Its syntax is `ObjectContext.SetAbort( )`.
SetComplete Method	Indicates that from the viewpoint of the script, the transaction has completed successfully. If all other components participating in the transaction also call SetComplete, the transaction can be committed. Its syntax is `ObjectContext.SetComplete( )`.

Request

Gives you access to the client's HTTP request header and body, as well as to some information about the server handling the request. The members of the Request object are listed in Table 5-4. All collections are read-only. The Request object also maintains a sort of "super-collection" that allows you to search for any members of the QueryString, Form, Cookies, ClientCertificate, and ServerVariables collections using the syntax:

```
vValue = Request("name")
```

Table 5-4. Members of the Request object

Name	Description
BinaryRead Method	Returns a SAFEARRAY structure containing data retrieved from the client. This method is primarily for C/C++ programmers.
ClientCertificate Collection	Contains the fields stored in the client certificate that is sent in the HTTP request, if there is one.
Cookies Collection	Contains the cookies sent in the HTTP request.
Form Collection	Contains form elements sent in the HTTP request body.
QueryString Collection	Contains the values of variables sent in the HTTP query string.
ServerVariables Collection	Contains predefined environment variables and their values.
TotalBytes Property	Indicates the total number of bytes sent by the client in the body of the request; read-only.

The collections of the Request object support the members shown in Table 5-5.

Table 5-5. Members of the Request object's collections

Name	Description
Count Property	A read-only property that returns the total number of members in the collection. The property is not available for the ClientCertificate collection, whose members are predefined.
Item Property	A read-only property that returns the value of a specific element in the collection. Its syntax is `oCollec.Item(Index)` where `Index` can be either the one-based ordinal position of the item in the collection or its key.
Key Property	A read-only property that returns the name or key value of a specific element in the collection. Its syntax is `oCollec.Item(Index)` where `Index` is the one-based ordinal position in the collection of the key whose name you want to retrieve.

Retrieving and then outputting raw user input from the Request object's Form and QueryString collections leaves a site open to cross-site security scripting attacks. For details on what these security holes are and how to avoid them, see an article written by Michael Howard at *http://msdn.microsoft.com/library/default. asp?url=/library/en-us/dncode/html/secure07152002.asp*.

Response

Allows you to control the output sent back to the requestor. The Response object's members are shown in Table 5-6.

Table 5-6. Members of the Response object

Name	Description
AddHeader Method	Adds a custom HTTP response header and its corresponding value to the HTTP output stream. Its syntax is Response.AddHeader strName, strValue where strName is the name of the response header and strValue is its value.
AppendToLog Method	Adds a string to the server's log entry for the current client request. Its syntax is Response.AppendToLog strLogEntry where strLogEntry is a string of up to 80 characters without commas that will be appended to the log.
BinaryWrite Method	Writes information directly to the response body without any character conversion. Its syntax is Request.BinaryWrite arbyteData where arbyteData is an array containing the binary bytes to be written.
Buffer Property	Determines whether script output is included in the HTML stream all at once (Buffer = True) or a line at a time (Buffer = False).
CacheControl Property	A string value that determines whether proxy servers serving your pages can cache your page. If set to "Public," pages can be cached; if set to "Private," pages cannot be cached.
Charset Property	Specifies a character set for the HTTP response content. The default character set is ISO-LATIN.
Clear Method	Clears any part of the response body that's been written to the output buffer. Its syntax is Response.Clear. The use of this method requires that the Buffer property of the Response object be set to True.
ContentType Property	Defines the value of the Content-Type in the HTTP response header, which determines the type of data sent in the response body. The default value of the ContentType property is "Text/HTML."
Cookies Collection	Defines or accesses cookies to be written to the client machine. It has the same members as the Cookies collection of the Request object, except the Item property can be used to add a cookie to the collection as well as to retrieve an existing cookie.
End Method	Closes the output buffer, sends its contents to the client, and stops the web server from processing additional code. Its syntax is Response.End.
Expires Property	Specifies the number of minutes that the client may cache the current page.
ExpiresAbsolute Property	Provides a date and time after which the content of the current page should no longer be cached by the client.
Flush Method	Immediately sends all content in the output buffer to the client. Its syntax is Response.Flush.
IsClientConnected Property	A read-only property that indicates whether the client is still connected to the server (its value is True) or not (its value is False).
PICS Property	Provides a PICS (Platform for Internet Content Selection) label to the HTTP response header.

Table 5-6. Members of the Response object (continued)

Name	Description
Redirect Method	Redirects the client's request to another URL. Its syntax is `Response.Redirect strURL` where `strURL` is the URL of the resource to which the client will be redirected.
Status Property	Defines the HTTP status line that is returned to the client. Its default value is "200 OK."
Write Method	Writes information directly to the HTTP response body. Its syntax is `Response.Write strData` where `strData` is the data to be written to the output stream.

Server

Provides miscellaneous functionality, including the ability to instantiate ActiveX components and to get any information from the server necessary for properly handling your application. The Server object has the members listed in Table 5-7.

Table 5-7. Members of the Server object

Name	Description
CreateObject Method	Instantiates an object on the server. Its syntax is `Set obj = Server.CreateObject(strProgID)` where `strProgID` is the programmatic identifier of the object to be instantiated, as defined in the system registry. You should use the Server object's CreateObject method to instantiate an external component (like ADO, CDO, or one of the custom components included with IIS) rather than calling the VBScript *CreateObject* function.
Execute Method	Calls an *.asp* file and processes it as if it were part of the calling script. Its syntax is `Server.Execute strPath` where `strPath` is the location of the *.asp* file to execute. Available with IIS 5.0 and later.
GetLastError Method	Returns an ASPError object providing information about the last error. Its syntax is `Server.GetLastError( )`. The method (as well as the ASPError object) is new to IIS 5.0. The ASPError object itself has the following members: *ASPCode* Returns the error code generated by IIS. *ASPDescription* For ASP-related errors, returns a longer description of the error than that provided by the Description property. *Category* Returns a string indicating whether the source of the error was IIS, the scripting language, or a component. *Column* Indicates the column within the *.asp* file that generated the error. *Description* Returns a short description of the error. *File* Returns the name of the *.asp* file that was being processed when the error occurred. *Line* Indicates the line within the *.asp* file that generated the error. *Number* Returns a standard COM error code. *Source* If available, returns the source code on the line containing the error.

VBScript with ASP

Table 5-7. Members of the Server object (continued)

Name	Description
HTMLEncode Method	Sends the actual HTML source to the output stream. Its syntax is `Server.HTMLEncode strHTMLString` where `strHTMLString` is the string whose HTML code is to be displayed on the client.
MapPath Method	Returns the physical path on the server that corresponds to a virtual or relative path. Its syntax is `Server.MapPath strPath` where `strPath` is a complete virtual path or a path relative to the current script's directory.
ScriptTimeout Property	Defines the maximum number of seconds that the web server will continue processing a script. Its default value is 90 seconds.
Transfer Method	Sends all of the information available to one *.asp* file—its Application and Session objects and variables as well as all information from the client request—to a second *.asp* file for processing. Its syntax is `Server.Transfer strPath` where `strPath` is the path and name of the *.asp* file to which control is to be transferred. New to IIS 5.0.
URLEncode Method	Applies URL encoding to a string so that it can be sent as a query string. Its syntax is `Server.URLEncode strURL` where `strURL` is the string to be encoded.

Session

A Session is created for every visitor to your web site. You can use this object to store Session-specific information and to retain "state" throughout the client session. The Session object has the members listed in Table 5-8.

Table 5-8. Members of the Session object

Name	Description
Abandon Method	Releases the memory used by the web server to maintain information about a given user session. Its syntax is Session.Abandon.
CodePage Property	Sets or retrieves the code page that the web server uses to display content in the current page.
Contents Collection	Contains all session-scoped variables and objects added by script.
LCID Property	Sets or returns a valid local identifier that the web server uses to display content to the client.
OnEnd Event	Fired when the user session ends.
OnStart Event	Fired when the new user session starts.
SessionID Property	A read-only value of type Long that uniquely identifies each current user session.
StaticObjects Collection	Contains all session-scoped variables and objects added by the `<OBJECT>` tag.
TimeOut Property	A Long that defines the number of minutes the web server will maintain a user's session without the user requesting or refreshing a page. Its default value is 20 minutes.

The Session object's Contents and StaticObjects collections have the members listed in Table 5-9.

Table 5-9. Members of the Session objects Contents and StaticObjects collections

Name	Description
Count Property	Indicates the number of members in the collection.
Item Property	Retrieves a member by its ordinal position in the collection or its name. Its syntax is oCollec.Item(*index*) where *index* is the one-based position of the member in the collection or its name.
Key Property	Returns the name of a particular element in the collection that's found at a specified ordinal position. Its syntax is oCollec.Key(*index*) where *index* is the one-based position of the member in the collection.
Remove Method	Removes a designated member from the Contents collection; it is not supported for the StaticObjects collection. Its syntax is oCollec.Key(*index*) where *index* is the one-based position of the member in the collection or its name. Available in IIS 5.0 only.
RemoveAll Method	Removes all the members from the Contents collection; it is not supported for the StaticObjects collection. Available in IIS 5.0 only.

For more detailed information about the ASP Object Model, refer to *ASP in a Nutshell*, Second Edition, by A. Keyton Weissinger (O'Reilly).

VBScript
with ASP

6

Programming Outlook Forms

Until the release of Microsoft Office 2000, Microsoft Outlook was clearly an idiosyncratic member of the Office suite. First released in Office 97 and later released in an interim version as Outlook 98, Outlook was the sole member of the Office family to feature VBScript as its programming language. Outlook 2000 finally added support for VBA and for the VBA-integrated development environment. However, in Outlook 2000 and Outlook 2002, VBScript remains as the programming language behind Outlook's custom forms.

Designing and programming Outlook forms is a large topic that has been the sole focus of a number of books, most notably *Building Applications with Microsoft Outlook*, published by Microsoft Press and available in various editions covering different versions of Outlook. Our focus in this chapter will not be on designing, creating, or modifying Outlook forms, but rather on programming those forms with VBScript.

Why Program Outlook Forms?

As a general purpose personal information management system (or PIM), Microsoft Outlook includes most of the general features that an individual or a group must perform, including such tasks as reading, sending, and organizing email, scheduling meetings, keeping notes, and maintaining a contacts list. The emphasis here, though, is on *general*; Outlook offers the basic set of features that most users require. In order to make Outlook capable of addressing the particular needs of individual users or groups of users, Microsoft added a number of customization and extensibility features to the product. These include Outlook's programmability (at an application level using VBA or a forms level using VBScript) and the ability to create custom forms.

By attaching VBScript code to either existing forms or new forms, you can modify the appearance or the behavior of the form, thus making it suitable for special applications. For example, you can:

- Change the recipient of an email message based on the content of the message to which you are replying

- Display or hide particular elements of a form depending on the attributes or content of a message, an appointment, or a contact

- Automatically store an item in a nondefault folder based on the item's attributes or content

- Get at data in some other document—like a Word document or an Excel spreadsheet—to include as your form's data

- Manipulate data stored in Outlook to summarize or display in an Outlook form

The Form-Based Development Environment

Although this chapter will discuss attaching code to Outlook forms, rather than creating and modifying Outlook forms themselves, we'll begin by looking at how the Outlook object model views the Outlook user interface and by briefly examining how you access and work with Outlook forms in design mode; both topics provide background that is necessary in order to begin coding. Then we'll look at Outlook's rather primitive VBScript environment.

Interfaces and Objects

Figure 6-1 shows a more-or-less standard Outlook window with Outlook displaying a mail folder. The Outlook window is divided into three parts, which correspond to four elements of the Outlook object model.

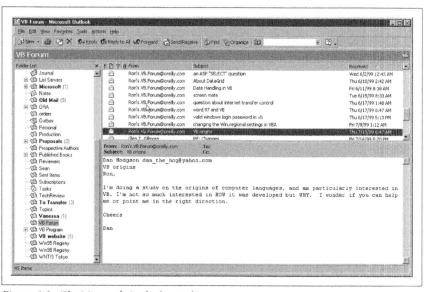

Figure 6-1. The Microsoft Outlook interface

The Folder List

On the left of the Outlook window is the Folder List. In the Outlook object model, this corresponds to the NameSpace object, which has a Folders collection in which each Folder object represents a folder in the MAPI store.

The Explorer

On the upper right of the Outlook window is the Explorer pane. (The term "Explorer" here is unrelated to Windows Explorer, the utility for displaying the Windows namespace and filesystem.) The Explorer pane is responsible for listing the items in the current folder. Each type of item has its own Explorer object, which is a member of the Explorers collection.

The Inspector

On the lower right of the Outlook window is the Preview pane. In other cases, when the entire right side of the Outlook window is occupied by the Explorer pane, the Preview pane appears when the user selects an item in the Explorer pane. The Preview pane is responsible for displaying the item selected in the Explorer pane and corresponds to an Inspector object in the Outlook object model. Note that the Inspector object uses an Outlook form to present a particular view of an Outlook data item.

An item

An item is one of several different object types that hold information. Outlook items include mail messages, appointments, and contacts. In the Outlook object model, these correspond to objects of specific kinds. For instance, a mail message is represented by a MailItem object, while an appointment is represented by an AppointmentItem object and a contact is represented by a ContactItem object. Table 6-1 lists the items available in Outlook and their corresponding objects in the Outlook object model.

Table 6-1. Outlook items and their objects

Item type	Outlook object
appointment	AppointmentItem object
contact	ContactItem object
distribution list	DistListItem object
document	DocumentItem object
journal entry	JournalItem object
mail message	MailItem object
mail nondelivery report	ReportItem object
meeting	MeetingItem object
note	NoteItem object
post	PostItem object
remote mail message	RemoteItem object
task	TaskItem object
task acceptance notification	TaskRequestAcceptItem object
task rejection notification	TaskRequestDeclineItem object
task assignment request	TaskRequestItem object
task assignment update	TaskRequestUpdateItem object

With this basic (and frequently nonintuitive) terminology out of the way, we return to the discussion of accessing the environment for developing Outlook forms.

Outlook Form Design Mode

Outlook requires that a form be in design mode rather than in run (or display) mode before you can attach code to it. You can select the form that you'd like to program and open it in run mode in any of the following ways:

- Select File → New from Outlook's main menu and choose the form type you'd like to create, modify, or code from the available menu items (Mail Message, Appointment, etc.).
- Select File → New → Choose Form from Outlook's main menu. Outlook opens the Choose Form dialog, which allows you to select an existing form.
- Select Tools → Forms → Choose Form from Outlook's main menu. Outlook opens the Choose Form dialog, which allows you to select an existing form.

You can then place the form in design mode by selecting Tools → Forms → Design This Form from the form's menu.

You can also open a form and place it in design mode in either of the following ways:

- Select Tools → Forms → Design a Form from Outlook's main menu. Outlook opens the Design Form dialog, which allows you to select the form you'd like to open. Outlook then opens the form you select in design mode.
- Select Tools → Forms → Design a Form from the menu of an Outlook form either when it is in design mode or in run mode. Outlook opens the Design Form dialog, which prompts you for the form you'd like to open. Outlook then opens the form in design mode.

Since Outlook's form-based development environment is somewhat idiosyncratic, let's review some of the basics of working with Outlook forms:

- You can't create a new Outlook form directly. To create a new form, you have to open an existing form, modify it, and save it as a new form.
- You can modify an existing form by simply overwriting it. However, Outlook won't permit you to overwrite forms in the Standard Forms Library, where Outlook stores its "hardcoded" forms.
- You can create or modify any type of Outlook form except for a note. Notes cannot be customized, nor are they programmable, presumably because of their extreme simplicity.
- You don't "save" a form that you've modified or created. Instead, you "publish" it by clicking on the Publish Form button on the item's toolbar or by selecting the Tools → Forms → Publish Form or Tools → Form → Publish Form As option from the item's menu.
- You can retrieve forms from and save forms to a variety of locations:

  The Standard Forms library
  > These are the "out of the box" forms provided by Outlook. The library is read-only; if you modify its forms, you have to save them elsewhere.

The Personal Forms library

These are customized forms stored in the current user's personal store (*.pst*) file. As a result, they are inaccessible to other users.

The Organizational Forms library

For organizations using Microsoft Exchange, these forms are stored on the server and are accessible to all Outlook users with access to the server and with the necessary permissions. The library is unavailable for Outlook clients not using Microsoft Exchange.

An Outlook folder

Forms stored in Outlook folders are accessible only in that folder. If the folder is a public one, then the form is available to all users with access to the folder. Otherwise, the form is stored in the user's *.pst* file and is accessible only to him.

- Outlook forms use the controls found in the MS Forms library—the same set of controls used in Microsoft Office UserForms. The controls are displayed on the control toolbox, which becomes visible when you click on the Control Toolbox button on a form's toolbar, or when you select Form → Control Toolbox from a form's menu.

- Just as in Visual Basic and in the VBA-hosted environments, you work with controls by setting their properties. The standard properties sheet is displayed when you select Form → Advanced Properties from the form's menu. A more user-friendly Properties dialog is displayed when you select Form → Properties from the form's menu.

- You can choose the data fields that your form displays by selecting them from the Field Chooser. The Field Chooser can be made visible by clicking on the Field Chooser button on the form's toolbar or by selecting the Form → Field Chooser option from the form's menu.

The VBScript Environment

To write code for your form, open the VBScript editor by clicking on the View Code button on the form's toolbar or select the View Code option from the form's Form menu. Outlook will open the VBScript editor, which is shown in Figure 6-2.

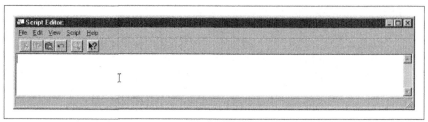

Figure 6-2. The VBScript editor

If you're familiar with the rich development environments of Visual Basic or the hosted versions of VBA, you'll recognize the VBScript editor as an extremely poor cousin. In fact, the editor is distinctly Notepad-like, without any of the amenities of the VBA IDE. Syntax is not checked automatically, nor are auto list members, auto quick info, or auto data tips available. In fact, the editor does not even have an option that allows you to require variable declaration. This feature, which is available in the VB and VBA IDEs, automatically adds an Option Explicit statement to each code module.

In keeping with its minimalist approach, the VBScript editor offers an object browser, though it lacks most of the ease-of-use features of the Object Browser found in the VBA IDE. To open it, select Script → Object Browser from the VBScript Editor's menu. The VBScript object browser is shown in Figure 6-3. It lacks the icons that help identify elements in the VBA Object Browser. (For instance, the entries that begin "Ol" in the Classes list box are enumerations; casual inspection might lead you to completely overlook that fact.) Nor is the VBScript object browser searchable, which is a serious limitation. Finally, in the case of form-level events (which the object browser depicts as members of the ItemEvents object), the prototypes displayed by the object browser in the status bar are not completely consistent with the shells that the editor creates for them. For experienced programmers, this discrepancy will most probably go unnoticed. For inexperienced programmers, it serves as another source of needless confusion.

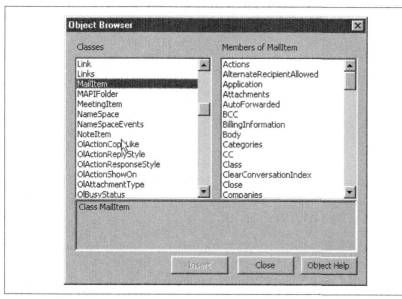

Figure 6-3. The VBScript object browser

If you need to browse the Outlook object model while you're programming, it's best to use the VBA Object Browser. It's available by opening the VBA IDE (select Tools → Macro → Visual Basic Editor from the Outlook menu) and pressing F2.

Running Your Code

The "hook" that allows your code to run is an *event handler* or an *event procedure*. Outlook recognizes particular external events—like an instance of a form

being opened, or the user clicking on the Send button to send a mail message—
and responds by firing an event. If a procedure exists to handle that event, its code
is executed automatically. The event procedure can in turn call other procedures
or functions, which can also call other procedures and functions, and so on.

Using VBScript, you are able to access only form-level events and control-level
events; events at other levels, such as the application or even the Items collection
level, cannot be trapped within the scripted environment. You can examine a list
of some of the available events in the VBScript editor by selecting Script → Event
Handler. The editor opens the Insert Event Handler dialog like the one shown in
Figure 6-4. If you select one of the events from the list box, the editor automatically creates the code shell for the event procedure. For example, if you were to
select the Open item (which is fired just before a form is opened) in Figure 6-4,
the editor would automatically generate the following code:

```
Function Item_Open( )

End Function
```

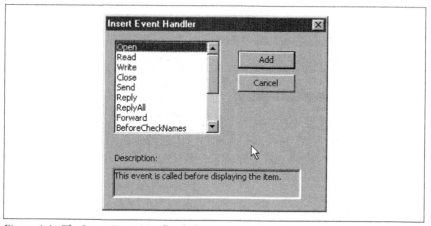

Figure 6-4. The Insert Event Handler dialog

Note that Outlook identifies the object whose Open event is being fired as "Item."
Each form represents a particular kind of Item object—an email message, for
instance, is represented by a MailItem object, while an appointment is represented by an AppointmentItem object. In other words, "Item" generically
identifies the current item in much the same way that "Form" in Visual Basic
identifies the current form. Each of the Outlook item object types listed in
Table 6-1 supports the events for which the VBScript editor automatically generates a code shell.

If any arguments are passed by Outlook to your event handler, they are shown in
the code shell created by the editor. For example, if you were to select the Attach-
mentAdd item, the editor would generate the following code automatically:

```
Sub Item_AttachmentAdd(ByVal NewAttachment)

End Sub
```

In this case, a single argument, which is referred to as *NewAttachment* within the event handler, is passed by value to the event handler; it represents the name of the file to be attached to a mail message.

Note that the editor identified the handler for the Item_Open event as a function, while it identified the handler for the Item_AttachmentAdd event as a subroutine. The difference is significant: a subroutine (defined with the Sub keyword) does not return a value, while a function (defined with the Function keyword) does. In the case of the Open event, the function returns a Boolean value that, if True, indicates that the form should be opened and, if False, cancels the open operation. So if the statement:

```
Item_Open = False
```

is executed within the function, the Item_Open event procedure will return a value of False, and Outlook will not open the item.

Table 6-2 lists the events that you can select from the Insert Event Handler dialog and for which you can write event handlers. In addition, the table notes the types of items to which the event applies, lists any arguments passed to the handler, and, in the case of functions, notes their possible return values.

Table 6-2. Events automatically recognized by the VBScript editor

Event	Description
AttachmentAdd	Fired when an attachment is added to an item.
	Parameter: *NewAttachment*, a reference to an Attachment object passed by value that represents the newly attached file.
AttachmentRead	Fired when an attachment is opened.
	Parameter: *ReadAttachment*, a reference to an Attachment object passed by value that represents the attachment.
BeforeAttachmentSave	Fired before an attachment is saved.
	Parameter: *SaveAttachment*, a reference to an Attachment object passed by value that represents the attachment to save.
BeforeCheckNames	Fired before Outlook begins to check the names in the Recipients collection, which contains all the recipients of an item.
	Return Value: If False, the default value, Outlook checks recipients' names. If set to True, the names check is cancelled.
Close	Fired before the Inspector (the window that displays an item) associated with the item is closed.
	Return Value: If True, the default value, the Inspector is closed. If set to False, cancels the close operation and keeps the Inspector open.
CustomAction	Fired when a custom action of an Outlook item executes.
	Parameters: *Action*, a reference to an Action object passed by value that defines the custom action; *NewItem*, a ByVal reference to the object created as a result of the custom action.
	Return Value: If True (the default), allows the custom action to complete. If set to False, the custom action is not complete.
	Optional: False when the event occurs. If the event procedure sets this argument to True, the custom action is not completed.
CustomPropertyChange	Fired when the value of a custom property is changed.
	Parameter: *Name*, a string passed by value containing the name of the custom property whose value was changed.

Event	Description
Forward	Fired when the user attempts to forward the item to one or more recipients.
	Parameter: ForwardItem, a reference passed by value to the new item to be forwarded.
	Return Value: If True (the default), the new item to be forwarded is displayed; if set to False, the operation is cancelled and the item is not displayed.
Open	Fired when an Outlook item is being opened in an Inspector but before the Inspector is displayed.
	Return Value: If True (the default), the item is opened; if set to False, the Open operation is cancelled.
PropertyChange	Fired when the value of a standard property is changed.
	Parameter: Name, a string passed by value containing the name of the standard property whose value was changed.
Read	Fired when an existing item is opened in a view that supports editing. This contrasts with the Open event, which is fired whenever a new or an existing item is opened. The Read event is fired before the Open event. And although the VBScript editor treats Item_Read as a function, setting its return value cannot cancel the read operation.
Reply	Fired when the user attempts to reply to an item.
	Parameter: Response, a reference passed by value to the new item to be sent in response to the original message.
	Return Value: If True (the default), the reply is displayed; if set to False, the operation is cancelled and the new item is not displayed.
ReplyAll	Fired when the user selects the Reply All option in response to an item.
	Parameter: Response, a reference passed by value to the new item to be sent in response to the original message.
	Return Value: If True (the default), the reply is displayed; if set to False, the operation is cancelled and the new item is not displayed.
Send	Fired when the user attempts to send an item.
	Return Value: If True (the default), the item is sent; if set to False, the Send operation is cancelled but the Inspector remains open.
Write	Fired when an item is about to be saved.
	Return Value: If True (the default), the item is saved; if set to False, the save operation is cancelled.

In addition to these form-level events, there is a single control event that you can trap in your code that will automatically be executed. This is the Click event, which is fired whenever the user clicks any of the following controls:

    CommandButton control
    Frame control
    Image control
    Label control
    Page tab of form
    Page tab of MultiPage control

In addition, the Click event is also fired whenever the user changes the values of any of the following controls:

    CheckBox control
    ComboBox control
    ListBox control
    OptionButton control (when the value changes to True only)
    ToggleButton control

The remaining standard controls (TextBox, ScrollBar, SpinButton, TabStrip, and TextBox) do not support the Click event.

 If you're accustomed to working with controls either in Visual Basic or in Microsoft Office (or even with intrinsic elements in HTML forms), you'll be very surprised (and probably disappointed) by an Outlook form's support only for the Click event. The diverse events that developers have come to rely on are simply not trapped in Outlook's scripted environment.

VBScript does not automatically create a code shell for these control or page Click events as it does for form events. Instead, you have to create the code shell. Its general form is:

```
Sub ControlName_Click( )

End Sub
```

where *ControlName* is the string assigned to the control's Name property.

The MultiPage control is somewhat unusual in that, while the control itself does not support the Click event, its individual pages do. (Individual pages are represented by Page objects that are contained in the Pages collection, which in turn is returned by the MultiPage control's Pages property.) Strangely, clicks on the page proper are detected, while clicks on the page's tab are not. The general format of a page's Click event is:

```
Sub PageName_Click( )

End Sub
```

where *PageName* is the name of the page as defined by its Name property (and not the string that appears on the page's tab, which is defined by its Caption property). This, of course, requires coding a separate event handler for each page of the control.

But taking advantage of the hook that automatically runs the code on your form isn't very useful unless Outlook will automatically load the form itself. This, however, is quite easy. Outlook loads forms on a folder-by-folder basis, with the form to be used defined by the "When posting to this folder, use" dropdown combo box on the General tab of a folder's Properties dialog (see Figure 6-5). The dialog is accessible by right-clicking on a folder and selecting Properties from the popup menu.

In the case of mail messages, that approach won't work, since Outlook expects that a Post message form will be used to display messages for all mail folders. A user can be given the choice of loading some form other than the default, however. To do this, publish the form to the folder in which you want to be available. The user can then create a form of that type by selecting Actions → New *formname* from the Outlook menu.

Control References in Code

Note that if you want to reference a control in code other than in the shell of its Click event handler, you either have to provide a complete object reference that identifies the control or instantiate an object variable that references the control. For instance, if you wanted to populate a list box named *lstFavoriteColors* with the names of some colors, you might use the following code fragment:

```
' This is a public variable so we don't have to instantiate
' it over and over
public lstFavoriteColors

' The Open event handler is executed before the form is
' opened
Function Item_Open( )

set lstFavoriteColors = _
   Item.GetInspector.ModifiedFormPages("P.2").lstFavoriteColors

lstFavoriteColors.AddItem "Red"
lstFavoritecolors.AddItem "Green"
lstFavoritecolors.AddItem "Black"
lstFavoritecolors.AddItem "Pink"
0
End Function
```

Strangely, even if you reference the control in its own event handler, you must still retrieve a reference to it. For example, the following click event generates a syntax error if *cmdVerify* is not a public variable:

```
Sub cmdVerify_Click( )
    If InStr(1, cmdVerify.Caption, "On") > 0 Then
        cmdVerify.Caption = "Verify: Off"
    Else
        cmdVerify.Caption = "Verify: On"
    End If
End Sub
```

Instead, code like the following is needed to recognize *cmdVerify* as a valid object:

```
Sub cmdVerify_Click( )
    Dim cmdVerify
    Set cmdVerify = _
        Item.GetInspector.ModifiedFormPages("P.4").cmdVerify

    If InStr(1, cmdVerify.Caption, "On") > 0 Then
        cmdVerify.Caption = "Verify: Off"
    Else
        cmdVerify.Caption = "Verify: On"
    End If
End Sub
```

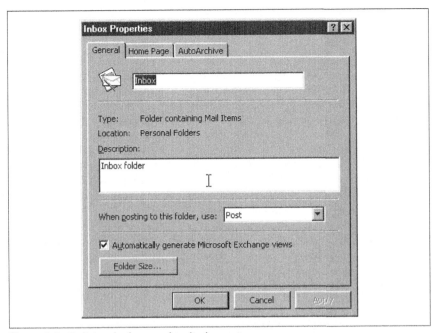

Figure 6-5. Defining the form used to display an item

Program Flow

As we have seen, the entry point into an Outlook program is an event handler, which is executed automatically based on some user action or other event. Program flow proceeds sequentially through the event procedure, with branches to all procedures and functions called by the event procedure (and of course, with branches to all procedures and functions called by those procedures or functions, and so on).

The code behind an Outlook form is finite, and consists of the code displayed by the VBScript editor for a single form. That is to say, Outlook forms provide no facility for importing or including additional code. Nor can the code in one form be called by the code in another form; the flow of program control is confined to the code behind a single Outlook form.

The code in an Outlook form itself consists of three components:

Global code
> Code outside of any procedure or function. Generally, this code appears anywhere from the beginning of the script to the script's first procedure or function. All of this code is executed when the form first loads, and before the Item_Load event procedure (if one is present) is invoked. In Visual Basic and VBA, this is known as a module's *general declarations section*, and it can contain only constant and variable declarations (such as Const, Dim, Private, Public, and Declare statements). In Outlook, it can contain a far larger range of statements; object assignments and access to the Outlook object model,

however, tend to be problematic if their code is placed here. All variables defined in global code, regardless of whether they are defined using the `Dim`, `Private`, or `Public` keywords, are public to the script.

Code for event procedures

Event procedures, as we discussed in the earlier section "Running Your Code," are functions or procedures that are automatically executed based on some event, typically one that results from some action of the user. The scope of all variables declared in event procedures or in supporting procedures and functions is limited to that routine itself; in order to be visible in some routine other than the one in which they are declared, they must be explicitly passed as arguments. Finally, variables in event procedures and in supporting procedures and functions must be declared using the `Dim` statement; the use of both the `Public` and `Private` keywords generates a syntax error.

Code for supporting procedures and functions

Unlike event procedures, other procedures and functions are not invoked automatically. Instead, they must be called by an event procedure or by another supporting procedure or function when it is being executed. The scope of variables declared in supporting procedures and functions is the same as for variables declared in event procedures.

The Outlook Object Model

Although VBScript allows you only to program an Outlook form, it nevertheless gives you relatively complete access to the Outlook object model, which is shown in Figure 6-6. Since the object model is fairly large, we'll focus only on some of its highlights here, and in particular on those objects that you are most likely to use when programming an Outlook form. You can explore the Outlook object model by opening the object browser in the VBScript editor, or by using the Object Browser included with the VBA-integrated development environment.

Note that when you're attempting to access the Outlook object model using VBScript, the context of your script is the current item, which can be represented by the `Item` keyword. In other words, as your script is executing, the Item object is the current object; to access other objects in the object model, you have to navigate to them from the Item object.

This also means that a reference to the current item is assumed in any attempt to navigate the object model or access a particular object, property, or method. For example, the code:

```
MsgBox Item.Application.Version
```

is identical to the code:

```
MsgBox Application.Version
```

This second line of code is interpreted as an attempt to retrieve the value of the Application object of the current item, and to retrieve its Version property.

If you're making extensive use of the properties and methods of other objects, your script's performance can be enormously improved by establishing references to those objects. For example, if your script involves accessing the object representing the form's current page, rather than having to navigate downward

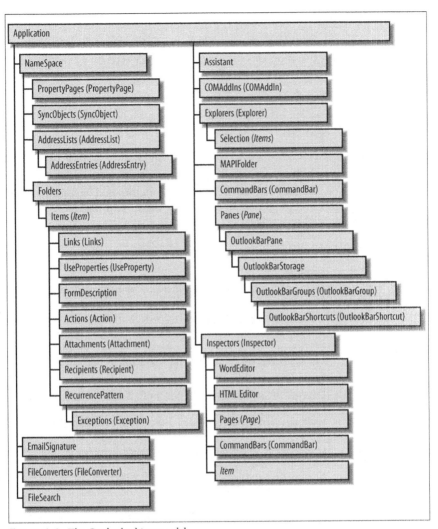

Figure 6-6. The Outlook object model

through the object model each time you want to access it, you can define an object reference, as the following code does:

```
Dim objPage
Set objApp = Item.Application
```

You could then use the *objApp* object variable to access the controls on the page.

Although the Outlook Application object is a global object in VBA (that is, its properties and methods can be called without prefacing them with a reference to the Application object), this is not true of VBScript. In VBScript, you must explicitly reference the Application object in order to access its members.

The Current Item

The current item that the form displays is represented by one of the item object types listed in Table 6-1. You can determine the object type by passing a reference to it to the VBA *TypeName* function. For example:

```
strClass = TypeName(Me)
```

or:

```
strClass = TypeName(Item)
```

where Item is an Outlook/VBScript keyword representing the current item.

You can call the general properties and methods that are suitable for any item (see Tables 6-3 and 6-4, respectively), as well as the properties and methods appropriate for an item of that particular type. The latter, unfortunately, are too numerous to mention in this chapter.

Table 6-3. General item properties

Property	Description
Actions[a]	Returns the Actions collection, which consists of one Action object for each custom action defined for the item.
Application	Returns a reference to the Application object, Outlook's top-level object.
Attachments	Returns the Attachments collection, which consists of the Attachment objects stored to the item.
BillingInformation	A read-write string intended to hold billing information associated with the item.
Body	A read-write string containing the item's body text.
Categories	A read-write string containing the categories assigned to the item. If multiple categories are present, they are separated from one another by a comma and a space.
Class	A read-only value represented by a member of the OlObjectClass enumeration that indicates the item's class.
Companies	A read-write string designed to contain information about the company or companies associated with the item.
ConversationIndex	Returns the index of the item's conversation thread.
ConversationTopic	Returns the topic of the item's conversation thread.
CreationTime	Returns the date and time that the item was created.
EntryID	Returns the item's identifier, which is unique to the items in a particular folder.
FormDescription	Returns a FormDescription object that describes the form used to display the item.
GetInspector	Returns an Inspector object that represents the window pane that contains the item.
Importance	A read-write constant of the OlImportance enumeration; indicates the item's importance. Enumeration members: olImportanceHigh (2), olImportance Low (0), and olImportanceNormal (1).
LastModificationTime	Date and time the item was last modified.
Links	Returns the read-only collection of Link objects representing contacts to which the item is linked.
MessageClass	A read-write string indicating the item's message class, which links it to a particular Outlook form.
Mileage	A read-write string field designed to store the mileage associated with an item for purposes of reimbursement.
NoAging	A read-write Boolean that indicates whether the item should not be aged.

Table 6-3. General item properties (continued)

Property	Description
OutlookInternalVersion	A read-only Long containing the build number of Outlook associated with the item.
OutlookVersion	A read-only string containing the major and minor version of Outlook associated with the item.
Parent	Returns a reference to the item's parent object.
Saved	A read-only flag that indicates whether the item has not been modified since it was last saved.
Sensitivity	A constant of the `OlSensitivity` enumeration (`olConfidential`, `olNormal`, `olPersonal`, or `olPrivate`) that indicates the item's sensitivity.
Session	Returns the Namespace object for the current session.
Size	Returns the item's size in bytes.
Subject	A string containing the subject of the item. It is the default member of all item types. In the case of NoteItem objects, it is read-only and is calculated from the content of the NoteItem object's Body property.
Unread	A read-write flag indicating if the item hasn't been opened.
UserProperties	Returns the UserProperties collection representing all the item's user properties.

^a Does not apply to the NoteItem object.

Table 6-4. General item methods

Method	Description
Close	Closes the item and its inspector and optionally saves changes. Its syntax is `Item.Close(SaveMode)` where *SaveMode* is a constant of the `OlInspectorClose` enumeration (`olDiscard`, `olPromptForSave`, `olSave`).
Copy	Creates a copy of the object. The new object is returned by the method call.
Delete	Deletes the item.
Display	Displays the item in a new Inspector object. Its syntax is `Item.Display(Modal)` where *Modal* is a Boolean that indicates whether the Inspector should be modal; its default value is `False`.
Move	Moves the item to a new folder. Its syntax is `Item.Move DestFldr` where *DestFldr* is a reference to the MAPIFolder object to which the item should be moved.
PrintOut	Prints the item using the default settings.
Save	Saves the item to the current folder or, in the case of a new item, to the default folder for that type of item.
SaveAs	Saves the item to a specified location in a specified format. Its syntax is `Item.SaveAs Path, [Type]` where *Path* is the path to the location in which the item should be saved, and the optional *Type* parameter is a constant of the `OlSaveAsType` enumeration: `olDoc`, `olHTML`, `olMSG` (the default), `olRTF`, `olTemplate`, `olTXT`, `olVCal`, or `olVCard`.

The Inspector Object

The Inspector object represents the window in which a particular Outlook item is displayed. A reference to the current item's Inspector object is returned by its GetInspector property. The Inspector object supports the properties shown in Table 6-5 and the methods shown in Table 6-6.

Table 6-5. Properties of the Inspector object

Property	Description
Application	Returns a reference to the Application object, Outlook's top-level object.
Caption	A read-only string that defines the caption in the inspector's titlebar.
Class	A read-only value that indicates the inspector's class. Its value is always olInspector, or 35.
CommandBars	Returns a reference to the CommandBars collection, which represents all the menus and toolbars available to the inspector.
CurrentItem	Returns the current item that the inspector is displaying.
EditorType	A read-only member of the OlEditorType enumeration: olEditorHTML (2), olEditorRTF (3), olEditorText (1), or olEditorWord (4).
Height	A read-write value that determines the height in pixels of the inspector window.
HTMLEditor	Returns the HTML Document Object Model of the displayed message. This property is valid only if the value of EditorType is olEditorHTML. In addition, since the object reference returned by this property is temporary, it should not be stored for later use.
Left	A read-write value that determines the distance in pixels between the left edge of the screen and the left edge of the inspector window.
ModifiedForm-Pages	Returns the Pages collection, which consists of the pages of the current form.
Parent	Returns a reference to the inspector's parent object, which is the Outlook Application object.
Session	Returns the NameSpace object for the current session.
Top	A read-write value that determines the distance in pixels between the top edge of the screen and the top edge of the inspector window.
Width	A read-write value that determines the width in pixels of the inspector window.
WindowState	A read-write constant of the OlWindowState enumeration (olMaximized, 1; olMinimized, 2; olNormal, 3) that determines the state of the inspector's window.
WordEditor	Returns the Word Document Object Model of the displayed message. This property is valid only if the value of EditorType is olEditorWord. In addition, since the object reference returned by this property is temporary, it should not be stored for later use.

Table 6-6. Methods of the Inspector object

Method	Description
Activate	Brings the inspector window to the foreground and gives it the focus.
Close	Closes the inspector window and optionally saves changes to the current item. Its syntax is oInspector.Close(SaveMode) where SaveMode is a constant of the OlInspectorClose enumeration (olDiscard, olPromptForSave, or olSave).
Display	Displays a new Inspector object for the item. Its syntax is Inspector.Display(Modal) where Modal is a Boolean that indicates whether the Inspector should be modal; its default value is False.
HideFormPage	Hides a page of the form displayed in the inspector. Its syntax is oInspector.HideFormPage PageName where PageName is a string that designates the name of the page to be hidden.
IsWordMail	Returns a Boolean that specifies whether the mail message associated with an inspector is displayed in an inspector or in Microsoft Word. If True, the value of the inspector's EditorType property is olEditorWord.
SetCurrentForm-Page	Displays a particular page of the current form. Its syntax is oInspector.SetCurrent-FormPage PageName where PageName is the name of the page to be displayed.
ShowFormPage	Shows a form page in the inspector. Its syntax is oInspector.ShowFormPage PageName where PageName is a string containing the name of the page to be shown.

The Pages Collection

The Pages collection represents the pages in the form that you want to access in order to customize. The Pages collection is returned by the ModifiedFormPages property of the Inspector object. Initially, the Pages collection is empty. Individual form pages are added to the collection either explicitly, by calling the collection's Add method, or implicitly, by referencing a control on one of the forms.

The Pages collection supports the properties shown in Table 6-7 and the methods listed in Table 6-8.

Table 6-7. Properties of the Pages collection

Property	Description
Application	Returns a reference to the Application object, Outlook's top-level object.
Class	A read-only value that indicates the page's class. Its value is always olPages, or 36.
Count	A read-only value that indicates the number of pages in the Pages collection.
Parent	Returns a reference to the collection's parent object, which is the Inspector object in which the form is displayed.
Session	Returns the NameSpace object for the current session.

Table 6-8. Methods of the Pages collection

Method	Description
Add	Adds a new page to the Pages collection. Its syntax is oPages.Add *Name* where *Name* is the name of the page to be added. The method returns a reference to the added page. Initially, the pages collection is empty, and there is a limit of five customizable pages per form.
Item	Retrieves an individual page from the Pages collection. Its syntax is oPages.Item *Index* where *Index* is either the one-based ordinal position of the page in the Pages collection or the name of the page.
Remove	Removes a page from the collection. Its syntax is oPages.Remove *Index* where *Index* is the one-based ordinal position of the page in the Pages colletion.

The FormDescription Object

The FormDescription object represents the form used to display a particular item in an inspector. It is returned by the current item's FormDescription property. The FormDescription object has 22 properties (shown in Table 6-9) and a single method (shown in Table 6-10).

Table 6-9. Properties of the FormDescription object

Property	Description
Application	Returns a reference to the Application object, Outlook's top-level object.
Category	The category assigned to the form description. It corresponds to the Category drop-down list box on the form's Properties page in design mode.
CategorySub	The subcategory assigned to the form description. It corresponds to the Sub-Category dropdown list box on the form's Properties page in design mode.

Table 6-9. Properties of the FormDescription object (continued)

Property	Description
Class	A read-only value that indicates the form description's class. Its value is always olFormDescription, or 37.
Comment	Sets or returns the comment associated with the form description. It corresponds to the Description text box on the form's Properties page in design mode.
ContactName	Sets or returns the name of the person to contact for information regarding the custom form. It corresponds to the Contact text box on the form's Properties page in design mode.
DisplayName	Defines the text that will be used to name the form in the Choose Forms dialog. Setting the DisplayName property also sets the Name property if it is empty (and vice versa).
Hidden	Determines whether a custom form is hidden (i.e., it does not appear in the Choose Form dialog box and is used only if designated as the response form for another custom form). Its default value is False; custom forms are not hidden. This property corresponds to the "Use form only for responses" checkbox on the form's Properties page in design mode.
Icon	Contains the name of the icon file to be displayed for the form. By default, its value is a temporary icon file generated by Outlook and placed in the Windows temporary directory.
Locked	Determines whether the form is read-only. Its default value is False; the form is read-write. It corresponds to the "Protect form design" checkbox on the form's Properties page in design mode.
MessageClass	The form's message class, which links the form to the type of items it can display.
MiniIcon	Contains the name of the icon file to be displayed for the form. By default, its value is a temporary icon file generated by Outlook and placed in the Windows temporary directory.
Name	The name of the form. This property must be set before calling the PublishForm method.
Number	Defines the number for the form. It corresponds to the Form Number text box on the form's Properties page in design mode.
OneOff	Determines whether the form is discarded after one-time use (True) or retained as a custom form (False). Its default value is False.
Parent	Returns a reference to the form's parent object, which is the item that the form displays.
Password	Sets or returns the password needed to modify the form. It is retrievable programmatically as clear text.
ScriptText	Returns a string containing all the VBScript code attached to the form.
Session	Returns the NameSpace object for the current session.
Template	Sets or returns the name of the Word template (*.dot file) for use with the form.
UseWordMail	A Boolean that determines whether Microsoft Word is the default editor for the form.
Version	Returns or sets the version number. It corresponds to the Version text box on the form's Properties page in design mode.

Table 6-10. Method of the FormDescription object

Method	Description
PublishForm	Saves the form definition. Its syntax is oFormDescription.PublishForm(Registry,[Folder]) where Registry determines the location to which the form should be saved and can be olDefaultRegistry (0), olFolderRegistry (3), olOrganizationRegistry (4), or olPersonalRegistry (2). If Registry is olFolderRegistry, Folder is a reference to a MAPIFolder object that defines the folder to which the form will be published.

The NameSpace Object

The NameSpace object represents the root object for accessing Outlook data. In other words, from an Outlook form, the NameSpace object is important because it gives access to the MAPIFolder objects that comprise Outlook's folder system.

The NameSpace object is returned by the GetNameSpace ("MAPI") method of the Application object. It has the properties shown in Table 6-11 and the methods listed in Table 6-12.

Table 6-11. Properties of the NameSpace object

Property	Description
AddressLists	Returns a collection of address lists available for the session.
Application	Returns a reference to the Application object, Outlook's top-level object.
Class	A read-only value that indicates the NameSpace object's class. Its value is always olNamespace, or 1.
CurrentUser	Returns a Recipient object representing the currently logged in user.
Folders	Returns the Folders collection, which represents all the Folder objects contained in the NameSpace.
Parent	Returns a reference to the namespace's parent object, which is the Application object.
Session	Returns the NameSpace object for the current session.
SyncObjects	Returns a collection containing all synchronization profiles.
Type	Returns the string "MAPI" to indicate the type of the NameSpace object.

Table 6-12. Methods of the NameSpace object

Method	Description
AddStore	Adds a personal folder file (.pst) to the current profile. Its syntax is oNameSpace. AddStore Store where Store is the path and name of the .pst file.
CreateRecipient	Creates and returns a Recipient object. Its syntax is oNameSpace.CreateRecipient RecipientName where RecipientName is the display name of the recipient.
GetDefaultFolder	Returns a MAPIFolder object that represents the default folder of a particular type. Its syntax is oNameSpace.GetDefaultFolder FolderTypeEnum where FolderTypeEnum is a member of the OlDefaultFolders enumeration: olFolderCalendar (9), oFolderContacts (10), oFolderDeletedItems (3), oFolderDrafts (16), oFolderInbox (6), oFolderJournal (11), oFolderNotes (12), oFolderOutbox (4), oFolderSentMail (5), oFolderTasks (13).
GetFolderFromID	Returns the MAPIFolder object that has a particular ID. Its syntax is oNamespace. GetFolderFromID(EntryIDFolder, [StoreID]) where EntryIDFolder is a string containing the folder's entry ID, and StoreID is an optional string containing the folder's store ID. These values are accessible through MAPI and CDO.
GetItemFromID	Returns the item in a folder that has a particular ID. Its syntax is oNameSpace.GetItem-FromID(EntryIDItem, [StoreID]) where EntryIDItem is a string containing the item's entry ID, and StoreID is an optional string containing the item's store ID. These values are readily accessible through MAPI and CDO.
GetRecipientFromID	Returns a Recipient object that has a particular ID. Its syntax is oNameSpace. GetRecipientFromID(EntryID) where EntryID is a string containing the recipient's entry ID. This value is readily accessible through MAPI and CDO.

Table 6-12. Methods of the NameSpace object (continued)

Method	Description
GetShared-DefaultFolder	Returns the MAPIFolder object that represents a particular type of default folder for a specified user. This method is most useful when one user has given another user access to one or more default folders. Its syntax is: `oNameSpace.GetSharedDefaultFolder(RecipientObject,FolderTypeEnum)` where `RecipientObject` is a Recipient object representing the owner of the folder, and `FolderTypeEnum` is a constant from the OlDefaultFolder enumeration (see the `GetDefaultFolder` method for a list of its members).
Logoff	Logs the user off from the current MAPI session.
Logon	Logs the user onto MAPI and begins a MAPI session. Its syntax is oNameSpace.Logon [*Profile*] [*Password*], [*ShowDialog*], [*NewSession*] where *Profile* is the name of the profile to use for the session, *Password* is an optional (and usually omitted) string containing the password associated with the profile, *ShowDialog* is an optional Boolean that indicates whether the MAPI logon dialog should be displayed if *Profile* is incorrect or unavailable, and *NewSession* is an optional Boolean that determines whether a new session should be created even if there is an existing session. (Within Outlook, however, multiple sessions are not supported.)
PickFolder	Displays the Pick Folder dialog and returns the MAPIFolder object representing the folder selected by the user. If the user cancels the dialog, the method returns Nothing.

The MAPIFolder Object

Given a reference to a MAPIFolder object, you can begin to programmatically manipulate the items that the folder contains. MAPIFolder objects are returned by the NameSpace object's Folders property, as well as by its GetDefaultFolder, GetSharedDefaultFolder, and PickFolder methods.

The properties of the MAPIFolder object are shown in Table 6-13, while its methods appear in Table 6-14.

Table 6-13. Properties of the MAPIFolder object

Property	Description
Application	Returns a reference to the Application object, Outlook's top-level object.
Class	A read-only value that indicates the NameSpace object's class. Its value is always olFolder, or 2.
DefaultItemType	Returns the default Outlook item type that the folder stores. It can be one of the following OlItemType constants: olAppointmentItem (1), olContactItem (2), olJournalItem (4), olMailItem (0), olNoteItem (5), olPostItem (6), or olTaskItem (3).
DefaultMessageClass	A read-only string containing the default message class of items in the folder.
Description	A read-write string containing the folder's description. It corresponds to the Description text box in the folder's Properties dialog.
EntryID	Returns the folder's unique entry ID that was assigned by MAPI when the folder was created.
Folders	Returns the Folders collection, which contains one Folder object for each subfolder in the current folder.
Items	Returns the collection of items in the folder.
Name	The name of the folder.

Table 6-13. Properties of the MAPIFolder object (continued)

Property	Description
Parent	Returns a reference to the folder's parent object, which is either the MAPI NameSpace object or a MAPIFolder object.
Session	Returns the NameSpace object for the current session.
StoreID	Returns or sets the folder's StoreID.
UnReadItemCount	A read-only value; indicates the number of unread items.
WebViewAllowNavigation	A Boolean that determines whether the user can navigate using the Back and Forward buttons.
WebViewOn	A Boolean that determines whether Outlook displays the web page specified by the WebViewURL property.
WebViewURL	A string containing the web page assigned to the folder.

Table 6-14. Methods of the MAPIFolder object

Method	Description
CopyTo	Copies the current folder. Its syntax is oFolder.CopyTo(*DestFldr*) where *DestFldr* is a MAPIFolder object representing the destination folder.
Delete	Deletes the folder.
Display	Displays a new Explorer object for the folder.
GetExplorer	Returns a new inactive Explorer object in which the current folder is the folder whose GetExplorer method is called. The method is useful for creating a new Explorer object to display a folder rather than changing the folder displayed in the active Explorer. Its syntax is GetExplorer([*DisplayMode*]) where *DisplayMode* is an optional constant of the OlFolderDisplayMode enumeration; its members are olFolderDisplay-FolderOnly (1), olFolderNoNavigation (2), or olFolderDisplayNormal (0, the default).
MoveTo	Moves the current folder.

Outlook Constants

The object model for Outlook 2000 defines 275 constants in 49 different enumerations. Unfortunately, though they are available to Outlook VBA, they are not available to VBScript. If you want to use the constants defined in Outlook's type library, you'll need to define them yourself using the Const statement. In addition, however, VBScript does not support the Enum statement, which allows you to define a group of constants. So you'll have to define each constant separately, as in the following code, which makes the members of the OlInpectorClose enumeration available to a script:

```
Const olDiscard = 1
Const olPromptForSave = 2
Const olSave = 0
```

In general, it's best to define all constants with global scope, which makes them available everywhere in your script.

Accessing Other Object Models

Although most of the programming done with Outlook forms is likely to involve the Outlook object model, there may be times when you want to access data from some other application or draw on some system service provided by a particular object model. The VBScript *CreateObject* function is used for this purpose to access the object model of some other application, while the VBScript *GetObject* function is the only means available to get a reference to an existing instance of an application—that is, to a running application. (For the syntax of both functions, see their entries in Chapter 10.)

 The *GetObject* function exists solely within VBScript, and is not implemented as a method of the Outlook Application object.

As Table 6-15 shows, you can instantiate objects like the following using these methods:

ActiveX Data Objects (ADO)
> ADO is a data access technology that offers a uniform methodology for accessing data regardless of location or format. ADO has a relatively "flat" object model, and many objects (like the Recordset object or the Connection object) can be instantiated independently of one another.

Data Access Objects (DAO)
> DAO is a data access technology intended primarily for use with Access databases. Its top-level object is named DBEngine.

The Dictionary object
> A part of the Scripting Runtime Library, the Dictionary object provides high-performance access to data sets that have identifiable keys.

The Excel Application object
> The Excel object model is useful for extracting data from spreadsheets or for manipulating charts. Its top-level object is the Application object.

The FileSystemObject object
> A part of the Scripting Runtime Library, the FileSystemObject provides access to the local filesystem.

The Word Application object
> The Word object model makes it easy to manipulate Word *.doc* files as well as Rich Text Format (*.rtf*) files. Its top-level object is the Application object.

Table 6-15. Some object models and their programmatic identifiers

Object	ProgID	Description
Connection	ADODB.Connection	An ADO database connection
DBEngine	DAO.DBEngine	The DAO object model, primarily for Access databases
Dictionary	Scripting.Dictionary	A high-performance alternative to arrays and collections for keyed data
Excel	Excel.Application	The Microsoft Excel application, for manipulating spreadsheets and charts
FileSystemObject	Scripting.FileSystemObject	Represents the local filesystem
Recordset	ADODB.Recordset	An ADO recordset
Word	Word.Application	The Microsoft Word application for manipulating documents

7

Windows Script Host 5.6

Windows Script Host (WSH) is designed to eliminate one of the major limitations of the Win32 platform: it has no real batch or macro language that allows common processes (such as creating shortcuts, writing to and reading from the registry, or getting information on the filesystem) to be automated. Windows' predecessor, the character-based DOS operating system, for instance, included the DOS batch language. And Windows 3.0 included the idiosyncratic and unsuccessful Recorder, which allowed the user to "record" keystrokes and mouse clicks and later repeat them.

When you execute a WSH script, WSH uses *WScript.exe* as the runtime engine for scripts that run within the Windows environment and *CScript.exe* as the runtime engine for scripts that execute within a Command Prompt window. WSH is language-independent; it can be used with any language with a Windows Script–compatible script engine. The language most commonly used to write WSH scripts, however, is VBScript.

Why Use WSH?

WSH exposes a relatively small but very significant portion of the functionality of the 32-bit Windows family of operating systems. In addition, WSH allows you to tap into other object models (such as the FileSystemObject object model provided by the Scripting Runtime library) that allow you to access additional features of either the operating system or individual applications.

The advantage of any script is that it allows repetitive tasks—including complex ones that require multiple steps—to be performed more or less automatically. This makes scripting suitable for batch operations—that is, for repetitive operations that do not require user intervention. In addition, if you are writing your scripts in VBScript, you can allow user interaction through the standard VBScript *InputBox* and *MsgBox* functions, as well as by instantiating components that support more sophisticated forms of interaction. Support for user interaction enhances the scripting environment's flexibility and increases the range of applications for which it is suitable.

Although the flexibility and power of WSH means that its actual uses are limited only by the imagination, we can nevertheless identify some areas in which WSH clearly excels:

Access to network resources
Although Windows makes automatic (and therefore more or less permanent) access to network resources at logon very easy, transitory access to network resources is not. WSH can be used to connect to network drives and printers for a short period, perform some operation, and then disconnect from the network resource.

System administration
A single script that is run locally on the user's machine or that is run from the system administrator's system and iterates network systems can enormously facilitate the tasks of administering a networked system.

Simple installation scripts
If your installation routine needs merely to check available disk space, determine whether any files are likely to be overwritten, copy some files, and add some registry settings, writing a WSH script can be as effective as a professional installation program while involving much less overhead.

File operations
By instantiating the FileSystemObject object, you can gain access to the local computer's filesystem, including attached network drives. This allows you to perform repetitive file operations, as well as to determine the status, capability, and storage space available on individual drives.

Software automation
Using WSH and VBScript, you can access the object model of an application program or a system service to perform some repetitive operation. For instance, you might use CDO to send a batch of emails with Microsoft Outlook, use Microsoft Word and Access to print mailing labels, or use Microsoft Excel to update monthly sales data and print the results in chart form.

Running WSH Scripts

Typically, WSH scripts have a file extension of *.vbs* (if they are written in VBScript) or *.wsf* (a Windows Script File, which contains XML elements along with script written in a language defined by the XML <script> tag), both of which are associated with the Windows Script Host executable in the registry. This allows the user to simply double-click on the file in an Explorer window in order to execute the script. If the script is a *.wsf* file containing multiple jobs, only the executable script in the first job (which must be delimited by the <job>...</job> tags) is executed.

It is also possible to run a script from the command line by using the syntax:

```
CScript.exe filename [//options] [/arguments]
```

or from the Run dialog or a Windows shortcut by using the syntax:

```
WScript.exe [//options] [/arguments]
```

where *//options* is one or more of the WSH features shown in Table 7-1, each of which must be preceded by double slashes.

Table 7-1. WSH options switches

Switch	Description
//B	Batch mode (prevents script errors and user interface elements such as those produced by the *MsgBox* and *InputBox* functions from displaying).
//D	Enables debugging. Automatically launches the debugger if an unhandled exception occurs.
//E:engine	Uses *engine* (which can be either Jscript or VBScript) for executing script. The switch is useful if your script is in a file, such as a *.txt* file, whose extension does not indicate the scripting language.
//H:cscript	Changes the default script host to *CScript.exe*.
//H:wscript	Changes the default script host to *WScript.exe*; this is the default value and the opposite of //H:cscript. You have to be an administrator to change the default.
//I	Interactive mode; this is the default and the opposite of //B.
//Job:xxxx	Allows a single job (delimited by the <job>...</job> statements) to be run from a file containing multiple jobs.
//Logo	Displays an opening banner; this applies to only *CScript.exe* and is the default switch.
//Nologo	The opposite of //Logo, it suppresses the opening banner; applies to *CScript.exe* only.
//S	Saves the current command-line options for the current user.
//T:nn	Time out in seconds; maximum time a script is permitted to run before the scripting engine automatically terminates it.
//U	Generates Unicode command-line output on Windows NT and Windows 2000 systems.
//X	Launches the debugger and executes the script in it.
//?	Displays help information on command-line options.

Finally, scripts can be launched from an Explorer window or as shortcuts on the desktop by dragging and dropping files onto them. In this case, each of the dropped files is passed as a command-line parameter to the script and can be retrieved from its WshArguments collection (see "The WshArguments Object" later in this chapter).

Program Flow

WSH supports two kinds of script files: *simple script files*, which were supported by WSH 1.0 and are suitable for simple scripting applications; and *script files with XML*, which are more structured, far more powerful, and have a number of features of interest to more advanced programmers. In this section, we'll examine how both types of script files can be used.

Simple Script Files

Simple script files written in VBScript usually have a *.vbs* extension and contain only VBScript language elements, along with references to the properties, methods, and events belonging to objects instantiated by the script. XML tags are not permitted within simple script files.

The program entry point of a simple script is the global area at the top of the file, and program execution terminates after the last line of code that is not contained within a function or a procedure has executed. This is illustrated by the simple script in Example 7-1. Program flow begins with the Dim statement on the first line and ends with the *MsgBox* function call on the fourth line. The fourth line also causes the *AddTwo* user-defined function to be executed before the *MsgBox* function. The *MultTwo* function is never executed, since it is not explicitly called by the first four lines of code.

Example 7-1. Program flow in a simple WSH script

```
Dim iVar1, iVar2

iVar1 = 1
iVar2 = 2
MsgBox AddTwo(iVar1, iVar2)


' Multiplies two numbers
Function MultTwo(var1, var2)
   MultTwo = var1 * var2
End Function


' Adds two numbers
Function AddTwo(var1, var2)
   AddTwo = var1 + var2
End Function
```

This top-down flow of control in WSH scripts has a very important implication: all variables defined outside of subroutines in a script file are global variables; that is, they are globally available to all of the routines stored in the file. To see what this means, let's take a look at the code in Example 7-2. The variable *fs*, which represents a FileSystemObject object, is automatically visible to the *ShowStorage* routine; it does not have to be passed as a parameter in order to be visible to the routine.

Example 7-2. WSH global variables

```
Dim fs
Set fs = CreateObject("Scripting.FileSystemObject")

ShowStorage

Public Sub ShowStorage( )
   Dim strMsg, dr

   For Each dr In fs.Drives
      strMsg = strMsg & dr.DriveLetter & ": " & _
            dr.FreeSpace & vbcrlf
   Next

   MsgBox strMsg
End Sub
```

This means, of course, that any modifications to the variable that the routine makes, whether they are deliberate or inadvertent, are reflected in the variable's value once control returns to the main code block.

To prevent this, parameter lists can be used to make sure that arguments are explicitly passed to called routines. If those arguments are passed by value, using the ByVal keyword, their value will remain unchanged when control returns to the calling routine, even if their value has been changed in a subordinate routine. This is illustrated by the script in Example 7-3, which assigns the values 5 and 10 to two variables—*intX* and *intY*, respectively—before calling *AddTwo* with these two variables as arguments. *AddTwo* contains a common assignment error: rather than assigning the sum of the arguments to a new variable, the sum is assigned to the *intX* parameter, effectively overwriting its value. However, when control returns to the calling routine and the sum of *intX* and *intY* is displayed, it remains as it was before the call to the *AddTwo* subroutine, since the changes made to the value of *intX* in *AddTwo* does not affect its value once the routine ends.

Example 7-3. Passing arguments by value

```
Dim intX, intY

intX = 5
intY = 10

AddTwo intX, intY

MsgBox "intX + intY = " & intX + intY


Sub AddTwo(ByVal intX, ByVal intY)
   intX = intX + intY
   MsgBox intX
End Sub
```

Script Files with XML Code

As of Version 2.0, WSH allows you to create *.wsf* files, which must contain one or more jobs that are designated by the XML <job>...</job> tag. In addition, you can include files containing script by using the <script>...</script> tag and including its src attribute. (See "WSH Language Elements" later in this chapter for details on XML tags.)

Any script file with a *.wsf* extension must contain the XML tags needed for the script to run. At a minimum, these are the <job>... </job> and, if script is present, the <script> ...</script> tags.

In a *.wsf* file that contains multiple jobs, each job is independent of others. In other words, the public variables and the public subroutines and functions of one job are not available to other jobs in the same *.wsf* file. Program flow begins at the beginning of the global script in the job designated by the //Job: switch when the script was launched, and continues until the </job> tag is encountered. If the //Job: switch was not used, program flow begins with the global script belonging to the first job in the file.

If a script file is included using the src attribute of the <script> tag, it must contain only script and no XML tags. The entire script file is read, and any global code blocks within the file are executed at the point that the <script> tag is encountered. Any variables defined in its global code blocks will be visible to the original job, and any functions or subroutines contained in the included file can be called from code in the job.

The WSH Object Model

When using VBScript to write WSH scripts, you use VBScript to access the WSH object model. The Windows Script Host object model, a small and fairly shallow object model with a number of createable objects, is shown in Figure 7-1.

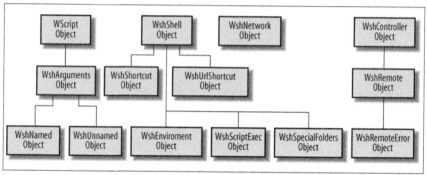

Figure 7-1. The Windows Scripting Host object model

WSH is not intended to be a self-contained, all-encompassing object model. It focuses on three major areas:

- Providing resources necessary to support script execution. For instance, the WScript object reports on the interpreter and version of WSH in use, while the WshShell object allows shortcuts and Internet shortcuts to be created.

- Enhancing the ease with which a system can connect to and disconnect from network resources. This functionality is supported by the WshNetwork object.

- Supporting functionality that is not readily available in other object models. For example, the WshShell object allows access to environment variables and to the location of Windows system folders.

Through the CreateObject and GetObject methods of the WScript object, WSH allows you to take advantage of the functionality supported by other objects that support COM automation. This topic is discussed in "Accessing Other Object Models" later in this chapter. The remainder of this section provides concise documentation on the objects that form the WSH object model, along with their properties and methods.

The WScript Object

The WScript object, the top-level object in the WSH object model, provides information about the script host (that is, about *WScript.exe* or *CScript.exe*) and the script file it is executing as well as provides access to other objects. This object is instantiated automatically by the host whenever a WSH script is launched; you don't have to retrieve a reference to it. (In fact, calls to either *CreateObject* or *GetObject* will fail to return a reference to the WScript object.) The properties of the WScript object are listed in Table 7-2, while its methods appear in Table 7-3.

Table 7-2. Properties of the WScript object

Property	Description
Application	Returns a reference to the WScript object itself, which can be passed as an argument to external routines.
Arguments	Returns a WshArguments object consisting of several collections of strings containing the command-line arguments (both named and unnamed) passed to the script when it was invoked; see the entry for the WshArguments object later in this chapter for details.
Fullname	The full path and filename of the script host file (which is usually either *WScript.exe* or *CScript.exe*).
Name	The friendly name of the script host file. For example, the friendly name of both *WScript.exe* and *CScript.exe* is "Windows Script Host." It is the default property of the WScript object.
Path	The full path (without the filename) to the script host.
ScriptFullName	The full path and filename of the script being executed.
ScriptName	Returns a string containing the filename of the script file being executed.
StdErr	Returns a reference to a write-only TextStream object that provides access to the script's standard error stream when *CScript.exe* is the WSH host. Typically, the error output stream is sent to the console.
	The TextStream object is part of the File System object model available from the Microsoft Scripting Runtime Library. Because it is write-only, the TextStream object returned by the StdErr property supports only the following methods:
	Close
	Write
	WriteBlankLines
StdIn	Returns a reference to a read-only TextStream object that provides access to the script's standard input stream when *CScript.exe* is the WSH host. Typically, standard input to a program comes from the keyboard, though it can also be provided by a source defined by the command-line redirection character. For example, in the following statement, the standard input is the contents of the file *Greeting.txt*:
	`CScript.exe ShowGreeting.vbs < Greeting.txt`
	Any attempt to read input that is unavailable causes the respective read method to block. The read-only TextStream object returned by the StdIn property supports the following properties and methods:
	AtEndOfLine
	AtEndOfStream
	Column
	Line
	Close
	Read
	ReadAll
	ReadLine
	Skip

Table 7-2. Properties of the WScript object (continued)

Property	Description
StdOut	Returns a reference to a write-only TextStream object that provides access to the script's standard output stream when *CScript.exe* is the WSH interpreter. Typically, standard output from a program goes to the screen; it can also go to a device defined by the command-line redirection character. For example, the output is redirected to the first parallel printer: `CScript.exe ShowGreeting.vbs > Greeting.txt` The TextStream object returned by StdOut supports these: Close Write WriteBlankLines
Version	The version of the script host.

Table 7-3. Methods of the WScript object

Method	Description

CreateObject	Instantiates a new instance of a class. Its syntax is `WScript.Create-rObject(strProgID[,strPrefix])` where `strProgID` is the programmatic identifier of the object to be created as defined in the registry and `strPrefix` is an optional string that instructs WSH to trap the object's events (if it has any) and to fire *public* event handlers whose names begin with `strPrefix` concatenated with the event name. The method returns a reference to the new object. For example:
	`Set oRate = _`
	`    WScript.CreateObject("Component1.Rate", "oRate_")`
	
	`Public Sub oRate_RateChanged( )`
	`    WScript.Echo "RateChanged event fired!"`
	`End Sub`
	
	The chief difference between the VBScript *CreateObject* function and the WScript CreateObject method is that the latter allows you to trap the events raised by an object.

ConnectObject	Connects an object's events to functions beginning with a designated prefix. Its syntax is `WScript.ConnectObject strobject, strPrefix` where `strobject` is a reference to the object whose events are to be trapped, and `strPrefix` is the prefix of the event handler for the events. Note that the documentation incorrectly indicates that `strObject` is the *name* of the object whose events are to be trapped. The event handler whose name is a concatenation of `strPrefix` and the event name is automatically invoked; for example:
	`WScript.ConnectObject oRate, "oRate_"`
	
	`Public Sub oRate_RateChanged( )`
	`    WScript.Echo "RateChanged event fired!"`
	`End Sub`
	
	Calling the ConnectObject method is equivalent to supplying a `strPrefix` parameter when retrieving an object reference using either the CreateObject or GetObject method of the WScript object. In addition, ConnectObject allows you to handle events raised by objects not createable by the CreateObject or GetObject methods.
	
	Some objects that source events do not allow runtime discovery of those events. Such objects cannot be connected with either the CreateObject or the ConnectObject methods of the WScript object.

DisconnectObject	This method simply "disconnects" an event sync; that is, it "disconnects" the object "connected" by the ConnectObject method. Its syntax is `WScript.DisconnectObject obj` where `obj` is a reference to the object whose events are no longer to be handled. If the events raised by `obj` are not currently being trapped, calling the method has no effect.

Table 7-3. Methods of the WScript object (continued)

Method	Description
Echo	Sends output to a dialog box (if the host is *WScript.exe*) or the console (for *CScript.exe*). Its syntax is `WScript.Echo [arg1, [arg2...]]` where `arg1` and `arg2` are the expressions to be output. If multiple arguments are present, a space is used to separate them. If none are present, the method outputs a blank line.
GetObject	Returns a reference to an existing instance of a class. Its syntax is `WScript.GetObject(strPathname [,strProgID], [strPrefix])` where `strPathname` is the path and name of the file containing the object to retrieve, `strProgID` is the programmatic identifier of the object to be created as defined in the registry, and `strPrefix` is an optional string that instructs WSH to trap the object's events (if it has any) and to fire *public* event handlers whose names begin with `strPrefix` concatenated with the event name. The method returns a reference to the object.
Quit	Terminates script execution and raises an error. Its syntax is `WScript.Quit [intErrorCode]` where `intErrorCode` is the number of the error to raise.
ShowUsage	Displays help information explaining how to use a script.
Sleep	Suspends script execution for a specified number of milliseconds. Its syntax is `WScript.Sleep(intTime)` where `intTime` is the number of milliseconds to wait. Events continue to fire and event handlers continue to run while sleeping.

The WshArguments Object

The WshArguments object is a collection object returned by the Arguments property of the WScript object; it cannot be created by calls to the WScript object's CreateObject or GetObject methods. The following statement returns a WshArguments collection object:

```
Dim oArgs
Set oArgs = WScript.Arguments
```

It consists of one string for each command-line argument passed to the script when it was invoked. You can iterate the arguments as follows:

```
Dim arg
For Each arg in oArgs
    ' Do something with arg, the individual argument
Next
```

Or you can retrieve an individual argument using code like the following, which retrieves the first argument in the collection:

```
Dim arg
arg = WScript.Arguments.Item(0)
```

WSH supports both named and unnamed arguments. *Named arguments* are passed to a script by using the syntax:

```
scriptname /ArgName:ArgValue
```

ArgName, the argument name, is preceded by a single slash, while the argument name and *ArgValue*, the value of the named argument, are separated from one another by a colon. *Unnamed arguments* are entered on the command line as values only, with no special syntax; for example:

```
scriptname ArgValue
```

Both named and unnamed arguments are included in the collection. The arguments can be filtered into named and unnamed arguments by using the WshArguments object's Named and Unnamed properties.

The properties of the WshArguments object are shown in Table 7-4.

Table 7-4. Properties of the WshArguments object

Property	Description
Count	Indicates the number of arguments in the collection.
Item	Returns a string argument given its ordinal position (or index) in the collection. The first argument is at position 0. Item is the default member of the WshArguments collection.
length	Like the Count method, returns the number of arguments in the collection.
Named	Returns a WshNamed object containing the named arguments passed to the script when it was invoked. For details, see the entry for the WshNamed object later in this chapter.
Unnamed	Returns a WshUnnamed object containing the unnamed arguments passed to the script when it was invoked. For details, see the entry for the WshUnnamed object later in this chapter.

The WshController Object

The WshController object, which is new to WSH 5.6, allows for the creation of a remote script process. WshController is a createable object that must be instantiated with a code fragment like the following:

```
Dim cnt
Set cnt = WScript.CreateObject("WSHController")
```

The WshController object has a single method, CreateScript, as shown in Table 7-5. It is this method that accesses the script to be run remotely and returns a WshRemote object that provides some control over the resulting script process. For an example of using remote scripting, see "The WshRemote Object" later in this chapter.

Table 7-5. Method of the WshController object

Name	Description
CreateScript	Returns a WshRemote object, which represents a remote script process. Its syntax is *object*. CreateScript(*CommandLine*,[*MachineName*]) where *object* is a reference to a WshConnection object, *CommandLine* provides the name of the script to execute (along with an optional path and any command-line switches and parameters), and *MachineName* is an optional parameter containing the UNC name of the system on which the script is to execute. If *MachineName* is omitted, the script executes on the system on which the WshController object is instantiated. If *CommandLine* identifies a different system than *MachineName*, the script is loaded from the system identified by *CommandLine* but run on the system identified by *MachineName*.

The WshEnvironment Object

The WshEnvironment object is a collection object returned by the Environment property of the WshShell object; it cannot be created by calls to the WScript object's CreateObject or GetObject methods.

WshEnvironment is a collection of strings containing a set of environment variables. Windows systems maintain two such sets of environment variables, either of which can be returned by the Environment property of the WshShell object:

- A system table, which is retrieved by supplying the string System as an argument to the Environment property of the WshShell object. The system table contains the environment variables available to all processes running on the system.

- A process table, which is retrieved by supplying the string Process as an argument to the Environment property of the WshShell object. The process table contains the environment variables defined for the individual process. It also includes the environment variables in the system table.

The members of the WshEnvironment object are shown in Table 7-6.

Since the WshEnvironment object is a child of the WshShell object, it requires that a WshShell object be instantiated. This requires that you access the WshEnvironment collection through a code fragment like the following:

```
Dim wsh, env
Set wsh = WScript.CreateObject("WScript.Shell")
Set env = wsh.Environment
```

You can then iterate the collection as follows:

```
Dim str
For Each str in env
    sMsg = sMsg & str & vbCrLf
Next

WScript.Echo sMsg
```

Table 7-6. Members of the WshEnvironment object

Name	Type	Description
Count	Property	Indicates the number of environment variables in the collection.

Item	Property	Returns an environment variable's name/value pair (separated by an equals sign) if passed a string containing its name (or key). Item is the default member of the WshEnvironment collection. Hence, the code:
		`WScript.Echo(WshShell.Environment.Item("Path"))`
		is functionally identical to the code:
		`WScript.Echo(WshShell.Environment("Path"))`

length	Property	Indicates the number of environment variables in the collection.
Remove	Method	Removes an environment variable from the collection. Its syntax is WshEnvironment.Remove *strName* where *strName* is a String representing the name of the environment variable. Attempting to delete a variable based on its ordinal position in the collection has no effect.

The WshNamed Object

The WshNamed object, which is new to WSH 5.6, is a collection object that contains named command-line arguments. (A named argument is entered on the command line with the syntax /name:value.) WshNamed is not a createable object, and is returned by the Named property of the WshArguments object.

The following statement returns a WshNamed collection object:

```
Dim namedArgs
Set namedArgs = WScript.Arguments.Named
```

It consists of one string for each named command-line argument passed to the script when it was invoked. You can iterate the arguments as follows:

```
Dim arg
For Each arg in namedArgs
    ' Do something with arg, the individual named argument
Next
```

Or you can retrieve an individual argument using code like the following, which retrieves the first named argument in the collection:

```
Dim arg
arg = WScript.Arguments.Named(0)
```

The members of the WshNamed object are listed in Table 7-7.

Table 7-7. Members of the WshNamed object

Name	Type	Description
Count	Method	Returns an integer indicating the number of named arguments in the collection. Its syntax is *object*.Count( ).
Exists	Method	Returns a Boolean indicating whether a particular named argument exists in the collection. Its syntax is *object*.Exists(*strArgName*) where *strArgName* is a String containing the argument name.
Item	Property	Returns a String containing the value of a particular named command line argument. Its syntax is: object.Item(*strArgName*) where *strArgName* is a String containing the argument name. If *strArgName* is not found in the collection, the property returns an empty string.
		Since Item is the default member of the WshNamed object, it need not be called explicitly. Hence, the following two lines of code function identically:
		strVal = oNamed.Item("name")
		strVal = oNamed("name")
length	Property	Returns an integer indicating the number of named arguments in the collection.

The WshNetwork Object

The WshNetwork object represents network resources that are available to a client computer. You can create a WshNetwork object with a code fragment like the following:

```
Dim oNet
Set oNet = WScript.CreateObject("WScript.Network")
```

The WshNetwork object supports the three properties shown in Table 7-8 and the eight methods shown in Table 7-9.

Table 7-8. Properties of the WshNetwork object

Property	Description
ComputerName	Returns a String containing the name of the local computer.
UserDomain	Returns a String containing the name of the user domain.
UserName	Returns a String containing the username.

Table 7-9. Methods of the WshNetwork object

Method	Description
AddPrinterConnection	Maps a remote printer to a local resource name. Its syntax is WshNetwork.AddPrinterConnection *strLocalName, strRemoteName* [,*bUpdateProfile*] [, *strUser*][, *strPassword*] where *strLocalName* is the local resource name, *strRemoteName* is the name of the remote resource, *bUpdateProfile* is an optional Boolean that indicates whether the user profile is to be updated to contain this mapping, *strUser* is the optional name of the user for whom the printer is being mapped, and *strPassword* is the password of the user for whom the printer is mapped.
AddWindows-PrinterConnection	Adds a printer connection. Its syntax for Windows NT/2000/XP is WshNetwork.AddWindowsPrinterConnection(*strPrinterPath*) where *strPrinterPath* is the path to the printer. Under Windows 95/98/ME, its syntax is: WshNetwork.AddWindowsPrinterConnection(*strPrinterPath, strDriverName*[, *strPort*]): where *strPrinterPath* is the path to the printer, *strDriverName* is the name of the printer driver to use, and *strPort* is the optional name of the port to which to attach the printer. The default value of *strPort* is LPT1. This method differs from the AddPrinterConnection method by not requiring that the printer be assigned a local port.

EnumNetworkDrives	Returns a zero-based collection of strings containing the current network drive mappings. All members having even index values are local names (drive letters), and all having odd index values are the remote names of the immediately preceding local drive. The collection returned by the method supports the following properties:
	Count
	    The number of items in the collection
	Item
	    Returns an individual item from the collection
	length
	    The number of items in the collection

EnumPrinter-Connections	Returns a zero-based collection of strings containing the current network printer mappings. All members having even index values are the ports, and all members having odd index values are the network mappings of the preceding port. The collection returned by the method has the following members:
	Count
	    The number of items in the collection
	Item
	    Returns an individual item from the collection
	length
	    The number of items in the collection

MapNetworkDrive	Maps a network share to a local resource. Its syntax is WshNetwork.MapNetworkDrive *strLocalName*, *strRemoteName*, [*bUpdateProfile*], [*strUser*], [*strPassword*] where *strLocalName* is the local resource, *strRemoteName* is the network resource, *bUpdateProfile* is a Boolean value that indicates whether the user's profile should be updated to include the mapping, *strUser* is the optional name of the user for whom the printer is being mapped, and *strPassword* is the optional password of the user for whom the printer is being mapped.

Table 7-9. Methods of the WshNetwork object (continued)

Method	Description
RemoveNetworkDrive	Removes a current resource connection. Its syntax is WshNetwork.RemoveNetwork- Drive *strName*, [*bForce*], [*bUpdateProfile*] where *strName* must be either a local name (if the remote drive is mapped to a local name) or a remote name, *bForce* is a Boolean value that indicates whether the connection should be removed even if the resource is in use, and *bUpdateProfile* is a Boolean that indicates whether the mapping should be removed from the user profile.
RemovePrinter- Connection	Removes the connection to a network printer. Its syntax is WshNetwork.Remove- PrinterConnection *strName*, [*bForce*], [*bUpdateProfile*] where *strName* must be a local name (if the printer is mapped to a local name) or a remote name, *bForce* is a Boolean value that indicates whether the printer should be removed even if it is in use, and *bUpdateProfile* is a Boolean that indicates whether the connection should be removed from the user profile.
SetDefaultPrinter	Sets the default printer to a remote printer. Its syntax is WshNetwork. SetDefaultPrinter *strPrinterName* where *strPrinterName* is the name of the remote printer. The names of available remote printers can be retrieved with the Enum- PrinterConnection method.

The WshRemote Object

The WshRemote object, which is new to WSH 5.6, allows for control over a remote script by the launching script. It is returned by the CreateScript method of the WshController object. The WshRemote object supports the members shown in Table 7-10. Note that, unlike most of the objects in the Windows Script Host object model, the WshRemote object supports three events: Start, End, and Error.

Configuring Remote Scripting

Before you can launch a script remotely, the system on which it runs has to be configured to support remote scripting. This requires that Windows Script Host 5.6 be installed on the remote machine, that the user launching the remote script be a member of the remote machine's Local Administrators group, and that remote scripting be enabled in the registry. The HKEY_LOCAL_MACHINE\ Software\Microsoft\Windows Script Host\Settings key has a value entry named Remote. If its value is 1, remote scripting is enabled; if 0, disabled. The following script enables the key:

```
Dim oShell, regKey, regValue

Set oShell = CreateObject("WScript.Shell")
regKey = "HKLM\Software\Microsoft\Windows Script Host\Settings\Remote"
regValue = oShell.RegRead(regKey)

If regValue = "0" Then
   regValue = "1"
   oShell.RegWrite regKey, regValue, "REG_SZ"
End If
```

Table 7-10. Members of the WshRemote object

Name	Type	Description
End	Event	Fired when a remote script completes execution either because the WshRemote object's Terminate method is called or because the script has itself terminated.
Error	Property	Returns a WshRemoteError object that, if retrieved from the WshRemote object's Error event handler, provides information about the error that caused a remote script to terminate.
Error	Event	Fired when an error occurs in the remote script. No parameters are passed to the event handler.
Execute	Method	Starts the execution of a remote script. Its syntax is: *object*.Execute( ).
Start	Event	Fired when the WshRemote object's Execute method is called to begin execution of a remote script.
Status	Property	Returns the status of the remote script. Possible values are NoTask (0), Running (1), and Finished (2).
Terminate	Method	Prematurely terminates the execution of a remote script.

The following example illustrates the use of remote scripting and the WshRemote object. A controller script launches remote scripts on a number of systems in order to assemble a report listing those systems with drives whose free space is under 200 MB. The following *.wsf* file launches the remote scripts:

```
<package>
<reference guid="{6F201540-B482-11D2-A250-00104BD35090}" />
<reference guid="{F935DC20-1CF0-11D0-ADB9-00C04FD58A0B}" />
<reference guid="{563DC060-B09A-11D2-A24D-00104BD35090}" />

<job id="GatherDiskInfo">
<reference guid="{420B2830-E718-11CF-893D-00A0C9054228}" />
<runtime>
   <description>
   This script uses remote scripting to examine the disk drives
   of designated systems and reports those with less than
   200MB free.
   </description>
</runtime>
<script language="VBScript">
Option Explicit

Const fn = "MachineList.txt"
Const NoTask = 0
Const WshRunning = 1
Const WshFinished = 2

Dim fs, ts
Dim ctrl, remote, sh
Dim machineName

' Retrieve file listing machines to examine
Set fs = CreateObject("Scripting.FileSystemObject")
Set ts = fs.OpenTextFile(fn, ForReading, False)
Set sh = CreateObject("WScript.Shell")
Set ctrl = CreateObject("WSHController")
```

```
Do While Not ts.AtEndOfStream
   machineName = ts.ReadLine( )
   Set remote = ctrl.CreateScript("freespace.vbs " & machineName, _
              machineName)
   WScript.ConnectObject remote, "remote_"

   remote.Execute( )
   Do While remote.Status = WshRunning
      WScript.Sleep 100
   Loop
   WScript.DisconnectObject remote
Loop

Sub remote_Start( )
   sh.LogEvent 0, "Started remote script on " & machineName
End Sub

Sub remote_End( )
   sh.LogEvent 0, "Ended remote script on " & machineName
End Sub

Sub remote_Error( )
   Dim wshErr
   Set wshErr = remote.Error
   sh.LogEvent 1, "Error " & wshErr.Number & ": " & wshErr.Description
   WScript.Quit -1
End Sub
</script>
</job>
</package>
```

The script reads a text file, *MachineList.txt*, which contains a list of the systems whose drives are to be checked for available space, one system per line. For each machine, it calls the WshController object's CreateScript method, which returns a reference to a WshRemote object. The first parameter to the CreateScript method is the name of the script to be run along with an unnamed argument, the machine name. The argument is included because this makes it very easy for the remote script to identify the system on which it is running. The second parameter of the CreateScript method is once again the name of the system on which the remote script is to run.

The call to the CreateScript method returns a reference to a WshRemote object, which is then used in the call to the WScript object's ConnectObject method so that the script can receive event notifications. The script then executes the following remote script and enters a loop until the remote script has completed, at which point it disconnects the event handler and reads another line if one is present in *MachineList.txt*:

```
Option Explicit

Const ForAppending = 8
Const ForReading = 1
Const ForWriting = 2
Const Fixed = 2
Const fn = "c:\books\vbscript ian\wsh\freespace.txt"
```

```
Dim fs, drives, drive
Dim overWrite
Dim freeSpace
Dim msg

' Retrieve object references
Set fs = CreateObject("Scripting.FileSystemObject")
Set drives = fs.Drives

overWrite = True
 ' Enumerate drives
For Each drive In drives
    ' Examine only fixed drives
  If drive.IsReady And drive.DriveType = Fixed Then
      freeSpace = drive.FreeSpace
      ' Log if under 200MB free
      If freeSpace < 200000000 Then
         ' Form message string
         msg = msg & "System: " & WScript.Arguments.Unnamed(0) & "  "
         msg = msg & "Drive " & drive.DriveLetter & ": " & _
             FormatNumber(drive.FreeSpace, 0, False, True, True) _
             & " free"
         msg = msg & "   Date: " & Date() & " " & Time()
         WriteToFile msg
         overwrite = False
      End If
  End If
Next

Sub WriteToFile(strToWrite)

    Dim mode, create
    Dim ts

    mode = ForAppending
    create = False

    Set ts = fs.OpenTextFile(fn, mode, create)
    ts.WriteLine strToWrite
    ts.Close
End Sub
```

When the remote script begins and ends, its Start and End events, respectively, are fired. This executes the remote_Start and remote_End event handlers in the controller script, which write information about the beginning and end of the remote script to the controller's event log. If an error occurs, information about it is also written to the controller's event log.

The WshRemoteError Object

The WshRemoteError object provides access to information about the error that caused a remote script to terminate execution. The object is new to WSH 5.6. The WshRemoteError object is not createable; instead, it is returned by the Error property of the WshRemote object. The property's value is typically retrieved in the Error event handler of the WshRemote object. To see the use of the WshRemoteError object in a script, see the example in "The WshRemote Object" earlier in this chapter.

The properties of the WshRemoteError object are listed in Table 7-11.

Table 7-11. Properties of the WshRemoteError object

Property	Description
Character	Returns the character position in a line at which the error occurred, or a 0 if a line and character position could not be identified as containing the source of the error.
Description	Returns a String containing a brief description of the error, or an empty string if none is available.
Line	Returns the number of the line on which the error occurred, or a 0 if a line containing the source of the error could not be identified.
Number	Returns a Long containing the error number.
Source	Identifies the COM object in which the error occurred.
SourceText	Returns the line of script containing the error, or an empty string if no line could be identified.

The WshScriptExec Object

The WshScriptExec object represents a local script or application launched by calling the *WshShell.Exec* method. Its members provide status information and allow you to access the script or application's standard input, output, and error streams. The WshScriptExec object is new to WSH 5.6.

The members of the WshScriptExec object are listed in Table 7-12.

Table 7-12. Members of the WshScriptExec object

Name	Type	Description
Status	Property	Returns status information about a script or application run using the *WshShell. Exec* method. Possible values are WshRunning (0) and WshFinished (1).
StdErr	Property	Provides access to the WshScriptExec's standard error stream.
StdIn	Property	Provides access to the WshScriptExec's standard input stream.
StdOut	Property	Provides access to the WshScriptExec's standard output stream.
Terminate	Method	Sends a WM_CLOSE message to a process (a script or an application) launched by calling the *WshShell.Exec* method. How the message is handled depends on the application: it can ignore the message, or it can terminate.

The WshShell Object

The WshShell object provides access to a wide variety of shell services, such as registry access, access to environment variables and to the location of system folders, and the ability to create shortcuts and to start processes. You can instantiate a WshShell object with a code fragment like the following:

```
Dim wsh
Set wsh = WScript.CreateObject("WScript.Shell")
```

The WShell object supports the 3 properties shown in Table 7-13 and the 11 methods listed in Table 7-14.

Table 7-13. Properties of the WshShell object

Property	Description
CurrentDirectory	A read-write property that determines the script's current directory.
Environment	Returns a WshEnvironment collection containing the system or process environment variables and their values. Its syntax is `oShell.Environment([strType])` where `strType` is an optional string indicating which table of environment variables (System or Process) the property should return. For details, see the WshEnvironment object. If omitted, the property returns the system environment variables on Windows NT/2000/XP and the process environment variables on Windows 95/98/ME.
SpecialFolders	Returns a WshSpecialFolders collection containing the names of system folders and their locations; for details, see the WshSpecialFolders object.

Table 7-14. Methods of the WshShell object

Method	Description
AppActivate	Activates an application window. Its syntax is `WshShell.AppActivate title` where `title` is the caption of the application to be activated. If there is no exact match, WSH will attempt to match `title` with the application window whose caption begins with title. The documentation mentions that title can also be the task ID, which is returned by the Shell function; the Shell function, however, is present in VB but not in VBScript or WSH.
CreateShortcut	Returns a reference to a new or an existing WshShortcut object. Its syntax is `WshShell CreateShortcut-(strPathname)` where `strPathname` is the path and filename of an existing or a new Windows shortcut file (a file with an extension of *.lnk). (If `strPathname` has an extension of *.url, the method returns a reference to a WshUrlShortcut object instead.)

Once you retrieve the object reference, you can create or modify the physical shortcut file by calling the WshShortcut object's Save method. |
Exec	Runs a script or application as a separate process and returns a WshScriptExec object that provides access to its standard input, standard output, and standard error. The method is new to WSH 5.6.
Expand-EnvironmentStrings	Expands an environment variable and returns its value. Its syntax is `WshShell.Expand-EnvironmentStrings (strString)` where `strString` is a string that includes the name of an environment variable delimited by a beginning and closing percentage sign (%).
LogEvent	Logs an event. Its syntax is `WshShell.LogEvent(intType, strMessage [,strTarget])` where `intType` defines the type of event and is one of the values in Table 7-15, `strMessage` is the text of the event message, and, for Windows NT/2000/XP only, `strTarget` is the optional name of the system on which the event should be logged. If `strTarget` is omitted, the event is logged on the local system. Under Windows NT/2000/XP, events are logged in the Windows NT event log. Under Windows 95/98/ME, they're logged in the *WSH.log* file in the user's Windows directory; each entry contains the date and timestamp, the event type, and the text of the log message. The method returns True if successful and False otherwise.
Popup	Displays a popup message box. Its syntax is:

`intButton = WshShell.Popup(strText, [natSecondsToWait], [strTitle], [natType])`

where `strText` is the text of the message to appear in the pop up, `natSecondsToWait` is the optional number of seconds to wait before automatically closing the pop up, `strTitle` is the optional pop-up dialog's caption (it defaults to "Windows Script Host" if omitted), and `natType` defines the types of buttons and icons to use in the pop-up window and has the same values as the Win32 *MessageBox* function. This can consist of any one icon type combined with (i.e., logically Or'ed with) any one button set shown in Table 7-16. The method returns one of the integers shown in Table 7-17, which indicates which button is pressed to close the pop up. |

Table 7-14. Methods of the WshShell object (continued)

Method	Description
RegDelete	Deletes a key or value from the registry. Its syntax is WshShell.RegDelete *strName* where *strName* is the path to the key or value to delete. If *strName* ends in a backslash, it denotes a key; otherwise, it denotes a value. The default (or unnamed) value of a key cannot be deleted; it must be replaced with an empty string ("") by using the RegRead method. The abbreviations for the top-level registry keys are shown in Table 7-18.
RegRead	Returns a registry value. Its syntax is WshShell.RegRead- (*strName*) where *strName* is the path to the value to read. If *strName* ends in a backslash, the method reads the key's default value; otherwise, it reads a named value. The abbreviations for the top-level keys are shown in Table 7-18; keys not listed must be accessed by their full name (e.g., HKEY_CURRENT_CONFIG). The RegRead method can read the data types shown in Table 7-19; other data types are not supported. Note that the RegRead method does not expand environment strings in REG_EXPAND_SZ data; this requires a separate call to the WshShell object's ExpandEnvironmentStrings method.
RegWrite	Writes a registry value. Its syntax is WshShell.RegWrite *strName*, *anyValue* [,*strType*] where *strName* is that path to the value to write. If *strName* ends in a backslash, the method writes the key's default value; otherwise, it writes a named value. The abbreviations for the top-level registry keys are shown in Table 7-18; keys not listed must be accessed by their full names (e.g., HKEY_USERS).The RegWrite method can read the data types shown in Table 7-19; other data types are not supported.
Run	Creates a new process. Its syntax is WshShell.Run (*strCommand*, [*intWindowStyle*], [*bWaitOnReturn*]) where *strCommand* represents the command to execute, along with any command-line parameters. Any environment variable in it will be expanded automatically. *intWindowStyle* is an optional integer that defines the window style of the new process (for a list of valid window styles, see Table 7-20), and *bWaitOnReturn* is an optional Boolean synchronization flag that determines whether control returns to the script only after the process ends; by default, control returns to the script immediately after the Run method is called. The value returned by the function is 0 if *bWaitOnReturn* is False; otherwise, the method returns any error code returned by the application.
SendKeys	Sends keystrokes to the active window as if they were typed at the keyboard. Its syntax is SendKeys *string* where *string* is a string expression that specifies the keystrokes to send. Except for the special symbols shown in Table 7-21, each keyboard character is represented in *string* by itself.
	The SendKeys method cannot be used to send keystrokes to a non-Windows application. Nor can SendKeys be used to send the Print Screen key to any window.

Table 7-15. Values of the intType parameter of the LogEvent method

Value	Description
0	Success
1	Error
2	Warning
4	Information
8	Audit_Success
16	Audit_Failure

Table 7-16. Values of the natType parameter of the Popup method

Type	Value	Description
Button	0	OK
Button	1	OK and Cancel

Table 7-16. Values of the natType parameter of the Popup method (continued)

Type	Value	Description
Button	2	Abort, Retry, Ignore
Button	3	Yes, No, Cancel
Button	4	Yes, No
Button	5	Retry, Cancel
Icon	16	Stop
Icon	32	Question
Icon	48	Exclamation
Icon	64	Information

Table 7-17. Return values of the Popup method

Value	Description
1	OK button
2	Cancel button
3	Abort button
4	Retry button
5	Ignore button
6	Yes button
7	No button

Table 7-18. Abbreviations for the top-level registry keys

Abbreviation	Key
HKCU	HKEY_CURRENT_USER
HKLM	HKEY_LOCAL_MACHINE
HKCR	HKEY_CLASSES_ROOT

Table 7-19. Data types supported by the WshShell registry methods

Data type	RegWrite string constant	RegRead/RegWrite variant type
string	"REG_SZ"	String
string with macros	"REG_EXPAND_SZ"	String
string array	not supported	String array
long integer	"REG_DWORD"	Long
binary data (byte array)	"REG_BINARY"	Variant array of bytes

Table 7-20. Values of the intWindowStyle parameter of the Run method

Value	Description
0	Hides the window and activates another window.
1	Activates and displays a window. If the window is minimized or maximized, the system restores it to its original size and position. This flag should be used when specifying an application for the first time.

Table 7-20. Values of the intWindowStyle parameter of the Run method (continued)

Value	Description
2	Activates the window and displays it minimized.
3	Activates the window and displays it maximized.
4	Displays a window in its most recent size and position. The active window remains active.
5	Activates the window and displays it in its current size and position.
6	Minimizes the specified window and activates the next top-level window in the Z order.
7	Displays the window as a minimized window. The active window remains active.
8	Displays the window in its current state. The active window remains active.
9	Activates and displays the window. If it is minimized or maximized, the system restores it to its original size and position. An application should specify this flag when restoring a minimized window.
10	Sets the show state based on the state of the program that started the application.

Table 7-21. Special characters for use with the SendKeys method

Key	String	Key	String
Shift	+	Scroll Lock	{SCROLLLOCK}
Ctrl	^	Tab	{TAB}
Alt	%	Up Arrow	{UP}
Backspace	{BACKSPACE}, {BS}, or {BKSP}	F1	{F1}
Break	{BREAK}	F2	{F2}
Caps Lock	{CAPSLOCK}	F3	{F3}
Delete	{DELETE} or {DEL}	F4	{F4}
Down Arrow	{DOWN}	F5	{F5}
End	{END}	F6	{F6}
Enter	{ENTER} or ~	F7	{F7}
Esc	{ESC}	F8	{F8}
Help	{HELP}	F9	{F9}
Home	{HOME}	F10	{F10}
Insert	{INSERT} or {INS}	F11	{F11}
Left Arrow	{LEFT}	F12	{F12}
Num Lock	{NUMLOCK}	F13	{F13}
Page Down	{PGDN}	F14	{F14}
Page Up	{PGUP}	F15	{F15}
Print Screen	{PRTSC}	F16	{F16}
Right Arrow	{RIGHT}		

The WshShortcut Object

The WshShortcut object represents a shortcut—that is, a link to a file or other resource on the local system or local network. A new or existing WshShortcut object is returned by the CreateShortcut method of the WshShell object, as in the following code fragment:

```
Set WshShell = WScript.CreateObject("WScript.Shell")
Set oSCut = WshShell.CreateShortcut("Startup Script.lnk")
```

 A WshShortcut object exists in memory only and not in the filesystem until it is saved by calling the object's Save method.

When a new shortcut object is created, its FullName property is assigned the value specified by the *strPathname* parameter. The remaining properties assume their default values and must be changed programmatically before calling the WshShortcut object's Save method.

The WshShortcut object supports the eight properties shown in Table 7-22 and the single method shown in Table 7-23.

Table 7-22. Properties of the WshShortcut object

Property	Description
Arguments	Sets or returns a single String representing the arguments passed to the shortcut.
Description	Sets or returns a String representing a description of the shortcut. The Description property is not visible from the Windows user interface.
FullName	Returns a String containing the full path and filename of the shortcut file. Shortcut files have a file extension of *.lnk*.
Hotkey	Sets or returns a String containing the keyboard shortcut that executes the shortcut file; hotkeys apply only to shortcuts located on the Windows desktop or on the Start menu. Multiple keys are joined by a "+" sign. For example, a Hotkey value of "Alt+Ctrl+A" indicates that the shortcut's hotkey is the Alt + Ctrl + A key combination.
	According to the documentation, strings indicating alphabetic keys are case-sensitive ("A" is an uppercase A, but "a" is lowercase), although this does not appear to be the case. The strings that represent some common nonalphanumeric hotkeys are listed in Table 7-24.
IconLocation	Defines the location of the shortcut's icon. Typically, its value is the complete path and filename to the file containing the icon followed by a comma and the zero-based position of the icon within the file. If the default icon is used, the value of IconLocation is " ,0".
TargetPath	Sets or returns the path and filename to the shortcut's executable file. Note that the value of the TargetPath property can also include a data file that's associated with an executable file.
WindowStyle	Defines the window style of the application launched by the shortcut. Valid values are shown in Table 7-25.
WorkingDirectory	Defines the shortcut's working directory (i.e., the directory in which the shortcut will start).

Table 7-23. Method of the WshShortcut object

Method	Description
Save	Saves the Shortcut object to the filesystem at the location specified by the FullName property. Its syntax is WshShortcut.Save.

Table 7-24. Some common nonalphanumeric hotkey strings

Hotkey String	Description
Alt	Alt key
Back	Backspace key

Table 7-24. Some common nonalphanumeric hotkey strings (continued)

Hotkey String	Description
Ctrl	Ctrl key
Escape	Esc key
Shift	Shift key
Space	Space key
Tab	Tab key

Table 7-25. Values of the WindowStyle property

Value	Description
1	Activates and displays a window.
3	Activates the window and displays it maximized.
7	Displays the window as a minimized window. The active window remains active.

The WshSpecialFolders Object

WshSpecialFolders is a collection object that stores strings that indicate the location of Windows system folders, like the Desktop folder of the Windows System folder. The collection is returned by the SpecialFolders property of the WshShell object, as the following code fragment shows:

```
Dim oShell, oSpFolders

Set oShell = WScript.CreateObject("WScript.Shell")
Set oSpFolders = oShell.SpecialFolders
```

Note that the location of a particular WshSpecialFolders object can be accessed by using its key, as discussed in the entry for the object's Item property in Table 7-26.

The WshSpecialFolders object supports the standard three properties of a WSH collection object, as shown in Table 7-26.

Table 7-26. Properties of the WshSpecialFolders object

Property	Description
Count	Indicates the number of items in the collection.
Item	Returns an individual item from the collection; each item is a string that indicates the location of a particular special folder. If the member doesn't exist, the Item property returns an empty variant. An item is retrieved from the collection either by its ordinal position in the collection or by its key; valid key values are: AllUsersDesktop, AllUsersStartMenu, AllUsersPrograms, AllUsersStartup, Desktop, Favorites, Fonts, MyDocuments, NetHood, PrintHood, Programs, Recent, SendTo, StartMenu, Startup, and Templates.
length	Indicates the number of items in the collection.

The WshUnnamed Object

The WshUnnamed object, which is new to WSH 5.6, is a collection object that contains unnamed command-line arguments. (An unnamed argument is entered on the command line by itself with no special syntax.) WshUnnamed is not a createable object, and is returned by the Unnamed property of the WshArguments object.

The following statement returns a WshUnnamed collection object:

```
Dim unnamedArgs
Set unnamedArgs = WScript.Arguments.Unnamed
```

It consists of one string for each unnamed argument passed to the script when it was invoked. You can iterate the arguments as follows:

```
Dim arg
For Each arg in unnamedArgs
    ' Do something with arg, the individual argument
Next
```

Or you can retrieve an individual argument using code like the following, which retrieves the first unnamed argument in the collection:

```
Dim arg
arg = WScript.Arguments.Unnamed(0)
```

The members of the WshUnnamed object are shown in Table 7-27.

Table 7-27. Members of the WshUnnamed object

Name	Type	Description
Count	Method	Returns an integer indicating the number of unnamed arguments in the collection. Its syntax is: `object.Count( )`.
Item	Property	Returns a String containing the value of a command-line argument at a particular ordinal position in the collection. Its syntax is: `object.Item(intPos)` where `intPos` is an Integer indicating the ordinal position of the argument. If `intPos` is outside of the range of the collection, an error occurs.
		Since Item is the default member of the WshUnnamed object, it need not be explicitly referenced. Hence, the following two lines of code function identically:
		`strVal = oUnnamed.Item(2)`
		`strVal = oUnnamed(2)`
length	Property	Returns an integer indicating the number of named arguments in the collection.

The WshUrlShortcut Object

The WshUrlShortcut object represents an Internet shortcut—an Internet link to an Internet resource. A new or an existing WshUrlShortcut object is returned by the CreateShortcut method of the WshShell object, as in the following code fragment:

```
Set WshShell = WScript.CreateObject("WScript.Shell")
Set oURL = WshShell.CreateShortcut("Favorite Website.url")
```

 A WshUrlShortcut object exists in memory only and not in the filesystem until it is saved by calling the object's Save method.

When a new WshUrlShortcut object is created, its FullName property is assigned the value specified by the *strPathname* parameter.

Its remaining property, TargetPath, must be changed programmatically before calling the WshUrlShortcut object's Save method.

The WshUrlShortcut object supports the three members shown in Table 7-28.

Table 7-28. Members of the WshUrlShortcut object

Member type	Member name	Description
Property	FullName	Returns a String containing the full path and filename of the Internet shortcut file. Shortcut files have a file extension of *.url.
Property	TargetPath	Sets or returns a String containing the complete URL of the Internet resource to which the Internet shortcut is linked.
Method	Save	Saves the Internet shortcut object to the filesystem at the location specified by the FullName property. Its syntax is WshUrlShortcut.Save.

WSH Language Elements

All the language elements listed in Table 7-29 have been added to Windows Script Host as of Version 2.0. They are XML elements that can be used in *.wsf* files and allow metadata about script-based applications to be embedded in the same file as the script

Table 7-29. WSH language elements

Element	Description
`<?job ?>`	Defines error handling. It syntax is `<?job error="`*`flag`*`" debug="`*`flag`*`" ?>` where *flag* is the string "True" or "False", "Yes" or "No", or the integers 1 or 0. The error attribute defines whether the user will be notified of errors; the debug attribute determines whether a debugger is launched when an error is raised. By default, both attributes are false.
`<?xml ?>`	Indicates that the contents of a file should be parsed as XML. Its syntax is `<?XML version="`*`version`*`" [standalone="`*`DTDflag`*`"] ?>` where *version* is a string in the format *n.n* that indicates the XML level of the file, and *DTDflag* is a Boolean value that indicates whether the XML file includes a reference to an external DTD. Since script files do not include DTDs, the value of this attribute must always be "yes." The `<?xml ?>` tag must be the first element in the file, and cannot be preceded by any blank lines. Its most common use is to indicate that the script file can be edited by an XML editor.
`<description>` *descriptiveText* `</description>`	Defines the purpose of a script. It is displayed when the WScript.ShowUsage method is called or the user adds the `/?` command-line switch when running the script. It is enclosed within the `<runtime>...</runtime>` element.
`<example>` *exampleScript* `</example>`	Provides an example of a script's usage. It is displayed when the WScript.ShowUsage method is called or the user adds the `/?` command-line switch when running the script. It is enclosed within the `<runtime>...</runtime>` element.
`<job>` *script* `</job>`	Defines an individual job within a script file containing one or more jobs. Its syntax is `<job id="`*`jobid`*`">` where *jobid* is a string identifier that's unique within the file. Every element that appears within a `<job>...</job>` tag applies to that job. An individual job can be invoked using the `//Job` command-line switch.
`<named` `name=`*`name`* `helpstring=`*`hlp`* `type=`*`type`* `required=`*`req`* `/>`	Provides information about a named argument to a script. It is displayed when the WScript.ShowUsage method is called or the user adds the `/?` command-line switch when running the script. *name* is the argument's name. *hlp* describes the argument. *type* indicates the argument's type and can be string, boolean, or simple. *req* is a Boolean that indicates whether the argument is required or optional. The `<named>` element must be enclosed within the `<runtime>...</runtime>` element. The required element is used in displaying usage information, and name and helpstring are used to describe the named argument.

Table 7-29. WSH language elements (continued)

Element	Description
`<object />`	Defines a global object. Its syntax is `<object id="objID" [classid="clsid:GUID" | progid="progID"] />` where *objID* is the name by which the object will be referred in the script or scripts, *GUID* is the CLSID of the class from which the object was created (as defined in HKEY_CLASSES_ROOT\CLSID), and *progID* is the programmatic identifier of the class. Either one of *GUID* or *ProgID* must be present, but not both.
`<package>` *script* `</package>`	Indicates that a Windows Script Host (.ws) file contains multiple job definitions, as defined by the `<job>...</job>` element. If a file contains only a single job, the element is optional.
`<reference />`	Adds a reference to a type library, making its constants available to the script. Its syntax is `<reference [object="progid" | guid="LibID"] [version="version"] />` where *progid* is the programmatic identifier of the type library, *LibID* is its GUID, and *version* is its version number. Either *progid* or *TypeLibGUID* must be present, but not both. Typically, this is element causes a good deal of difficulty, although it does work. While individual classes within type libraries do have programmatic identifiers, most type libraries do not, which means that you should specify the GUID by determining its value from a subkey of the HKEY_CLASSES_ROOT\ TypeLib key in the registry. In addition, *version* defaults to 1.0, which is rarely the version you'd want to use. Available versions are listed as subkeys of HKEY_CLASSES_ ROOT\TypeLib*LibID*, where *LibID* is the type library's GUID.
`<resource id=id>` *text or number* `</resource>`	Defines a string or number as a resource that can be retrieved by its identifier rather than "hard-coded" throughout script. Among other uses, resources are invaluable in localizing applications. Resources can be retrieved using the getResource method, whose syntax is getResource(id) where *id* is the ID of the resource. The method returns a string containing the resource value.
`<runtime>` *runtimeInfo* `</runtime>`	Provides runtime information about a script when the `WScript.ShowUsage` method is called or the user adds the /? command-line switch when running the script. It must appear within the `<job>...</job>` element and therefore can apply to only a single script. It in turn can contain `<description>`, `<usage>`, `<example>`, `<named>`, and `<unnamed>` elements.
`<script>` *script* `</script>`	Defines the language in which a code block is written and optionally imports that code block from another file. Its syntax is `<script language="lang" [scr="strfile"]>` where *lang* is a COM-compliant scripting language such as "VBScript" or "JScript" and *strfile* is the path and name of the file to be included.
`<unnamed` *name=unnamed helpstring=hlp many=many required=req* `/>`	Provides information about an unnamed argument to a script. It is displayed when the `WScript.ShowUsage` method is called or the user adds the /? command-line switch when running the script. *name* is the name used for the unnamed argument. *hlp* describes the argument. *many* is a Boolean that indicates whether the argument can be specified more times than the required attribute. type. *req* is a Boolean that indicates how many times the argument should appear on the command line.
`<usage>` *descriptiveText* `</usage>`	Provides information about a script that is displayed when the `WScript.ShowUsage` method is called or the user adds the /? command-line switch when running the script. It allows the typical usage display to be overridden, since if it is present, all other tags contained by the `<runtime>` element are ignored. The `<usage>` element must be enclosed within the `<runtime>...</runtime>` element.

Accessing Other Object Models

On the whole, the functionality of WSH is strictly limited. For instance, WSH itself provides almost no access to the filesystem, nor does it support any application services. This is a deliberate omission; the designers of Windows Script Host intended that you could draw on the functionality of other object models when writing WSH scripts.

The "hooks" into other object models are provided by the WScript object's CreateObject and GetObject methods; the former method creates a new instance of an object, while the latter retrieves a reference to an existing instance. As Table 7-30 shows, using these methods, you can instantiate objects like the following:

Active Directory Service Interface (ADSI)
ADSI provides a single set of directory service interfaces for managing network resources.

ActiveX Data Objects (ADO)
ADO is a data access technology that offers a uniform methodology for accessing data regardless of location or format. ADO has a relatively "flat" object model, and many objects (like the Recordset object, or the Connection object) can be instantiated independently of one another.

Collaborative Data Objects (CDO)
CDO is an object model that uses MAPI to create mail-enabled applications. The Session object is its top-level object.

Data Access Objects (DAO)
DAO is a data access technology intended primarily for use with Access databases and the Jet database engine. Its top-level object is named DBEngine.

The Dictionary object
A part of the Scripting Runtime Library, the Dictionary object provides access to data sets that have identifiable keys.

The Excel Application object
The Excel object model is useful for extracting data from spreadsheets or for manipulating charts. Its top-level object is the Application object.

The FileSystemObject object
A part of the Scripting Runtime Library, the FileSystemObject provides access to the local filesystem.

Windows Management Instrumentation (WMI)
WMI is Microsoft's implementation of Web-Based Enterprise Management (WBEM), a technology that aims at standardizing access to management information in an enterprise environment.

The Word Application object
The Word object model makes it easy to manipulate Word *.doc* files as well as Rich Text Format (*.rtf*) files. Note that its top-level object is the Application object.

Table 7-30. Some object models and their programmatic identifiers

Object	ProgID	Description
Access	Access.Application	The forms and reports (primarily) of an Access table
Connection	ADODB.Connection	An ADO database connection
DBEngine	DAO.DBEngine	The DAO object model, primarily for Access databases
Dictionary	Scripting.Dictionary	A high-performance alternative to arrays and collections for keyed data

Object	ProgID	Description
Excel	`Excel.Application`	The Microsoft Excel application, for manipulating spreadsheets and charts
FileSystemObject	`Scripting.FileSystemObject`	Represents the local filesystem
Recordset	`ADODB.Recordset`	An ADO recordset
Session	`MAPI.Session`	A Session object using Collaborative Data Objects (CDO)
SWbemLocator	`WbemScripting.SWbemLocator`	A WMI object that provides access to WMI on a particular local or remote host computer
SWbemObjectPath	`WbemScripting.SWbemObjectPath`	A WMI object that constructs and validates object paths
SWbemServices	`winmgmts:`	A WMI object whose InstancesOf method provides access to WMI class instances
Word	`Word.Application`	The Microsoft Word application for manipulating documents

8

VBScript with Internet Explorer

VBScript was initially intended for client-side scripting. It provided a Visual Basic–like method for HTML developers to add interactivity to their web pages. The hope was that since many developers were familiar with Visual Basic, a scripting language modeled after the application development tool would have a wide audience. The basic concept proved to be correct, although client-side scripting with VBScript never achieved the popularity its developers had hoped for. This is because client-side scripting with VBScript has a major downside: VBScript is supported only in Internet Explorer. This means that you have to either force your users to a specific browser (which is really only possible on intranets), or script with both VBScript and some flavor of ECMAScript to make sure that you are providing the same functionality to all users. This, however, does not mean that scripting in ECMAScript will answer all of your compatibility issues, either. Netscape Navigator and Internet Explorer each have their own flavor of ECMAScript, which, while mostly similar, still have their differences. Anyway, we'll assume that if you are reading this chapter that you are interested in client-side scripting in Internet Explorer.

The <SCRIPT> Tag

Very much like the <A> tag is used to delimit a hyperlink on your web page, the <SCRIPT> tag is used to contain your script. The <SCRIPT> tag allows scripts to be written inline with the rest of your HTML document, and indicates where the embedded scripting code begins. It also indicates the scripting language, and therefore serves to identify which particular scripting engine is responsible for handling the code. As with nearly all HTML tags, there is a corresponding end tag (</SCRIPT>) to close the script.

<SCRIPT> Attributes

The <SCRIPT> tag has one main attribute, LANGUAGE, which is optional. There are also two additional attributes, SRC and FOR, that give the <SCRIPT> tag a specialized meaning.

The LANGUAGE attribute

LANGUAGE is used to specify to the browser which scripting language engine is to compile and execute the code contained within the script tags. In order to indicate that a script should be handled by the VBScript language engine, either of the following two forms of the <SCRIPT> tag are acceptable:

```
<SCRIPT LANGUAGE="vbscript">
<SCRIPT LANGUAGE="vbs">
```

Unless otherwise stated, HTML tags or elements and attributes are *not* case-sensitive. Therefore, it would be legal to include the following <SCRIPT> tag in an HTML document:

```
<script language="VBSCRIPT">
```

As we saw earlier, the language attribute is actually optional. However, if you do not specify the language, Internet Explorer will, by default, treat the script as though it were JScript, and use the JScript language engine when compiling and executing it.

Instead of the LANGUAGE attribute, it is possible to use the TYPE attribute to specify the scripting language. The value of the TYPE attribute must be the MIME type of a scripting engine. The valid MIME types for VBScript are text/VBScript and text/VBS. Hence, the following two <SCRIPT> tags are functionally identical:

```
<script language="VBSCRIPT">
<script type="text/VBScript">
```

The SRC attribute

The <SCRIPT> tag itself need not contain script. Instead, the <SCRIPT> tag, when used with the SRC attribute, can designate a script file to be included at that point in the HTML stream. The SRC attribute's value is the URL of the script file to be included. When the SRC attribute is present, the LANGUAGE attribute should also be used. Otherwise, Internet Explorer interprets the included script file as having the same language as the *last* script block parsed; if there is no previous script block, it defaults to JScript. In addition, the </SCRIPT> end tag should immediate follow the <SCRIPT> tag. For instance, the following tag includes a file named *Include1.htm*:

```
<SCRIPT SRC="Include1.htm" LANGUAGE="VBScript"> </SCRIPT>
```

The file designated by the SRC attribute should be purely a script file containing source code in the designated scripting language; that is, it should contain no embedded HTML tags, not even the <SCRIPT> tag. Otherwise, an error results.

Note that the file designated by the SRC attribute is included in the HTML stream and is treated by the scripting engine as if it were part of the HTML file in which it is included. This means, for instance, that attempting to "hide" global variables from the scripts in the calling HTML document by declaring them private will not succeed, since the scripting engine will see them as having been defined in the document from which you're trying to hide them.

The SRC attribute can be extremely useful in allowing you to make a code library accessible to your web pages. You simply relocate all of the functions and procedures that you use in multiple web pages to a single script file and include it in all of the web pages that require its functions and procedures. One of the obvious advantages of this approach is that it leaves you with only a single copy of the source code to maintain, rather than with innumerable frequently incompatible copies in a multiplicity of locations.

The FOR attribute

Strictly speaking, FOR is an attribute of the <SCRIPT> tag. However, we like to separate <SCRIPT> and <SCRIPT FOR> in our minds, at least, since they are used somewhat differently. <SCRIPT FOR> is used to enclose the script for a single event belonging to a single object or control, whereas <SCRIPT> can contain numerous functions, procedures, events, etc. You can see this clearly in the full <SCRIPT FOR> tag. Unlike all the other <SCRIPT> tags you have seen thus far, this line attaches its script to a specific event of a specific control:

```
<SCRIPT FOR="myButton" EVENT="onClick" LANGUAGE="vbscript">
```

The FOR attribute specifies which control (usually an intrinsic HTML object) the code is to be attached to, and the EVENT attribute tells the scripting engine what event handler the <SCRIPT FOR> tag script is defining. To put it another way, the <SCRIPT FOR> tag allows you to define an event handler for a control event without having to name that event explicitly. For instance, Example 8-1 defines an event handler for the myButton_onClick event.

Example 8-1. The <SCRIPT FOR> tag

```
<HTML>
<BODY BGCOLOR="white">
<FORM NAME="myForm">
  <INPUT TYPE=text NAME="myText">
  <INPUT TYPE=button NAME="myButton">
    <SCRIPT FOR="myButton" EVENT="onClick" LANGUAGE="vbscript">
      alert Document.myForm.myText.Value
    </SCRIPT>
</FORM>
</BODY>
</HTML>
```

As you can see from Example 8-1, the VBScript Sub...End Sub construct is not required, since the event and object have been specified in the <SCRIPT FOR> tag, and the script itself consists of a complete procedure. If you attempt to use the Sub...End Sub construct, the VBScript compiler displays an error message. This means, incidentally, that the procedure defined by the <SCRIPT FOR> tag does not have a name; consequently, it cannot be called from any other part of a VBScript program. Also note that to improve readability, it is usual to place a <SCRIPT FOR> construct directly after the object to which it relates.

Where to Place the <SCRIPT> Tag

The <SCRIPT> tag can be placed anywhere within the <HEAD> or <BODY> sections of an HTML document. There's also no limitation on the number of <SCRIPT> sections you can place within a HTML file; you can have as many combinations of

<SCRIPT>...</SCRIPT> as you want. You may choose to bundle all your proce-
dures together into one large <SCRIPT> section and place this at the end of the BODY
section, out of the way of the main HTML coding, or you could quite easily split
the procedures into their own <SCRIPT> sections, placing them near to or directly
after the HTML elements they refer to (or are called from). The three models or
templates that appear in Examples 8-2 through 8-4 show where you can place the
<SCRIPT> tag within your HTML document.

Example 8-2. Using a single <SCRIPT> section as part of the <HEAD> section

```
<HTML>
  <HEAD>
    <SCRIPT LANGUAGE="vbscript">
    various scripted procedures
    </SCRIPT>
  </HEAD>
<BODY>
various html coding, etc.
</BODY>
</HTML>
```

Example 8-3. Using a single <SCRIPT> section at the end of the <BODY> section

```
<HTML>
  <HEAD>
  </HEAD>
<BODY>
 various html coding, etc.
  <SCRIPT LANGUAGE="vbscript">
 various scripted procedures
  </SCRIPT>
</BODY>
</HTML>
```

Example 8-4. Using multiple <SCRIPT> sections within the <BODY> section

```
<HTML>
  <HEAD>
  </HEAD>
<BODY>
  various html coding, etc.
  <SCRIPT LANGUAGE="vbscript">
 various scripted procedures
  </SCRIPT>
  Various HTML coding etc.
  <SCRIPT LANGUAGE="vbscript">
 various scripted procedures
  </SCRIPT>
  various html coding, etc.
  <SCRIPT LANGUAGE="vbscript">
 various scripted procedures
  </SCRIPT>
</BODY>
</HTML>
```

Internet
Explorer

Using <!----> with <SCRIPT>

Although certainly not mandatory, Microsoft recommends that you "comment out" the contents of the <SCRIPT> section by using the HTML comment tags <!-- and -->. This prevents older browsers that do not recognize the <SCRIPT> tag from interpreting the script as plain text and displaying it on the HTML page, as illustrated in Figure 8-1.

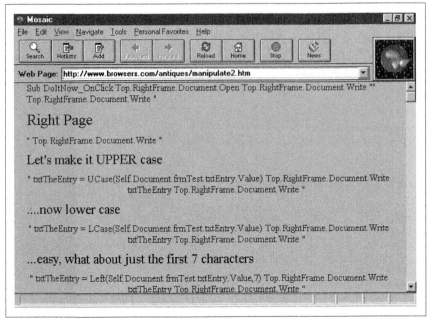

Figure 8-1. An older browser displaying uncommented script as text

The comment tags <!-- and --> must be placed within the <SCRIPT> tags, as the following code fragment shows:

```
<SCRIPT LANGUAGE="vbscript">
<!--
  Sub DoAScript
    .......
  End Sub
-->
</SCRIPT>
```

Otherwise, the <SCRIPT> tags themselves will be ignored by all browsers. Since browsers are expected to overlook tags that they don't understand, older browsers will skip over the <SCRIPT> tag. But since they don't "know" that the <SCRIPT> tag marks the beginning of executable content, rather than of displayable text, they'll display the text unless the comment tags are present. On the other hand, browsers that support the <SCRIPT> tag use the scripting engine to interpret all text between the <SCRIPT> and </SCRIPT> tags. The HTML comment tags are ignored by the script engine, so that it "sees" only the actual code. However, any additional comment tags, or any comment tags in any other position within the <SCRIPT> and </SCRIPT> tags, are interpreted as script, and generate a syntax error. This means that if you need to add comments to your code, don't use the HTML comment tags; use either REM or a single quotation mark (') at the start of the line.

What Can You Do with Client-Side Scripting?

The three main things that you can do with client-side scripting are:

- Interact with the client
- Handle events
- Validate data entry

These tasks are accomplished by manipulating the Internet Explorer Document Object Model (DOM). We'll examine each of these uses in turn.

Interacting with the Client

First, let's take a look at a small script that displays a message to the user when the web page loads, as shown in Figure 8-2; its HTML source is shown in Example 8-5. Don't worry about the code now; we'll take a more in-depth look at it later.

Example 8-5. A little VBScript interactivity

```
<HTML>
<HEAD>
<Script Language = "VBSCRIPT">
sub window_onload
    msgbox "Welcome to my Website"
end sub
</SCRIPT>
</HEAD>

<BODY>
<H1>Matt's Wonderful World of Web</H1>
</BODY>
</HTML>
```

This simple example will pop up a message box to the client when the page loads in the window. Not too complex, but a nice touch—and more importantly, not something you can do without a scripting language. Let's take a little closer look at what is happening here.

First, we declare the subroutine in the <HEAD> section of the HTML page. This isn't required, but we highly recommend it as good practice. Better to have all of your code in one place so you can find the subroutines faster when you need to make corrections or changes.

The next section is the actual VBScript that has been written for this event:

```
sub window_onload
    msgbox "Welcome to my Website"
end sub
```

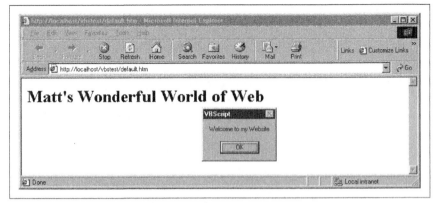

Figure 8-2. Web page produced by Example 8-5

This should be a common sight for anyone who has written any VB or VBA code. Here we have declared a subroutine that will fire when the page is being loaded. In this case, it will display a simple message box to the user welcoming them to our site.

From this small example, it is easy to see how VBScript allows you to add some flavor and depth to your web pages.

Now that you've seen a small example, let's expand on it and add a little more interactivity. Our HTML source code is shown in Example 8-6.

Example 8-6. A simple interactive web page

```
<HTML>
<HEAD>
<Script Language = VBSCRIPT>

sub window_onload
    msgbox "Welcome to my Website"
end sub

sub cmdMessage_onclick
    msgbox "Hello " & txtName.value
end sub

</SCRIPT>
</HEAD>

<BODY>
<H1>Matt's Wonderful World of Web</H1>
<input type = "Text" Name = "txtName"/>
<BR>
<Input Type = "Button" Name = "cmdMessage" VALUE = "Submit"/>
</BODY>
</HTML>
```

You'll notice that there are now two different subroutines in the <HEAD> section of the HTML document. In addition to the original one from Example 8-1, there is now a new one that is tied to a button that we have placed on the page. Again, nothing too complex here, so we will walk through the new code quickly.

You can see that we have added a button to the form with the following line of HTML:

```
<Input Type = "Button" Name = "cmdMessage" VALUE = "Submit">
```

We have named the button cmdMessage, and in the <HEAD> section of the document, we have created an event handler for this button called cmdMessage_ onclick. This event will fire every time this button is clicked. Let's take a look at what the code does:

```
sub cmdMessage_onclick
    msgbox "Hello " & txtName.value
end sub
```

This should seem familiar to you by now. We are again calling the *MsgBox* function, but this time we are appending a variable value to our message. In this code, we are referencing the value of the input box directly, but we could have also used a declared variable as well:

```
sub cmdMessage_onclick
    dim txtUser
    txtUser = txtName.value
    msgbox "Hello " & txtUser
end sub
```

There is no real advantage to using a variable in this instance, but most of your code won't be this simple, so it is a good idea to get used to handling user input or other information with variables.

Handling Events

The previous section demonstrated some simple code based on events that can be triggered from within a web page. Before we discuss data validation, we should touch on the idea of event-driven programming and look at how we can use VBScript to handle events that take place on your web pages. Table 8-1 displays some common HTML intrinsic controls and their associated events.

Table 8-1. HTML intrinsic controls and their events

Control	Event
Button	OnClick
Check Box	OnClick
Image	OnClick
Form	OnReset
	OnSubmit
Radio	OnClick
Submit	OnClick

Table 8-1. HTML intrinsic controls and their events (continued)

Control	Event
Text	OnBlur
	OnChange
	OnFocus
	OnSelect
Textarea	OnBlur
	OnChange
	OnFocus
	OnSelect
Window	OnLoad

This is by no means an exhaustive list, just some of the more common events that are available to you. For a complete list of all of the HTML controls and their corresponding events, we recommend *HTML & XHTML: The Definitive Guide*, Fifth Edition, by Chuck Musciano and Bill Kennedy (O'Reilly).

Most of the code that you write will be in response to some sort of action that the user takes. When you write code for a specific event, it is called an *event handler*. In other words, you have created code that will be executed in response to a specific event. The concept of event-driven programming is what makes VB and VBA so popular. In client-side scripting, you have laid the framework with HTML, and you are using VBScript to respond to the way the user interacts with the web page.

The code in Example 8-6 handles two different events, one when the window is loaded into the browser, and the other when the user clicks on a button. Both of these event handlers use the method of appending the name of the event being handled to the object name; the VBScript parser knows to associate this code with the proper event. In the case of the button, it looked like this:

```
Sub btnUser_onclick
Msgbox "Display a message"
End Sub
```

This method is familiar to VB and VBA developers, since it is how event handlers are named within those two environments.

In addition, you can use the <SCRIPT FOR> tag to explicitly declare the event that the code will be associated with. For example:

```
<SCRIPT FOR="btnUser" EVENT="onclick" LANGUAGE="vbscript"
MsgBox "Display a message"
</SCRIPT>
```

As in most coding, this is really a matter of which style you prefer. Developers who have worked with VB and VBA may prefer the implicit style, while HTML programmers adding VBScript to their toolbox may prefer the explicit method. There is no functional difference between the two, so the choice is yours.

Now that we've had a look at how to write code for the events, let's look at putting that into a little more useful practice. Next we'll take a look at data validation and how we can use VBScript to make sure that the user has entered the correct data before we do anything important with it.

Data Validation

One of the best uses of client-side scripting is to check user input before processing it. Let's build on our earlier example and add a simple routine to check whether data entered by the user meets our requirements. Example 8-7 asks the user to enter a user ID and then checks to make sure that she has entered only numeric data.

Example 8-7. Simple data validation in client-side script

```
<HTML>
<HEAD>
<Script Language = VBSCRIPT>
sub window_onload
    msgbox "Welcome to my Website"
end sub

sub cmdMessage_onclick
    dim txtUser
    txtUser = txtName.value
    if isnumeric(txtUser) then
        msgbox "Number Accepted"
    else
        msgbox "Please enter a numeric value"
    end if
end sub
</SCRIPT>
</HEAD>

<BODY>
<H1>Matt's Wonderful World of Web</H1>
<input type = "Text" Name = "txtName">
 Enter your ID Number
<BR>
<Input Type = "Button" Name = "cmdMessage" VALUE = "Submit">
</BODY>
</HTML>
```

First, we've added some instructions to our HTML to let the user know that we want him or her to enter a numeric user ID. Second, we have made some changes to the onClick event for the Submit button. Now when the user submits the information, an If statement is executed that checks whether the value the user entered is a number. If it is, the user gets a message telling them that the value is correct; if not, the user is prompted to re-enter a correct value.

This is a good example of doing some basic data checking. Let's expand this and look at validating data that the user has entered into a form. In order to do this, we'll need to expand our HTML a bit and add some new elements. Example 8-8 shows the result.

Example 8-8. Validating form data

```
<HTML>
<HEAD>
```

Example 8-8. Validating form data (continued)

```vbscript
<Script Language = VBSCRIPT>

Function radUserChecked (grpState)
    dim intChkRadio
    radUserChecked = False
    For intChkRadio = 0 to grpState.Length -1
      If grpState(intChkRadio).Checked Then
      radUserChecked = True
      Exit Function
      end if
    Next
End Function


sub cmdMessage_onclick
  If radUserChecked(frmUser.radUserState) Then
    msgbox "Thank you for making a selection"
  else
    msgbox "Please select one of the choices"
  end if
end sub

</SCRIPT>
</HEAD>

<BODY>
<H1>Matt's Wonderful World of Web</H1>
<BR>
<BR>
<BR>
<Form method=post id=frmUser name=frmUser>
New User
<Input Type = "Radio" id=radUserState name=radUserState value="New User">
<BR>
Previous User
<Input Type = "Radio" id=radUserState name=radUserState value="Previous User">
<BR>
<BR>
<Input Type = "Button" Name = "cmdMessage" VALUE = "Submit">
</FORM>
</BODY>
</HTML>
```

Here we have added a form to the HTML document. Inside the form, we have
added two radio buttons. We want to make sure that the user has checked one of
the buttons before we submit any information. In order for all of the radio buttons
to be a group, you have to remember to give them the same name. Grouping the
buttons allows us to loop through the collection to make sure that one of them
has been selected. We achieve this by creating the *radUserChecked* function that
will return a value to let us know the state of the group.

Next, let's look at how to handle whether data is submitted to the server. Ultimately, this is the reason that you are performing data validation. Let's use the example of a web page that asks the user to submit an email address. First, we will need to determine whether the user has entered anything; second, we will parse the text looking for an @ somewhere in the string. The web page is shown in Example 8-9.

Example 8-9. Cancelling form submission

```
<HTML>
<HEAD>
<Script Language="VBSCRIPT">
Function frmEmail_onsubmit( )

Dim strEmail

strEmail = frmEmail.txtEmail.value

If strEmail = "" Then
   MsgBox "You must submit an email address"
   frmEmail_onsubmit = False
Else
   If InStr(1, strEmail, "@", vbTextCompare) = 0 Then
      MsgBox "You have not entered a valid email address"
      frmEmail_onsubmit = False
   Else
      MsgBox "Thanks for entering your Email"
   End If
End If

End Function

</Script>
</HEAD>
<BODY>
<Form action="getemail.asp" method=POST id=frmEmail
      name=frmEmail>
Please Enter Your Email Address
<BR>
<INPUT type="text" id="txtEmail" name="txtEmail">
<BR>
<INPUT type = "submit" value="Send Email" id=btnSubmit
      name=btnSubmit>
</Form>
</BODY>
</HTML>
```

In this example, we prevented the user from posting the form data without entering a valid email address. The event handler for the HTML Form object's OnSubmit event (frmEmail_OnSubmit in our example) is a function, rather than a subroutine, and the function's return value indicates whether the default action of the event—in the case of the OnSubmit event, that the form data be submitted to the URL defined by the ACTION attribute—should occur. If the function returns

True (its default value), the form data is submitted. But if it returns False, the submission is cancelled. In Example 8-9, when we detected that the user had not entered the correct data, we sent back a value of frmEmail_onsubmit = False, which cancels the submit action.

As you can see, you can check and handle most user interaction with VBScript. The previous examples are pretty straightforward, but don't be fooled by them. You can build in incredibly complex client-side scripting as needed. Now let's move on to more interaction with the browser itself by taking a look at the Document Object Model.

Understanding the IE Object Model

Once the World Wide Web began to gain popularity, there was a great concern about preserving standards, so that the exchange of information would remain as open as possible. The Document Object Model (DOM), like HTML, is one of those standards. Basically, the Document Object Model provides a means for you to interact programmatically with the document displayed by the browser. Both Netscape Navigator and Internet Explorer have a document object model; however, there are some large differences between the two. Despite the presence of standards documents, there is always room for interpretation. (If you are interested in reading more about the Document Object Model standards, or any of the other standards that apply to the World Wide Web, see *http://www.w3.org*.)

We are going to take a look at the Internet Explorer Document Object Model. It is a rich environment that will allow you a measure of control over the document in the browser. Before we jump in, let's have a quick look at the Document Object Model itself and some of its parts. These are shown in Figure 8-3.

As you can see, the Window object is the parent of all of the other objects in this model. Each document will always have at least one Window object. A Window object will always have at least one Document object. Without the Document object, there would not be much for you to do with the Document Object Model. This figure shows the hierarchical nature of the Document Object Model. Like many of the object models that Visual Basic developers work with, you can access objects via their parent and use their properties to enhance your client-side development.

The object model is too extensive to document fully here. The next section displays some tables that describe the properties and methods of some of the objects that are programmatically available in the DOM. These tables are not exhaustive references to the objects; we have included the methods and properties that we consider to be the most useful and interesting. This will give you an idea of the scope and power of the Document Object Model.

The Window Object

The Window object is the top-level object in the object model. When you reference the Window object, you are actually interacting directly with the browser and the browser window itself. The Frame object in the object model is also just a particular type of Window object—the same properties and methods that apply to the Window object apply to the Frame object as well.

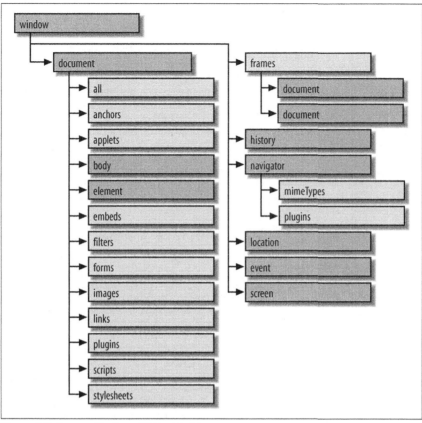

Figure 8-3. Internet Explorer Object Model

Some of the Window object's significant properties are shown in Table 8-2; its methods appear in Table 8-3.

Table 8-2. Some properties of the Window object

Property	Description
clientInformation	Returns the navigator (or clientInformation) object, which provides information about the browser.
closed	A Boolean value that can be checked to see if a window is still open.
event	Returns an event object that is accessible only from within an event handler. The event object itself conveys a wealth of information (such as mouse location or keyboard status) about the system environment when the event was fired.
history	Returns the History object for the current window or frame.
location	Sets or retrieves the URL of the document currently loaded in the window.
name	The name of a frame or window.
parent	Returns a reference to the parent window.
screen	Returns a reference to the screen object.
status	Returns or sets the text of the status bar in the browser.
top	Returns a reference to the browser window (i.e., the top-level Window object).

Table 8-3. Some methods of the Window object

Method	Description
alert	Displays a dialog box with a message. Its syntax is `Window.alert` *sMsg* where *sMsg* is an optional string containing the message.
blur	Removes the focus from the window and fires the onBlur event. Its syntax is `Window.blur`.
clearTimeout	Turns off the timeout delay counter set in a previous call to the setTimeout method. Its syntax is `Window.clearTimeout` *iTimeoutID* where *iTimeoutID* is the timeout setting returned by the previous call to setTimeout.
close	Closes the current window. Its syntax is `Window.close`.
execScript	Evaluates one or more script expressions in any scripting language embedded in the browser. Its syntax is `Window.execScript` *sExpression*, *sLanguage*, where *sExpression* is a string that specifies the code to be executed and *sLanguage* is an optional string that specifies the language of *sExpression*. The default value of *sLanguage* is JScript.
focus	Brings the window to the front of all regular browser windows and fires the onFocus event. Its syntax is `Window.focus`.
navigate	Loads a new document into the window or frame. Its syntax is `Window.navigate` *sURL*, where *sURL* is a string containing the URL of the document to be loaded.
open	Opens a new window (but does not close the original one). Its syntax is `Window.open(`*sURL*, *sName*, *sFeatures*, *bReplace*`)`, where *sURL* is the optional URL of the document to be opened in the window (if absent, the browser will open its default document), *sName* is the optional name of a window used as the value of the `TARGET` attribute of the `<FORM>` or `<A>` tag, *sFeatures* is an optional string that can contain a wide array of window configuration features, and *bReplace* is an optional Boolean that indicates whether the new URL should replace the existing one in the browser's history list (`True`) or whether an entry should be added (`False`). The method returns a reference to the new Window object.
print	Starts the printing process for the window or frame. Its syntax is `Window.print`.
scroll	Sets the scrolled position of the document inside the current window or frame. Its syntax is `Window.scroll` *ix*, *iy*, where *ix* and *iy* are the number of pixels to be offset horizontally and vertically in the upper-left corner of the window.
showHelp	Displays a help window with the document specified by the URL parameter. Its syntax is `Window.showHelp` *sURL*, *vContextID* where *sURL* is the URL of the help file and *vContextID* is an optional context identifier that identifies a particular item within the help file.

The Document Object

The Document object represents the document displayed in a window or frame. Its properties are shown in Table 8-4 and its methods are listed in Table 8-5.

Table 8-4. Some properties of the Document object

Property	Description
activeElement	Returns a reference to the object that currently has the focus within the document.
alinkColor	Retrieves or sets the color of the hypertext link as it is clicked.
bgColor	Retrieves or sets the background color of the element.
body	Returns a reference to the Body object defined by the `<BODY>` element within the document.
domain	Returns or sets the hostname of the server that served up the document.
fgColor	Retrieves or sets the foreground color for the document.
linkColor	Retrieves or sets the color of a hypertext link that hasn't been visited.
location	Returns a location object that allows the URL of the current document to be retrieved or set.
vlinkColor	Retrieves or sets the color of a link that has been visited recently.

Table 8-5. Some methods of the Document object

Method	Description
clear	Removes the document from the window or frame. Its syntax is `Document.clear`.
close	Closes the document writing stream to a window or frame. Its syntax is `Document.close`.
createStyleSheet	Creates and adds a new stylesheet for the document. Its syntax is `Document.createStyleSheet` *sURL, iIndex* where *sURL* is an optional string that specifies whether to add style information as a Link object or as a Style object, and *iIndex* is an optional integer that indicates where the new stylesheet is to be inserted in the styleSheets collection. By default, it is inserted at the end of the collection. The method returns a reference to the new styleSheet object.
open	Opens a new window to receive output from the Write and WriteLn methods. Its syntax is `Document.open(`*sMimeType, sReplace*`)`, where *sMimeType* must be "text/html," and *sReplace* is an optional string that indicates whether the new document replaces the existing one in the history list (`True`) or not (`False`, the default). The method returns the new Document object.
write	Allows for dynamic content to be added to the page. Must be called when the page is being opened. Its syntax is `Document.write` *sText*, where *sText* is the text and HTML to be written.

The Elements Collection and HTML Intrinsic Controls

The Elements collection is a collection of all the HTML intrinsic objects contained in a form. You can access the Elements collection with a code fragment like the following:

```
Dim oElements
Set oElements = Document.frmForm.Elements
```

where *frmForm* is the name of the form on which the Elements collection resides. The Elements collection has two read-only properties:

length
    Indicates the number of HTML intrinsic controls in the collection.

Item
    Retrieves a specific HTML intrinsic control based on either its name or its ordinal position in the collection, starting at 0. The highest ordinal position in the collection is one less than the value of the length property.

You can then access a particular control with a code fragment like:

```
Set oCtrl = Document.frmData.Elements.Item("txtName")
```

However, the Item property is the default member of the Elements collection, so this can be shortened to:

```
Set oCtrl = Document.frmData.Elements("txtName")
```

The default member of the Form collection is the Elements collection, though, so this statement can be further shortened to:

```
Set oCtrl = Document.frmData("txtName")
```

or, even more clearly:

```
Set oCtrl = Document.frmData.txtName
```

Unfortunately, the way in which you programmatically work with an HTML intrinsic control depends on the control type; HTML intrinsic controls do not have a uniform set of properties, methods, and events. Each, however, does have a type property, which allows you to determine the type of control with which you are working.

The following sections will examine the HTML intrinsic controls and their most important properties, methods, and events.

The textbox control

The HTML textbox control is defined by the `<INPUT TYPE=Text>` tag. Working with the textbox control is very straightforward, and closely resembles working with a Visual Basic TextBox control or a VBA UserForm TextBox control. The control's properties include the following:

Property	Description
defaultValue	The initial contents of the textbox, as defined by the VALUE attribute
name	The name assigned to the textbox by the NAME attribute
type	The type property of a textbox control is always "text"
value	The contents or text of the textbox

The most useful methods of the textbox control (none of which take any parameters) are:

Method	Description
Focus	Moves the focus to the textbox control if it does not have the focus and fires its onFocus event
Select	Selects or highlights all of the text contained in the control

Of the events supported by the textbox control, the following are most useful:

Event	Description
onChange	Fired when the contents of the textbox control have changed
onFocus	Fired when the control receives the input focus

The checkbox control

The HTML Checkbox control is defined by the `<INPUT TYPE=checkbox>` tag. Working with the Checkbox control is very straightforward, and closely resembles working with a Visual Basic checkbox control or a VBA UserForm checkbox control. The control's properties include the following:

Property	Description
checked	A Boolean that reflects whether the control is checked
name	The name assigned to the checkbox by the NAME attribute
type	The type property of a checkbox control is always "checkbox"

The most useful methods of the checkbox control (none of which take any parameters) are:

Method	Description
Click	Simulates a click by causing the OnClick event to fire
Focus	Moves the focus to the textbox control if it does not have the focus and fires its onFocus event

Of the events supported by the checkbox control, the following are most useful:

Event	Description
onClick	Fired when the user clicks on the checkbox
onFocus	Fired when the control receives the input focus
onReadyStateChange	Fired when the state of a checkbox has changed

The radio button control

The HTML radio button control is defined by the <INPUT TYPE=radio> tag. Because radio buttons reflect a set of two or more mutually exclusive choices, there is always more than one radio button with the same name on a form. The individual button's VALUE attribute determines which of those mutually exclusive choices the button represents, while the presence of the CHECKED attribute causes it to be the selected button of the set.

Since multiple radio buttons have the same name in the Elements collection, you cannot retrieve the selected radio button directly from the Elements collection. Instead, you must iterate the collection with the For Each...Next construct, extract the button whose Selected property is True, and retrieve its value. The code to do this looks something like the following:

```
Dim oElement, oElements, oRadio
Dim sValue

' Get reference to Elements collection
Set oElements = Document.frmTest.Elements

' Iterate collection looking for selected radio button
For Each oElement in oElements
   If oElement.Type = "radio" And oElement.Checked
      Set oRadio = oElement
      Exit For
   End If
Next

' Make sure a radio button was selected
If Not oRadio Is Nothing Then
   sValue = oRadio.Value
   ' Perform any other processing
End If
```

If the form has multiple sets of radio buttons, then you can look for the radio button of a particular name whose Checked property is True.

The radio button control's properties include the following:

Property	Description
checked	A Boolean that indicates whether the radio button is selected
name	The name assigned to the radio button by the NAME attribute
type	The type property of a radio button control is always "radio"
value	The option represented by this control in the set of radio button controls

The most useful methods of the radio button control (none of which take any parameters) are:

Method	Description
Click	Simulates a click by causing the OnClick event to fire
Focus	Moves the focus to the textbox control if it does not have the focus and fires its onFocus event

Of the events supported by the radio button control, the following are most useful:

Event	Description
onClick	Fired when the user clicks on a radio button
onFocus	Fired when the control receives the input focus
onReadyStateChange	Fired when the state of a radio button has changed

The list box

A list box is defined by the <SELECT>...</SELECT> tag, with its individual items defined by <OPTION> tags. Depending on whether the MULTIPLE attribute is present, multiple items can be selected at a single time. Each item in the list box is a member of the Options collection, which is returned by the list box's Options property. In a single-selection list, you can determine the item selected by examining the SelectedIndex property. In a multiple-selection list, you can determine which items are selected by iterating the Options collection and checking whether the item's Selected property is True. If it is, you can retrieve the value of its Index and Text properties. The following code fragment illustrates this by forming strings containing the index numbers of selected items and the text of selected items:

```
Dim oElements, oDropDown, oOption
Dim sSelected, sItems

Set oElements = Document.frmTest.Elements
Set oDropDown = oElements("lstColors")

For each oOption in oDropDown.Options
   If oOption.Selected Then
      sSelected = sSelected & cStr(oOption.index) & vbCrLf
      sItems = sItems & oOption.Text & vbCrLf
   End If
Next
```

The list box has the following properties:

Property	Description
length	The number of items in the list box.
multiple	A Boolean value that indicates whether multiple items can be selected at the same time.
name	The name of the drop-down list box, which corresponds to its NAME attribute.
options	A collection of Option objects, each of which represents an item in the list box.
selectedIndex	The index of the selected option. If the list box supports multiple selections, the selectedIndex property reflects the index of the first selected item in the list.
type	The type property of a drop-down list box is either "select-one" if the multiple property is False or "select-multiple" if the multiple property is True.

The list box's most useful methods (none of which take any parameters) are:

Method	Description
Click	Simulates a click by causing the OnClick event to fire
Focus	Moves the focus to the textbox control if it does not have the focus and fires its onFocus event

Of the events supported by the radio button control, the following are most useful:

Event	Description
onChange	Fired when a list box selection has changed
onClick	Fired when the user clicks on the list box
onFocus	Fired when the control receives the input focus
onScroll	Fired when the user scrolls the list box

Individual Option objects, which represent individual items in the list box, have the following properties:

Property	Description
index	The ordinal position of the item in the Options collection. The first item is at position 0, and the last is at 1 less than the value of the list box's length property.
selected	A Boolean value that indicates whether the item is selected. For single-selection lists, only one item can return a True value for the selected property.
text	The text used to describe the item in the list box.

Command button controls

HTML supports three types of buttons:

- The Submit button (defined with an <INPUT TYPE=submit> tag), which submits form data to a web server
- The Reset button (defined with an <INPUT TYPE=reset> tag), which resets form data to its default values
- A general-purpose command button (defined with an <INPUT TYPE=button> tag), whose function is defined programatically

The three button types share a common set of properties and methods. The most commonly used properties are:

Property	Description
name	The name assigned to the button by the NAME attribute
type	The type property of a button control is defined by the TYPE attribute and is either "submit," "reset," or "button"
value	The button's caption

The most commonly used methods are:

Method	Description
Click	Simulates a click by causing the OnClick event to fire
Focus	Moves the focus to the button if it does not have the focus and fires its onFocus event

Finally, the most commonly used events are:

Event	Description
onClick	Fired when the user clicks on a command button.
onFocus	Fired when the control receives the input focus.
onReset	Fired when the Reset button is clicked and before existing form data is reset to its default values. This event handler is a function rather than a subroutine; by setting its return value to False, the reset operation can be cancelled.
onSubmit	Fired when the Submit button is clicked and before form data is submitted to the web server. This event handler is a function rather than a subroutine; by setting its return value to False, submission of form data to the server can be cancelled.

The History Object

The History object represents the history list of recently opened documents. It has only one property, which is shown in Table 8-6, and three methods, which are listed in Table 8-7.

Table 8-6. Property of the History object

Property	Description
length	Returns the number of items in the history list

Table 8-7. Methods of the History object

Method	Description
back	Allows for bringing previously viewed document to be loaded into a target window or frame. Its syntax is History.back iDistance, where iDistance is the number of URLs to go back.
forward	Navigates to the next item in the history array. Its syntax is History.forward.
go	Navigates to a specific position in the history listing. Its syntax is History.go vLocation where vLocation can be an integer that indicates the relative position of the URL in the history list or a string that matches all or part of a URL contained in the browser's history.

The Event Object

The Event object can be accessed inside of an event handler and provides additional information about that event. Its major properties are listed in Table 8-8.

Table 8-8. Major properties of the Event object

Property	Description
altKey	A Boolean that indicates whether the Alt key was pressed when the event fired
button	For mouse events, indicates which mouse button set off the event
ctrlKey	A Boolean that indicates whether the Ctrl key was pressed when the event fired
fromElement	Returns a reference to the object where the cursor had just been prior to the onMouseOver or onMouseOut event
keyCode	The Unicode key value for the keyboard that triggered the onKeyUp, onKeyDown, and onKeyPress events
reason	Returns a code associated with the onDataSetComplete event signifying the state of a data transfer
shiftKey	A Boolean that indicates whether the Shift key was pressed when the event fired
srcElement	Returns a reference to the element object that fired the current event
type	Returns a string containing the name of the current event

Using the Document Object Model

Let's take a look at a simple example, Example 8-10, and then build on that until we are exploiting a few of the different options available. It's not the most useful piece of code ever written, but it does demonstrate a piece of the Document Object Model hierarchy.

Example 8-10. A simple example using the Document Object Model

```
<HTML>
<HEAD>
<Script Language = VBSCRIPT>

sub showme_onclick
    dim varTagName
    set varTagName = window.document.all(6)
    MsgBox varTagName.name
end sub

</SCRIPT>
</HEAD>
<BODY>
Demonstrates a simple use of the Document Object Model
<BR>
<input type = "button" value = "Get Tag Name" name = "showme">
</BODY>
</HTML>
```

First, we declare a variable called *varTagName* in the showme_onclick event procedure. We will set this variable equal to the value returned by the seventh member of the all collection, which corresponds to the seventh tag in the document. In this instance, this is the input button that we have created. When the user clicks the button, this page will generate a message box with the name of the tag. It is important to note here that tags are zero-based, so the first tag in the document will actually be tag 0. You can also refer to the tag by its name.

In Example 8-11, we are using the hierarchy to work into the individual elements of a table. First we reference the table by the tag name "table1," and then we can set the row and cell references after that. In this instance, we have given the table a tag name so that we can easily refer to it. If you do not give your tags names, then you must work with their index position on the page. If you look at the Name property of a tag with no name assigned, you will see the tag definition.

Example 8-11. Using client-side scripting to create a table

```
<HTML>
<HEAD>
<Script Language = VBSCRIPT>

sub showme_onclick
    dim varRowCon
    dim varTableCon
    dim varCellCon

    set varTableCon = document.all("table1")
    set varRowCon = varTableCon.all(1)
    set varCellCon = varRowCon.all(2)
    MsgBox varCellCon.InnerText
end sub

</SCRIPT>
</HEAD>
<BODY>
<Table border=1 id="table1" name="table1">
<TR>
    <TD> This is Cell One </TD>
    <TD> This is Cell Two </TD>
    <TD> This is Cell Three </TD
</TR>
<TR>
    <TD> This is Cell One, Row Two </TD>
    <TD> This is Cell Two, Row Two </TD>
    <TD> This is Cell Three, Row Two </TD>
</TR>
</TABLE>
<BR>
<BR>
<BR>
<input type = "button" value = "Show Cell" name = "showme">
</BODY>
</HTML>
```

The Document Object Model allows us to work with the individual elements on the page pretty effectively. You could apply this type of logic to make dynamic changes based on user interaction. This is the basis of Dynamic HTML (DHTML) coding. The Document Object Model is an active living concept, and there is currently an update to the standard being considered. The nice thing is that with each iteration of the standard, the DOM has become a more powerful tool for developers. For more information on DHTML, see *Dynamic HTML: The Definitive Reference*, Second Edition, by Danny Goodman (O'Reilly).

9

Windows Script Components

Windows Script Components (WSC) is a technology that allows programmers using scripting languages like VBScript to create COM components (that is, components based on Microsoft's Component Object Model technology). Ordinarily, COM component creation requires a compiled programming language, such as C++ or Visual Basic. Windows Script Components relies on a runtime module (*scrobj.dll*) that handles the implementation details of COM, while a script file parsed by the script engine contains the component definition.

The source code for a script component is stored in a Windows Script Component (*.wsc*) file. This is an XML file that contains the component definition, along with the code for the properties, methods, and events that the component exposes.

In addition, Windows Script Components supports *interface handlers*, which are compiled COM components that provide the implementation for particular interfaces. Windows Script Components automatically provides support for the interfaces necessary for COM automation, ASP, and DHTML.

Windows Scripts Components automates much of the process of creating a COM component by providing a wizard that collects information on the component to be created and writes it to a *.wsc* file. To illustrate the operation of the wizard, we'll create a simple math component.

The Script Component Wizard

The opening screen of the Script Component Wizard is shown in Figure 9-1. Although the dialog contains a number of text boxes, it is only necessary to enter the component name in the Name text box. The Script Component Wizard will then automatically use this information to complete the Filename and Prog ID text boxes. However, each of these text boxes, as well as the Version and Location text boxes, can be manually overridden. The text boxes are described in the following list:

Name

The name of the component.

Filename

The Windows Script Component (*.wsc*) file containing the component definition. If you specify an existing filename, WSC will overwrite it with the new component definition.

Prog ID

The component's programmatic identifier. The programmatic identifier can be any string and is defined in the system registry. Typically, it consists of two substrings separated by a period. For instance, the VBScript *CreateObject* function, which creates a new instance of an object, takes a programmatic identifier as an argument.

Version

The version number of the component. This has the format *MajorVersion. MinorVersion*.

Location

The path to the directory in which the *.wsc* file resides.

 WSC allows you to define multiple components within a single *.wsc* file. This feature is not supported, however, by the Script Component Wizard; if you attempt to assign a new component to an existing *.wsc* file, the wizard overwrites the file containing the original component. If you do want to create multiple components, you can use the wizard to define the first component, and then use a text editor to define all remaining components.

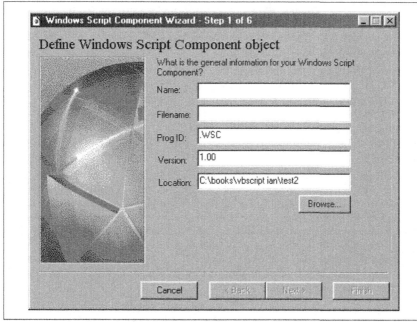

Figure 9-1. The component definition dialog of the Script Component Wizard

For our example, we'll name the component MathLib. Figure 9-2 shows the completed dialog after we enter the component name.

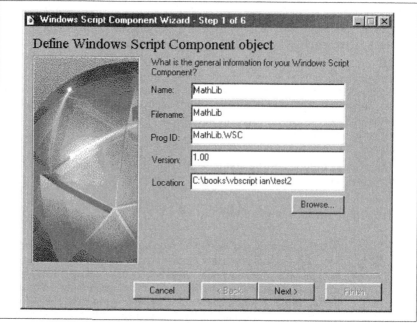

Figure 9-2. The component definition dialog for the MathLib component

The second screen, which is shown in Figure 9-3, allows you to define the general characteristics of the component, such as its scripting language, the interface handlers it uses, and whether error checking and debugging are available for the component at runtime.

By default, WSC supports three interface handlers: COM automation, ASP, and DHTML. Support for COM automation is automatically added whenever you define a property, method, or event for the component. If the component is to be used within Microsoft Internet Explorer, support for DHTML can be added by checking the "Use this scriptlet with DHTML behaviors" check box. If the component is to be used in generating ASP pages, check the Support Active Server Pages check box.

The runtime options check boxes allow you to determine whether any debugging features are enabled at runtime. The "Error checking" check box allows the component to display a descriptive error message should an error occur in the component when it is used. Ordinarily, the component will not display an error message, since recognizing and handling the error is the responsibility of the client that instantiates the component. The Debugging check box allows the Script Debugger to be launched if an error occurs. If this option is disabled, a runtime error simply terminates the program or script without prompting the user to open the Script Debugger.

In the case of our component, we'll uncheck the "Do you want special implements support" box to turn off support for the ASP and DHTML interface handlers. And we'll leave error checking and debugging enabled.

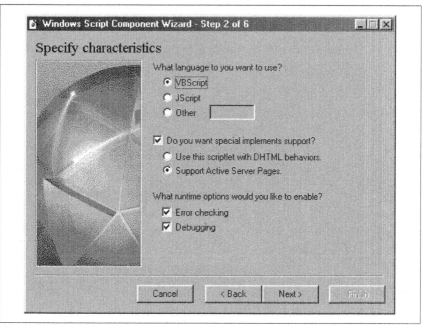

Figure 9-3. The component characteristics dialog of the Script Component Wizard

The third screen, which is shown in Figure 9-4, allows you to define component properties. Properties are attributes or descriptions of the state of component. Along with the property's name, you indicate whether the property is read/write, read-only, or write-only. In addition, you can assign an optional default value to the property. For our example MathLib component, define the properties as shown in Figure 9-4.

The fourth screen, which is shown in Figure 9-5, allows you to define component methods, along with their parameters. Each parameter is specified as a simple parameter name. Multiple parameters are separated from each other by commas. The methods for our example MathLib component are shown in Figure 9-5.

The fifth screen, shown in Figure 9-6, allows you to define the events raised by the component. This simply requires that you enter the name of the event. In the case of our example, we'll define one event, DivByZero. The sixth and final screen simply summarizes the information that you've entered about the component. Figure 9-7 shows the summary dialog for our MathLib component.

When you click the Finish button, the wizard generates the *.wsc* file that contains the skeleton code needed by your component. All that you have to do is to write the script required by your component's properties, methods, and events. In order to do this, however, it is useful to know something about the format of a *.wsc* file.

The *MathLib.wsc* file produced by the Script Component Wizard is shown in Example 9-1. It begins with an <?xml ?> tag, which is automatically inserted by the wizard and is required if the file is to be edited using an XML editor; otherwise, it is optional. Its presence indicates that the file is to be parsed using strict XML syntax.

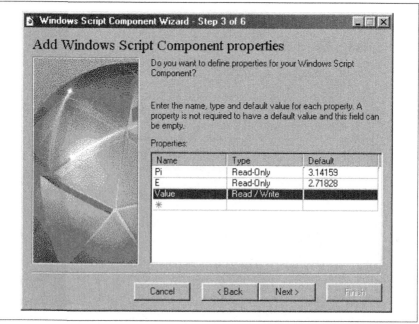

Figure 9-4. The properties definition dialog of the Script Component Wizard

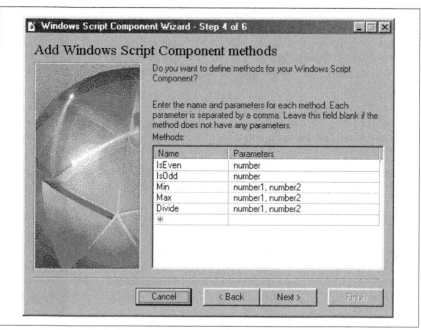

Figure 9-5. The methods definition dialog of the Script Component Wizard

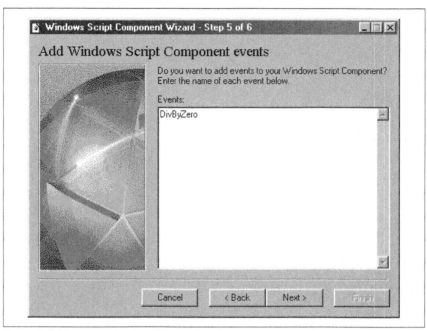

Figure 9-6. The events definition dialog of the Script Component Wizard

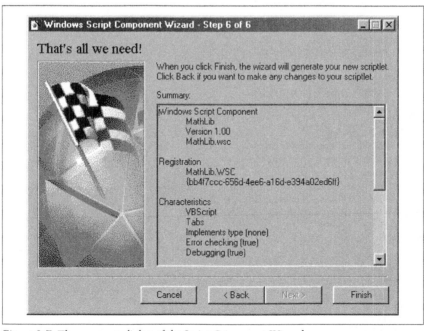

Figure 9-7. The summary dialog of the Script Component Wizard

Script
Components

Example 9-1. The MathLib.wsc file

```xml
<?xml version="1.0"?>
<component>

<?component error="true" debug="true"?>

<registration
    description="MathLib"
    progid="MathLib.WSC"
    version="1.00"
    classid="{ca624be4-9313-4d4a-9f1b-d585f50b321a}"
>
</registration>

<public>
    <property name="Pi">
        <get/>
    </property>
    <property name="E">
        <get/>
    </property>
    <property name="Value">
        <get/>
        <put/>
    </property>
    <method name="IsEven">
        <PARAMETER name="number"/>
    </method>
    <method name="IsOdd">
        <PARAMETER name="number"/>
    </method>
    <method name="Min">
        <PARAMETER name="number1"/>
        <PARAMETER name="number2"/>
    </method>
    <method name="Max">
        <PARAMETER name="number1"/>
        <PARAMETER name="number2"/>
    </method>
    <method name="Divide">
        <PARAMETER name="number1"/>
        <PARAMETER name="number2"/>
    </method>
</public>

<script language="VBScript">
<![CDATA[

dim Pi
Pi = 3.14159
dim E
E = 2.71828
dim Value
```

Example 9-1. The MathLib.wsc file (continued)

```
function get_Pi( )
   get_Pi = Pi
end function

function get_E( )
   get_E = E
end function

function get_Value( )
   get_Value = Value
end function

function put_Value(newValue)
   Value = newValue
end function

function IsEven(number)
   IsEven = "Temporary Value"
end function

function IsOdd(number)
   IsOdd = "Temporary Value"
end function

function Min(number1, number2)
   Min = "Temporary Value"
end function

function Max(number1, number2)
   Max = "Temporary Value"
end function

function Divide(number1, number2)
   Divide = "Temporary Value"
end function

]]>
</script>

</component>
```

Note that the beginning and end of our MathLib component definition is signaled by the <component> and </component> tags. If multiple components are stored in a single file, <package> and </package> tags that surround all component definition tags are required. The <?component ?> tag defines attributes for runtime error handling. It is only inserted by the wizard if either runtime error handling or debugging are enabled; otherwise, it is omitted. If you've selected the defaults and nevertheless want to add it, it takes the following form:

```
<?component error="false" debug="false" ?>
```

The <registration>...<registration> tag provides the registration information needed to identify and create an instance of the component. This includes a description or friendly name for the component, its programmatic identifier and version number, and finally a globally unique identifier (GUID) that uniquely identifies the component. Eventually, the information provided by the <registration> tag is entered into the system registry.

The <public>...</public> tag defines a component's public interface. Information on all of the properties (indicated by the <property> tag), methods (indicated by the <method> tag), and events (indicated by the <event> tag, which is not shown in Example 9-1) exposed by the component is stored here. The presence of the <public> tag also indicates that the component will use the COM automation interface handler.

The <property> tag has a name attribute that defines the property name, as well as one or two subelements. If the property is read-only, it has a <get> element, which indicates that a property value can be retrieved. If the property is write-only, it has a <put> element, which indicates that a property value can be assigned. And if the property is read-write, it has both a <get> and a <put> element.

The <method> tag has a name attribute as well as zero, one, or more <parameter> subelements that indicate the names of the method parameters.

The <public> tag can also have one or more <event> subelements that indicate the event name. This syntax means, incidentally, that we cannot define events that supply arguments to event handlers. But although we've defined an event for our MathLib component, as Figure 9-6 shows, the <event> element has not been added to our .wsc file. If we want our component to fire events, we have to add the <event> element manually.

The <property> and <method> elements are responsible for defining the public interface members of a component, but they do not provide an implementation. The actual operation of properties and methods is determined by code within the <script>...</script> tags. As Example 9-1 shows, in addition to providing the <script>...</script> tags, the Script Component Wizard creates a template for each of the component's properties and methods. Both member types, however, are implemented in code as methods. Property accessor methods (that is, methods responsible for retrieving a property value) are named by prepending the string get_ to the property name. Property mutator methods (methods responsible for assigning a value to a property) are named by prepending the string put_ to the property name. The value to be assigned to a property is represented by the newValue parameter.

In addition to providing a template in which we can supply code to define the operation of our component's public methods, the Script Component Wizard also handles defining a default value to a property. In the case of our read-only Pi property, for instance, it defines a variable named Pi (which is not the same as the Pi property) to which it assigns the default value 3.14159.

In the next section, we'll complete our component by writing the code for its public members. In the process, we'll look at some of the issues involved in developing components using WSC.

Writing Component Code

For the most part, Example 9-2, which shows the completed script block for our MathLib component, contains straightforward VBScript code. Only handling the DivByZero event, which will be discussed in the "Handling Events" section later in this chapter, requires comment.

Example 9-2. Script block for the MathLib component

```
<script language="VBScript">
<![CDATA[

dim Pi
Pi = 3.14159
dim E
E = 2.71828
dim Value

function get_Pi()
    get_Pi = Pi
end function

function get_E()
    get_E = E
end function

function get_Value()
    get_Value = Value
end function

function put_Value(newValue)
    Value = newValue
end function

function IsEven(number)
    IsEven = (number/2 = number\2)
end function

function IsOdd(number)
    IsOdd = Not IsEven(number)
end function

function Min(number1, number2)
    If number1 < number2 Then
        Min = number1
    Else
        Min = number2
    End If
end function

function Max(number1, number2)
    If number1 > number2 Then
        Max = number1
```

Example 9-2. Script block for the MathLib component (continued)

```
    Else
        Max = number2
    End If
end function

function Divide(number1, number2)
    If number2 = 0 Then
        fireEvent "DivByZero"
        Divide = 0
    Else
        Divide = number1/number2
    End If
end function

]]>
</script>
```

Using the Component

Once you've generated the *.wsc* file and written its code, there are two additional steps that may be required before you can use the component, depending precisely on how the component is to be used.

Registration

In most cases, unless the component is to be used exclusively to interface with DHTML in Microsoft Internet Explorer, it should be registered. The registration process stores information about the component that is needed to identify, locate, and activate it in the system registry. You can register your component in one of two ways:

- By right clicking on the file in Windows Explorer and selecting the Register option from the context menu.
- By typing the following from the command line:

    ```
    regsvr32 <componentFilename>
    ```

    where *componentFilename* is the name and extension of the *.wsc* file to be registered.

When registration has succeeded, a dialog appears that reads `DllRegisterServer` and `DllInstall in <path>\scrobj.dll succeeded.`

Instantiating the Component

If you're using the component from VBScript, you instantiate a script component like you would any other object—by calling the *CreateObject* function and passing it the programmatic identifier of the object to be created. You can then access the component's members. For instance, Example 9-3 shows a Windows Script Host script that instantiates the MathLib component and accesses each of its members. Programmatically, the scripted component is handled identically to a binary COM component.

Example 9-3. Using the MathLib component

```
Dim math, sMsg
' Instantiate script component
Set math = CreateObject("MathLib.WSC")
WScript.ConnectObject math, "math_"

' Set and retrieve Value property
math.Value = 12.121
sMsg = "Value: " & math.Value & vbCrLf

' Retrieve read-only properties
sMsg = sMsg & "Pi: " & math.Pi & vbCrLf
sMsg = sMsg & "E:" & math.E & vbCrLf

' Call Min/Max methods
sMsg = sMsg & "Min: " & math.Min(10, 10.3) & vbCrLf
sMsg = sMsg & "Max: " & math.Max(1000,200) & vbCrLf

' Call Divide method
sMsg = sMsg & "Divide by 10: " & math.Divide(100, 10) & vbCrLf
sMsg = sMsg & "Divide by 0: " & math.Divide(2, 0) & vbCrLf

' Call IsEven/IsOdd methods
sMsg = sMsg & "Even: " & math.IsEven(12) & vbCrLf
sMsg = sMsg & "Even: " & math.IsEven(1) & vbCrLf
sMsg = sMsg & "Odd: " & math.IsOdd(12) & vbCrlf
sMsg = sMsg & "Odd: " & math.IsOdd(3) & vbCrlf

MsgBox sMsg

Public Sub math_DivByZero
    Dim eMsg
    eMsg = "Division by Zero Error " & vbCrLf & vbCrLf
    eMsg = eMsg & Err.Number & ": " & Err.Description
    eMsg = eMsg & Err.Source
    MsgBox eMsg
End Sub
```

WSC Programming Topics

For the most part, the Script Component Wizard succeeds in automating the process of creating a script component so that you can focus on the code needed to implement your component's logic, rather than on the code needed to implement basic "plumbing" so that the component can work properly. In a number of areas, however, WSC offers functionality that either requires some additional coding or that extend the functionality of VBScript in significant ways. These include handling events, using interface handlers, taking advantage of resources, and building object models.

Handling Events

VBScript itself provides no native support for firing or handling custom events. Its support for events is limited to the Initialize and Terminate events, which are fired when a new instance of a class defined by the Class...End Class construct is created or destroyed, respectively. (And, in fact, they're not real events: the scripting runtime simply calls the routines if they're present.) Support for any other events must be provided by the environment in which VBScript is running.

In the case of Windows Script Components, WSC requires that an event be declared using the <event> element. Its syntax is:

```
<event name="event_name" dispid="dispid" />
```

where name defines the name of the event, and dispid is an optional attribute that assigns the event's dispatch ID. Ordinarily, WSC automatically provides a dispatch ID to identify an event. You might want to provide your own dispatch ID to map a custom event to a standard COM event, or to insure that dispatch IDs remain the same across different versions of your component.

Once the event is defined, you can fire it from your code. For this, you use the WSC fireEvent method. Its syntax is:

```
fireEvent eventName[,...]
```

where *eventName* is a string containing the name of the event to be fired. Multiple events can be fired by separating them from one another with a comma. The use of the fireEvent method is illustrated by the boldface line of code in Example 9-3.

Once the event is fired, it must also be handled by the client application using the event definition facilities provided by the client environment. Example 9-3, shown earlier in the "Instantiating the Component" section, illustrates how an event is handled in a WSH script. In the code, the ConnectObject method of the WScript object is invoked to indicate that the script should receive event notifications for the math object.

Using an Interface Handler: ASP

The <implements> element in a *.wsc* file allows you to define the interface handlers that are available to your script. The element's syntax is:

```
<implements type="handlerName" id="sourceCodeName" assumed=fAssumed >
</implements>
```

The <implements> element has the following attributes:

type

    The name of the interface handler. In *scrobj.dll* WSC provides an ASP handler for Active Server Pages and a Behavior handler for DHTML. A third handler for COM automation is automatically referenced without an <implements> element if the <public> element is encountered in a *.wsc* file.

id

    An optional element that defines the name by which the interface handler will be referenced in code. Since referenced interfaces are in the script's global namespace (that is, they do not have to be referenced through an interface object), id is typically used only to uniquely identify an object or member when there is a naming conflict between multiple interfaces.

assumed

An optional Boolean that determines whether the value of the `internalName` attribute is assumed in scripts, so that the referenced interface resides in the script's global namespace and does not have to be referenced through an object. By default, its value is `true`.

Ordinarily, once the interface handler is defined, interface classes and members can be referenced as if they were native to the component. In the case of ASP, for instance, an `implements` element like:

```
<implements type="ASP" id="ASP"/>
```

means that the ASP intrinsics are globally accessible to a WSC component. As a result, the number of items in the Contents collection of the Application object, for instance, can be retrieved with the following line of code, which is identical to the code that would be used within an Active Server Page itself:

```
Dim iCount = Application.Contents.Count
iCount = Application.Contents.Count
```

Example 9-4 shows a simple ASP component that displays information from the intrinsic ASP Request object. Although most of the code is straightforward, several features are worth noting:

- Since ASP objects are available in the component's global namespace, they can be accessed without referencing the interface handler. The user agent string in the ServerVariables collection, for instance, could be accessed as:

  ```
  ASP.Request.ServerVariables("Http_User_Agent")
  ```

  but is instead accessed in Example 9-4 as:

  ```
  Request.ServerVariables("Http_User_Agent")
  ```

- WSC supports parameterized properties. For instance, the Value property has a *name* parameter that contains the key whose value is to be retrieved. Implementing a parameterized property simply requires editing the *.wsc* file with a text editor to add a `<parameter>` element.

- In addition to scalar values, properties can return arrays, objects, or collections. In Example 9-4, for instance, the Values property returns the ASP Form collection object.

Example 9-4. A simple component for ASP

```
<?xml version="1.0"?>
<component>

<?component error="true" debug="true"?>

<registration
    description="ASPInfo"
    progid="ASPInfo.WSC"
    version="1.00"
    classid="{783106e5-f78e-402d-b16f-b78e20d2e0b2}"
>
</registration>
```

Script Components

Example 9-4. A simple component for ASP (continued)

```
<public>
   <property name="Browser">
      <get/>
   </property>
   <property name="ServerName">
      <get/>
   </property>
   <property name="RemoteAddress">
      <get/>
   </property>
   <property name="Value">
      <PARAMETER name="name"/>
      <get/>
   </property>
   <property name="Values">
      <get/>
   </property>

</public>

<implements type="ASP" id="ASP"/>

<script language="VBScript">
<![CDATA[

dim Browser
dim RemoteAddress
dim Values

function get_Browser( )
   get_Browser = Request.ServerVariables("HTTP_USER_AGENT")
end function

function get_ServerName( )
   get_ServerName = Request.ServerVariables("SERVER_NAME")
end function

function get_RemoteAddress( )
   get_RemoteAddress = Request.ServerVariables("REMOTE_ADDR")
end function

function get_Value(name)
   get_Value = Server.HtmlEncode(Request.Form.Item(name))
end function

function get_Values( )
   set get_Values = Request.Form
end function


]]>
```

Example 9-4. A simple component for ASP (continued)

```
</script>

</component>
```

Example 9-5 provides the HTML source for a page that requests the ASP page whose listing appears in Example 9-6.

Example 9-5. An HTML page

```
<HTML>
<HEAD><TITLE>Using an ASP Component</TITLE></HEAD>
<BODY>
Enter your name:
<FORM METHOD="POST" ACTION="AspInterface.asp">
<INPUT TYPE="text" NAME="name" SIZE=20> <P>
<INPUT TYPE="submit" VALUE="Submit">
</FORM>
</BODY>
</HTML>
```

Example 9-6. An ASP page that uses a Windows Script Component

```
<%
Dim info
Set info = CreateObject("ASPInfo.WSC")
Response.Write "<b>Your Browser:</b> " & Info.Browser  & "<BR>"
Response.Write "<b>Server Name:</b> " & info.ServerName & "<BR>"
Response.Write "<b>Your IP Address:</b> " & info.RemoteAddress & "<BR>"
Response.Write "<b>Your Name:</b> " & Server.HTMLEncode(info.Value("name")) &
"<BR>"
%>
```

Using Resources

Typically, strings are handled by hardcoding their values throughout one or more scripts. This creates a maintenance nightmare when the strings need to be modified or localized. To deal with this problem, WSC offers the <resource> element, which allows a value to be associated with a resource identifier. The syntax of the resource element is:

```
<resource id="resourceID">value</resource>
```

resourceID must be a string that uniquely identifies the resource in the component; it is, in other words, a key value. *value* is the string or number that is associated with the resource identifier.

Example 9-7 illustrates one possible way to use resources. The component has a SayHello method that returns a string in one of four languages. The language name serves as the key or resource ID that provides access to the localized string. The user can then select his native language from a drop-down list box (see the HTML page in Example 9-8). An ASP page (see Example 9-9) instantiates the component, retrieves the user's name and language choice from the Request object's Form collection, and uses the language as the key to look up the localized version of the greeting.

Script
Components

Example 9-7. A component that uses resources

```
<?xml version="1.0"?>
<component>

<registration
    description="Greeting"
    progid="Greeting.WSC"
    version="1.00"
    classid="{6c7d1aec-fed2-42b1-bc79-2e87cf34ad9b}" >
</registration>

<public>
    <method name="SayHello">
        <PARAMETER name="language"/>
    </method>
</public>

<resource id="English">Good day</resource>
<resource id="Croat">Dobar dan</resource>
<resource id="French">Bonjour</resource>
<resource id="German">Guten tag</resource>

<script language="VBScript">
<![CDATA[

function SayHello(language)
    SayHello = getResource(language)
end function

]]>
</script>

</component>
```

Example 9-8. HTML page allowing the user to select a language

```
<HTML>
<HEAD><TITLE>Using a Resource</TITLE></HEAD>
<BODY>
Enter your name:
<FORM METHOD="POST" ACTION="Resource.asp">
<INPUT TYPE="text" NAME="name" SIZE=20> <P>
Your native language:
<SELECT NAME="language" size="1">
    <OPTION>English
    <OPTION>French
    <OPTION>Croat
    <OPTION>German
</SELECT> <P>
<INPUT TYPE="submit" VALUE="Submit">
</FORM>
</BODY>
</HTML>
```

Example 9-9. ASP page that uses the Greeting component

```
<%
Dim greet, lang, name

Set greet = CreateObject("Greeting.WSC")

lang = Request.Form.Item("language")
name = Request.Form.Item("name")
If Not name = "" Then
   Response.Write greet.SayHello(lang) & ", " & name
Else
   Response.Write "You have failed to provide us with your name."
End If
%>
```

Building an Object Model

Often when you work with your component, you don't want to instantiate just one object. Instead, you want to instantiate a parent object, which in turn builds a hierarchy of child objects.

To build an object model in this way with Windows Script Component, you can include multiple components in your *.wsc* file. This requires some modification to the basic *.wsc* file created by the Script Component Wizard:

- If multiple components are defined in the same *.wsc* file, a `<package>` tag within which all `<component>` tags are nested must be included.
- Each `<component>` tag must include the optional `id` attribute, which defines the name by which the component is referenced within the *.wsc* file.

You can then instantiate all but the parent or top-level component by calling the Windows Script Component's createComponent method. Its syntax is:

```
Set object = createComponent(componentID)
```

where *object* is the variable that will contain the object reference, and *componentID* is the name assigned to the component by the `id` attribute of the `<component>` element.

Example 9-10 illustrates the use of the createComponent method to instantiate child components. A parent Workgroup object contains a Users component, which in turn contains zero or more User components. When the workgrp component is instantiated, a users object is also automatically instantiated; it is accessible only through the workgrp object's Users property. When the users object's Add method is called, a user object is added to the array held by the users object.

Example 9-10. A three-component object model

```
<?xml version="1.0"?>
<package>
<component id="workgrp">
<registration
    description="Workgroup"
    progid="Workgrp.WSC"
```

Example 9-10. A three-component object model (continued)

```
    version="1.00"
    classid="{6f4d2531-a891-4e8e-9b17-e05603eefee2}"
>
</registration>

<public>
   <property name="Users">
      <get/>
   </property>
   <property name="name">
      <get/>
   </property>
</public>

<script language="VBScript">
<![CDATA[

dim Users, workgroupName

workgroupName = "MyWorkgroup"
Set users = createComponent("Users")

Function get_Users()
   set get_Users = users
End Function

Function get_name()
   get_name = workgroupName
End Function
]]>
</script>

</component>

<component id="Users">

<registration progid="users.wsc" />

<public>
   <method name="Add" />
   <method name="Item" dispid="0">
      <parameter name="index" />
   </method>
</public>

<script language="VBScript">
<![CDATA[

Dim ctr, userArray(10)

Sub Add()
   Dim username
```

Example 9-10. A three-component object model (continued)

```vbscript
    username = InputBox("Enter name of user: ", "User Name")

    If Not username = "" Then

        Set usr = createComponent("user")

        usr.Name = username

        If ctr > 0 And ctr Mod 10 = 0 Then
            ReDim Preserve userArray(UBound(userArray)+10)
        End If

        Set userArray(ctr) = usr

        ctr = ctr + 1
    End If
End Sub

Function Item(index)
    Set Item = userArray(index)
End Function

]]>
</script>

</component>

<component id="user">

<registration progid="user.wsc" />

<public>
    <property name="Name">
        <get />
        <put />
    </property>
</public>

<script language="VBScript">
<![CDATA[

Dim userName

Function get_Name( )
    get_Name = userName
End Function

Function put_Name(newValue)
    userName = newValue
End Function
```

Example 9-10. A three-component object model (continued)

```
]]>
</script>

</component>

</package>
```

Reference

This section consists of only a single very long chapter, Chapter 10, *The Language Reference*, which contains an alphabetic reference to VBScript language elements.

The chapter documents the following:

- Statements, like Dim or For Each.
- Functions, like *Format* or *InStr*.
- The Scripting Runtime object models: the File System object model and the Dictionary object model. Here you'll find complete documentation of all of the objects, along with their properties and methods.

When you're looking for a particular language element but don't quite remember what it's called, an alphabetic reference is of little value. For this reason, we've included Appendix A.

Finally, VBScript operators aren't included in this section. Instead, you'll find them discussed in Appendix C.

10

The Language Reference

The elements of the VBScript language can be broken into four main areas: statements, functions, operators, and object models.

Statements

Statements form the cornerstone of the language. You'll notice in Appendix A that the largest concentration of statements is in the program structure section. Statements are used mainly for such tasks as declaring variables or procedures.

Functions

In general, functions return a value, although, as with any function, you can choose to ignore the return value.

Operators

An operator connects or performs some operation upon one or more language elements to form a single expression. For example, in the code fragment:

```
strResult = 16 + int(lngVar1)
```

the addition operator (+) combines 16 and the value returned by int(lngVar1) into a single expression whose value is assigned to the variable *strResult*. Operators are not documented in this chapter but are listed in Appendix C.

Object models

An integral part of VBScript is the Microsoft Scripting Runtime, which provides an add-on library containing the Dictionary object (which is similar to a Perl associative array) and the FileSystemObject object (which provides access to a local filesystem). Because of their significance, both object models are fully documented in this book.

VBScript is a high-level language and, like all high-level languages, it is a large yet rich language. While this means that it takes time for new users to understand the intricacies of the functions and statements available to them, at the same time, the language's syntax is straightforward, logical, and easy to understand.

To speed the process of finding the right function or statement to perform a particular task, you can use Appendix A to determine what language elements are available for the purpose you require.

Abs Function

Syntax

result = Abs(*number*)

number

    Use: Required   Data Type: Any valid numeric expression

    A number or a string representation of a number.

Return Value   The absolute value of *number*. The data type is the same as that passed to the function if *number* is numeric, and Double if it is not.

Description   Returns the absolute value of a number (i.e., its unsigned magnitude). For example, Abs(-1) and Abs(1) both return 1.

Rules at a Glance

- *number* can be a number, a string representation of a number, an object whose default property is numeric, or a Null or Empty.
- If *number* is Null, the function returns Null.
- If *number* is an uninitialized variable or Empty, the function returns zero.

See Also   IsNumeric Function

Array Function

Syntax

Array([*element1*], [*elementN*],....)

element

    Use: Optional   Data Type: Any

    The data to be assigned to the first array element.

elementN

    Use: Optional   Data Type: Any

    Any number of data items you wish to add to the array.

Return Value   A variant array consisting of the arguments passed into the function.

Description   Returns a variant array containing the elements whose values are passed to the function as arguments.

The code fragment:

```
Dim vaMyArray
vaMyArray = Array("Mr", "Mrs", "Miss", "Ms")
```

is similar to writing:

```
Dim vaMyArray(3)
vaMyArray(0) = "Mr"
vaMyArray(1) = "Mrs"
vaMyArray(2) = "Miss"
vaMyArray(3) = "Ms"
```

Because *Array* creates a variant array, you can pass any data type, including objects, to the *Array* function. You can also pass the values returned by calls to other *Array* functions to create multidimensional arrays; these kinds of arrays are called "ragged" arrays.

Rules at a Glance

- Although the array you create with the *Array* function is a variant array data type, the individual elements of the array can be a mixture of different data types.
- The initial size of the array you create is the number of arguments you place in the argument list and pass to the *Array* function.
- The lower bound of the array created by the *Array* function is 0.
- The array returned by the *Array* function is a dynamic rather than a static array. Once created, you can redimension the array using `Redim`, `Redim Preserve`, or another call to the *Array* function.
- If you don't pass any arguments to the *Array* function, an empty array is created. Although this may appear to be the same as declaring an array in the conventional manner with the statement:

  ```
  Dim myArray( )
  ```

  the difference is that you can then use the empty array with the *Array* function again later in your code.

Example

```
<%
Dim myArray
myArray = Array(100, 2202, 3.3, 605, 512)
Response.Write myArray(2)
%>
```

Programming Tips and Gotchas

- The *Array* function was not present in the first version of VBScript and was added to the language in Version 2.
- You cannot assign the return value of *Array* to a variable previously declared as an array variable. Therefore, *don't* declare the variant variable as an array using the normal syntax:

  ```
  Dim MyArray( )
  ```

  Instead, simply declare a variant variable, such as:

  ```
  Dim MyArray
  ```

- The *Array* function is ideal for saving space and time and for writing more efficient code when creating a fixed array of known elements, for example:

  ```
  Dim Titles
  Title = Array("Mr", "Mrs", "Miss", "Ms")
  ```

- You can use the *Array* function to create multidimensional arrays. However, accessing the elements of the array needs a little more thought. The following code fragment creates a simple two-dimensional array with three elements in the first dimension and four elements in the second:

  ```
  Dim vaListOne

  vaListOne = Array(Array(1, 2, 3, 4), _
                    Array(5, 6, 7, 8), _
                    Array(9, 10, 11, 12))
  ```

Surprisingly, the code you'd expect to use to access the array returns a "Subscript out of range" error:

```
'This line generates a Subscript out of range error
Response.Write vaListOne(1, 2)
```

Instead, since this is an array stored within an array (that is, a ragged array), you can access it as follows:

```
Response.Write vaListOne(1)(2)
```

- Because you declare the variant variable to hold the array as a simple variant, rather than an array and can then make repeated calls to *Array*, the function can create dynamic arrays. For example, the following code fragment dimensions a variant to hold the array, calls *Array* to create a variant array, then calls *Array* again to replace the original variant array with a larger variant array:

```
Dim varArray
varArray = Array(10,20,30,40,50)
...
varArray = Array(10,20,30,40,50,60)
```

The major disadvantage of using this method is that while it makes it easy to replace an array with a different array, it doesn't allow you to easily expand or contract an existing array.

VBA/VBScript Differences
Unlike Visual Basic, VBScript does not contain an Option Base statement; therefore, arrays created in VBScript using the *Array* function have a lower boundary of 0. That is, the first element of the array will always be accessed using an index value of 0.

See Also   Dim Statement, LBound Function, ReDim Statement, UCase Function

---

Asc, AscB, AscW Functions

Syntax
```
Asc(string)
AscB(string)
AscW(string)
```

string
    Use: Required   Data Type: String

    Any expression that evaluates to a string.

Return Value   An integer that represents the character code of the first character of the string.

Description   Returns the ANSI (in the case of *Asc*) or Unicode (in the case of *AscW*) character code that represents the first character of the string passed to it. All other characters in the string are ignored. The *AscB* function returns the first byte of a string.

Rules at a Glance

- The string expression passed to the function must contain at least one character, or a runtime error (either "Invalid use of Null" or "Invalid procedure call or argument") is generated.

- Only the first character of the string is evaluated by *Asc*, *AscB*, and *AscW*.

- Use the *AscW* function to return the Unicode character of the first character of a string.

- Use the *AscB* function to return the first byte of a string containing byte data.

Example

```
<%
Dim sChars
Dim iCharCode

sChars = Request.Form("chars")
If Len(sChars) > 0 Then
    CharCode = Asc(sChars)
    If iCharCode >= 97 And iCharCode <= 122 Then
        Response.Write "The first character must be uppercase"
    Else
        Response.Write iCharCode
    End If
End If
%>
```

Programming Tips and Gotchas

- Always check that the string you are passing to the function contains at least one character using the *Len* function, as the following example shows:

```
If Len(sMyString) > 0 Then
    iCharCode = Asc(sMyString)
Else
    Response.Write "Cannot process a zero-length string"
End If
```

- Surprisingly, although the VBScript documentation shows that the data type of the parameter passed to the *Asc* function is String, it can actually be any data type. Evidently the *Asc* routine converts incoming values to strings before extracting their first character. Try this quick example for yourself:

```
<%
sChars = 123
Response.Write Asc(sChars)
%>
```

- Use *Asc* within your data validation routines to determine such conditions as whether the first character is upper- or lowercase and whether it's alphabetic or numeric, as the following example demonstrates:

```
Function CheckText (sText)

Dim iChar

If Len(sText) > 0 Then
    iChar = Asc(sText)
```

```
      If iChar >= 65 And iChar <= 90 Then
         CheckText = "The first character is UPPERCASE"
      ElseIf iChar >= 97 And iChar <= 122 Then
         CheckText = "The first character is lowercase"
      Else
          CheckText = "The first character isn't alphabetical"
      End If
   Else
      CheckText = "Please enter something in the text box"
   End If

   End Function
```

See Also   Chr, ChrB, ChrW Functions

Atn Function

Syntax

Atn(*number*)

number

    Use: Required   Data Type: Numeric

    Any numeric expression, representing the ratio of two sides of a right angle triangle.

Return Value   The return value is a Double representing the arctangent of *number* in the range –pi/2 to pi/2 radians.

Description   Takes the ratio of two sides of a right triangle (*number*) and returns the corresponding angle in radians. The ratio is the length of the side opposite the angle divided by the length of the side adjacent to the angle.

Rules at a Glance

- If no number is specified, a runtime error is generated.
- The return value of *Atn* is in radians, not degrees.

Example

```
<%
Const Pi = 3.14159
 Dim dblSideAdj, dblSideOpp
 Dim dblRatio, dblAtangent, dblDegrees

 dblSideAdj = 50.25
 dblSideOpp = 75.5

 dblRatio = dblSideOpp / dblSideAdj
 dblAtangent = Atn(dblRatio)
 ' convert from radians to degrees
 dblDegrees = dblAtangent * (180 / Pi)
 Response.Write dblDegrees & " Degrees"
%>
```

Programming Tips and Gotchas

- To convert degrees to radians, multiply degrees by pi/180.
- To convert radians to degrees, multiply radians by 180/pi.
- Don't confuse *Atn* with the cotangent. *Atn* is the inverse *trigonometric* function of *Tan*, as opposed to the simple inverse of *Tan*.

See Also   Tan Function

Call Statement

Syntax

```
[Call] procedurename [argumentlist]
```

Call
    Use: Optional

procedurename
    Use: Required   Data Type: n/a

    The name of the subroutine being called.

argumentlist
    Use: Optional   Data Type: Any

    A comma-delimited list of arguments to pass to the subroutine being called.

Description   Passes program control to an explicitly named procedure or function.

Rules at a Glance

- The Call statement requires that the procedure being called be named explicitly. You cannot assign the subroutine name to a variable and provide that as an argument to the Call statement. For example, the following is an illegal use of Call:

```
Dim sProc
sProc = "PrintRoutine"
Call sProc(sReport)        ' Illegal: sProc is a variable
```

The following code fragment shows a valid use of the Call statement:

```
Call PrintRoutine(sReport)        ' Legal usage
```

- You aren't required to use the Call keyword when calling a function procedure. However, if you use the Call keyword to call a procedure that requires arguments, *argumentlist* must be enclosed in parentheses. If you omit the Call keyword from the procedure call, you must also omit the parentheses around *argumentlist*.

Example

The WSH code fragment shows a call to a procedure that passes two arguments: a string array and a string. Note that while the call to the *ShowList* procedure uses the Call keyword, the equivalent call to the *MsgBox* function within the ShowList procedure does not:

```
Dim aList, sCaption

aList = Array("One", "Two", "Three", "Four")
sCaption = "Array Contents"
```

```
Call ShowList(aList, sCaption)

Sub ShowList(arr( ), s2)
    Dim mem, sMsg

    For Each mem In arr
        sMsg = sMsg & mem & vbCrLf
    Next

    MsgBox sMsg, ,s2
End Sub
```

Programming Tips and Gotchas

- You can use the Call keyword to call a function when you're not interested in the function's return value.

- The use of the Call keyword is considered outdated. We suggest not using the keyword, as it is unnecessary and provides no value.

- If you remove the Call statement but fail to remove the parentheses from a call to a subroutine with a single argument, then that argument is passed by value rather than by reference. This can have unintended consequences.

VBA/VBScript Differences

VBA (as of Version 6.0) supports the *CallByName* function, which allows you to call a public procedure in a VBA object module by assigning the procedure name to a variable. VBScript does not support the *CallByName* function and requires that you provide the name of the function or sub procedure in the Call statement.

CBool Function

Syntax

```
CBool(expression)
```

expression
    Use: Required   Data Type: String or Numeric

    Any numeric expression or a string representation of a numeric value.

Return Value   *expression* converted to a type of Boolean (True or False).

Description   Casts *expression* as aa Boolean type. Expressions that evaluate to 0 are converted to False (0), and expressions that evaluate to nonzero values are converted to True (−1).

Rules at a Glance

If the expression to be converted is a string, the string must act as a number. Therefore, CBool("ONE") results in a type mismatch error, yet CBool("1") converts to True.

Programming Tips and Gotchas

- You can check the validity of the expression prior to using the *CBool* function by using the *IsNumeric* function.

- When you convert an expression to a Boolean, an expression that evaluates to 0 is converted to False (0), and any nonzero number is converted to True (–1). Therefore, a Boolean False can be converted back to its original value (i.e., 0), but the original value of the True expression can't be restored unless it was originally –1.

See Also   IsNumeric Function

CByte Function

Syntax

```
CByte(expression)
```

expression
    Use: Required   Data Type: Numeric or String

    A string or numeric expression that evaluates between 0 and 255.

Return Value   *expression* converted to a type of Byte.

Description   Converts *expression* to a Byte data type. The Byte type is the smallest data storage device in VBScript. Being only one byte in length, it can store unsigned numbers between 0 and 255.

Rules at a Glance

- If *expression* is a string, the string must be capable of being treated as a number.
- If *expression* evaluates to less than 0 or more than 255, an overflow error is generated.
- If *expression* isn't a whole number, *CByte* rounds the number prior to conversion.

Example

```
If IsNumeric(sMyNumber) Then
    If val(sMyNumber) >= 0 and val(sMyNumber) <= 255 Then
        BytMyNumber = Cbyte(sMyNumber)
    End If
End If
```

Programming Tips and Gotchas

- Check that the value you pass to *CByte* is neither negative nor greater than 255.
- Use *IsNumeric* to insure the value passed to *CByte* can be converted to a numeric expression.
- When using *CByte* to convert floating-point numbers, fractional values up to but not including 0.5 are rounded down, while values greater than 0.5 are rounded up. Values of 0.5 are rounded to the nearest even number (i.e., they use the Banker's Rounding Algorithm).

See Also   IsNumeric Function

CCur Function

Syntax

    CCur(expression)

expression

    Use: Required   Data Type: Numeric or String

    A string or numeric expression that evaluates to a number between −922,337,203,685,477.5808 and 922,337,203,685,477.5807.

Return Value   *expression* converted to a type of Currency.

Description   Converts an expression into a type of Currency.

Rules at a Glance

- If the expression passed to the function is outside the range of the Currency data type, an overflow error occurs.

- Expressions containing more than four decimal places are rounded to four decimal places.

- The only localized information included in the value returned by *CCur* is the decimal symbol.

Example

    If IsNumeric(sMyNumber) Then
        curMyNumber = CCur(sMyNumber)
    End If

Programming Tips and Gotchas

- *CCur* doesn't prepend or append a currency symbol; for this, you need to use the *FormatCurrency* function. *CCur* does, however, correctly convert strings that include a localized currency symbol. For instance, if a user enters the string "$1234.68" into a text box whose value is passed as a parameter to the *CCur* function, *CCur* correctly returns a currency value of 1234.68.

- *CCur* doesn't include the thousands separator; for this, you need to use the *FormatCurrency* function. *CCur* does, however, correctly convert currency strings that include localized thousands separators. For instance, if a user enters the string "1,234.68" into a text box whose value is passed as a parameter to the *CCur* function, *CCur* correctly converts it to a currency value of 1234.68.

See Also   FormatCurrency, FormatNumber, FormatPercent Functions

CDate Function

Syntax

    CDate(expression)

expression

    Use: Required   Data Type: String or Numeric

    Any valid date expression.

Return Value   *expression* converted into a Date type.

Description   Converts *expression* to a Date type. The format of *expression*—the order of day, month, and year—is determined by the locale setting of your computer. To be certain of a date being recognized correctly by *CDate*, the month, day, and year elements of *expression* must be in the same sequence as your computer's regional settings; otherwise, the *CDate* function has no idea that in the *expression* "04/01/01," 4 is supposed to be the 4th of the month, not the month of April, for example.

CDate also converts numbers to a date. The precise behavior of the function, however, depends on the value of *expression*:

- If *expression* is less than or equal to 23 and includes a fractional component less than 60, the integer is interpreted as the number of hours since midnight, and the fraction is interpreted as the number of seconds.

- In all other cases, the integer portion of *expression* is converted to a date that interprets the integer as the number of days before (in the case of negative numbers) or after December 31, 1899, and its fractional part is converted to the time of day, with every .01 representing 864 seconds (14 minutes 24 seconds) after midnight.

Rules at a Glance

- *CDate* accepts both numerical date expressions and string literals. You can pass month names into *CDate* in either complete or abbreviated form; for example, "31 Dec 1997" is correctly recognized.

- You can use any of the date delimiters specified in your computer's regional settings; for most systems, this includes , / - and the space character.

- The oldest date that can be handled by the Date data type is 01/01/100, which in VBScript terms equates to the number –657434. Therefore, if you try to convert a number of magnitude greater than –657434 with *CDate*, an error ("Type mismatch") is generated.

- The furthest date into the future that can be handled by the Date data type is 31/12/9999, which in VBScript terms equates to the number 2958465. Therefore, if you try to convert a number higher than 2958465 with *CDate*, an error ("Type mismatch") is generated.

- A "Type mismatch" error is generated if the values supplied in *expresssion* are invalid. *CDate* tries to treat a month value greater than 12 as a day value.

Programming Tips and Gotchas

- Use the *IsDate* function to determine if *expression* can be converted to a date or time.

- A common error is to pass an uninitialized variable to *CDate*, in which case midnight will be returned

- A modicum of intelligence has been built into the *CDate* function. It can determine the day and month from a string regardless of their position, but only where the day number is larger than 12, which automatically distinguishes it from the number of the month. For example, if the string "30/12/97" were passed into the *CDate* function on a system expecting a date format of mm/dd/yy, *CDate* sees that 30 is obviously too large for a month number and treats it as the day. It's patently impossible for *CDate* to second guess what you mean by "12/5/97"—is it the

12th of May, or 5th of December? In this situation, *CDate* relies on the regional settings of the computer to distinguish between day and month. This can also lead to problems, as you may have increased a month value to more than 12 inadvertently in an earlier routine, thereby forcing *CDate* to treat it as the day value. If your real day value is 12 or less, no error is generated, and a valid, albeit incorrect, date is returned.

- If you pass a two-digit year into *CDate*, how does it know which century you are referring to? Is "10/20/97" 20 October 1997 or 20 October 2097? The answer is that two-year digits less than 30 are treated as being in the 21st Century (i.e., 29 = 2029), and two-year digits of 30 and over are treated as being in the 20th Century (i.e., 30 = 1930).

- Don't follow a day number with "st," "nd," "rd," or "th," since this generates a type mismatch error.

- If you don't specify a year, the *CDate* function uses the year from the current date on your computer.

VBA/VBScript Differences

If you pass an initialized variable to the *CDate* function in VBA, the return value is 31 December 1899. In VBScript, the function's return value is 12:00:00 AM.

See Also   FormatDateTime Function

CDbl Function

Syntax

```
CDbl(expression)
```

expression

Use: Required   Data Type: Numeric or String

$-1.79769313486232E308$ to $-4.94065645841247E-324$ for negative values; $4.94065645841247E-324$ to $1.79769313486232E308$ for positive values.

Return Value   *expression* cast as a Double type.

Description   Converts *expression* to a Double type.

Rules at a Glance

- If the value of *expression* is outside the range of the double data type, an overflow error is generated.

- Expression must evaluate to a numeric value; otherwise, a type mismatch error is generated.

Example

```
Dim dblMyNumber as Double
If IsNumeric(sMyNumber) then
    dblMyNumber = CDbl(sMyNumber)
End If
```

Programming Tips and Gotchas

Use *IsNumeric* to test whether *expression* evaluates to a number.

See Also   IsNumeric Function

Chr, ChrB, ChrW Functions

Syntax

```
Chr(charactercode)
ChrB(charactercode)
ChrW(charactercode)
```

charactercode
    Use: Required   Data Type: Long

    An expression that evaluates to either an ANSI or Unicode character code.

Return Value   *Chr*, *ChrB*, and *ChrW* return a variant of the string type that contains the character represented by *charactercode*.

Description   Returns the character represented by *charactercode*.

Rules at a Glance

- *Chr* returns the character associated with an ANSI character code.
- *ChrB* returns a one-byte string.
- *ChrW* returns a Unicode character.

Programming Tips and Gotchas

- Use Chr(34) to embed quotation marks inside a string, as shown in the following example:

```
sSQL = "SELECT * from myTable where myColumn = " & Chr(34) & _
            sValue & Chr(34)
```

- You can use the *ChrB* function to assign binary values to String variables.
- The following table lists some of the more commonly used character codes that are supplied in the call to the *Chr* function:

Code	Value	Description
0	NULL	For C/C++ string functions, the null character required to terminate standard strings; equivalent to the vbNullChar constant.
9	TAB	Equivalent to the vbTab constant.
10	LF	Equivalent to the vbLf constant.
13	CR	Equivalent to the vbCr constant.
13 & 10	CRLF	Equivalent to the CWlocal constant.
34	"	Quotation mark. Useful to embed quotation marks within a literal string, especially when forming SQL query strings.

See Also   Asc, AscB, AscW Functions, CStr Function

CInt Function

Syntax

```
CInt(expression)
```

expression

   Use: Required   Data Type: Numeric or String

   The range of expression is –32,768 to 32,767; fractions are rounded.

Return Value   *expression* cast as an integer type.

Description   Converts *expression* to a type of integer; any fractional portion of
expression is rounded.

Rules at a Glance

- *expression* must evaluate to a numeric value; otherwise, a type mismatch error is generated.
- If the value of *expression* is outside the range of the Integer data type, an overflow error is generated.
- When the fractional part of *expression* is exactly 0.5, *CInt* always rounds to the nearest even number. For example, 0.5 rounds to 0, and 1.5 rounds to 2.

Example

```
<HTML>
<HEAD>
<SCRIPT LANGUAGE="VBScript">
Option Explicit

Sub cmdAdd_OnClick( )

    Dim iSum, sNum1, sNum2

    sNum1 = Window.Document.frmAdd.txtText1.Value
    sNum2 = Window.Document.frmAdd.txtText2.Value
    If IsNumeric(sNum1) And IsNumeric(sNum2) Then
        iSum = CInt(sNum1) + CInt(sNum2)
        Alert "The sum is: " & iSum
    Else
        Alert "The values you enter in the text boxes must be numeric."
    End If
End Sub
</SCRIPT>
</HEAD>

<BODY>
<FORM NAME="frmAdd">
    <INPUT TYPE="text" NAME="txtText1"><BR>
    <INPUT TYPE="text" NAME="txtText2"><BR>
    <INPUT TYPE="button" NAME="cmdAdd" VALUE="Sum">
</FORM>
</BODY>
</HTML>
```

Programming Tips and Gotchas

- Use *IsNumeric* to test whether *expression* evaluates to a number before performing the conversion.

- *CInt* differs from the *Fix* and *Int* functions, which truncate, rather than round, the fractional part of a number. Also, *Fix* and *Int* always return a value of the same type as was passed in.

- In client-side scripts, *CInt* is useful in converting the string in an HTML intrinsic text box control to a number. This is illustrated in the example.

See Also   CLng Function, Fix Function, FormatCurrency, FormatNumber, FormatPercent Functions, Int Function, IsNumeric Function

Class Statement

Syntax

```
Class name
    'statements
End Class
```

name

     Use: Required   Data Type: n/a

     The name of the class

Description   Defines a class and delimits the statements that define that class's member variables, properties, and methods.

Rules at a Glance

- *name* follows standard Visual Basic variable naming conventions.

- *statements* can consist of the following:

  — Private variable definitions. These variables are accessible within the class but not outside it.

  — Public variable definitions. (If variables are declared using the Dim keyword without an explicit indication of their accessibility, they are Public by default.) These variables become public properties of the class.

  — Public functions and subroutines defined with the Function...End Function or Sub...End Sub statements. The scope of routines not explicitly defined by the Public or Private keywords is public by default. These routines become the public methods of the class.

  — Private function and subroutines defined with the Function...End Function or Sub...End Sub statements. They are visible within the Class...End Class code block, but not to code outside the class.

  — Public properties defined using the Property Let, Property Get, and Property Set statements. Properties defined without an explicit Public or Private statement are also Public by default. They, along with any public variables, form the public properties of the class.

  — Private properties defined using the Property Let, Property Get, and Property Set statements. They are visible within the class, but inaccessible outside of it.

- The default member of the class can be defined by specifying the `Default` keyword in the member's `Function`, `Sub`, or `Property Get` statement.
- The Initialize event is fired and the Class_Initialize event procedure is executed, if it is present, when the class is instantiated.
- The Terminate event is fired and the Class_Terminate event procedure is executed, if it is present, when an instance of the class is destroyed. This occurs when the last variable or property holding the object reference is set to `Nothing` or when it goes out of scope. Note that, even if all the variables are destroyed, there are situations (such as circular references) in which the object persists until the script engine is destroyed. Hence, the Terminate event procedure may not be called until very late.
- The class can be instantiated by using the Set statement with the New keyword. For example, if a class named `CObject` is defined with the `Class...End Class` construct, the following code fragment instantiates an object belonging to the class:

```
Dim oObj
Set oObj = New CObject
```

Example

The example defines a class, CCounter, with one read-only property, Value, and one method, ShowCount, as well as an Initialize event procedure and one private variable:

```
Dim oCtr
Set oCtr = New CCounter

oCtr.Increment
oCtr.Increment
MsgBox "Count: " & oCtr.ShowCount

' definition of CCounter class
Class CCounter
    Private lCtr

    Private Sub Class_Initialize()
        lCtr = 1
    End Sub

    Public Sub Increment()
        lCtr = lCtr + 1
    End Sub

    Public Function ShowCount()
        ShowCount = Me.Value
    End Function
End Class
```

Programming Tips and Gotchas

- A property defined as a simple public variable cannot be designated as the class's default member.
- Public properties should be defined using the `Property Let`, `Property Get`, and `Property Set` statements, since they allow the value of a property to be modified in a controlled and predictable way. Defining a public variable that becomes accessible outside of the class (that is, defining a variable using either the `Dim` or `Public` keywords) is considered poor programming practice.

- The Me Keyword can be used within the Class...End Class construct to reference the object instance.
- The Initialize event procedure can be used to initialize variables and property values.
- The Terminate event procedure can be used to perform cleanup, such as releasing references to child objects, or closing database connections or recordsets. But be very careful about what code you run in the Terminate event terminator. Any code that results in the object being referenced again results in the terminated object's continued existence.
- A VBScript object instance should never be stored to the Session object in an ASP application. Since VBScript object instances are apartment-threaded, this has the effect of locking down the application to a single thread of execution.

VBA/VBScript Differences

The Class...End Class construct, which is the scripted equivalent of VBA class modules, is not supported in VBA.

See Also   Dim Statement, Function Statement, Initialize Event, Private Statement, Property Get Statement, Property Let Statement, Property Set Statement, Public Statement, Set Statement, Sub Statement, Terminate Event

---

CLng Function

Syntax

```
CLng(expression)
```

expression
    Use: Required   Data Type: Numeric or String

    The range of *expression* is –2,147,483,648 to 2,147,483,647; fractions are rounded.

Return Value   *expression* cast as a type of Long.

Description   Converts *expression* to a type of Long; any fractional element of *expression* is rounded.

Rules at a Glance

- *expression* must evaluate to a numeric value; otherwise, a type mismatch error is generated.
- If the value of *expression* is outside the range of the long data type, an overflow error is generated.
- When the fractional part is exactly 0.5, *CLng* always rounds it to the nearest even number. For example, 0.5 rounds to 0, and 1.5 rounds to 2.

Example

```
<HTML>
<HEAD>
<SCRIPT LANGUAGE="VBScript">
Option Explicit
```

```
Sub cmdAdd_OnClick( )

    Dim lSum, sNum1, sNum2

    sNum1 = Window.Document.frmAdd.txtText1.Value
    sNum2 = Window.Document.frmAdd.txtText2.Value
    If IsNumeric(sNum1) And IsNumeric(sNum2) Then
        lSum = CLng(sNum1) + CLng(sNum2)
        Alert "The sum is: " & lSum
    Else
        Alert "The values you enter in the text boxes must be numeric."
    End If
End Sub
</SCRIPT>
</HEAD>

<BODY>
<FORM NAME="frmAdd">
    <INPUT TYPE="text" NAME="txtText1"><BR>
    <INPUT TYPE="text" NAME="txtText2"><BR>
    <INPUT TYPE="button" NAME="cmdAdd" VALUE="Sum">
</FORM>
</BODY>
</HTML>
```

Programming Tips and Gotchas

- Use *IsNumeric* to test whether *expression* evaluates to a number.

- *CLng* differs from the *Fix* and *Int* functions, which truncate, rather than round, the fractional part of a number. Also, *Fix* and *Int* always return a value of the same type as was passed in.

- In client-side scripts, *CLng* is useful in converting the string in an HTML intrinsic text box control to a number. This is illustrated in the example.

See Also   CInt Function, Fix Function, FormatCurrency, FormatNumber, FormatPercent Functions, Int Function, IsNumeric Function

---

Const Statement

Syntax

        [Public|Private] Const *constantname* = *constantvalue*

constantname
    Use: Required

    The name of the constant.

constantvalue
    Use: Required   Data Type: Numeric or String

    A constant value, and optionally, the + and - unary operators. Unlike variables, constants must be initialized.

Description   Declares a constant value; i.e., its value can't be changed throughout the life of the program or routine. One of the ideas of declaring constants is to make code easier to both write and read; it allows you to replace a value with a recognizable word.

Rules at a Glance

- The rules for *constantname* are the same as those of any variable: the name can be up to 255 characters in length and can contain any alphanumeric character or an underscore, although it must start with an alphabetic character. As is the case with variable names, these rules can be overridden by placing brackets around the constant name.

- *constantvalue* can be a string or numeric literal. It can be only a single value (a simple constant); that is, it cannot be an expression that includes a call to an intrinsic or user-defined function, property, or method, nor can it contain any arithmetic or string operators or variables. In addition, a constant can't be defined in terms of another constant, as in the statement:

```
Public Const CDATE = CSTART_DATE    ' Invalid
```

Example

```
Private Const  my_Constant = 3.1417
```

Programming Tips and Gotchas

- The recommended coding convention for constants is the same as variables: use camel casing. This places the first letter of the first word in lowercase, and the first letter of subsequent words in uppercase. All other characters are in lowercase. To improve readability, you can also use underscores to separate words. For example, myConstant or my_Constant are constant names that adhere to this coding convention.

- One of the benefits of long variable and constant names (of up to 255 characters) in VBScript is that you can make your constant names as meaningful as possible while using abbreviations sparingly. After all, you may know what abbreviations mean, but will others?

- Rather than having to explicitly define constants found in type libraries, you can access the type library definitions from Windows Script Hosts by using the XML <reference> element in an *.wsf* file (for details, see Chapter 7), and from Active Server Pages by using the <METADATA> tag in the application's *global.asa* file.

VBA/VBScript Differences

- VBA allows you to explicitly define the data type of the constant. VBScript, since it does not support strong typing, does not.

- VBA supports complex constants; that is, VBA allows you to define constants using other constants, as well as using expressions containing absolute values, operators, and constants. In contrast, VBScript supports only simple constants; that is, it allows you to define a constant using only an absolute value.

See Also   Private Statement, Public Statement

Cos Function

Syntax

    Cos(number)

number
> Use: Required   Data Type: Numeric expression
>
> An angle in radians.

Return Value   A type of Double denoting the cosine of an angle.

Description   Takes an angle specified in radians and returns a ratio representing the length of the side adjacent to the angle divided by the length of the hypotenuse.

Rules at a Glance

The cosine returned by the function is between –1 and 1.

Example

    Dim dblCosine as Double
    dblCosine = Cos(dblRadians)

Programming Tips and Gotchas

- To convert degrees to radians, multiply degrees by pi/180.
- To convert radians to degrees, multiply radians by 180/pi.

See Also   Atn Function, Sin Function, Tan Function

CreateObject Function

Syntax

    CreateObject(servername, progID [, location])

servername
> Use: Required   Data Type: String
>
> The name of application providing the object.

ProgID
> Use: Required   Data Type: String
>
> The programmatic identifier (ProgID) of the object to create, as defined in the system registry.

Location
> Use: Optional   Data Type: String
>
> The name of the server where the object is to be created.

Return Value   A reference to an ActiveX object.

Description   Creates an instance of an OLE Automation (ActiveX) object. Prior to calling the methods, functions, or properties of an object, you are required to create an instance of that object. Once an object is created, you reference it in code using the object variable you defined.

Rules at a Glance

- In order to assign the object reference to a variable, you must use the Set keyword. For example:

```
Dim oDoc
Set oDoc = CreateObject("Word.Document")
```

- Programmatic identifiers use a string to identify a particular COM component or COM-enabled application. They are included among the subkeys of HKEY_CLASSES_ROOT in the system registry.

- Some common programmatic identifiers are shown in the following table:

ProgID	Description
ADODB.Connection	An ActiveX Data Objects connection
ADODB.Recordset	An ActiveX Data Objects recordset
DAO.DBEngine	Data Access Objects
Excel.Application	Microsoft Excel
Excel.Chart	A Microsoft Excel chart
Excel.Sheet	A Microsoft Excel workbook
MAPI.Session	Collaborative Data Objects
Outlook.Application	Microsoft Outlook
Scripting.Dictionary	Dictionary object
Scripting.FileSystemObject	File System object model
Word.Application	Microsoft Word
Word.Document	A Microsoft Word document

- If an instance of the ActiveX object is already running, *CreateObject* may start a new instance when it creates an object of the required type.

Example

The following WSH example places text in the first cell of an Excel spreadsheet document, changes the font to bold, saves the document to the *MyDocuments* folder, and closes the Excel application. In this example, Excel must already be running for the code to work (the code uses the *CreateObject* function to create a new workbook, but not to open Excel itself), but you can just as easily use the *CreateObject* function to open an application:

```
' Get MyDocuments folder
Dim oShell
Dim docfolder
Set oShell = WScript.CreateObject ("WScript.Shell")
docfFolder = oShell.SpecialFolders ("MyDocuments")

'Create and save Excel worksheet
Dim XLObj, XLBook, XLSheet
Set XLObj = CreateObject ("Excel.Application")
XLObj.Application.Visible = True
XLObj. Workbooks.Add( )
Set XLSheet = XLObj.ActiveSheet
XLSheet.Cells(1,1) = "Insert Text Here"
XLSheet.Cells(1,1).Font.Bold = True
XLSheet.SaveAs docFolder & "\Test.xls"
XLObj.Application.Quit
```

Programming Tips and Gotchas

- In a scripted environment, it's sometimes preferable to use the host application's object model to instantiate new objects rather than to use the VBScript *CreateObject* function. For instance, using the CreateObject method of the IIS Server object instead of the VBScript *CreateObject* function allows ASP to track the object instance and allows the object to participate in MTS or COM+ transactions. In Windows Script Host, using the CreateObject method of the WScript object instead of the VBScript *CreateObject* function allows WSH to track the object instance and to handle the object's events. When using VBScript to develop an Outlook form, the CreateObject method of the Application object is the preferred way to instantiate an external class.

- The *CreateObject* function does not succeed in client-side Internet Explorer scripts if the code attempts to create a dangerous object or the user's security policy does not allow it. In order to instantiate an object, use the HTML <OBJECT> tag.

- VBScript offers the ability to reference an object on another network server. Using the *Location* parameter, you can pass in the name of a remote server and the object can be referenced from that server. This means that you could even specify different servers depending upon prevailing circumstances, as this short example demonstrates:

```
Dim sMainServe
Dim sBackUpServer

sMainServer = "NTPROD1"
sBackUpServer = "NTPROD2"

If IsOnline(sMainServer) Then
    CreateObject("Sales.Customer",sMainServer)
Else
    CreateObject("Sales.Customer",sBackUpServer)
End If
```

- To use a current instance of an already running ActiveX object, use the *GetObject* function.

- If an object is registered as a single-instance object (i.e., an out-of-process ActiveX EXE), only one instance of the object can be created; regardless of the number of times *CreateObject* is executed, you will obtain a reference to the same instance of the object.

- An urban programming legend says it's necessary to release unused object references by setting them to Nothing when the reference is no longer needed. But since unused object references are released when they go out of scope, this step is not necessary. In general, object variables need to be explicitly released only to free circular references.

- Using the *CreateObject* function's location parameter to invoke an object remotely requires that the object be DCOM-aware. As an alternative, scripts can be run remotely using Remote Windows Script Host, a technology briefly discussed in Chapter 7.

- A apartment-threaded COM object instantiated using the *CreateObject* function should never be stored to the Session object in an ASP application, since doing so locks down the ASP application to a single thread of execution.

VBA/VBScript Differences

- In VBA, the *CreateObject* function is just one of the language constructs that you can use to instantiate a new object; you can also use the New keyword in either the object variable declaration or the object assignment. Because VBScript supports only late binding, however, *CreateObject* (along with a similar method in the target object model that you're using) is the only method available to instantiate objects that are external to the script.

- While *CreateObject* under VBA is an intrinsic part of the language, you cannot assume that *CreateObject* is necessarily available in a particular scripted environment. In Internet Explorer, for instance, calls to the CreateObject method generate a runtime error.

See Also   GetObject Function, Set Statement

CSng Function

Syntax

```
CSng(expression)
```

expression
: Use: Required   Data Type: Numeric or String

  The range of *expression* is −3.402823E38 to −1.401298E-45 for negative values; 1.401298E-45 to 3.402823E38 for positive values.

Return Value   *expression* cast as a type of Single.

Description   Returns a single-precision number.

Rules at a Glance

- *expression* must evaluate to a numeric value; otherwise, a type mismatch error is generated.
- If the value of *expression* is outside the range of the Single data type, an overflow error is generated.

Example

```
Dim sngMyNumber
If IsNumeric(sMyNumber) then
    sngMyNumber = CSng(sMyNumber)
End If
```

Programming Tips and Gotchas

- If you need to use a floating-point number in VBScript, there is no reason to use a Single; use a Double instead. Generally, a Single is used because it offers better performance than a Double, but this is not true in VBScript. Not only is a Single not smaller than a Double in the VBScript implementation, but the processor also converts Singles to Doubles, performs any numeric operations, and then converts Doubles back to Singles.

- Test that *expression* evaluates to a number by using the *IsNumeric* function.

See Also   FormatCurrency, FormatNumber, FormatPercent Functions, IsNumeric Function

CStr Function

Syntax

```
CStr(expression)
```

expression
    Use: Required   Data Type: Any

    Any expression that is to be converted to a string.

Return Value   *expression* converted to a String.

Description   Returns a string representation of *expression*.

Rules at a Glance

Almost any data can be passed to *CStr* to be converted to a string.

Example

```
Dim sMyString
SMyString = CStr(100)
```

Programming Tips and Gotchas

- The string representation of Boolean values is either True or False, as opposed to their underlying values of 0 and –1.
- An uninitialized variable passed to *CStr* returns an empty string.
- An object reference cannot be passed to the *CStr* function. Attempting to do so generates a runtime error.

Date Function

Syntax

```
Date
```

Return Value   Date returns a Date.

Description   Returns the current system date.

Rules at a Glance

They don't come any easier than this!

Programming Tips and Gotchas

To return both the current date and time in one variable, use the *Now* function.

See Also   IsDate Function, Now Function

DateAdd Function

Syntax

    DateAdd(*interval*, *number*, *date*)

interval

   Use: Required   Data Type: String

   An expression denoting the interval of time you need to add or subtract (see the following table "Interval Settings").

number

   Use: Required   Data Type: Any numeric type

   An expression denoting the number of time intervals you want to add or subtract.

date

   Use: Required   Data Type: Date

   The date on which to base the DateAdd calculation.

Interval Settings

Setting	Description
yyyy	Year
q	Quarter
m	Month
y	Day of year
d	Day
w	Weekday
ww	Week
h	Hour
n	Minute
s	Second

Return Value   A Date.

Description   Returns a Date representing the result of adding or subtracting a given number of time periods to or from a given date or time. For instance, you can calculate the date 178 months before today's date, or the date and time 12,789 minutes from now.

Rules at a Glance

- Specify the interval value as a string enclosed in quotation marks (e.g., "ww").
- If *number* is positive, the result will be after *date*; if *number* is negative, the result will be before *date*.
- The *DateAdd* function has a built-in calendar algorithm to prevent it from returning an invalid date. For example, if you add 10 minutes to 31 December 1999 23:55, *DateAdd* automatically recalculates all elements of the date to return a valid date—in this case, 1 January 2000 00:05. In addition, the calendar algorithm takes the presence of 29 February into account for leap years.

Example

```
Dim lNoOfIntervals
lNoOfIntervals = 100
Msgbox DateAdd("d", lNoOfIntervals, Now)
```

Programming Tips and Gotchas

- When working with dates, always check that a date is valid using the *IsDate* function prior to passing it as a parameter to the function.

- To add a number of days to *date*, use either the day of the year "y", the day "d", or the weekday "w".

- The Variant date type can handle only dates as far back as 100 A.D. *DateAdd* generates an error (runtime error number 5, "Invalid procedure call or argument") if the result precedes the year 100.

- The Variant date type can handle dates as far into the future as 9999 A.D.—from a practical application standpoint, a virtual infinity. If the result of *DateAdd* is a year beyond 9999 A.D., the function generates runtime error number 5, "Invalid procedure call or argument."

- If *number* contains a fractional value, it's rounded to the nearest whole number before being used in the calculation.

See Also   DateDiff Function, DatePart Function, DateSerial Function, IsDate Function

---

DateDiff Function

Syntax

```
DateDiff(interval, date1, date2[, firstdayofweek[, firstweekofyear]])
```

interval
>   Use: Required   Data Type: String
>
>   The units of time used to express the result of the difference between *date1* and *date2* (see the following "Interval Settings" table).

date1
>   Use: Required   Data Type: Date
>
>   The first date you want to use in the differential calculation.

date2
>   Use: Required   Data Type: Date
>
>   The second date you want to use in the differential calculation.

firstdayofweek
>   Use: Optional   Data Type: Integer
>
>   A numeric constant that defines the first day of the week. If not specified, Sunday is assumed (see the following table "First Day of Week Constants").

firstweekofyear
>   Use: Optional   Data Type: Integer
>
>   A numeric constant that defines the first week of the year. If not specified, the first week is assumed to be the week in which January 1 occurs (see the following table "First Week of Year Constants").

Interval Settings

Setting	Description
yyyy	Year
q	Quarter
m	Month
y	Day of year
d	Day
w	Weekday
ww	Week
h	Hour
n	Minute
s	Second

First Day of Week Constants

Constant	Value	Description
vbUseSystem	0	Use the NLS API setting
vbSunday	1	Sunday (default)
vbMonday	2	Monday
vbTuesday	3	Tuesday
vbWednesday	4	Wednesday
vbThursday	5	Thursday
vbFriday	6	Friday
vbSaturday	7	Saturday

First Week of Year Constants

Constant	Value	Description
vbUseSystem	0	Use the NLS API setting
vbFirstJan1	1	Start with the week in which January 1 occurs (default)
vbFirstFourDays	2	Start with the first week that has at least four days in the new year
vbFirstFullWeek	3	Start with first full week of the year

Return Value   A Long specifying the number of time intervals between two dates.

Description   The *DateDiff* function calculates the number of time intervals between two dates. For example, you can use the function to determine how many days there are between 1 January 1980 and 31 May 1998.

Rules at a Glance

- The calculation performed by *DateDiff* is always *date2*–*date1*. Therefore, if *date1* chronologically follows *date2*, the value returned by the function is negative.
- If *interval* is Weekday "w", *DateDiff* returns the number of weeks between *date1* and *date2*. *DateDiff* totals the occurrences of the day on which *date1* falls, up to

and including *date2*, but not including *date1*. Note that an *interval* of "w" doesn't return the number of weekdays between two dates, as you might expect.

- If *interval* is Week "ww", *DateDiff* returns the number of calendar weeks between *date1* and *date2*. To achieve this, *DateDiff* counts the number of Sundays (or whichever other day is defined to be the first day of the week by the *firstdayofweek* argument) between *date1* and *date2*. *date2* is counted if it falls on a Sunday, but *date1* isn't counted, even if it falls on a Sunday.

- The *firstdayofweek* argument affects only calculations that use the "ww" (week) interval values.

Example

```
Dim dtNow, dtThen
Dim sInterval
Dim lNoOfIntervals

dtNow = Date
dtThen = #01/01/1990#
sInterval = "m"

lNoOfIntervals = DateDiff(sInterval, dtThen, dtNow)

MsgBox lNoOfIntervals
```

Programming Tips and Gotchas

- When working with dates, always check that a date is valid using the *IsDate* function prior to passing it as a function parameter.

- When comparing the number of years between December 31 of one year and January 1 of the following year, *DateDiff* returns 1, although in reality, the difference is only one day.

- *DateDiff* considers the four quarters of the year to be January 1–March 31, April 1–June 30, July 1–September 30, and October 1–December 31. Consequently, when determining the number of quarters between March 31 and April 1 of the same year, for example, *DateDiff* returns 1, even though the latter date is only one day after the former.

- If *interval* is "m", *DateDiff* simply counts the difference in the months on which the respective dates fall. For example, when determining the number of months between January 31 and February 1 of the same year, *DateDiff* returns 1, even though the latter date is only one day after the former.

- To calculate the number of days between *date1* and *date2*, you can use either Day of year "y" or Day "d".

- In calculating the number of hours, minutes, or seconds between two dates, if an explicit time isn't specified, *DateDiff* provides a default value of midnight (00:00:00).

- If you specify *date1* or *date2* as strings within quotation marks (" ") and omit the year, the year is assumed to be the current year, as taken from the computer's date. This allows the same code to be used in different years.

See Also

DateAdd Function, DatePart Function, IsDate Function

DatePart Function

Syntax

```
DatePart(interval, date[,firstdayofweek[, firstweekofyear]])
```

interval
    Use: Required   Data Type: String

The unit of time to extract from within *date* (see the following table "Interval Settings").

date
    Use: Required   Data Type: Date

The Date value that you want to evaluate.

firstdayofweek
    Use: Optional   Data Type: Integer

A numeric constant that defines the first day of the week. If not specified, Sunday is assumed (see the following table "First Day of Week Constants").

firstweekofyear
    Use: Optional   Data Type: Integer

A numeric constant that defines the first week of the year. If not specified, the first week is assumed to be the week in which January 1 occurs (see the following table "First Week of Year Constants").

Interval Settings

Setting	Description
yyyy	Year
q	Quarter
m	Month
y	Day of year
d	Day
w	Weekday
ww	Week
h	Hour
n	Minute
s	Second

First Day of Week Constants

Constant	Value	Description
vbUseSystem	0	Use the NLS API setting
vbSunday	1	Sunday (default)
vbMonday	2	Monday
vbTuesday	3	Tuesday
vbWednesday	4	Wednesday
vbThursday	5	Thursday

Constant	Value	Description
vbFriday	6	Friday
vbSaturday	7	Saturday

First Week of Year Constants

Constant	Value	Description
vbUseSystem	0	Use the NLS API setting
vbFirstJan1	1	Start with week in which January 1 occurs (default)
vbFirstFourDays	2	Start with the first week that has at least four days in the new year
vbFirstFullWeek	3	Start with first full week of the year

Return Value   An Integer.

Description   Extracts an individual component of the date or time (like the month or the second) from a date/time value. It returns an Integer containing the specified portion of the given date. *DatePart* is a single function encapsulating the individual *Year*, *Month*, *Day*, *Hour*, *Minute*, and *Second* functions.

Rules at a Glance

- The *firstdayofweek* argument affects only calculations that use either the "w" or "ww" *interval* values.

- The *firstdayofweek* argument affects only calculations that use the "ww" *interval* value.

Example

```
Dim sTimeInterval
Dim dtNow

sTimeInterval = "n" 'minutes
dtNow = Now

MsgBox DatePart(sTimeInterval, dtNow)
```

Programming Tips and Gotchas

- When working with dates, always check that a date is valid using the *IsDate* function prior to passing it as a function parameter.

- If you specify *date* within quotation marks (" ") omitting the year, the year is assumed to be the current year taken from the computer's date.

- If you attempt to extract either the hours, the minutes, or the seconds, but *date1* doesn't contain the necessary time element, the function assumes a time of midnight (0:00:00).

See Also   DateSerial Function, Day Function, Month Function, Year Function, Minute Function, Hour Function, Second Function

DateSerial Function

Syntax

```
DateSerial(year, month, day)
```

year

Use: Required   Data Type: Integer

Number between 0 and 9999, inclusive.

month

Use: Required   Data Type: Integer

Any numeric expression to express the month between 1 and 12.

day

Use: Required   Data Type: Integer

Any numeric expression to express the day between 1 and 31.

Return Value   A Date.

Description   Returns a Date from the three date components (year, month, and day). For the function to succeed, all three components must be present and all must be numeric values.

Rules at a Glance

- If the value of a particular element exceeds its normal limits, *DateSerial* adjusts the date accordingly. For example, if you tried DateSerial(96,2,31)—February 31, 1996—*DateSerial* returns March 2, 1996.

- You can specify expressions or formulas that evaluate to individual date components as parameters to *DateSerial*. For example, DateSerial (98,10+9,23) returns 23 March 1999. This makes it easier to use *DateSerial* to form dates whose individual elements are unknown at design time or that are created on the fly as a result of user input.

Example

```
Dim iYear, iMonth, iday

iYear = 1987
iMonth = 3 + 11
iday = 16

MsgBox DateSerial(iYear, iMonth, iday)
```

Programming Tips and Gotchas

- If any of the parameters exceed the range of the Integer data type (–32,768 to 32,767), an error (runtime error 6, "Overflow") is generated.

- The Microsoft documentation for this function incorrectly states, "For the year argument, values between 0 and 99, inclusive, are interpreted as the years 1900–1999." In fact, *DateSerial* handles two-digit years in the same way as other Visual Basic date functions. A year argument between 0 and 29 is taken to be in the 21st Century (2000 to 2029); year arguments between 30 and 99 are taken to be in the 20th Century (1930 to 1999). Of course, the safest way to specify a year is to use the full four digits.

See Also   DateAdd Function

DateValue Function

Syntax
```
DateValue(stringexpression)
```
stringexpression
    Use: Required   Data Type: String expression
    Any of the date formats recognized by *IsDate*.

Return Value   Variant of type Date.

Description   Returns a Date variant containing the date represented by *stringexpression*. *DateValue* can successfully recognize a *stringexpression* in any of the date formats recognized by *IsDate*. *DateValue* doesn't return time values in a date/time string; they are simply dropped. However, if *stringexpression* includes a valid date value but an invalid time value, a runtime error results.

Rules at a Glance
- The order of the day, the month, and the year within *stringexpression* must be the same as the sequence defined by the computer's regional settings.
- Only those date separators recognized by *IsDate* can be used.
- If you don't specify a year in your date expression, *DateValue* uses the current year from the computer's system date.

Example
```
Dim dateExpression

dateExpression = #10 March 2003#

If IsDate (dateExpression) Then
    MsgBox DateValue(dateExpression)
Else
    MsgBox "Invalid date"
End If
```

Programming Tips and Gotchas
- When working with dates, always check that a date is valid using the *IsDate* function prior to passing it as a function parameter.
- If *stringexpression* includes time information as well as date information, the time information is ignored; however, if only time information is passed to *DateValue*, an error is generated.
- *DateValue* handles two-digit years in the following manner: year arguments between 0 and 29 are taken to be in the 21st Century (2000 to 2029), and year arguments between 30 and 99 are taken to be in the 20th Century (1930 to 1999). The safest way to specify a year is to use the full four digits.

- The current formats being used for dates are easier to discover on Windows NT than on Windows 9x. On Windows NT, the date formats are held as string values in the following registry keys:

    Date Separator
    HKEY_CURRENT_USER\Control Panel\International, sDate value entry

    Long Date
    HKEY_CURRENT_USER\Control Panel\International, sLongDate value entry

    Short Date
    HKEY_CURRENT_USER\Control Panel\International, sShortDate value entry

- The more common approach to date conversion is to use the *CDate* function. Microsoft also recommends using *CDate* and the other *C...* conversion functions due to their enhanced capabilities and their locale awareness.

See Also   CDate Function, DateSerial Function, IsDate Function

Day Function

Syntax

    Day(*dateexpression*)

dateexpression
    Use: Required   Data Type: Any valid date expression
    Any expression capable of conversion to a Date.

Return Value   Variant of type Integer.

Description   Returns a variant integer data type that can take on a value ranging from 1 to 31, representing the day of the month of *dateexpression*. *dateexpression*, the argument passed to the *Day* function, must be a valid date/time or time value.

Rules at a Glance

- *dateexpression* can be any variant, numeric expression, or string expression that represents a valid date.
- The range of *dateexpression* is 1/1/100 to 12/31/9999.
- If *dateexpression* is Null, Null is returned.

Programming Tips and Gotchas

- When working with dates, always check that a date is valid using the *IsDate* function prior to passing it as a function parameter.
- If *dateexpression* omits the year, *Day* still returns a valid day.
- If the day portion of *dateexpression* is outside its valid range, the function generates runtime error 13, "Type mismatch." This is also true if the day and month portion of *dateexpression* is 2/29 for a nonleap year.
- To return the day of the week, use the *WeekDay* function.

See Also   DatePart Function, Weekday Function, WeekdayName Function, Month Function, Year Function

Dictionary Object

Createable   Yes

Library   Microsoft Scripting Runtime

Description   The Dictionary object is similar to a Collection object, except that it's loosely based on the Perl associative array. Like an array or a Collection object, the Dictionary object holds elements, called *items* or *members*, containing data. A Dictionary object can contain any data whatsoever, including objects and other Dictionary objects. Access the value of these dictionary items by using unique *keys* (or named values) that are stored along with the data, rather than by using an item's ordinal position as you do with an array. This makes the Dictionary object ideal when you need to access data that is associated with a unique named value.

You can access each item stored to a Dictionary object by using the For Each ...Next construct. However, rather than returning a variant containing the data value stored to the Dictionary object as you would expect, it returns a variant containing the key associated with the member. You then have to pass this key to the Item method to retrieve the member, as the following example shows:

```
Dim vKey
Dim sItem, sMsg
Dim oDict

Set oDict = CreateObject("Scripting.Dictionary")
oDict.Add "One", "Engine"
oDict.Add "Two", "Wheel"
oDict.Add "Three", "Tire"
oDict.Add "Four", "Spanner"

For Each vKey In oDict
   sItem = oDict.Item(vKey)
   sMsg = sMsg & sItem & vbCrLf
Next

MsgBox sMsg
```

Dictionary Object Properties

The Dictionary object includes the following four properties:

Property	Description
CompareMode	Determines the order of text comparisons in the Item property
Count	Indicates the total number of items in the dictionary
Item	Sets or retrieves a particular item of data in the dictionary
Key	Renames an existing key

Dictionary Object Methods

The Dictionary object supports the following five methods:

Property	Description
Add	Adds an item and its associated key to the dictionary
Exists	Determines whether a particular key exists in the dictionary
Keys	Returns all keys in the dictionary
Remove	Removes an item from the dictionary
Remove All	Removes all the data from the dictionary

Dictionary.Add Method

Syntax

```
dictionaryobject.Add key, item
```

dictionaryobject
    Use: Required   Data Type: Dictionary object

    A reference to a Dictionary object.

key
    Use: Required   Data Type: Any

    A key value that's unique in the Dictionary object.

item
    Use: Required   Data Type: Any

    The item to be added to the dictionary.

Description   Adds a key and its associated item to the specified Dictionary object.

Rules at a Glance

- If the key isn't unique, runtime error 457, "This key is already associated with an element of this collection," is generated.
- *item* can be of any data type, including objects and other Dictionary objects.

Example

The example uses a Dictionary object to store state abbreviations and their corresponding state names:

```
Dim StateCode, StateName
Dim StateDict
Dim Key

Set StateDict = CreateObject("Scripting.Dictionary")

StateCode = "CA"
StateName = "California"
StateDict.Add StateCode, StateName

StateCode = "NY"
StateName = "New York"
StateDict.Add StateCode, StateName
```

```
StateCode = "MI"
StateName = "Michigan"
StateDict.Add StateCode, StateName

Key = "NY"
MsgBox StateDict.Item(Key)
```

Programming Tips and Gotchas

- The order of members within a Dictionary object is officially undefined. That is, you can't control the position of individual members, nor can you retrieve individual members based on their position within the Dictionary object. Your code, in short, should make no assumptions about the position of individual elements within the Dictionary objects.

- Once you add a key and its associated data item, you can change the key by using the write-only Key property.

- Use the Dictionary object to store tables of data, and particularly to store single items of data that can be meaningfully accessed by a key value.

- The use of the Dictionary object to store multifield data records is not recommended; instead, classes offer a better programmatic alternative. Typically, you would store a record by adding an array representing the record's field values to the dictionary. But assigning arrays to items in the Dictionary object is a poor programming practice, since individual elements of the array cannot be modified directly once they are assigned to the dictionary.

See Also   Dictionary.Key Property

Dictionary.CompareMode Property

Data Type
Long

Description   Sets or returns the mode used to compare the keys in a Dictionary object.

Rules at a Glance

- CompareMode can be set only on a dictionary that doesn't contain any data.
- The CompareMode property can have either of the following two values:

    0, Binary
    > This is the default value. It compares the keys with a string byte-per-byte to determine whether a match exists.

    1, Text
    > Uses a case-insensitive comparison when attempting to match keys with a string.

    In addition, the value of CompareMode can be greater than 2, in which case it defines the locale identifier (LCID) to be used in making the comparison.

Programming Tips and Gotchas

- You need to explicitly set the CompareMode property only if you do not wish to use the default binary comparison mode.

- The Scripting Runtime type library defines constants (BinaryCompare and TextCompare) that can be used in place of their numeric equivalents. You can do this in one of three ways. You can define the constants yourself by adding the following code to your script:

```
Const BinaryCompare = 0
Const TextCompare = 1
```

  You can also use the equivalent vbBinaryCompare and vbTextCompare constants that are defined in the VBScript library.

  Finally, if you're an ASP programmer, you can use the METADATA directive to access the Scripting Runtime type library; if you're developing a Windows Script Host script, you can include the following line in a Windows Script Host (.wsf) file in order to access the constants from the Scripting Runtime type library:

```
<reference GUID="{420B2830-E718-11CF-893D-00A0C9054228}" />
```

- Practically, the CompareMode property indicates whether the comparison between existing key names and the *key* argument of the Dictionary object's Add method, Exists method, Item property, or Key property will be case-sensitive (BinaryCompare) or case-insensitive (TextCompare). By default, comparisons are case-sensitive.

Dictionary.Count Property

Data Type
Long

Description   A read-only property that returns the number of key/item pairs in a Dictionary object.

Rules at a Glance
This property returns the actual number of items in the dictionary. So if you use the Count property to iterate the items in the dictionary, you would use code like the following:

```
Dim ctr
For ctr = 0 to dictionary.Count - 1
    ' do something
Next
```

Dictionary.Exists Method

Syntax

```
dictionaryobject.Exists(key)
```

dictionaryobject
    Use: Required   Data Type: Dictionary object
    A reference to a Dictionary object.

key
    Use: Required   Data Type: String
    The key value being sought.

Return Value   Boolean

Description   Determines whether a given key is present in a Dictionary object.

Rules at a Glance

Returns True if the specified key exists in the Dictionary object; False if not.

Programming Tips and Gotchas

- If you attempt to use the Item property to return the item of a nonexistent key, or if you assign a new key to a nonexistent key, the nonexistent key is added to the dictionary, along with a blank item. To prevent this, you should use the Exists property to ensure that the Key is present in the dictionary before proceeding.

- The way in which *key* is compared with the existing key values is determined by the setting of the Dictionary object's CompareMode property.

Example

```
If oDict.Exists(strOldKey) Then
    oDict.Key(strOldKey) = strNewKey
End If
```

Dictionary.Item Property

Syntax

The syntax for setting an item is:

dictionaryobject.Item(*key*) = *item*

The syntax for returning an item is:

value = *dictionaryobject*.Item(*key*)

dictionaryobject
Use: Required   Data Type: Dictionary object
A reference to a Dictionary object.

key
Use: Required   Data Type: String
A unique string key for this Dictionary object.

item
Use: Optional   Data Type: Any
The data associated with *key*.

Data Type

Any

Description   Sets or returns the data item to be linked to a specified key in a Dictionary object.

Rules at a Glance

- The Item property is the default member of the Dictionary object.
- The data type is that of the item being returned.
- Unlike the Item property of most objects, the Dictionary object's Item property is read/write. If you try to set *item* to a nonexistent key, the key is added to the dictionary, and the item is linked to it as a sort of "implicit add."

Programming Tips and Gotchas

- The Dictionary object doesn't allow you to retrieve an item by its ordinal position.

- If you provide a nonexistent key when trying to retrieve an item, the dictionary exhibits rather strange behavior: it adds *key* to the Dictionary object along with a blank item. You should therefore use the Exists method prior to setting or returning an item, as the example shows.

- If the item to be assigned or retrieved from the Dictionary object is itself an object, be sure to use the Set keyword when assigning it to a variable or to the Dictionary object.

- The comparison of *key* with member keys is defined by the value of the Dictionary object's CompareMode property.

- Although the read/write character of the Dictionary object's Item property has its drawbacks, it also has its advantages. In particular, it makes it easy to overwrite or replace an existing data item, since its Item property is read/write: simply assign the new value like you would with any other property.

- The Dictionary object should never be used to store HTML form or query data in Session scope in an ASP application. Since the Dictionary object is an apartment-threaded COM object, this has the effect of locking down the application to a single thread of execution.

Example

The example uses the Dictionary object as a lookup table to retrieve the state name that corresponds to the state code entered by the user. The HTML page that submits user information to the server is as follows:

```
<HTML>
<HEAD><TITLE>Dictionary Object Example</TITLE></HEAD>
<BODY>
Enter your name and location: <P>
<FORM METHOD=POST ACTION=dictobj.asp>
Your name:
<INPUT TYPE="Text" NAME="VisitorName" /><P>
Your location:
<INPUT TYPE="Text" NAME="City" />,
<INPUT TYPE="Text" NAME="State" SIZE=2 /> <P>
<INPUT TYPE="Submit" VALUE="Submit" />
</FORM>
<BODY>
</HTML>
```

The ASP page that retrieves the information submitted by the user, encodes it, and uses the Dictionary object to retrieve the full state name is as follows:

```
<HTML>
<HEAD>
<TITLE>ASP Page for the Dictionary Object Example</TITLE>
</HEAD>
<BODY>

        <% Show Greeting %>

<SCRIPT LANGUAGE="VBScript" RUNAT="Server">
```

```
Sub ShowGreeting( )
    Dim StateDict
    Dim ClientName, ClientState

    ' Initialize dictionary
    Set StateDict = Server.CreateObject("Scripting.Dictionary")
    StateDict.Add "NY", "New York"
    StateDict.Add "CA", "California"
    StateDict.Add "FL", "Florida"
    StateDict.Add "WA", "Washington"
    StateDict.Add "MI", "Michigan"
    StateDict.Add "MA", "Massachusetts"
    StateDict.Add "MN", "Minnesota"
    ' add other states

    ClientName = Server.HTMLEncode(Request.Form("VisitorName"))
    ClientState = Server.HTMLEncode(Request.Form("State"))

    Response.Write("Hello, " & ClientName & ". <P>")
    Response.Write("We are pleased to have a visitor from ")
        Response.Write(StateDict.Item(ClientState) & "!")
    End Sub
</SCRIPT>
</BODY>
</HTML>
```

Dictionary.Items Method

Syntax

```
dictionaryobject.Items
```

dictionaryobject

    Use: Required   Data Type: Dictionary object

    A reference to a Dictionary object.

Return Value   A Variant array.

Description   Returns an array containing all the items in the specified Dictionary object.

Rules at a Glance

The returned array is always a zero-based variant array whose data type matches that of the items in the Dictionary object.

Programming Tips and Gotchas

- The only way to directly access members of the Dictionary is via their key values. However, using the Items method, you can "dump" the data from the Dictionary into a zero-based variant array. The data items can then be accessed like an array in the normal way, as the following code shows:

```
Dim vArray
vArray = DictObj.Items
For i = 0 to DictObj.Count -1
    Response.Write vArray(i) & "<P>"
Next I
```

- The Items method retrieves only the items stored in a Dictionary object; you can retrieve all the Dictionary object's keys by calling its Keys method.

See Also   Dictionary.Keys Method

Dictionary.Key Property

Syntax

```
dictionaryobject.Key(key) = newkey
```

dictionaryobject
    Use: Required   Data Type: Dictionary object

    A reference to a Dictionary object.

key
    Use: Required   Data Type: String

    The key of an existing dictionary item.

newkey
    Use: Required   Data Type: String

    A new unique key for this dictionary item.

Data Type

A String.

Description   Replaces an existing key with a new one.

Rules at a Glance

- The Key property is write-only.
- *key*, the existing key value, must exist in the dictionary or an error results.
- *newkey* must be unique and must not already exist in the dictionary or an error results.
- The comparison of *key* and *newkey* with existing key values is defined by the Dictionary object's CompareMode property.

Example

```
Private Function ChangeKeyValue(sOldKey, sNewKey)
'Assumes oDictionary is a public object
    If oDictionary.Exists(sOldKey) Then
        oDictionary.Key(sOldKey) = sNewKey
        ChangeKeyValue = True
    Else
        ChangeKeyValue = False
    End If
End Function
```

Programming Tips and Gotchas

- Use the Key property to change the name of an existing key. Use the Add method to add a new key and its associated value to the Dictionary object. Use the Keys method to retrieve the names of all keys; this is especially useful when you don't know the names or the contents of the dictionary in advance.

- Attempting to retrieve the key name (a nonsensical operation, since this amounts to providing the key's name in order to retrieve the key's name) generates an error, as does attempting to modify a key name that hasn't already been added to the dictionary.

- Using a For Each...Next loop to iterate the members of a Dictionary object involves an implicit call to the Key property. In other words, each iteration of the loop returns a key, rather than a data item. To retrieve the member's data, you then must use its key value to access its data through the Item property. This is illustrated in the example for the Dictionary.Item property.

Dictionary.Keys Method

Syntax

```
dictionaryobject.Keys
```

dictionaryobject
    Use: Required   Data Type: Dictionary object

    A reference to a Dictionary object.

Return Value   An array of strings.

Description   Returns an array containing all the Key values in the specified Dictionary object.

Rules at a Glance

The returned array is always a 0-based variant array whose data type is String.

Programming Tips and Gotchas

The Keys method retrieves only the keys stored in a Dictionary object. You can retrieve all the Dictionary object's items by calling its Items method. You can recall an individual data item by using the Dictionary object's Item property.

Example

```
Dim vArray
vArray = DictObj.Keys
For i = 0 to DictObj.Count -1
    Response.Write vArray(i) & "<BR>"
Next
```

Dictionary.Remove Method

Syntax

```
dictionaryobject.Remove key
```

dictionaryobject
    Use: Required   Data Type: Dictionary object

    A reference to a Dictionary object.

key
    Use: Required   Data Type: String

    The key associated with the item to be removed.

Description   Removes both the specified key and its associated data (i.e., its item) from the dictionary.

Rules at a Glance

If *key* doesn't exist, runtime error 32811, "Element not found," occurs.

Dictionary.RemoveAll Method

Syntax

```
dictionaryobject.RemoveAll
```

dictionaryobject
    Use: Required   Data Type: Dictionary object

    A reference to a Dictionary object.

Description   Clears out the dictionary; in other words, removes all keys and their associated data from the dictionary.

Programming Tips and Gotchas

If you want to remove a selected number of members rather than the entire contents of the dictionary, use the Remove method.

Dim Statement

Syntax

```
Dim varname[([subscripts])], varname[([subscripts])]
```

varname
    Use: Required

    Your chosen name for the variable.

subscripts
    Use: Optional

    Dimensions of an array variable.

Description   Declares and allocates storage space in memory for variables. The Dim statement is used either at the start of a procedure or the start of a global script block. In the first case, the variable declared using Dim is local to the procedure. In the second, it's available throughout the module.

Rules at a Glance

- You can declare multiple variables in a single Dim statement, as long as you use a comma to delimit them.
- When variables are first initialized with the Dim statement, they have a value of Empty. In addition, if a variable has been initialized but not assigned a value, the following expressions will both evaluate to True:

```
If vVar = 0 Then
If vVar = "" Then
```

- To declare array variables, use the following syntax:

  Fixed length, single dimension
  > Dim *arrayname*(*upper*)

  > Example: Dim myArray(10)

  Fixed length, multidimensional
  > Dim *arrayname*(*upper*, *upper*, ...)

  > Example: Dim MyArray(20,30)

  Variable length, single or multidimensional
  > Dim *arrayname*( )

  > Example: Dim myArray( )

- You can declare a multidimensional array with up to 60 dimensions.
- Variable-length arrays can be resized using the ReDim statement. Fixed-length arrays can't be resized.

Example

The example shows how to use the Dim statement to define a variable that receives an array returned by a function:

```
Dim Input, NumArray

Input = InputBox("Enter three numbers separated by commas: ")
NumArray = Split(Input, ",")
If IsEmpty(NumArray) Then
    MsgBox "No numbers were entered."
Else
    Dim Sum, Element
    For Each Element in NumArray
        If IsNumeric(Element) Then Sum = Sum + CDbl(Element)
    Next
    MsgBox "The total of the numbers is: " & Sum
End If
```

Programming Tips and Gotchas

- It's accepted practice to place all the Dim statements to be used in a particular procedure at the beginning of that procedure, and to place all Dim statements for global variables at the beginning of the script block.
- Variables declared with Dim in the global script block are available to all procedures within the script. At the procedure level, variables are available only within the procedure.

VBA/VBScript Differences

- VBA allows you to instantiate objects of a particular type through early binding by using the New keyword. VBScript does not support the New keyword when used with Dim statement, nor does it support strong typing of objects.
- VBA supports the use of the WithEvents keyword, which allows VBA code to trap the events fired by an object of a particular type (that is, by a strongly typed object). VBScript does not support the keyword and hence does not allow you to trap events that are not otherwise supported by the host object model. For instance, you can trap the Application_OnStart, Application_OnEnd, OnTransactionCommit, OnTransactionAbort, Session_OnStart, and Session_OnEnd events in an ASP application. (For details on events supported by each object

model, see Chapters 5 through 8, which discuss the object models of each host environment that supports VBScript.) A partial exception to this lack of support for external events is Windows Script Host, which allows you to trap an object's events by supplying an extra parameter to the WScript.CreateObject method or by calling the WScript.ConnectObject method.

- In VBA, only variables explicitly declared as variants and variables whose data type has not been declared are reported by the *IsEmpty* function to be empty, and return True when compared to zero or to a null string. This is true of all variables in VBScript, because it does not support strong typing.

See Also Const Statement, Private Statement, Public Statement, ReDim Statement

---

Do ... Loop Statement

Syntax

```
Do [{While | Until} condition]
    [statements]
[Exit Do]
    [statements]
Loop
```

or:

```
Do
    [statements]
[Exit Do]
    [statements]
Loop [{While | Until} condition]
```

condition
Use: Optional   Data Type: Boolean expression

An expression that evaluates to True or False.

statements
Use: Optional

Program statements that are repeatedly executed while, or until, *condition* is True.

Description Repeatedly executes a block of code while or until a condition becomes True.

Rules at a Glance

- On its own, Do...Loop repeatedly executes the code that is contained within its boundaries indefinitely. You therefore need to specify under what conditions the loop is to stop repeating. Sometimes, this requires modifying the variable that controls loop execution within the loop. For example:

```
Do
    intCtr = intCtr + 1   ' Modify loop control variable
    Response.Write "Iteration " & intCtr & _
        " of the Do loop..." & "<BR>"
    ' Compare to upper limit
    If intCtr = 10  Then Exit Do
Loop
```

Failure to do this results in the creation of an endless loop.

- Adding the Until keyword after Do instructs your program to Do something Until the condition is True. Its syntax is:

```
Do Until condition
    code to execute
Loop
```

If *condition* is True before your code gets to the Do statement, the code within the Do...Loop is ignored.

- Adding the While keyword after Do repeats the code while a particular condition is True. When the condition becomes False, the loop is automatically exited. The syntax of the Do While statement is:

```
Do While condition
 code to execute
Loop
```

Again, the code within the Do...Loop construct is ignored if *condition* is False when the program arrives at the loop.

- In some cases, you may need to execute the loop at least once. You might, for example, evaluate the values held within an array and terminate the loop if a particular value is found. In that case, you'd need to execute the loop at least once. To do this, place the Until or While keyword along with the condition *after* the Loop statement. Do...Loop Until always executes the code in the loop at least once and continues to loop until the condition is True. Likewise, Do...Loop While always executes the code at least once, and continues to loop while the condition is True. The syntax of these two statements is as follows:

```
Do
 code to execute
Loop Until condition
```

```
Do
 code to execute
Loop While condition
```

- A Null *condition* is treated as False.
- Your code can exit the loop at any point by executing the Exit Do statement.

Programming Tips and Gotchas

- Inexperienced programmers often think that a loop exits as soon as the condition that terminates the loop is met. In fact, however, it exits whenever the conditional statement that evaluates the loop control expression is executed and that expression is True. For example, in the code:

```
Do While X <> 10
    ' This always executes if the loop is entered

    ' Set loop termination variable
    X = 10

    ' Any code here still executes. There is nothing
    ' monitoring X
Loop
```

all statements following the assignment execute until the condition at the top of the loop is evaluated.

- You'll also encounter situations in which you intend to continually execute the loop while or until a condition is True, except in a particular case. This type of exception is handled using the Exit Do statement. You can place as many Exit Do statements within a Do...Loop structure as you require. As with any exit from a Do...Loop, whether it's exceptional or normal, the program continues execution on the line directly following the Loop statement. The following code fragment illustrates the use of Exit Do:

```
Do Until condition1
  'code to execute
    If condition2 Then
       Exit Do
    End if
    'more code to execute—only if condition2 is false
Loop
```

See Also   For Each . . . Next Statement, For . . . Next Statement, While . . . Wend Statement

---

Drive Object

Returned by

File.Drive property
FileSystemObject.Drives.Item property

Createable   No

Library   Microsoft Scripting Runtime

Description   Represents a single drive connected to the current machine, including a network drive. By using the Drive object, you can interrogate the system properties of any drive. In addition, you can use the Folder object returned by the Drive object's RootFolder property as your foothold into the physical drive's filesystem.

A new instance of the Drive object cannot be created. Instead, a Drive object that represents an existing physical drive typically is retrieved from the FileSystemObject object's Drives collection, as in the following code fragment, which retrieves an object reference that represents the C: drive:

```
Dim oFS, oDrive
Set oFS = CreateObject("Scripting.FileSystemObject")
set oDrive = oFS.Drives("C")
```

For an overview of the File System object model, including the library reference needed to access it, see the "File System Object Model" entry.

Properties

All Drive object properties are read-only. In addition, removable media drives must be ready (i.e., have media inserted) for the Drive object to read certain properties.

AvailableSpace

Data Type: Long

Returns the number of bytes unused on the disk. Typically, the AvailableSpace property returns the same number as the Drive object's FreeSpace property, although differences may occur on systems that support quotas. In early versions of the Scripting Runtime, AvailableSpace was capable of storing only values that ranged from 0 to 2^31, or 2,147,483,648; in other words, in the case of drives with over 2 GB free, it failed to accurately report the amount of available free space.

In order to check the amount of available space on the drive, the drive must be ready. Otherwise, an error is likely to result. This makes it worthwhile to check the value of the IsReady property before attempting to retrieve a drive's free space, particularly if your script is iterating the Drives collection.

DriveLetter

Data Type: String

The drive letter used for this drive on the current machine (e.g., C). In addition, its value is an empty string ("") if the drive is a network share that has not been mapped to a local drive letter.

DriveType

Data Type: Long

A value (see the following table) indicating the type of drive. Any remote drive is shown only as remote. For example, a shared CD-ROM or Zip drive that is both remote and removable is shown simply as remote (i.e., it returns a value of 3) on any machine other than the machine on which it's installed.

Constant	Value
CDROM	4
Fixed	2
RAMDisk	5
Remote	3
Removable	1
Unknown	0

The Scripting Runtime type library defines the constants shown in the above table's Constant column that can be used in place of their numeric equivalents. You can take advantage of these constants in your scripts in one of two ways. You can define the constants yourself by adding the following code to your script:

```
Const Unknown = 0
Const Removable = 1
Const Fixed = 2
Const Remote = 3
Const CDRom = 4
Const RAMDisk = 5
```

You can also use the ASP METADATA tag to access the constants from the type library, or you can include the following line in a Windows Script Host (.wsf) file in order to access the constants from the Scripting Runtime type library:

```
<reference GUID="{420B2830-E718-11CF-893D-00A0C9054228}" />
```

The DriveType property does not require that the drive be ready to return a value.

FileSystem

Data Type: String

The installed filesystem; returns FAT, FAT32, NTFS, or CDFS. In order to determine that the filesystem in place, a device must be present on removable drives or runtime error 71, "Disk not ready," results.

FreeSpace

Data Type: Long

The number of bytes unused on the disk. Typically, its value is the same as the Drive object's AvailableSpace property, although differences may occur on computer systems that support quotas.

In early versions of the scripting Runtime, the property was capable of storing only values that ranged from 0 to 2^{31}, or 2,147,483,648. In other words, in the case of drives with over 2 GB free, it failed to accurately report the amount of available free space.

IsReady

Data Type: Boolean

For hard drives, this should always return True. For removable media drives, True is returned if media is in the drive; otherwise, False is returned.

A number of Drive object properties raise an error if the drive they represent is not ready. You can use the IsReady property to check the status of the drive and prevent your script from raising an error.

Path

Data Type: String

The drive name followed by a colon (e.g., C:). (Note that it does not include the root folder.) This is the default property of the Drive object.

RootFolder

Data Type: Folder object

Gives you access to the rest of the drive's filesystem by exposing a Folder object representing the root folder.

SerialNumber

Data Type: Long

The serial number of the drive, an integer that uniquely identifies the drive or disk. If a disk or CD-ROM has been assigned a serial number, you can use this property to insure that the correct disk is present in a drive that has removable media.

ShareName

Data Type: String

For a network share, returns the machine name and share name in UNC format (e.g., \\NTSERV1\TestWork). If the Drive object does not represent a network drive, the ShareName property returns a zero-length string ("").

TotalSize

Data Type: Double

The total size of the drive in bytes. In early versions of the Scripting Runtime, the TotalSize property was capable of storing only values that ranged from 0 to 2^{31}, or 2,147,483,648. In other words, in the case of drives larger than 2 GB, it failed to accurately report the total drive size.

In order to check the amount of total space on the drive, the drive must be ready. Otherwise, a "Disk not ready" error is likely to result. This makes it worthwhile to check the value of the IsReady property before attempting to retrieve a drive's free space, particularly if your script is iterating the Drives collection.

VolumeName

Data Type: String

The drive's volume name, if one is assigned (e.g., *DRIVE_C*). If a drive or disk has not been assigned a volume name, the VolumeName property returns an empty string (""). This is the only read/write property supported by the Drive object.

In order to retrieve the volume name, the drive must be ready. Otherwise, a "Disk not ready" error is likely to result. This makes it worthwhile to check the value of the IsReady property before attempting to retrieve a drive's volume name, particularly if your script is iterating the Drives collection.

Drives Collection Object

Returned by   FileSystemObject.Drives property

Createable   No

Library   Microsoft Scripting Runtime

Description   All drives connected to the current machine are included in the Drives collection, even those that aren't currently ready (like removable media drives with no media inserted in them). The Drives collection object is read-only.

The Drives collection cannot be created; instead, it is returned by the Drives property of the FileSystemObject object, as the following code fragment illustrates:

```
Dim oFS, oDrives
Set oFS = CreateObject("Scripting.FileSystemObject")
Set oDrives = oFS.Drives
```

For an overview of the filesystem object model, including the library reference needed to access it, see the "File System Object Model" entry.

Properties

Count

Data Type: Long

Returns the number of Drive objects in the collection.

Item

Syntax: oDrives.Item(*key*)

Data Type: Drive object

Returns a Drive object whose key is *key*, the drive letter. This is an unusual collection, since the drive's index value (its ordinal position in the collection) can't be used; attempting to do so generates runtime error 5, "Invalid procedure call or argument." Since attempting to retrieve a Drive object for a drive that doesn't exist generates runtime error 68, it's a good idea to call the FileSystemObject object's DriveExists method beforehand.

Example

```
Dim ofsFileSys  As FileSystemObject
Dim ofsDrives As Drives
Dim ofsDrive As Drive

Set ofsFileSys = New FileSystemObject
Set ofsDrives = ofsFileSys.Drives
Set ofsDrive = ofsDrives.Item("C")
MsgBox ofsDrive.DriveType
```

See Also   Drive Object, FileSystemObject.Drives Property

End . . . Statement

Syntax

```
End Class
End Function
End If
End Property
End Select
End Sub
End With
```

Description   Ends a procedure or a block of code.

Rules at a Glance

The End statement is used as follows:

Statement	Description
End Class	Marks the end of a class definition
End Function	Marks the end of a Function procedure
End If	Marks the end of an If...Then...Else statement
End Property	Marks the end of a Property Let, Property Get, or Property Set procedure within a Class. ..End Class construct
End Select	Marks the end of a Select Case statement
End Sub	Marks the end of a Sub procedure
End With	Marks the end of a With statement

Programming Tips and Gotchas

The End statement used by itself to terminate the program is not supported within a VBScript script or procedure. Instead you should terminate execution of a procedure prematurely using the Exit... statement. You can also terminate the script or application by calling a method belonging to an object of the object model you are using. These are shown in the following table:

Environment	Method
ASP	Response.End or Session.Abandon
IE	Application.Quit

Environment	Method
Outlook form	Item.Close
Windows Script Host	WScript.Quit

VBA/VBScript Differences

VBA supports the End statement, which immediately terminates execution of code and, in the case of Visual Basic, terminates the application. The End statement, however, is not supported in VBScript.

See Also   Exit Statement

Erase Statement

Syntax

```
Erase arraylist
```

arraylist
>   Use: Required   Data Type: Variant array
>
>   A list of array variables to clear.

Description   Resets the elements of an array to their initial (unassigned) values. In short, Erase "clears out" or empties an array.

Rules at a Glance

- Specify more than one array to be erased by using commas to delimit *arraylist*.

- Fixed array variables remain dimensioned; on the other hand, all memory allocated to dynamic arrays is released.

- After the Erase statement executes, TypeName returns "Variant( )" for a fixed-length array; in addition, the *IsEmpty* function returns True when individual members of the array are passed to it, and comparisons of an individual member of the array with an empty string ("") and with zero both return True. On the other hand, the *TypeName* function returns Empty for a dynamic array, and comparisons of the array with an empty string ("") and zero also return True.

Programming Tips and Gotchas

Once you use Erase to clear dynamic arrays, they must be redimensioned with ReDim before being used again. This is because Erase releases the memory storage used by the dynamic array back to the operating system, which sets the array to have no elements.

VBA/VBScript Differences

Because VBA can be strongly typed, the behavior of the Erase statement in clearing a fixed array varies, depending on the array's data type. The effect of the Erase statement on a fixed variant array in VBScript is described earlier in the "Rules at Glance" section.

See Also   Dim Statement, ReDim Statement

Err Object

Description   The Err object contains properties and methods that allow you to obtain information about a single runtime error in a VBScript script. It also allows you to generate errors and to reset the error object. Because the Err object is an intrinsic object (which means that it's part of every VBScript script you create) with global scope, you don't need to create an instance of it within your code.

When an error is generated in your application—whether it's handled or not—the properties of the Err object are assigned values you can then access to gain information about the error that occurred. You can even generate your own errors explicitly using the Err.Raise method. You can also define your own errors to unify the error-handling process.

When your program reaches an On Error Resume Next or On Error Goto 0 statement, the Err object is cleared and its properties reinitialized. This can also be achieved explicitly using the Err.Clear method.

Properties

Property name	Description
Description	The string associated with the given error number
HelpContext	A context ID within a VBScript Help file
HelpFile	The path to a VBScript Help file
Number	A long integer used to describe an error (i.e., an error code)
Source	Either the name of the current project or the class name of the application that generated the error

Methods

Method name	Description
Clear	Resets all the properties of the Err object
Raise	Forces an error with a particular error code to be generated

Programming Tips and Gotchas

The VBScript Err object isn't a collection; it contains only information about the last error, if one occurred. You could, however, implement your own error collection class to store a number of errors by copying error information from the Err object into an object array that holds error information.

VBA/VBScript Differences

- The VBA Err object includes one additional property, LastDLLError, that reports the last error code generated by a call to a DLL routine.

- In VBA, the Err object is automatically reset whenever an Exit Function, Exit Sub, Exit Property, Resume, or On Error statement is encountered, the Err object is cleared, and its properties reinitialized. In VBScript, this occurs only when an On Error Resume Next or an On Error Goto 0 statement is executed.

See Also   Err.Clear Method, Err.Raise Method, On Error Statement

Err.Clear Method

Syntax

```
Err.Clear
```

Description   Explicitly resets all the properties of the Err object after an error has been handled.

Rules at a Glance

You need to clear the Err object only if you need to reference its properties for another error within the same subroutine or before another On Error Resume Next statement within the same subroutine.

Example

```
On Error Resume Next

i = oObjectOne.MyFunction(iVar)

If Err.Number <> 0 Then
    MsgBox "The Error : " & Err.Description & vbCrLf _
          & " was generated in " & Err.Source
    Err.Clear
End If

j = oObjectTwo.YourFunction(iVar)

If Err.Number <> 0 Then
    MsgBox "The Error : " & Err.Description & vbCrLf _
          & " was generated in " & Err.Source
    Err.Clear
End If
```

Programming Tips and Gotchas

- Resetting the Err object explicitly using the Clear method is necessary when you use On Error Resume Next and test the value of *Err.Number* repeatedly. Unless you reset the Err object, you run the very real risk of catching the previously handled error, the details of which are still lurking in the Err object's properties.

- The Err object is automatically reset when an On Error Resume Next or On Error Goto 0 statement is executed.

- It is also possible to set the Err.Number property to 0 instead of calling up the Err.Clear method. However, this doesn't reset the remaining properties of the Err object.

- When testing the value of *Err.Number*, don't forget that OLE servers often return "negative" numbers. Actually internally they're not really negative, but are unsigned longs. However, since VBScript has no unsigned long data type, its value is represented as a negative number.

VBA/VBScript Differences

In VBA, the Err object is automatically reset by an Exit Function, Exit Sub, Exit Property, Resume, or On Error statement. In VBScript, it's reset only by an On Error statement.

See Also   Err Object, Err.Raise Method, On Error Statement

Err.Description Property

Data Type   String

Description   A read/write property containing a short string describing a runtime error.

Rules at a Glance

- When a runtime error occurs, the Description property is automatically assigned the standard description of the error.
- If there is no error (that is, if the value of Err.Number is 0), the value of the Description property is an empty string.
- For user-defined errors (that is, for errors that you define in your own scripts), you must assign a string expression to the Description property or the error won't have an accompanying textual message.
- You can override the standard description by assigning your own description to the Err object for both VBScript errors and user-defined errors.

Example

This example uses the description parameter of the Err.Raise method to return an error message when validating information from an HTML form. The web page containing the form is:

```
<HTML>
<HEAD>
<TITLE>Register</TITLE>
</HEAD>
<BODY>
<CENTER><H1>Welcome!</H1></CENTER>
Enter Your Name:
<FORM NAME="frmName" METHOD="POST" ACTION="Err_Desc2.asp" >
<INPUT TYPE="text" NAME="txtName">
<INPUT TYPE="submit">
</FORM>
</BODY>
</HTML>
```

The source code for *Err_Desc2.asp* is:

```
<HTML>
<HEAD>
<TITLE>Welcome to our Web Page</TITLE>
<SCRIPT LANGUAGE="VBSCRIPT" RUNAT="Server">
Function ValidateString(sString)
    If sString = "" Then
        Err.Raise 61000,,
            "<H4>Please press the Back button and enter your name.</H4>"
    Else
        ValidateString = sString
    End If
End Function
</SCRIPT>
</HEAD>
```

```
<BODY>
<%
    On Error Resume Next
    Dim sFormName, sName

    sFormName = Server.HTMLEncode(Request.Form.Item("txtName"))
    sName = ValidateString(sFormName)
    If Err.Number = 0 Then
        Response.Write "<H1><CENTER>Welcome, " & sName & "."
    Else
        Response.Write "We encounter an error in the information you
submitted: " & _
"<P>" & Err.Description
    End If
%>
</BODY>
</HTML>Chapter 7
```

Programming Tips and Gotchas

- If you raise an error with the Err.Raise method that does not correspond to a VBScript error and don't set the Description property, the Description property is automatically set to "Unknown runtime error."
- You can also pass the Err.Description to a logging device such as a log file in Windows 95/98/ME or the application log in Windows NT/2000/XP by using the Windows Script Host WSHShell.LogEvent method; for details, see Chapter 7.
- The best way to set the Description property for your own application-defined errors is to use the *description* argument with the Raise method:

  ```
  Err.Raise 65444,, "Meaningful Error Description"
  ```

VBA/VBScript Differences

In VBA, user-defined errors that do not have descriptions are automatically assigned a description of "Application Defined or Object Defined Error." In VBScript, the description is "Unknown runtime error."

See Also   Err Object, Err.Number Property, Err.Raise Method

Err.HelpContext Property

Data Type   Long

Description   A read/write property that either sets or returns a long integer value containing the context ID of the appropriate topic within a Help file.

Rules at a Glance

- The HelpContext property can be set either directly or by supplying the fifth parameter (the *helpcontext* parameter) to the Err.Raise method.
- HelpContext IDs are decided upon when writing and creating a Windows help file. Once the Help or HTML help file has been compiled, the IDs can't be changed. Each ID points to a separate Help topic.

Example

```
On Error Resume Next

Dim i

i = 8
MsgBox (i / 0)
If Err.Number <> 0 Then
    Err.Description = "You are attempting to divide by zero."
    Err.Helpfile = "C:\Windows\help\CustomApp.CHM"
    Err.HelpContext = 1000000 + Err.Number
    MsgBox Err.Description, vbMsgBoxHelpButton, "Error", Err.HelpFile, _
            Err.HelpContext
End If
```

Programming Tips and Gotchas

- You can display a topic from a help file by supplying values to the Err.HelpFile and Err.HelpContext properties, using the *MsgBox* function with the vbMsgBoxHelpButton constant and passing *Err.HelpContext* as the *HelpContext* argument (as shown in the previous example).

- If you supply a HelpContext ID that can't be found in a Windows Help file, the contents page for the Help file should be displayed. However, what actually happens is that a Windows Help error is generated, and a message box is displayed that informs the user to contact their vendor. If you supply a HelpContextID that cannot be found in an HTML Help file, VBScript displays an error message indicating that the Help file is either invalid or corrupted.

- In ASP applications, the HelpContext and HelpFile properties should not be used, since context-sensitive help on the server is undesirable. In Internet Explorer applications, particularly those that are accessible over the Internet, use of the HelpContext and HelpFile properties is not advisable, since you can't be certain that the appropriate help file is available on the client.

VBA/VBScript Differences

- At runtime, the HelpFile and HelpContext properties are automatically set when a VBA runtime error is encountered either because of an actual error or because of a call to the Err.Raise method. When a VBScript-defined error is encountered, on the other hand, these property values are not updated, since it may not make sense to supply help in a scripted environment.

- An invalid HelpContext ID to an HTML Help file causes VBA to display the file's Contents page. It causes VBScript to display an error message noting that the file either is not a help file or has been corrupted.

See Also   MsgBox Function, Err.HelpFile Property, Chapter 4

Err.HelpFile Property

Data Type   String

Description   A read/write string property that contains the fully qualified path of a Windows Help or HTML Help file.

Rules at a Glance

The HelpFile property can be set either directly or by supplying the fourth parameter (the *helpfile* parameter) to the Err.Raise method.

Example

See Err.HelpContext.

Programming Tips and Gotchas

- Some objects you may use within your application have their own help files, which you can access using HelpFile to display highly focused help to your users.

- Remember that once the program encounters an On Error statement, all the properties of the Err object are reset; this includes HelpFile. You must therefore set the Err.HelpFile property each time your application needs to access the help file.

- In ASP applications, the HelpContext and HelpFile properties should not be used, since context-sensitive help on the server is undesirable. In IE applications, particularly those that are accessible over the Internet, use of the HelpContext and HelpFile properties is not advisable, since you can't be certain that the appropriate help file is available on the client.

VBA/VBScript Differences

Much of the utility of the HelpFile and HelpContext properties in VBA stems from the fact that, for errors recognized by the runtime engine, these values are automatically supplied to the Err object and can in turn be passed to the *MsgBox* function. In VBScript, however, these values are not updated automatically; if you want to use a help file or implement context-sensitive help, you have to supply these values yourself.

See Also   Err.HelpContext Property, Err.Number Property, Chapter 4

Err.Number Property

Data Type   Long

Description   A read/write property containing a type Long value that represents the error code for the last error generated.

Rules at a Glance

- When a runtime error is generated within the program, the error code is automatically assigned to Err.Number.

- The Number property is updated with an application-defined error whose code is passed as an argument to the Err.Raise method.

- When using the Err.Raise method in normal code, your user-defined error codes can't be greater than 65536 or less than 0. (See the final note in the "Programming Tips and Gotchas" section of the entry for the Err.Raise method.)

- VBScript uses error numbers in the range of 1–1058 as well as 32766–32767 and 32811 for its own trappable errors. In implementing a series of application-defined errors, your error handlers should either translate application errors into VBScript trappable errors or, preferably, assign a unique range to application-defined errors.

- If your code instantiates an ActiveX server, its error codes should be increased by the value of the VBScript intrinsic constant vbObjectError. When control returns to the local application after an error has been raised by the OLE server, the application can determine that the error originated in the OLE server and extract the error number with a line of code like the following:

```
Dim lError
If ((Err.Number And &HFF00) And vbObjectError) Then
    lError = Err.Number XOr vbObjectError
```

Err.Raise Method

Syntax

```
Err.Raise number, [source], [description], _
            [[helpfile], helpcontext]
```

number
    Use: Required   Data Type: Long integer

    A numeric identifier of the particular error.

source
    Use: Optional   Data Type: String

    The name of the object or application responsible for generating the error.

description
    Use: Optional   Data Type: String

    A useful description of the error.

helpfile
    Use: Optional   Data Type: String

    The fully qualified path of a Microsoft Windows Help or HTML Help file containing help or reference material about the error.

helpcontext
    Use: Optional   Data Type: Long

    The context ID within *helpfile*.

Description   Generates a runtime error.

Rules at a Glance

- To use the Raise method, you must specify an error number.

- If you supply any of the *number*, *source*, *description*, *helpfile*, and *helpcontext* arguments when you call the Err.Raise method, they are supplied as values to the Err object's Number, Source, Description, HelpFile, and HelpContext properties, respectively. Refer to the entries for the individual properties for full descriptions of and rules for each property.

Programming Tips and Gotchas

- The Raise method doesn't reinitialize the Err object prior to assigning the values you pass in as arguments. This can mean that if you Raise an error against an Err object that hasn't been cleared since the last error, any properties you don't specify values for still contain the values from the last error.

- As well as using Raise in a runtime scenario, you can put it to good use in the development stages of your program to test the viability of your error-handling routines under various circumstances.
- The fact that Err.Number accepts only numbers in the range 0–65536 may appear to be strange at first because the data type of the Error Number parameter in the Raise event is a Long; however, deep in the recesses of the Err object, the error code must be declared as an unsigned integer, which is a data type not supported by VBScript.
- When you raise an error in a scripted environment, it may not make sense to supply arguments to the *helpfile* and *helpcontext* parameters. They have no relevance to ASP applications; in IE applications, the help file itself may not be available on the host computer.

See Also   Err Object, Err.Clear Method, Err.HelpContext Property, Err.Number Property, Chapter 4

Err.Source Property

Data Type   String

Description   A read/write string property containing the name of the application or the object that has generated the error.

Rules at a Glance
- When a runtime error occurs in your code, the Source property is automatically assigned the string "Microsoft VBScript runtime error."
- If the error occurs in an ActiveX component instantiated by your application, the Source property usually contains the class name or the programmatic identifier of the component that raised the error.

Programming Tips and Gotchas
Knowing what type of error has occurred within a program is often of little use if you don't know where the error was generated. However, if you enhance the standard Source property by adding the name of the procedure, class, property, or method when you raise an error, your debugging time can be cut dramatically.

See Also   Err Object, Chapter 4

Escape Function

Syntax
```
Escape (string)
string
```

string
    Use: Optional   Data Type: String

    The String to be encoded.

Return Value   An encoded Variant of Type string.

Description   Returns an encoded version of *string*.

Rules at a Glance

- All Unicode characters 255 and below are converted to %xx format except for A–Z, a–z, 0–9, and _*+-./@. For example, a space is replaced by %20.

Programming Tips and Gotchas

- The Escape function is not documented in the VBScript documentation.
- The function corresponds to the JScript escape method.
- You can use the Escape function to encode an HTML document so that a web browser displays the HTML source rather than interprets it. Alternatively, you can use the HTMLEncode method of the ASP Server object to achieve a similar (and more readable) result.
- You can use the Escape function to encode an HTTP query string before returning it to a web server.
- If *string* contains no spaces, punctuation characters, accented characters, or non-ASCII characters, the Escape function simply returns *string* unchanged.

Example

The following is a very simple routine that allows you to experiment with encoding character strings:

```
Option Explicit

Dim sIn, sOut
Do While True
    sIn = InputBox("Enter a string:", "UnescapedString", "")
    If sIn = " Then Exit Do

    sOut = Escape(sIn)

    msgbox "In: " & sIn & vbcrlf & _
Loop
```

For example, the string:

```
This is a level-1 head: <H1>Hello!</H1>
```

returns the string:

```
This%20is%20a%20level-1%20head%3A%20%3CH1%3EHello%21%3C/H1%3E
```

VB/VBA Differences

This function is not supported in VBA.

See Also   Unescape Function

Eval Function

Syntax

```
[result = ]Eval(expression)
```

result
    Use: Optional   Data Type: Any

    A variable to hold the result of the Eval function.

---

expression

> Use: Required   Data Type: String

> The expression to be evaluated.

Return Value   Any

Description   Evaluates an expression and returns the results.

Rules at a Glance

- *Eval* follows the rules of precedence in evaluating *expression*.
- If an equals sign (=) occurs in *expression*, it is interpreted as a comparison oper-ator rather than as an assignment operator. In this case, *Eval* returns True if the parts of *expression* are equal and False if they are not.

Example

In this example, the first result will always evaluate to False, since the variables are not equal, and the second will always evaluate to True, since *Test1* is in fact less than *Test2*:

```
Dim Test1, Test2, Result

Test1 = 4
Test2 = 5
Result = Eval("Test1 = Test2")
MsgBox Result
Result = Eval("Test1 < Test2")
MsgBox Result
Result = Eval("Test1 / Test2")
MsgBox Result
Result = Eval("Test1 - Test2")
MsgBox Result
```

Programming Tips and Gotchas

You may wonder why you'd want to bother with *Eval* when you can do the same thing without it. For example:

```
lVar1 = 2
lVar2 = 3
lResult = lVar1 + lVar2
```

is the same as:

```
lVar1 = 2
lVar2 = 3
lResult = Eval(lVar1 + lVar2)
```

But the significance of *Eval* is that it evaluates expressions stored to strings. For example, the code:

```
Dim sExp, result, a, b, c

a = 10
b = 20
c = 30

sExp = "a + b + c"

result = eval(sExp)
```

returns 60. This means that you can build expressions and assign them to strings dynamically, then have them evaluated by passing them to the *Eval* function.

VBA/VBScript Differences
The *Eval* function is not supported in VBA.

See Also   Execute Statement

Execute Statement

Syntax
```
Execute statement
```
statement
>   Use: Required   Data Type: String expression

>   A string expression containing one or more statements for execution.

Description   Executes one or more statements.

Rules at a Glance
- *statement* must evaluate to a string that contains one or more executable statements. An executable statement is any call to a user-defined procedure or function, or any intrinsic VBScript command.
- You can put multiple statements in the expression; separate them with colons.
- You can also separate the arguments with embedded line breaks.
- If *statement* includes an equal sign, it is interpreted as an assignment rather than an evaluation. For example, x = 3 assigns the value 3 to the variable x, rather than comparing the value of the variable x with 3.
- In VBScript, a program fragment such as x=3 can be interpreted as both an assignment statement (assigning the value 3 to the variable x) or as a comparison expression (for example If x = 3 Then...) The Execute and ExecuteGlobal statements always treat strings of the form a = b as assignment statements. Use *Eval* to interpret strings of this form as expressions.

Example
The following is a corrected version of an example appearing in online help that appears to do nothing. In this case, the Execute statement is used to execute a procedure named Proc2, and the entire source code for the procedure is also stored to the string S that is passed to the Execute statement:

```
dim S

S = "Proc2 : "
S = S & "Sub Proc2 : "
S = S & "Dim x : "
S = S & "x = 10 : "
S = S & "MsgBox X : "
S = S & "End Sub "

Execute S
```

But since the Execute statement only defines Proc2 as a procedure that's visible within the script block but does not execute it, we must also execute Proc2 as follows:

```
dim S

S = "Sub Proc2 : "
S = S & "Dim x : "
S = S & "x = 10 : "
S = S & "MsgBox X : "
S = S & "End Sub "

Execute S
Proc2
```

Programming Tips and Gotchas
- The Execute statement does for executable statements what the *Eval* function does for expressions: it allows you to dynamically (i.e., at runtime) assign code to a string and execute it by passing it to the Execute statement.
- Be careful with this technique, since it can lead to very hard-to-read code.

VBA/VBScript Differences
The Execute statement is not supported by VBA. However, it is not unlike the *Call-ByName* function, which appeared for the first time in VBA 6.0. *CallByName* allows you to execute a routine whose name you store to a variable; hence, the name of the routine need not be determined at design time.

See Also   Eval Function, ExecuteGlobal Statement

ExecuteGlobal Statement

Syntax
```
ExecuteGlobal statement
```
statement
    Use: Required   Data Type: String
    A string expression containing zero or more statements for execution.

Description   Executes zero or more statements in the global namespace of a script.

Rules at a Glance
- *statement* must evaluate to a string containing one or more executable statements. An executable statement is any call to a user-defined procedure or function, or to an intrinsic VBScript command.
- If statement contains multiple statements or lines of code, you can separate them with colons.
- You can also separate statements or lines of code with embedded line breaks (i.e., vbCrLf).
- If *statement* includes an equal sign, it is interpreted as an assignment rather than an evaluation. For example, x = 3 assigns the value 3 to the variable x, rather than comparing the value of the variable x with 3.

- Code created by ExecuteGlobal is executed in the script's *global namespace*. The global namespace is the following:
  - In ASP and IE, code within a <SCRIPT>...</SCRIPT> tag, but outside of individual functions or procedures.
  - In Outlook, form-level code outside of individual event handlers, functions, or procedures.
  - In WSH, code outside of individual functions and procedures.

Example

The example WSH script illustrates the difference between Execute and ExecuteGlobal. Each is called within the *MainProc* procedure to define a subroutine. Execute creates a procedure named Proc2; however, it is only visible if called from *MainProc*. ExecuteGlobal creates a procedure named Proc1 which is globally available throughout the script.

```
Option Explicit

Dim x
x = 10

MainProc
EndProc
'Proc2              ' procedure not visible

Sub MainProc
   Dim x
   x = 20
   ExecuteGlobal "Sub Proc1 : MsgBox x : End Sub"
   Execute "Sub Proc2 : MsgBox x : End Sub"
   Proc2              ' only callable from MainProc
   Proc1
End Sub

Sub EndProc
   Proc1
End Sub
```

Note that both Proc1 and Proc2 access the public variable x, even though a local variable x was visible in *MainProc* when the Execute statement created the Proc2 procedure. If we wanted to pass the local variable x to our routine, we'd have to redefine Proc2 to accept it as a parameter, as follows:

```
Execute "Sub Proc2(ByVal a) : MsgBox a : End Sub"
```

Programming Tips and Gotchas

- While the Execute statement executes code that inherits the scope of the procedure in which it was declared, ExecuteGlobal always executes code in the script's global scope. This has two major implications:
  - After the ExecuteGlobal statement runs, functions, procedures, or classes defined using ExecuteGlobal can be accessed from anywhere within the script.
  - Any variables accessed from code defined by the ExecuteGlobal statement must have global scope. In other words, when using ExecuteGlobal in a local scope, ExecuteGlobal will not see local variables.

VBA/VBScript Differences

The ExecuteGlobal statement is not supported by VBA.

See Also   EvalFunction, Execute Statement

Exit Statement

Syntax

```
Exit Do
Exit For
Exit Function
Exit Property
Exit Sub
```

Description   Prematurely exits a block of code.

Rules at a Glance

Exit Do

> Exits a Do...Loop statement. If the current Do...Loop is within a nested Do...Loop, execution continues with the next Loop statement wrapped around the current one. If, however, the Do...Loop is standalone, program execution continues with the first line of code after the Loop statement.

Exit For

> Exits a For...Next loop. If the current For...Next is within a nested For...Next loop, execution continues with the next Next statement wrapped around the current one. If, however, the For...Next loop is standalone, program execution continues with the first line of code after the Next statement.

Exit Function

> Exits the current function.

Exit Property

> Exits the current property procedure.

Exit Sub

> Exits the current sub procedure.

Programming Tips and Gotchas

- Traditional programming theory recommends one entry point and one exit point for each procedure. However, you can improve the readability of long routines by using the Exit statement. Using Exit Sub can save having to wrap almost an entire subroutine (which could be tens of lines long) within an If...Then statement.

  With Exit Sub:

  ```
  Sub MyTestSub(iNumber)
      If iNumber = 10 Then
          Exit Sub
      End If
      ...'code
  End Sub
  ```

  Without Exit Sub:

  ```
  Sub MyTestSub(iNumber)
      If iNumber <> 10 Then
  ```

```
        ...'code
    End If
End Sub
```

- In the case of the Exit Function, Exit Property, and Exit Sub statements, the point in the program to which program flow returns depends on the caller of the property, function, or sub, respectively, and not on the property, function, or sub itself.

See Also   Do . . . Loop Statement, For . . . Next Statement, For Each . . . Next Statement, Function Statement, Property Get Statement, Property Let Statement, Property Set Statement, Sub Statement

Exp Function

Syntax

```
Exp(number)
```

number

    Use: Required   Data Type: Number

    Any valid numeric expression.

Return Value   A Double representing the antilogarithm of *number*.

Description   Returns the antilogarithm of a number; the antilogarithm is the base of natural logarithms, *e* (whose value is the constant 2.7182818), raised to a power.

Rules at a Glance

The maximum value for *number* is 709.782712893.

Programming Tips and Gotchas

Exp is the inverse of the *Log* function.

See Also   Log Function

File Object

Createable   No

Returned by

    Files.Item property
    FileSystemObject.GetFile method

Library   Microsoft Scripting Runtime

Description   The File object represents a disk file that can be a file of any type and allows you to interrogate the properties of the file and to move upward in the filesystem hierarchy to interrogate the system on which the file resides. The process of instantiating a File object—for example, assigning a reference from the File object's Item property to a local object variable—doesn't open the file. An open file is represented in the File System object model by a TextStream object, which can be generated by the File object's OpenAsTextStream method.

There are several methods of retrieving a reference to an existing File object:

- If you want to work with a particular file, you can retrieve a reference to it directly by calling the GetFile method of the FileSystemObject object. For example:

```
Dim oFS, oFile
Set oFS = CreateObject("Scripting.FileSystemObject")
Set oFile = oFS.GetFile("C:\Documents\MyReport.doc")
```

allows you to retrieve a reference to a File object representing the *MyReport.doc* file without having to use the File System object model to navigate the filesystem.

- If you want to work with a file as a member of a folder or of a set of files, you can retrieve a reference to a File object that represents it from the Item property of the Files collection. (The Files collection is returned by the Files property of a Folder object.) The following code fragment, for instance, retrieves a reference to a file named *MyReport.doc* that is a member of the Documents folder:

```
Dim oFS, oFile
Set oFS = CreateObject("Scripting.FileSystemObject")
Set oFile = oFS.Drives("C").RootFolder.SubFolders("Documents"). _
            Files("MyReport.doc")
```

Note that a File object represents an existing file; you cannot create a File object representing a new file. (You can, however, create a new TextStream object that represents a new text file by calling the Folder object's CreateTextFile method.)

Properties

Attributes

Data Type: Long

Sets or returns the file's attributes. The value of the property represents a bit mask consisting of six flags in the case of a File object, each of which represents a particular file attribute. These values are:

Value	Description
1	Read-only
2	Hidden
4	System
32	Archive
1024	Alias
2048	Compressed

All flags are read/write except for the alias and compressed flags. A value of 0 (normal) indicates that no flags are set.

The attribute flags are represented by the constants of the FileAttribute enumeration in the Scripting Runtime library. You can access them from an ASP page by including the METADATA tag, or from a WSH script by including the following line in a Windows Script Host (*.wsf*) file:

```
<reference GUID="{420B2830-E718-11CF-893D-00A0C9054228}" />
```

You can also add Const statements that define the attribute constants.

DateCreated

    Data Type: Date

    The date and time the file was created; the property is read-only.

DateLastAccessed

    Data Type: Date

    The date and time the file was last accessed. Whether the property includes the date and time or only the date depends on the operating system; Windows 95, Windows 98, and Windows ME, for instance, only return the date, while Windows NT, Windows 2000, and Windows XP return the date and time. The property is read-only.

DateLastModified

    Data Type: Date

    The date and time the file was last modified; the property is read-only.

Drive

    Data Type: Drive object

    Returns a Drive object representing the drive on which the file resides; the property is read-only.

Name

    Data Type: String

    The name of the file. Modifying the value of a File object's Name property renames the file.

ParentFolder

    Data Type: Folder object

    Returns a Folder object representing the folder in which the file resides; the property is read-only.

Path

    Data Type: String

    Returns the full path to the file from the current machine, including drive letter or network path/share name; the property is read-only. Path is the default property of the File object.

ShortName

    Data Type: String

    Returns a DOS 8.3 filename.

ShortPath

    Data Type: String

    Returns a DOS 8.3 folder name. The property is read-only.

Size

    Data Type: Long

    Returns the size of the file in bytes. The property is read-only.

    The Size property holds a long integer, meaning that it accurately reports file sizes from 0 to 2,147,483,648 bytes. In previous versions of VBScript, the property failed to accurately report the size of large files of over 2 GB.

Type

Data Type: String

Returns a string containing the registered type description. This is the type string displayed for the file in Windows Explorer. If a file doesn't have an extension, the type is simply "File." When a file's type isn't registered, the type appears as the extension and "File." The property is read-only.

Methods

Copy
Move
Delete
OpenAsTextStream

File.Copy Method

Syntax

```
oFileObj.Copy Destination [, OverwriteFiles]
```

oFileObj

Use: Required   Data Type: File object

A File object.

Destination

Use: Required   Data Type: String

The path and, optionally, the filename of the copied file.

OverwriteFiles

Use: Optional   Data Type: Boolean

True if the copy operation can overwrite an existing file, False otherwise.

Description   Copies the file represented by *oFileObj* to another location.

Rules at a Glance

Wildcard characters can't be used in *Destination*.

Programming Tips and Gotchas

- If the *Destination* path is set to read-only, the Copy method fails regardless of the *OverwriteFiles* setting and generates a "Permission denied" error.
- If *OverwriteFiles* is False and the file already exists in *Destination*, runtime error 58, "File Already Exists," is generated.
- If the user has adequate rights, *Destination* can be a network path or share name. For example:

```
MyFile.Copy "\\NTSERV1\d$\RootTwo\"
MyFile.Copy "\\NTSERV1\RootTest"
```

See Also   FileSystemObject.CopyFile Method

File.Delete Method

Syntax

oFileObj.Delete [*Force*]

oFileObj
    Use: Required   Data Type: File object

    A File object.

Force
    Use: Optional   Data Type: Boolean

    If set to True, ignores the file's read-only flag (if it's on), and deletes the file.

Description   Removes the current file.

Rules at a Glance

- The Delete method deletes a file permanently; it does not move it to the Recycle Bin.
- If the file is open, the method fails with a "Permission Denied" error.
- The default setting for *Force* is False.
- If *Force* is set to False, and the file is read-only, the method will fail.

Programming Tips and Gotchas

- Unlike the FileSystemObject object's DeleteFile method, which accepts wildcard characters in the path parameter and can therefore delete multiple files, the Delete method deletes only the single file represented by *oFileObj*.
- As a result of the Delete method, the Files collection object containing *oFileObj* is automatically updated, the deleted file is removed from the collection, and the collection count is reduced by one. You shouldn't try to access the deleted file object again; you should set *oFileObj* to Nothing.

See Also   FileSystemObject.DeleteFile Method

File.Move Method

Syntax

oFileObj.Move *destination*

oFileObj
    Use: Required   Data Type: File object

    A File object.

destination
    Use: Required   Data Type: String

    The path to the location where the file is to be moved.

Description   Moves a file from one folder to another.

Rules at a Glance

- The file represented by *oFileObj* must not be open or an error occurs.
- Wildcard characters can't be used in *Destination*.
- *Destination* can be either an absolute or a relative path.

Programming Tips and Gotchas

- If a fatal system error occurs during the execution of this method (like a power failure), the worst that can happen is that the file is copied to the destination but not removed from the source. There are no rollback capabilities built into the File.Move method; however, because the copy part of this two-stage process is executed first, the file can't be lost.
- If a folder or a file by the same name already exists in *destination*, the method generates runtime error 58, "File exists." To prevent this, you can use the FileSystemObject's FileExists and GetAbsolutePath methods prior to calling the Move method.
- Unlike the FileSystemObject's MoveFile method, which accepts wildcard characters in the path parameter and can therefore move multiple files, the Move method moves only the single file represented by *oFileObj*.
- As a result of the Move method, the Files collection object originally containing *oFileObj* is automatically updated, the file is removed from it, and the collection count is reduced by one. You shouldn't try to access the moved file object again in the same Folders collection object.
- *oObj*, the File object reference, remains valid after the file has been moved. Its relevant properties (the Drive, ParentFolder, Path, and ShortPath properties, for example) are all updated to reflect the file's new path after the move.
- If the user has rights, *destination* can be a network path or share name:

  ```
  oFile.Move "\\NTSERV1\d$\RootTwo\myfile.doc"
  ```

See Also   FileSystemObject.MoveFile Method

File.OpenAsTextStream Method

Syntax

```
oFileObj.OpenAsTextStream ([IOMode[, Format]])
```

oFileObj
> Use: Required   Data Type: File object
>
> A File object.

IOMode
> Use: Optional   Data Type: Long
>
> A constant specifying the purpose for opening the file.

Format
> Use: Optional   Data Type: Long
>
> A constant specifying ASCII or Unicode format.

Return Value   A TextStream object.

Description   Opens the referenced text file for reading or writing.

Rules at a Glance

- *IOMode* can be one of the following values:

Constant	Value	Description
ForAppending	8	Opens the file in append mode; that is, the current contents of the file are protected, and new data written to the file is placed at the end of the file.
ForReading	1	Opens the file for reading; you can't write to a file that has been opened for reading.
ForWriting	2	Opens the file for writing; all previous file content is overwritten by new data.

The default value is 1, ForReading.

- The Scripting Runtime type library defines constants of the IOMode enumeration that can be used in place of their numeric equivalents for the *IOMode* argument. You can use them in your scripts in either of two ways. You can define the constants yourself by adding the following code to your script:

```
Const ForReading = 1
Const ForWriting = 2
Const ForAppending = 8
```

You can also include the ASP METADATA tag in *global.asa* or include the following line in a Windows Script Host (*.wsf*) file in order to access the constants from the Scripting Runtime type library:

```
<reference GUID="{420B2830-E718-11CF-893D-00A0C9054228}" />
```

- *Unicode* can be one of the following values:

Constant	Value	Description
TristateUseDefault	−2	Open as System default
TristateTrue	−1	Open as Unicode
TristateFalse	0	Open as ASCII

The default value is 0 or ASCII (TristateFalse).

- The Scripting Runtime type library defines constants of the Tristate enumeration that can be used in place of their numeric equivalents for the *Unicode* argument. You can use them in your scripts in either of two ways. You can define the constants yourself by adding the following code to your script:

```
Const TristateFalse = 0
Const TristateTrue = -1
Const TristateUseDefault = -2
```

You can also include the ASP METADATA tag in *global.asa* or include the following line in a Windows Script Host (*.wsf*) file in order to access the constants from the Scripting Runtime type library:

```
<reference GUID="{420B2830-E718-11CF-893D-00A0C9054228}" />
```

- If another process has opened the file, the method fails with a "Permission Denied" error.

- The TextStream object is so named for a very good reason: it is designed to work with text files rather than binary files. Although it is possible to use the OpenAs

TextStream method to open a binary file, an enormous number of subtle bugs may crop up when you manipulate binary data as text. Because of this, if you want to work with binary files, you should use some technology (like the ADO binary file object) or programming language (like C/C++) that's more amenable to processing binary files.

See Also   FileSystemObject.OpenTextFile Method, TextStream Object

File System Object Model

Library to Reference
Microsoft Scripting Runtime (*SCRRUN.DLL*)

Description   The FileSystemObject is a boon for all developers using any variety of Visual Basic (VBScript, VBA, and VB). It simplifies the task of dealing with any type of file input and output and for dealing with the system file structure itself. Rather than resorting to complex calls to the Win32 API (or, in the case of VBScript, not being able to access the filesystem altogether), this object allows the developer to easily handle files and navigate the underlying directory structures. This is especially useful for those developers or administrators who are creating scripts that are used for system administration or maintenance.

The File System object model is available to both VB and VBA developers, but it is only intrinsically part of the VBScript scripting language. The File System object model allows you to interrogate, create, delete, and manipulate folders and text files.

To access the File System object model, you must first create an instance of the FileSystemObject object, the only externally createable object in the model. From there, you can navigate through the object model, as shown in the object hierarchy diagram in Figure 10-1. The FileSystemObject object can be instantiated with a code fragment like the following:

```
Dim oFS
Set oFS = CreateObject("Scripting.FileSystemObject")
```

It can also be instantiated using the object creation method of the host object model.

See Also   File Object, Files Collection Object, FileSystemObject Object, Folder Object, Folders Collection Object, TextStream Object

Files Collection Object

Createable   No

Returned by Folder.Files property

Library   Microsoft Scripting Runtime

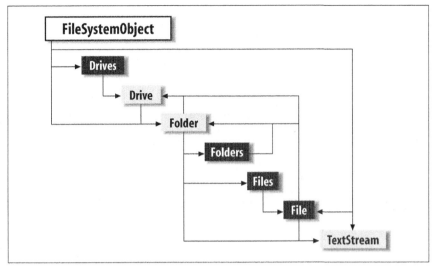

Figure 10-1. The File System object model

Description   The Files collection object is one of the objects in the File System object model; for an overview of the model, including the library reference needed to access it, see the "File System Object Model" entry.

The Files collection object is a container for File objects that is returned by the Files property of any Folder object. All files contained in the folder are included in the Files collection object. You can obtain a reference to a Files collection object using a code fragment like the following:

```
Dim oFS, oFiles

Set oFS = CreateObject("Scripting.FileSystemObject")
Set oFiles = oFS.Drives("C:").RootFolder. _
            SubFolders("Windows").Files
```

This code returns the Files collection for the Windows folder.

You can obtain a reference to an individual File object using the Files collection object's Item property; this takes the exact filename, including the file extension, as an argument. To iterate through the collection, you can use the For Each...Next statement. For details, see the entry for the File Object.

The Files collection object is read-only. Consequently, it supports only the following two properties.

Properties

Count   Data Type: Long

The number of File objects in the collection.

Item   Data Type: File object

Takes the filename (including the file extension) as a parameter and returns the File object representing the file with that name. Individual File objects can't be accessed by their ordinal position in the collection. Item is the Files collection object's default property. The code fragment shown next uses the Item property to retrieve the *autoexec.bat* File object.

```
Dim ofsFiles
Dim ofsFile

Set ofsFileSys = CreateObject("Scripting.FileSystemObject")
Set ofsFiles = ofsFileSys.Drives("C:").RootFolder.Files
Set ofsFile = ofsFiles.Item("autoexec.bat")
MsgBox ofsFile.DateCreated & vbCrLf & _
          ofsFile.DateLastModified & vbCrLf & _
          ofsFile.DateLastAccessed
```

See Also   File System Object Model, File Object

FileSystemObject Object

Createable   Yes

Library   Microsoft Scripting Runtime

Description   The FileSystemObject object is at the top level of the File System object model and is the only externally createable object in the hierarchy; that is, it's the only object you can create using the CreateObject function or the host object model's object creation facilities. For example, the following code instantiates a FileSystemObject object named *oFS*:

```
Dim oFS
Set oFS = CreateObject("Scripting.FileSystemObject")
```

The FileSystemObject object represents the host computer's filesystem as a whole. Its members allow you to begin navigation into the filesystem, as well as to access a variety of common filesystem services. For information about the FileSystemObject object's properties and methods, see the entry for each property and method.

For an overview of the file system object model, see the "File System Object Model" entry.

Properties   Drives (returns a Drives collection object).

Methods

BuildPath	FileExists	GetFileName
CopyFile	FolderExists	GetFolder
CopyFolder	GetAbsolutePathName	GetParentFolderName
CreateFolder	GetBaseName	GetSpecialFolderd
CreateTextFile	GetDrive	GetTempName
DeleteFile	GetDriveName	MoveFile
DeleteFolder	GetExtensionName	MoveFolder
DriveExists	GetFile	OpenTextFile

FileSystemObject.BuildPath Method

Syntax

`oFileSysObj.BuildPath(Path, Name)`

oFileSysObj
    Use: Required   Data Type: FileSystemObject object

    A FileSystemObject object.

Path
    Use: Required   Data Type: String

    A drive and/or folder path.

Name
    Use: Required   Data Type: String

    The folder or file path to append to *path*.

Return Value   A String.

Description   Creates a single string representing a path and filename or simply a path by concatenating the *path* parameter with the folder or filename, adding, where required, the correct path separator for the host system.

Rules at a Glance

- *Path* can be an absolute or relative path and doesn't have to include the drive name.
- Neither *Path* nor *Name* has to currently exist.

Programming Tips and Gotchas

- BuildPath is really a string concatenation method rather than a filesystem method; it does not check the validity of the new folder or filename. If you intend that the method's return value be a path, you should check it by passing it to the FolderExists method; if you intend that the method's return value be a path and filename, you should verify it by passing it to the FileExists method.
- The only advantage to using the BuildPath function as opposed to concatenating two strings manually is that the function selects the correct path separator.

FileSystemObject.CopyFile Method

Syntax

`oFileSysObj.CopyFile Source, Destination [, OverwriteFiles]`

oFileSysObj
    Use: Required   Data Type: FileSystemObject object

    A FileSystemObject object.

Source
    Use: Required   Data Type: String

    The path and name of the file to be copied. The path can be relative or absolute, and the filename (but not the path) can contain wildcard characters.

Destination

    Use: Required   Data Type: String

    The path and optionally the filename of the copy to make. *Destination* cannot include wildcard characters.

OverwriteFiles

    Use: Optional   Data Type: Boolean

    Flag indicating whether an existing file is to be overwritten (True) or not (False). It's default value is True; files of the same names in the target folder will be overwritten.

Description   Copies a file or files from one folder to another.

Rules at a Glance

- The default value for *OverwriteFiles* is True.
- The source path can be relative or absolute.
- The source filename can contain wildcard characters; the source path can't.
- Wildcard characters can't be included in *Destination*.

Programming Tips and Gotchas

- If the destination path or file is read-only, the CopyFile method fails, regardless of the value of *OverwriteFiles* and generates runtime error 70, "Permission Denied."
- If *OverwriteFiles* is set to False and the file exists in *Destination*, a trappable error—runtime error 58, "File Already Exists"—is generated.
- If an error occurs while copying more than one file, the *CopyFile* method exits immediately, thereby leaving the rest of the files uncopied. There is no rollback facility to undo copies made prior to the error.
- Both *Source* and *Destination* can include relative paths—that is, paths that are relative to the current folder. The *current folder* is the folder in which the script is stored, the folder specified in the "Start in" text box of a shortcut, or the folder from which the script is launched from the console mode. The symbol to indicate the parent of the current folder is (..); the symbol to indicate the current folder is (.).
- *Source* must include an explicit filename. For instance, under DOS, you could copy all of the files in a directory with a command in the format of:

```
Copy c:\data c:\bckup
```

    or:

```
Copy c:\data\ c:\bckup
```

    which would copy all the files from the *C:\data* directory to *C:\bckup*. The Source argument cannot take any of these forms; instead, you must include some filename component. For example, to copy all of the files from *C:\data*, the CopyFile statement would take the form:

```
oFS.CopyFile "C:\data\*.*", "C:\bckup"
```

- To specify multiple files, the *Source* argument can include the * and ? wildcard characters. Both are legacies from DOS. * matches any characters in a filename that follow those characters that are explicitly specified. For instance, a *Source* argument of File* matches *File01.txt*, *File001.txt,* and *File.txt*, since all three filenames begin with the string "File"; the remainder of the filename is ignored. ? is a wildcard that ignores a single character in a filename comparison. For instance, a *Source* argument of Fil?01.txt copies *File01.txt* and *Fil_01.txt*, since the fourth character of the filename is ignored in the comparison.

- If you want the source and the destination directories to be the same, you can copy only a single file at a time, since *Destination* does not accept wildcard characters.
- If the path specified in *Destination* does not exist, the method does not create it. Instead, it generates runtime error 76, "Path not found."
- If the user has adequate rights, the source or destination can be a network path or share name. For example:

```
CopyFile "c:\Rootone\*.*", "\\NTSERV1\d$\RootTwo\"
CopyFile "\\NTSERV1\RootTest\test.txt", "c:\RootOne"
```

- The CopyFile method copies a file or files stored in a particular folder. If the folder itself has subfolders containing files, the method doesn't copy these; use the CopyFolder method.
- The CopyFile method differs from the Copy method of the File object in two ways:
  - You can copy any file anywhere in a filesystem without having to first instantiate it as a File object.
  - You can copy multiple files in a single operation, rather than copying only the file represented by the File object.

See Also   FileSystemObject.CopyFolder Method, Folder.Copy Method

FileSystemObject.CopyFolder Method

Syntax

```
oFileSysObj.CopyFolder Source, Destination [, OverwriteFiles]
```

oFileSysObj
    Use: Required   Data Type: FileSystemObject object
    A FileSystemObject object.

Source
    Use: Required   Data Type: String
    The path and name of the folder to be copied from.

Destination
    Use: Required   Data Type: String
    The path for the folder where the copy is to be made.

OverwriteFiles
    Use: Optional   Data Type: Boolean
    Flag indicating whether existing files are to be overwritten (True) or not (False). Its default value is True; files of the same name will be overwritten if they already exist in *Destination*.

Description   Copies the contents of one or more folders, including their subfolders, to another location.

Rules at a Glance

- *Source* must end with either a wildcard character or no path separator. If it ends with a wildcard character, all matching subfolders and their contents will be copied. Wildcard characters can be used in *Source* only for the last component.

- Wildcard characters can't be used in `Destination`.

- All subfolders and files contained within the source folder are copied to *Destination* unless disallowed by the wildcard characters. That is, the Copy-Folder method is recursive.

- If *Destination* ends with a path separator or *Source* ends with a wildcard, Copy-Folder assumes that the folder stated in *Source* exists in *Destination* or should otherwise be created. For example, given the following folder structure:

```
C:\
    Rootone
        SubFolder1
        SubFolder2
    RootTwo
```

The code `FileSys.CopyFolder "c:\Rootone\*", "C:\RootTwo"` produces this folder structure:

```
C:\
    Rootone
        SubFolder1
        SubFolder2
    RootTwo
        SubFolder1
        SubFolder2
```

The code `FileSys.CopyFolder "c:\Rootone", "C:\RootTwo\"` produces this folder structure:

```
C:\
    Rootone
        SubFolder1
        SubFolder2
    RootTwo
        Rootone
            SubFolder1
            SubFolder2
```

Programming Tips and Gotchas

- If the destination path or any of the files contained in *Destination* are set to read-only, the CopyFolder method fails, regardless of the value of `OverwriteFiles`.

- If `OverwriteFiles` is set to `False`, and the source folder or any of the files contained in *Source* exists in *Destination*, runtime error 58, "File Already Exists," is generated.

- If an error occurs while copying more than one file or folder, the *CopyFolder* function exits immediately, leaving the rest of the folders or files uncopied. There is no rollback facility to undo the copies prior to the error.

- If the user has adequate rights, both the source or destination can be a network path or share name. For example:

```
CopyFolder "c:\Rootone", "\\NTSERV1\d$\RootTwo\"
CopyFolder "\\NTSERV1\RootTest", "c:\RootOne"
```

See Also   Folder.Copy Method

FileSystemObject.CreateFolder Method

Syntax

oFileSysObj.CreateFolder(*Path*)

oFileSysObj
    Use: Required   Data Type: FileSystemObject object

    A FileSystemObject object.

Path
    Use: Required   Data Type: String

    An expression that returns the name of the new folder to create.

Return Value   A Folder object.

Description   Creates a single new folder in the path specified and returns its Folder object.

Rules at a Glance

- Wildcard characters aren't allowed in *Path*.
- *Path* can be a relative or absolute path.
- If no path is specified in *Path*, the current drive and directory are used.
- If the last folder in *Path* already exists, the method generates runtime error, "File already exists."

Programming Tips and Gotchas

- If *Path* is read-only, the CreateFolder method fails.
- If *Path* already exists, the method generates runtime error 58, "File already exists."
- If the user has adequate rights, *Path* can be a network path or share name. For example:

```
CreateFolder "\\NTSERV1\d$\RootTwo\newFolder"
CreateFolder "\\NTSERV1\RootTest\newFolder"
```

- You must use the Set statement to assign the Folder object to an object variable. For example:

```
Dim oFileSys
Dim oFolder
Set oFileSys = CreateObject("Scripting.FileSystemObject")
Set oFolder = oFileSys.CreateFolder("MyFolder")
```

See Also   Folders.Add Method

FileSystemObject.CreateTextFile Method

Syntax

oFileSysObj.CreateTextFile *Filename* [, *Overwrite*[, *Unicode*]])

oFileSysObj
    Use: Required   Data Type: FileSystemObject object

    A FileSystemObject object.

Filename
> Use: Required   Data Type: String

> Any valid filename, along with an optional path.

Overwrite
> Use: Optional   Data Type: Boolean

> Flag indicating if an existing file of the same name should be overwritten.

Unicode
> Use: Optional   Variant Sub Type: Boolean

> Flag indicating if *Filename* is to be written in Unicode or ASCII.

Return Value   A TextStream object.

Description   Creates a new file and returns its TextStream object.

Rules at a Glance

- Wildcard characters aren't allowed in *Filename*.
- *Filename* can be a relative or absolute path.
- If no path is specified in *Filename*, the script's current drive and directory are used. If no drive is specified in *Filename*, the script's current drive is used.
- If the path specified in *Filename* doesn't exist, the method fails. To prevent this error, you can use the FileSystemObject object's FolderExists method to insure that the path is valid.
- The default value for *Overwrite* is False.
- If *Unicode* is set to True, the file is created in Unicode; otherwise, it's created as an ASCII text file. The default value for *Unicode* is False.

Programming Tips and Gotchas

- The newly created text file is automatically opened only for writing. If you subsequently wish to read from the file, you must first close it and reopen it in read mode.
- If the path referred to in *Filename* is set to read-only, the CreateTextFile method fails regardless of the value of *Overwrite*.
- If the user has adequate rights, *Filename* can contain a network path or share name. For example:

    ```
    FileSys.CreateTextFile "\\NTSERV1\RootTest\myFile.doc"
    ```

- You must use the Set statement to assign the TextStream object to your local object variable.
- The CreateTextFile method of the Folder object is identical in operation to that of the FileSystemObject object.

See Also   Folder.CreateTextFile Method, TextStream Object

FileSystemObject.DeleteFile Method

Syntax

oFileSysObj.DeleteFile *FileSpec* [, *Force*]

oFileSysObj
    Use: Required   Data Type: FileSystemObject object

    A FileSystemObject object.

FileSpec
    Use: Required   Data Type: String

    The name and path of the file or files to delete.

Force
    Use: Optional   Data Type: Boolean

    If set to True, the read-only flag on a file is ignored and the file deleted. Its default value is False; read-only files will not be deleted.

Description

Permanently removes a given file or files.

Rules at a Glance

- *FileSpec* can contain wildcard characters as the final path component, which allows multiple files to be deleted.
- *FileSpec* can be a relative or absolute path.
- If any of the files specified for deletion are open, the method fails with a "Permission Denied" error.
- If the specified file or files can't be found, the method fails.
- If only a filename is used in *FileSpec*, the application's current drive and directory is assumed.

Programming Tips and Gotchas

- If *FileSpec* specifies a path not ending in a path separator, the method will fail without generating an error. If *FileSpec* specifies a path that ends in a path separator, the method fails and generates runtime error 53, "File not found."
- The DeleteFile method differs from the Delete method of the File object in several respects. First, it allows you to delete a file directly, without first obtaining an object reference to it. Second, by supporting wildcards, it allows you to delete multiple files at once.
- If an error occurs while deleting more than one file, the DeleteFile method exits immediately, thereby leaving the rest of the files undeleted. There is also no rollback facility to undo deletions prior to the error.
- If the user has adequate rights, the source or destination can be a network path or share name. For example:

      DeleteFile "\\NTSERV1\RootTest\myFile.doc"

- DeleteFile permanently deletes files; it doesn't move them to the Recycle Bin.

See Also

Folder.Delete Method

FileSystemObject.DeleteFolder Method

Syntax

```
oFileSysObj.DeleteFolder FileSpec[, Force]
```

oFileSysObj
 Use: Required   Data Type: FileSystemObject object

 A FileSystemObject object.

FileSpec
 Use: Required   Data Type: String

 The name and path of the folders to delete.

Force
 Use: Optional   Data Type: Boolean

 If set to True, the read-only flag on a file is ignored and the file deleted. By default, its value is False; read-only files will not be deleted.

Description   Removes a given folder and all its files and subfolders.

Rules at a Glance

- *FileSpec* can contain wildcard characters as the final path component, which allows multiple folders that meet the file specification to be deleted.
- *FileSpec* can't end with a path separator.
- *FileSpec* can be a relative or absolute path.
- If any of the files within the specified folders are open, the method fails with a "Permission Denied" error.
- The DeleteFolder method deletes all contents of the given folder, including other folders and their contents.
- If the specified folder can't be found, the method fails.

Programming Tips and Gotchas

- If an error occurs while deleting more than one file or folder, the DeleteFolder method exits immediately, thereby leaving the rest of the folders or files undeleted. There is also no rollback facility to undo the deletions prior to the error.
- DeleteFolder permanently deletes folders and their contents; it doesn't move them to the Recycle Bin.
- The DeleteFolder method differs from the Delete method of the Folder object in two respects. First, it allows you to directly delete a folder, without first having to navigate to it or otherwise obtain an object reference to it. Second, it allows you to delete multiple folders, whereas the Delete method allows you to delete only the folder represented by the Folder object.
- If the user has adequate rights, the source or destination can be a network path or share name. For example:

    ```
    FileSys.DeleteFolder "\\NTSERV1\d$\RootTwo"
    ```

See Also   Folder.Delete Method

FileSystemObject.DriveExists Method

Syntax

oFileSysObj.DriveExists (*DriveSpec*)

oFileSysObj
 Use: Required   Data Type: FileSystemObject object

 A FileSystemObject object.

DriveSpec
 Use: Required   Data Type: String

 A path or drive letter.

Return Value Boolean (True or False).

Description Determines whether a given drive (of any type) exists on the local machine or on the network. The method returns True if the drive exists or is connected to the machine, and returns False if not.

Rules at a Glance

- If *DriveSpec* is a Windows drive letter, it doesn't have to include the colon. For example, "*C*" works just as well as "*C:*".

- Returns True if the drive exists or is connected to the machine, and returns False if not.

Programming Tips and Gotchas

- DriveExists doesn't note the current state of removable media drives; for this, you must use the IsReady property of the Drive object representing the given drive.

- If the user has adequate rights, *DriveSpec* can be a network path or share name. For example:

    ```
    If ofs.DriveExists("\\NTSERV1\d$") Then
    ```

- This method is ideal for detecting any current drive around the network before calling a function in a remote ActiveX server located on that drive.

FileSystemObject.Drives Property

Syntax

oFileSysObj.Drives

oFileSysObj
 Use: Required   Variant Type: FileSystemObject object

 A FileSystemObject object.

Return Value Drives collection object.

Description Drives is a read-only property that returns the Drives collection; each member of the collection is a Drive object, representing a single drive available on the system. Using the collection object returned by the Drives property, you can iterate all the drives on the system using a For...Next loop, or you can retrieve an individual Drive object, which represents one drive on the system, by using the Drives collection's Item method.

See Also   Drive Object, Drives Collection Object

FileSystemObject.FileExists Method

Syntax

```
oFileSysObj.FileExists(FileSpec)
```

oFileSysObj
    Use: Required   Data Type: FileSystemObject object

    A FileSystemObject object.

FileSpec
    Use: Required   Data Type: String

    A complete path to the file.

Return Value   Boolean (True or False).

Description   Determines if a given file exists.

Rules at a Glance

- Returns True if the file exists or is connected to the machine, and returns False if not.
- *FileSpec* can't contain wildcard characters.
- *FileSpec* can include either an absolute or a relative path—that is, a path that is relative to the current folder. The *current folder* is the folder in which the script is running, or the folder specified in the "Start in" text box of the shortcut used to launch the script. The symbol to indicate the parent of the current folder is (..); the symbol to indicate the current folder is (.). If *FileSpec* does not include a path, the current folder is used.

Programming Tips and Gotchas

If the user has adequate rights, *FileSpec* can be a network path or share name. For example:

```
If ofs.FileExists("\\TestPath\Test.txt") Then
```

See Also   FileSystemObject.FolderExists Method

FileSystemObject.FolderExists Method

Syntax

```
oFileSysObj.FolderExists(FolderSpec)
```

oFileSysObj
    Use: Required   Data Type: FileSystemObject object

    A FileSystemObject object.

FolderSpec
    Use: Required   Data Type: String

    The complete path to the folder.

Return Value   Boolean (True or False).

Description   Determines whether a given folder exists; the method returns True if the Folder exists, and returns False if not.

Rules at a Glance

- *FolderSpec* can't contain wildcard characters.
- *FolderSpec* cannot include a filename as well as a path. In other words, the entire *FolderSpec* string can only include drive and path information.
- If *FolderSpec* does not include a drive specification, the current drive is assumed.
- *FolderSpec* is interpreted as an absolute path if it begins with a drive name and a path separator, and it is interpreted as an absolute path on the current drive if it begins with a path separator. Otherwise, it is interpreted as a relative path.

Programming Tips and Gotchas

- If the user has adequate rights, *FolderSpec* can be a network path or share name. For example:

      If FileSys.FolderExists("\\NTSERV1\d$\TestPath\") Then

- Among its string manipulation methods, the Scripting Runtime library lacks one that will extract a complete path from a path and filename. The example provides the *GetCompletePath* function to perform this useful task, as well as to illustrate the use of the FolderExists method.

Example

```
Function GetCompletePath(sPath)

Dim oFS
Dim sFileName, sPathName
Dim lPos

Set oFS = CreateObject("Scripting.FileSystemObject")

' Check if no backslash is present
If Instr(1, sPath, "\") = 0 Then
    ' Determine if string is a filename
    If oFS.FileExists(sPath) Then
        ' Return current folder
        GetCompletePath = oFS.GetAbsolutePathName(".")
    Else
        ' Check if folder exists
        If oFS.FolderExists("\" & sPath) Then
            GetCompletePath = sPath
        Else
            ' Raise "Path not found" error
            Err.Raise 76
        End If
    End If
' At least one backslash is present
Else
    ' check if last character is a backslash
    If Right(sPath, 1) = "\" Then
```

```
            If oFS.FolderExists(sPath) Then
                GetCompletePath = sPath
            Else
                Err.Raise 76
            End If
      ' Extract prospective filename from path
      Else
          ' Check if the string includes a filename
          lPos = InstrRev(sPath, "\")
          sFileName = Mid(sPath, lPos + 1)
          If oFS.FileExists(sPath) Then
              GetCompletePath = Left(sPath, lPos)
          Else
              ' Generate file not found error
              Err.Raise 53
          End If
      End If
    End If
  End If

  End Function
```

See Also   FileSystemObject.DriveExists   Method,   FileSystemObject.FileExists
Method

FileSystemObject.GetAbsolutePathName Method

Syntax

   oFileSysObj.GetAbsolutePathName(*Path*)

oFileSysObj
   Use: Required   Data Type: FileSystemObject object
   A FileSystemObject object.

Path
   Use: Required   Data Type: String
   A path specifier.

Return Value   A string containing the absolute path of a given path specifier.

Description   Converts a relative path to a fully qualified path, including the drive letter.

Rules at a Glance

- (.) returns the drive letter and complete path of the current folder.
- (..) returns the drive letter and path of the parent of the current folder.
- If *Path* is simply a filename without a path, the method concatenates the complete path to the current directory with the filename. For example, if the current folder is *C:\Documents\MyScripts*, then the method call:

   sFileName = GetAbsolutePathName("MyFile.txt")

   produces the string "C:\Documents\MyScripts\MyFile.txt".

- All relative pathnames are assumed to originate at the current folder. This means, for example, that (.) returns the drive letter and complete path of the current folder, and that (..) returns the drive letter and path of the parent of the current folder.

- If a drive isn't explicitly provided as part of *Path*, it's assumed to be the current drive.
- Wildcard characters can be included in *Path* at any point.

Programming Tips and Gotchas
- An absolute path provides a complete route from the root directory of a particular drive to a particular folder or file. In contrast, a relative path describes a route from the current folder to a particular folder or file.
- For mapped network drives and shares, the method doesn't return the full network address. Rather, it returns the fully qualified local path and locally issued drive letter.
- The GetAbsolutePathName method is really a string conversion and concatenation method, rather than a filesystem method. It merely returns a string, but doesn't verify that a given file or folder exists in the path specified.

FileSystemObject.GetBaseName Method

Syntax
```
oFileSysObj.GetBaseName(Path)
```
oFileSysObj
    Use: Required   Data Type: FileSystemObject object

    A FileSystemObject object.

Path
    Use: Required   Data Type: String

    A path specifier.

Return Value   A string containing the last element in *Path*.

Description   Returns the name of the last path component, less any extension.

Rules at a Glance
The file extension of the last element in *Path* isn't included in the returned string.

Programming Tips and Gotchas
- GetBaseName doesn't verify that a given file or folder exists in *Path*.
- In stripping the "file extension" and returning the base name of *Path*, GetBaseName has no intelligence. That is, it doesn't know whether the last component of *Path* is a path or a filename. If the last component includes one or more dots, it simply removes the last one, along with any following text. Hence, GetBaseName returns a null string for a *Path* of (.) and it returns (.) for a *Path* of (..). It is, in other words, really a string manipulation function, rather than a file function.

See Also   FileSystemObject.GetExtensionName Method

FileSystemObject.GetDrive Method

Syntax

```
oFileSysObj.GetDrive(drivespecifier)
```

oFileSysObj
> Use: Required   Data Type: FileSystemObject object

> A FileSystemObject object.

drivespecifier
> Use: Required   Data Type: String

> A drive name, share name, or network path.

Return Value   A Drive object.

Description   Obtains a reference to a Drive object for the specified drive.

Rules at a Glance

- If *drivespecifier* is a local drive or the letter of a mapped drive, it can consist of only the drive letter (e.g., "C"), the drive letter with a colon ("C:"), or the drive letter and path to the root directory (e.g., "C:\") without generating a runtime error.

- If *drivespecifier* is a share name or network path, GetDrive ensures that it exists as part of the process of creating the Drive object; if it doesn't, the method generates runtime error 76, "Path not found."

- If the specified drive isn't connected or doesn't exist, runtime error 67, "Device unavailable," occurs.

Programming Tips and Gotchas

- Individual drive objects can be retrieved from the Drives collection by using the Drives property. This is most useful, though, if you want to enumerate the drives available on a system. In contrast, the GetDrive method provides direct access to a particular Drive object.

- If you are deriving the *drivespecifier* string from a path, you should first use GetAbsolutePathName to insure that a drive is present as part of the path. Then you should use FolderExists to verify that the path is valid before calling GetDriveName to extract the drive from the fully qualified path. For example:

```
Dim oFileSys, oDrive

Set oFileSys = CreateObject("Scripting.FileSystemObject")
sPath = oFileSys.GetAbsolutePathName(sPath)
If oFileSys.FolderExists(sPath) Then
    Set oDrive = oFileSys.GetDrive(oFileSys.GetDriveName(sPath))
End If
```

- If *drivespecifier* is a network drive or share, you should use the DriveExists method to confirm the required drive is available prior to calling the GetDrive method.

- You must use the Set statement to assign the Drive object to a local object variable.

See Also   Drives Collection Object

FileSystemObject.GetDriveName Method

Syntax

oFileSysObj.GetDriveName (*Path*)

oFileSysObj
    Use: Required   Data Type: FileSystemObject object

    A FileSystemObject object.

Path
    Use: Required   Data Type: String

    A path specifier.

Return Value   A String.

Description   Returns the drive name of a given path.

Rules at a Glance

If the drive name can't be determined from the given path, a zero-length string (" ") is returned.

Programming Tips and Gotchas

- For local and mapped drives, GetDriveName appears to look for the colon as a part of the drive's name to determine whether a drive name is present. For network drives, it appears to look for the computer name and drive name.

- GetDriveName is really a string-parsing method rather than a filesystem method. In particular, it does not verify that the drive name that it extracts from *Path* actually exists on the system.

- *Path* can be a network drive or share.

FileSystemObject.GetExtensionName Method

Syntax

oFileSysObj.GetExtensionName(*Path*)

oFileSysObj
    Use: Required   Data Type: FileSystemObject object

    A FileSystemObject object.

Path
    Use: Required   Data Type: String

    A path specifier.

Return Value   A String.

Description   Returns the extension of the file element of a given path.

Rules at a Glance

If the extension in *Path* can't be determined, a zero-length string (" ") is returned.

Programming Tips and Gotchas

- GetExtensionName is a string parsing method rather than a filesystem method. It does not verify that *Path* is valid, does not verify that the filename designated in *Path* exists, and does not even guarantee that the value it returns is a valid file extension. In other words, GetExtensionName has no intelligence. It simply parses a string and returns the text that follows the last dot of the last element.
- *Path* can be a network drive or share.

See Also   FileSystemObject.GetBaseName Method

FileSystemObject.GetFile Method

Syntax

> *oFileSysObj*.GetFile(*FilePath*)

oFileSysObj
    Use: Required   Data Type: FileSystemObject object

    A FileSystemObject object.

FilePath
    Use: Required   Data Type: String

    A path and filename.

Return Value   File object.

Description   Returns a reference to a File object.

Rules at a Glance

- *FilePath* can be an absolute or a relative path.
- If *FilePath* is a share name or network path, GetFile ensures that the drive or share exists as part of the process of creating the File object.
- If any part of the path in *FilePath* can't be contacted or doesn't exist, an error occurs.

Programming Tips and Gotchas

- The object returned by GetFile is a File object, not a TextStream object. A File object isn't an open file; the point of the File object is to perform methods such as copying or moving files and interrogating a file's properties. Although you can't write to or read from a File object, you can use the File object's OpenAsText-Stream method to obtain a TextStream object. You can also save yourself a step by calling the FileSystemObject object's OpenTextFile method.
- You should first use GetAbsolutePathName to create the required *FilePath* string.
- If *FilePath* includes a network drive or share, you could use the DriveExists method to confirm that the required drive is available prior to calling the GetFile method.
- Since GetFile generates an error if the file designated in *FilePath* doesn't exist, you should call the FileExists method before calling GetFile.
- You must use the Set statement to assign the File object reference to a local object variable.

See Also   FileSystemObject.GetFolder   Method,   FileSystemObject.GetDrive Method, FileSystemObject.OpenTextFile Method

---

FileSystemObject.GetFileName Method

Syntax

oFileSysObj.GetFileName(*Path*)

oFileSysObj
    Use: Required   Data Type: FileSystemObject object

    A FileSystemObject object.

Path
    Use: Required   Data Type: String

    A path specifier.

Return Value   A String.

Description   Returns the filename element of a given path.

Rules at a Glance

- If the filename can't be determined from the given *Path*, a zero-length string (" ") is returned.

- *Path* can be a relative or absolute reference.

Programming Tips and Gotchas

- GetFileName doesn't verify that a given file exists in *Path*.

- *Path* can be a network drive or share.

- Like all the Get*x*Name methods of the FileSystemObject object, the GetFileName method is more a string manipulation routine that an object-related routine. GetFileName has no built-in intelligence (and, in fact, seems to have even less intelligence than usual for this set of methods); it simply assumes that the last element of the string that is not part of a drive and path specifier is in fact a filename. For example, if *Path* is *C:\Windows*, the method returns the string "Windows"; if Path is *C:\Windows* (which unambiguously denotes a folder rather than a filename), the method still returns the string "Windows."

FileSystemObject.GetFileVersion Method

Syntax

oFileSysObj.GetFileVersion(*FileName*)

oFileSysObj
    Use: Required   Data Type: FileSystemObject object

    A reference to the FileSystemObject object.

FileName
    Use: Required   Data Type: String

    A path and filename.

Return Value   A String.

Description   Retrieves version information about the file specified in *FileName*.

Rules at a Glance

- *FileName* should include the path as well as the name of the file. The path component can be either an absolute or a relative path to the file.
- If path information is omitted, VBScript attempts to find *FileName* in the current folder.
- This function reports version information in the format:

  `Major_Version.Minor_Version.0.Build`

- If a file does not contain version information, the function returns an empty string (" ").

Programming Notes

- The files that can contain version information are executable files (*.exe*) and dynamic link libraries (*.dll*).
- If you're using VBScript to replace a private executable or DLL with another, be particularly careful with version checking, since it has been a particularly serious source of error. Ensuring that the new version of the file should be installed requires that any one of the following conditions be true:
  — It has the same major and minor version but a later build number than the existing file.
  — It has the same major version but a greater minor version number than the existing file.
  — It has a higher version number than the existing file.
- It's also a good idea to copy the replaced file to a backup directory, such as the Windows *Sysbckup* directory.
- If you're thinking of using VBScript to replace a system executable or DLL with another, it's best to use a professional installation program for this purpose.
- Although this function is listed in the type library and is actually implemented in the Scripting Runtime, no documentation for it is available in the HTML Help file.

See Also   ScriptEngineBuildVersion Function, ScriptEngineMajorVersion Function, ScriptEngineMinorVersion Function

---

FileSystemObject.GetFolder Method

Syntax

`oFileSysObj.GetFolder(FolderPath)`

oFileSysObj
    Use: Required   Data Type: FileSystemObject object

    A FileSystemObject object.

FolderPath
    Use: Required   Data Type: String

    A path to the required folder.

Return Value   A Folder object.

Description   Returns a reference to a Folder object.

Rules at a Glance

- *FolderPath* can be an absolute or relative path.
- If *FolderPath* is a share name or network path, GetFolder ensures that the drive or share exists as part of the process of returning the Folder object.
- If any part of *FolderPath* doesn't exist, an error occurs.

Programming Tips and Gotchas

- You should first use GetAbsolutePathName to create the required *FolderPath* string.
- If *FolderPath* includes a network drive or share, you could use the DriveExists method to confirm the required drive is available prior to calling the GetFolder method.
- Since GetFolder requires that *FolderPath* is the path to a valid folder, you should call the FolderExists method to verify that *FolderPath* exists.
- The GetFolder method allows you to directly obtain an object reference to a particular folder. You can also use the Item property of the Folders collection object for cases in which you must navigate the filesystem to reach a particular folder, or for those cases in which you're interested in enumerating the subfolders belonging to a particular folder.
- You must use the Set statement to assign the Folder object reference to a local object variable.

See Also   Folders Collection Object

FileSystemObject.GetParentFolderName Method

Syntax

```
oFileSysObj.GetParentFolderName(Path)
```

oFileSysObj
    Use: Required   Data Type: FileSystemObject object

    A FileSystemObject object.

Path
    Use: Required   Data Type: String

    A path specifier.

Return Value   A String.

Description   Returns the folder name immediately preceding the last element of a given path. In other words, if *Path* ends in a filename, the method returns the path to the folder containing that file. If *Path* ends in a folder name, the method returns the path to that folder's parent.

Rules at a Glance

- If the parent folder name can't be determined from *Path*, a zero-length string (" ") is returned.
- *Path* can be a relative or absolute reference.

Programming Tips and Gotchas

- GetParentFolderName doesn't verify that any element of *Path* exists.
- *Path* can be a network drive or share.
- GetParentFolderName assumes that the last element of the string that isn't part of a drive specifier is the parent folder. It makes no other check than this. As with all the Get*x*Name methods of the FileSystemObject object, the GetParentFolder-Name method is more a string parsing and manipulation routine than an object-related routine.

FileSystemObject.GetSpecialFolder Method

Syntax

```
oFileSysObj.GetSpecialFolder(SpecialFolder)
```

oFileSysObj
    Use: Required   Data Type: FileSystemObject object

    A FileSystemObject object.

SpecialFolder
    Use: Required   Data Type: Special folder constant

    A value specifying one of three special system folders.

Return Value   A Folder object.

Description   Returns a reference to a Folder object of one of the three special system folders: System, Temporary, and Windows.

Rules at a Glance

SpecialFolder can be one of the following special folder constants:

Constant	Value	Description
SystemFolder	1	The Windows system folder (*/windows/system* or */windows/system32*)
TemporaryFolder	2	The folder that stores temporary files (*../windows/temp*)
WindowsFolder	0	The root folder of the Windows system folder tree (*/windows* or */winnt*)

Programming Tips and Gotchas

- As the previous table shows, the Scripting Runtime type library defines constants of the SpecialFolderConst enumeration that can be used in place of their numeric equivalents. You can use them in your scripts in either of two ways. You can define the constants yourself by adding the following code to your script:

```
Const WindowsFolder = 0
Const SystemFolder = 1
Const TemporaryFolder = 2
```

You can also include a METADATA tag in an ASP *global.asa* file or include the following line in a Windows Script Host (*.wsf*) file in order to access the constants from the Scripting Runtime type library:

```
<reference GUID="{420B2830-E718-11CF-893D-00A0C9054228}" />
```

- Prior to the development of the Scripting Runtime Library with its support for the FileSystemObject, the only way to determine the location of system folders was via the Win32 API. This is a much simpler way of getting at that information. This is especially significant when using VBScript with the Windows Script Host, and adds an extremely powerful aspect to writing administrative or maintenance scripts with VBScript.

- You can use the Set statement to assign the Folder object reference to a local object variable. However, if you're interested only in retrieving the path to the special folder, you can do it with a statement like the following:

  ```
  sPath = oFileSys.GetSpecialFolder(iFolderConst)
  ```

  or:

  ```
  sPath = oFileSys.GetSpecialFolder(iFolderConst).Path
  ```

  The first statement works because the Path property is the Folder object's default property. Since the assignment isn't to an object variable, it's the default property's value, rather than the object reference, that is assigned to *sPath*.

- WSH includes a SpecialFolders collection. However, it does not duplicate the functionality of the GetSpecialFolder method.

FileSystemObject.GetStandardStream Method

Syntax

```
oFileSys.GetStandardStream(StandardStreamType, [Unicode])
```

oFileSys
Use: Required   Data Type: FileSystemObject object

A reference to the FileSystemObject object.

StandardStreamType
Use: Required   Data Type: Long

A constant indicating which standard stream (input, output, or error) should be returned by the function.

Unicode
Use: Optional   Data Type: Boolean

A Boolean indicating whether the stream should be Unicode or ASCII.

Return Value   A TextStream object.

Description   Allows you to read from the standard input stream and write to the standard output or standard error streams.

Rules at a Glance

- *StandardStreamType* can be one of the following constants defined in the Scripting Runtime type library:

Constant	Value	Description
StdIn	0	Standard input
StdOut	1	Standard output
StdErr	2	Standard error

- The Scripting Runtime type library defines constants of the StandardStreamTypes enumeration that can be used in place of their numeric equivalents for the *StandardStreamType* argument. You can use them in your scripts in either of two ways. You can define the constants yourself by adding the following code to your script:

```
Const StdIn = 0
Const StdOut = 1
Const StdErr = 2
```

You can also include an ASP METADATA tag in the *global.asa* file or the following line in a Windows Script Host (.*wsf*) file in order to access the constants from the Scripting Runtime type library:

```
<reference GUID="{420B2830-E718-11CF-893D-00A0C9054228}" />
```

- The Unicode parameter can be either Unicode (True) or ASCII (False).

Programming Tips and Gotchas

- The GetStandardStream method is available from a WSH script run in console mode using *CScript.exe* as the WSH engine. Otherwise, attempting to retrieve a reference to the TextStream object returned by the method generates an "Invalid handle" or (in ASP) a "Server.CreateObject failed" error message.

- Note that standard input is a read-only stream, while standard output and standard error are write-only streams.

- Although the function is implemented in the Scripting Runtime library, it is currently undocumented.

- This method is functionally equivalent to three methods in the WSH object model: the WScript.StdIn property, which returns a TextStream object representing the standard input; the WScript.StdOut property, which returns a TextStream object representing the standard output; the WScript.StdErr property, which returns a TextStream object representing the standard error stream.

See Also   TextStream Object

FileSystemObject.GetTempName Method

Syntax

```
oFileSysObj.GetTempName
```

oFileSysObj
    Use: Required   Data Type: FileSystemObject object
    A FileSystemObject object.

Return Value   A String.

Description   Returns a system-generated temporary file or folder name.

Rules at a Glance

GetTempName doesn't create a temporary file or folder; it simply provides a name you can use with the CreateTextFile method.

Programming Tips and Gotchas

- As a general rule, you shouldn't create your own temporary filenames. Windows provides an algorithm within the Windows API to generate the special temporary file and folder names so that it can recognize them later.

- If you are calling GetTempName as the first step in creating a temporary file, you can also call the GetSpecialFolder method to retrieve the path of the temporary directory, as follows:

```
Const TemporaryFolder = 2
Dim oFS, sTempPath
Set oFS = CreateObject("Scripting.FileSystemObject")
sTempPath = oFS.GetSpecialFolder(TemporaryFolder)
```

You can then form the complete path to the temporary folder as follows:

```
<CODE>sFullPath = sTempPath & "' & sTempFileName
```

FileSystemObject.MoveFile Method

Syntax

oFileSysObj.MoveFile *source, destination*

oFileSysObj
    Use: Required   Data Type: FileSystemObject object

    A FileSystemObject object.

source
    Use: Required   Data Type: String

    The path to the file or files to be moved.

destination
    Use: Required   Data Type: String

    The path to the location where the file or files are to be moved.

Description   Moves a file from one folder to another.

Rules at a Glance

- If *source* contains wildcard characters or if *destination* ends in a path separator, *destination* is interpreted as a path; otherwise, its last component is interpreted as a filename.

- If the destination file exists, an error occurs.

- *source* can contain wildcard characters, but only in its last component. This allows multiple files to be moved.

- *destination* can't contain wildcard characters.

- Both *source* and *destination* can be either absolute or relative paths.

- Both *source* and *destination* can be network paths or share names.

Programming Tips and Gotchas

- MoveFile resolves both arguments before beginning the operation.

- Any single file move operation is atomic; that is, any file removed from *source* is copied to *destination*. However, if an error occurs while multiple files are being moved, the execution of the function terminates, but files already moved aren't moved back to their previous folder. If a fatal system error occurs during the execution of this method (like a power failure), the worst that can happen is that the affected file is copied to the destination but not removed from the source. There are no rollback capabilities built into the File.Move method, since, because the copy part of this two-stage process is executed first, the file can't be lost. But while there is no chance of losing data, particularly in multifile operations, it's more difficult to determine whether the move operations have succeeded. This is because an error at any time while files are being moved causes the MoveFile method to be aborted.

- You can use the GetAbsolutePath, FolderExists, and FileExists methods prior to calling the MoveFile method to ensure its success.
- The MoveFile method differs from the File object's Move method by allowing you to directly designate a file to be moved rather than requiring that you first obtain an object reference to it. It also allows you to move multiple files rather than the single file represented by the File object.

See Also   FileSystemObject.CopyFile   Method,   FileSystemObject.FileExists Method, FileSystemObject.GetAbsolutePathName Method

FileSystemObject.MoveFolder Method

Syntax

```
oFileSysObj.MoveFolder source, destination
```

oFileSysObj

Use: Required   Data Type: FileSystemObject object

A FileSystemObject object.

source

Use: Required   Data Type: String

The path to the folder or folders to be moved.

destination

Use: Required   Data Type: String

The path to the location where the folder or folders are to be moved.

Description   Moves a folder along with its files and subfolders from one location to another.

Rules at a Glance

- *source* must end with either a wildcard character or no path separator.
- Wildcard characters can be used in *source*, but only for the last component.
- Wildcard characters can't be used in *destination*.
- All subfolders and files contained within the source folder are copied to *destination* unless disallowed by the wildcard characters. That is, the Move-Folder method is recursive.
- If *destination* ends with a path separator or *Source* ends with a wildcard, Move-Folder assumes the folder in *Source* exists in *Destination*. For example:

```
C:\
   Rootone
      SubFolder1
      SubFolder2
   RootTwo
```

The command MoveFolder "c:\Rootone*", "C:\RootTwo\" produces this folder structure:

```
C:\
    Rootone
    RootTwo
        SubFolder1
        SubFolder2
```

The command MoveFolder "c:\Rootone", "C:\RootTwo\" produces this folder structure:

```
C:\
    RootTwo
        Rootone
            SubFolder1
            SubFolder2
```

- *source* and *destination* can be either absolute or relative paths.
- *source* and *destination* can be network paths or share names.

Programming Tips and Gotchas

- MoveFolder resolves both arguments before starting the operation.
- If a fatal system error occurs during the execution of this method (like a power failure), the worst that can happen is that the file is copied to the destination but not removed from the source. There are no rollback capabilities built into the FileSystemObject.MoveFolder method, since, because the copy part of this two-stage process is executed first, the file can't be lost.
- Although there is no chance of actually losing data, it can be difficult to determine whether the operation has succeeded or failed in the event of an error when multiple folders are being moved. This is because an error in the middle of a multifile move operation causes the MoveFolder method to be abandoned and subsequent folder operations to be aborted.
- You can call the GetAbsolutePath and FolderExists methods before calling the MoveFile method to ensure its success.
- If the user has adequate rights, the source or destination can be a network path or share name. For example:

```
MoveFolder "c:\Rootone", "\\NTSERV1\d$\RootTwo\"
```

See Also FileSystemObject.CopyFile Method, FileSystemObject.FolderExists Method, FileSystemObject.GetAbsolutePathName Method

FileSystemObject.OpenTextFile Method

Syntax

```
oFileSysObj.OpenTextFile(FileName[, IOMode[, Create[, Format]]])
```

oFileSysObj
    Use: Required   Data Type: FileSystemObject object
    A FileSystemObject object.

FileName
    Use: Required   Data Type: String
    The path and filename of the file to open.

IOMode

    Use: Optional   Data Type: Long

    A constant specifying the purpose for opening the file.

Create

    Use: Optional   Data Type: Boolean

    A Boolean flag denoting whether the file should be created if it can't be found in the given path.

Format

    Use: Optional   Data Type: Long

    A constant specifying ASCII or Unicode format.

Return Value   A TextStream object.

Description   Opens (and optionally first creates) a text file for reading or writing.

Rules at a Glance

- File open (IOMode) values are:

Constant	Value	Description
ForAppending	8	Opens the file for appending; that is, the current contents of the file are protected and new data written to the file is placed at the end of the file.
ForReading	1	Opens the file for reading; ForReading files are read-only.
ForWriting	2	Opens the file for writing; all previous file content is overwritten by new data.

- Tristate (*Format*) values are:

Constant	Value	Description
TristateUseDefault	−2	Opens as System default
TristateTrue	−1	Opens as Unicode
TristateFalse	0	Opens as ASCII

- The path element of *FileName* can be relative or absolute.
- The default *IOMode* setting is ForReading (1).
- The default *Format* setting is ASCII (False).
- If another process has opened the file, the method fails with a "Permission Denied" error.

Programming Tips and Gotchas

- You can use the GetAbsolutePath and FileExists methods prior to calling the OpenTextFile method to ensure its success.
- As the table listing values for the *IOMode* parameter shows, the Scripting Runtime type library defines constants of the IOMode enumeration that can be used in place of their numeric equivalents. You can use them in your scripts in either of two ways. You can define the constants yourself by adding the following code to your script:

```
Const ForReading = 1
Const ForWriting = 2
Const ForAppending = 8
```

You can also include a METADATA tag in the ASP *global.asa* file or the following line in a Windows Script Host (*.wsf*) file in order to access the constants from the Scripting Runtime type library:

```
<reference GUID="{420B2830-E718-11CF-893D-00A0C9054228}" />
```

- The value of *IOMode* can be only that of a single constant. For example, a method call such as the following:

```
lMode = ForReading Or ForWriting
oFileSys.OpenTextStream(strFileName, lMode)   ' WRONG
generates runtime error 5, "Invalid procedure call or argument."
```

- As the table listing values for the *Format* parameter shows, the Scripting Runtime type library defines constants of the Tristate enumeration that can be used in place of their numeric equivalents. You can use them in your scripts in either of two ways. You can define the constants yourself by adding the following code to your script:

```
Const TristateFalse = 0
Const TristateTrue = -1
Const TristateUseDefault = -2
```

You can also include a METADATA tag in the ASP *global.asa* file or the following line in a Windows Script Host (*.wsf*) file in order to access the constants from the Scripting Runtime type library:

```
<reference GUID="{420B2830-E718-11CF-893D-00A0C9054228}" />
```

- If the user has adequate rights, the path element of *FileName* can be a network path or share name. For example:

```
OpenTextFile "\\NTSERV1\d$\RootTwo\myFile.txt"
```

See Also   File.OpenAsTextStream Method, TextStream Object

Filter Function

Syntax

```
Filter(SourceArray, FilterString[, Switch[, Compare]])
```

SourceArray

Use: Required   Data Type: String or numeric

An array containing values to be filtered.

FilterString

Use: Required   Data Type: String or numeric

The string of characters to find in the source array.

Switch

Use: Optional   Data Type: Boolean

A Boolean (True or False) value. If True, the default value, *Filter* includes all matching values in *result*; if False, *Filter* excludes all matching values (or, to put it another way, includes all nonmatching values).

Compare

Use: Optional   Data Type: Long

An optional constant (possible values are 0, vbBinaryCompare; 1, vbTextCompare) that indicates the type of string comparison to use. The default value is 0, vbBinaryCompare.

Return Value A String array of the elements filtered from *SourceArray*.

Description Produces an array of matching values from an array of source values that either match or don't match a given filter string. In other words, individual elements are copied from a source array to a target array if they either match or don't match a filter string.

Rules at a Glance

- The default *Switch* value is True.
- The default *Compare* value is 0, vbBinaryCompare.
- vbBinaryCompare is case-sensitive; that is, *Filter* matches both character and case. In contrast, vbTextCompare is case-insensitive, matching only character regardless of case.

Programming Tips and Gotchas

- *SourceArray* elements that are Empty or that contain zero-length strings ("") are ignored by the *Filter* function.
- The array you declare to assign the return value of *Filter* should be a simple variant, as the following code fragment illustrates:

```
Dim aResult
aResult = Filter(sNames, sCriteria, True)
```

- Although the *Filter* function is primarily a string function, you can also filter numeric values. To do this, populate a *SourceArray* with numeric values. Although *FilterString* appears to be declared internally as a variant string, a Long or Integer can be passed to the function. For example:

```
Dim varSource As Variant, varResult As Variant
Dim strMatch As String

strMatch = CStr(2)
varSource = Array(10, 20, 30, 21, 22, 32)
varResult = Filter(varSource, strMatch, True, _
                   vbBinaryCompare)
```

In this case, the resulting array contains four elements: 20, 21, 22, and 32.

- The *Filter* function is an ideal companion to the Dictionary object. The Dictionary object is a collection-like array of values, each of which is stored with a unique string key. The Keys method of the Dictionary object allows you to produce an array of these Key values, which you can then pass into the *Filter* function as a rapid method of filtering the members of your Dictionary, as the following example demonstrates.

Example

```
Dim sKeys
Dim sFiltered
Dim sMatch
Dim blnSwitch
```

```
Dim oDict

Set oDict = CreateObject("Scripting.Dictionary")

oDict.Add "Microsoft", "One Microsoft Way"
oDict.Add "AnyMicro Inc", "31 Harbour Drive"
oDict.Add "Landbor Data", "The Plaza"
oDict.Add "Micron Co.", "999 Pleasant View"

sKeys = oDict.Keys
sMatch = "micro"
blnSwitch = True
'find all keys that contain the string "micro" - any case
sFiltered = Filter(sKeys, sMatch, blnSwitch, _
                    vbTextCompare)
'now iterate through the resulting array
For i = 0 To UBound(sFiltered)
    sMsg = sMsg & sFiltered(i) & ", " & oDict.Item(sFiltered(i)) & _
           vbCrLf
Next
MsgBox sMsg
```

See Also   RegExp Object

Fix Function

Syntax

```
Fix(number)
```

number

> Use: Required   Data Type: Numeric

> Any valid numeric expression.

Return Value   The same data type as passed to the function containing only the integer portion of *number*.

Description   Removes the fractional part of a number. Operates in a similar way to the *Int* function.

Rules at a Glance

* If *number* is Null, *Fix* returns Null.

* The operations of *Int* and *Fix* are identical when dealing with positive numbers: numbers are rounded down to the next lowest whole number. For example, both Int(3.14) and Fix(3.14) return 3.

* If *number* is negative, *Fix* removes its fractional part, thereby returning the next greater whole number. For example, Fix(-3.667) returns –3. This contrasts with *Int*, which returns the negative integer less than or equal to *number* (or –4, in the case of our example).

Example

```
Dim dblTest
Dim varTest
```

```
dblTest = -100.9353
varTest = Fix(dblTest)
' returns -100
Msgbox   varTest & " " & TypeName(varTest)

dblTest = 100.9353
varTest = Fix(dblTest)
'returns 100
Msgbox.Print varTest & " " & TypeName(varTest)
```

Programming Tips and Gotchas

Fix doesn't round *number* to the nearest whole number; it simply removes the fractional part of *number*. Therefore, the integer returned by *Fix* is the nearest whole number less than (or greater than, if the number is negative) the number passed to the function.

See Also   Int Function, CInt Function, CLng Function, Round Function

---

Folder Object

Createable   No

Returned by

> Drive.RootFolder property
> FileSystemObject.CreateFolder method
> FileSystemObject.GetFolder method
> Folder.SubFolders.Item property
> Folders.Add method

Library   Microsoft Scripting Runtime

Description   The Folder object allows you to interrogate the system properties of the folder and provides methods that allow you to copy, move, and delete the folder. You can also create a new text file within the folder.

The Folder object is unusual because with it, you can gain access to a Folders collection object. The more usual method is to extract a member of a collection to gain access to the individual object. However, because the Drive object exposes only a Folder object for the root folder, you have to extract a Folders collection object from a Folder object (the collection represents the subfolders of the root). From this collection, you can navigate downward through the filesystem to extract other Folder objects and other Folders collections. A Boolean property, IsRootFolder, informs you of whether the Folder object you are dealing with currently is the root of the drive.

The Folder object is one of the objects in the Filesystem object model; for an overview of the model, see the "File System Object Model" entry.

Properties

Attributes

> Data Type: Long

> A set of flags representing the folder's attributes. The flags that apply to folders are:

Constant	Value
Archive	32
Directory	16
Hidden	2
ReadOnly	1
System	4

As the table shows, the Scripting Runtime type library defines constants of the `FileAttribute` enumeration that can be used in place of their numeric equivalents. You can use them in your scripts in either of two ways. You can define the constants yourself by adding the following code to your script:

```
Const Normal = 0
Const ReadOnly = 1
Const Hidden = 2
Const System = 4
Const Directory = 16
Const Archive = 32
```

Or you can take advantage of the host's facilities to make the constants accessible. In Active Server Pages, you can include the METADATA tag in the *global.asa* file and provide the type library identifier for the Scripting Runtime as follows:

```
<!-- METADATA TYPE="TypeLib"
    UUID="420B2830-E718-11CF-893D-00A0C9054228"
-->
```

In Windows Script Host, you can include the following line in a *.wsf* file in order to access the constants defined in the Scripting Runtime:

```
<reference GUID="{420B2830-E718-11CF-893D-00A0C9054228}" />
```

You can determine which flag is set by using a logical AND along with the value returned by the property and the value of the flag you'd like to test. For example:

```
If oFolder.Attributes And ReadOnly Then
    ' Folder is read-only
```

To clear a flag, And the value of the Attributes property with a Long in which the flag you want to clear is turned off. For example, the following code clears a Folder object's read-only flag:

```
oFile.Attributes = oFile.Attributes And (Not ReadOnly)
```

Date Created

Data Type: Date

The date and time the folder was created.

DateLastAccessed

Data Type: Date

The date and, if it's available from the operating system, the time that the folder was last accessed.

DateLastModified

Data Type: Date

The date and time the folder was last modified.

Drive

Data Type: Drive object

Returns a Drive object representing the drive on which this folder resides; the property is read-only.

Files

Data Type: Files collection object

Returns a read-only Files collection object representing all files in the current folder.

IsRootFolder

Data Type: Boolean

Returns True if the folder is the root folder of its drive.

Name

Data Type: String

Returns the name of the folder.

ParentFolder

Data Type: Folder object

Returns a folder object representing the folder that's the parent of the current folder. It returns Nothing if the current object is the root folder of its drive (i.e., if its IsRootFolder property is True).

Path

Data Type: String

Returns the complete path of the current folder, including its drive. It is the default property of the Folder object.

ShortName

Data Type: String

Returns a DOS 8.3 folder name without the folder's path. The property is read-only.

ShortPath

Data Type: String

Returns the complete path to a folder in DOS 8.3 format. The property is read-only.

Size

Data Type: Long

Returns the total size of all files, subfolders, and their contents in the folder structure, starting with the current folder. The property is read-only.

In previous versions of the Scripting Runtime, this property failed to accurately report the size of a folder whose files and subfolders occupied more than 2 GB of disk space.

Attempting to retrieve the value of a Folder object's Size property when that folder is a drive's root folder (that is, its IsRootFolder property returns True) generates a runtime error.

SubFolders

Data Type: Folders collection object

Returns a Folders collection object representing all subfolders within the current folder.

Type
    Data Type: String

    Returns the description of a filesystem object, as recorded in the system registry. For Folder objects, the property always returns "File Folder."

Methods
    Copy
    Create TextFile
    Delete
    Move

Folder.Copy Method

Syntax
    oFolderObj.Copy *Destination* [, *OverwriteFiles*]

oFolderObj
    Use: Required   Data Type: Folder object
    A Folder object.

Destination
    Use: Required   Data Type: String
    The path and, optionally, the filename of the copy to be made.

OverwriteFiles
    Use: Optional   Data Type: Boolean
    Indicates whether existing files and folders should be overwritten (True) or not (False).

Description   Copies the current folder and its contents, including other folders, to another location.

Rules at a Glance
- Wildcard characters can't be used in *Destination*.

- The folder and all subfolders and files contained in the source folder are copied to *Destination*. That is, the Copy method is recursive.

- Unlike the FileSystemObject.CopyFolder method, there is no operational difference between ending *Destination* with a path separator or not.

Programming Tips and Gotchas
- If the destination path or any of the files contained in the *Destination* structure are set to read-only, the Copy method will fail regardless of the value of *OverwriteFiles* and will generate a "Permission denied" error.

- If *OverwriteFiles* is set to False, and the source folder or any of the files contained in the *Destination* structure exists in the *Destination* structure, then trappable error 58, "File Already Exists," is generated.

- If an error occurs while copying more than one file, the Copy method exits immediately, leaving the rest of the files uncopied. There is also no rollback facility to undo the copies prior to the error.

- If the user has adequate rights, *Destination* can be a network path or share name. For example:

```
oFolder.Copy "\\NTSERV1\d$\RootTwo\"
```

Folder.CreateTextFile Method

Syntax

```
oFolderObj.CreateTextFile FileName[, Overwrite[, Unicode]])
```

oFolderObj
> Use: Required   Data Type: Folder object
>
> A Folder object.

FileName
> Use: Required   Data Type: String
>
> Any valid filename and optional path.

Overwrite
> Use: Optional   Data Type: Boolean
>
> Flag to indicate whether an existing file of the same name should be overwritten.

Unicode
> Use: Optional   Data Type: Boolean
>
> Flag to indicate whether file is to be written in Unicode or ASCII.

Return Value   A TextStream object.

Description   Creates a new file at the specified location and returns a TextStream object for that file.

Rules at a Glance

- *Filename* can be a relative or absolute path. Wildcard characters are not allowed in *FileName*.
- If no path is specified in *Filename*, the script's current drive and directory are used. If no drive is specified in *Filename*, the script's current drive is used.
- The default value for *Overwrite* is False.
- If *Unicode* is set to True, a Unicode file is created; otherwise it's created as an ASCII text file.
- The default value for *Unicode* is False.

Programming Tips and Gotchas

- If the path specified in *Filename* does not exist, the method fails. To prevent this error, you can use the FileSystemObject object's FolderExists method to be sure that the path is valid.
- The newly created text file is automatically opened only for writing. If you subsequently wish to read from the file, you must first close it and reopen it in read mode.
- If the file referred to in *Filename* already exists as a read-only file, the CreateTextFile method fails regardless of the value of *Overwrite*.

- You must use the Set statement to assign the TextStream object to a local object variable.
- If the user has adequate rights, *Filename* can contain a network path, or share name. For example:

    ```
    oFolder.CreateTextFile "\\NTSERV1\RootTest\myFile.doc"
    ```

- The CreateTextFile method in the Folder object is identical in operation to that in the FileSystemObject object.

See Also   FileSystemObject.CreateTextFile Method, TextStream Object

Folder.Delete Method

Syntax

```
oFolderObj.Delete [Force]
```

oFolderObj
  Use: Required   Data Type: Folder object

  A Folder object.

Force
  Use: Optional   Data Type: Boolean

  If set to True, any read-only flag on a file or a folder to be deleted is ignored and the file or folder is deleted. When set to False, a read-only flag prevents that folder or file from being deleted. Its default value is False.

Description   Removes the folder specified by the Folder object and all its files and subfolders.

Rules at a Glance

- If any of the files within the folder are open, the method fails with a "Permission Denied" error.
- The Delete method deletes all the contents of the given folder, including subfolders and their contents.
- The default setting for *Force* is False. If any of the files in the folder or its subfolders are set to read-only, the method will fail.
- If *Force* is set to False and any of the files in the folders are set to read-only, the method fails.

Programming Tips and Gotchas

- The Delete method deletes a folder and its files and subfolders permanently; it does not move the folder or its files and subfolders to the Recycle Bin.
- If an error occurs while deleting more than one file in the folder, the Delete method exits immediately, thereby leaving the rest of the folders or files undeleted. There is also no rollback facility to undo the deletions prior to the error.
- Unlike the FileSystemObject's DeleteFolder method, which accepts wildcard characters in the path parameter and can therefore delete multiple folders, the Delete method deletes only the single folder represented by the Folder object.

- Immediately after the Delete method executes, the Folder's collection object containing the Folder object is automatically updated. The deleted folder is removed from the collection, and the collection count is reduced by one. You shouldn't try to access the deleted Folder object again, and you should set the local object variable to Nothing, as the following code snippet demonstrates:

```
Set ofsSubFolder = ofsSubFolders.Item("roottwo")
    MsgBox ofsSubFolders.Count
    ofsSubFolder.Delete False
    MsgBox ofsSubFolders.Count
Set ofsSubFolder = Nothing
```

See Also   FileSystemObject.DeleteFile Method, FileSystemObject.DeleteFolder Method

Folder.Move Method

Syntax

```
oFolderObj.Move destination
```

oFolderObj
    Use: Required   Data Type: Folder object

    A Folder object.

destination
    Use: Required   Data Type: String

    The path to the location where the folder or folders are to be moved.

Description   Moves a folder structure from one location to another.

Rules at a Glance

- Wildcard characters can't be used in *destination*.
- If any of the files within the folder being moved are open, an error is generated.
- All subfolders and files contained within the source folder are copied to *destination*, unless disallowed by the wildcard characters. That is, the Move method is recursive.
- *destination* can be either an absolute or a relative path.

Programming Tips and Gotchas

- If a fatal system error (like a power failure) occurs during the execution of this method, the worst that can happen is that the folder is copied to the destination but not removed from the source. There are no rollback capabilities built into the Folder.Move method; since, the copy part of this two-stage process is executed first, the folder can't be lost.
- If an error occurs in the middle of a move operation, the operation is terminated, and the remaining files and folders in the folder aren't moved.
- If a folder or a file by the same name already exists in *destination*, the method generates runtime error 58, "File already exists." To prevent this, you can use the FileSystemObject's FolderExists and GetAbsolutePath methods prior to calling the Move method.

- Unlike the FileSystemObject's MoveFolder method, which accepts wildcard characters in the *source* parameter and can therefore move multiple folders, the Move method moves only the single folder represented by the Folder object and its contents.

- Immediately after the Move method executes, the Folders collection object containing the Folder object is automatically updated, the moved folder is removed from the collection, and the collection count is reduced by one. You shouldn't try to access the moved folder object again from the same Folders collection object.

- *oFolderObj*, the Folder object reference, remains valid after the folder has been moved. Its relevant properties (the Drive, ParentFolder, Path, and ShortPath properties, for example) are all updated to reflect the folder's new path after the move.

- If the user has adequate rights, the destination can be a network path or share name. For example:

  ```
  oFolder.Move "\\NTSERV1\d$\RootTwo\"
  ```

See Also   FileSystemObject.MoveFile Method, FileSystemObject.MoveFolder Method

---

Folders Collection Object

Createable

No

Returned by Folder.SubFolders property

Library Microsoft Scripting Runtime

Description   The Folders collection object is a container for Folder objects. Normally, you'd expect to access a single object from the collection of that object; for example, you'd expect to access a Folder object from the Folders collection object. However, things are the other way around here: you access the Folders collection object from an instance of a Folder object. This is because the first Folder object you instantiate from the Drive object is a Root Folder object, and from it you instantiate a subfolders collection. You can then instantiate other Folder and subfolder objects to navigate through the drive's filesystem.

The Folders collection is a subfolder of any Folder object. For instance, the top-level Folders collection (representing all of the folders in the root directory of a particular drive) can be can be instantiated as follows:

```
Dim oFS, oFolders
Set oFS = CreateObject("Scripting.FileSystemObject")
Set oFolders = oFS.Drives("C").RootFolder.SubFolders
```

The Folders collection object is one of the objects in the File System object model; see the File System object model entry for an overview of the model, including the library reference needed to access it.

Properties

Item

> Data Type: Folder object

> Retrieves a particular Folder object from the Folders collection object. You can access an individual folder object by providing the exact name of the folder without its path. However, you can't access the item using its ordinal number. For example, the following statement returns the Folder object that represents the *roottwo* folder:

```
Set ofsSubFolder = ofsSubFolders.Item("roottwo")
```

Count

> Data Type: Long

> The number of Folder objects contained in the Folders collection.

Methods

> Add

See Also

> Folders.Add Method, Folder Object

Folders.Add Method

Syntax

> *oFoldersCollObj*.Add *newfoldername*

oFoldersCollObj

> Use: Required   Data Type: Folders collection object

> Any object variable returning a Folders collection object.

newfoldername

> Use: Required   Data Type: String

> The name of the new folder.

Return Value   Folder object.

Description   Creates a new folder. The location of the new folder is determined by the parent to which the Folders collection object belongs. For example, if you are calling the Add method from a Folders collection object that is a child of the root Folder object, the new folder is created in the root (i.e., it's added to the root's subfolders collection). For example:

```
Dim oFileSys
Dim oRoot, oChild
Dim oRootFolders

Set oFileSys = CreateObject("Scripting.FileSystemObject")
Set oRoot = oFileSys.Drives("C").RootFolder
Set oRootFolders = oRoot.SubFolders
Set oChild = oRootFolders.Add("Downloads")
```

Rules at a Glance

You can't use a path specifier in *newfoldername*; you can use only the name of the new folder.

See Also   FileSystemObject.CreateFolder Method

For . . . Next Statement

Syntax

```
For counter = initial_value To maximum_value [Step stepcounter]
  code to execute on each iteration
    [Exit For]
Next
```

counter
> Use: Required   Data Type: Numeric
>
> A variable to be used as the loop counter.

initial_value
> Use: Required   Data Type: Numeric
>
> Any valid numeric expression that specifies the loop counter's initial value.

maximum_value
> Use: Required   Data Type: Numeric
>
> Any valid numeric expression that specifies the loop counter's maximum value.

stepcounter
> Use: Optional (required if Step used)   Data Type: Numeric
>
> Any valid numeric expression that indicates how much the loop counter should be incremented with each new iteration of the loop.

Description   Defines a loop that executes a given number of times, as determined by a loop counter. To use the For...Next loop, you must assign a numeric value to a counter variable. This counter is either incremented or decremented automatically with each iteration of the loop. In the For statement, you specify the value that is to be assigned to the counter initially and the maximum value the counter will reach for the block of code to be executed. The Next statement marks the end of the block of code that is to execute repeatedly, and also serves as a kind of flag that indicates the counter variable is to be modified.

Rules at a Glance

- If *initial_value* is greater than *maximum_value*, and no Step keyword is used or the step counter is positive, the For...Next loop is ignored and execution commences with the first line of code immediately following the Next statement.
- If *initial_value* and *maximum_value* are equal and *stepcounter* is 1, the loop executes once.
- *counter* can't be a variable of type Boolean or an array element.
- *counter* is incremented by one with each iteration unless the Step keyword is used.

- If the Step keyword is used, *stepcounter* specifies the amount *counter* is incremented if *stepcounter* is positive or decremented if it's negative.

- If the Step keyword is used, and *stepcounter* is negative, *initial_value* should be greater than *maximum_value*. If this isn't the case, the loop doesn't execute.

- The For...Next loop can contain any number of Exit For statements. When the Exit For statement is executed, program execution commences with the first line of code immediately following the Next statement.

Example

This example demonstrates how to iterate from the end to the start of an array of values:

```
sArray=Array(10, 12, 14, 16, 18, 20, 22, 24)
For  i = UBound(sArray) To LBound(sArray) Step -1
  total = total +sArray(i)
Next
```

This example demonstrates how to select only every other value from an array of values:

```
sArray=Array(10, 12, 14, 16, 18, 20, 22, 24)
For  i = LBound(sArray) To UBound(sArray) Step 2
  total = total +sArray(i)
Next
```

Programming Tips and Gotchas

- You can also nest For...Next loops:

```
    For iDay = 1 to 365
        For iHour = 1 to 23
            For iMinute = 1 to 59
                ...
            Next
        Next
    Next
```

- You should avoid changing the value of *counter* in the code within the loop. Not only can this lead to unexpected results, but it also makes for code that's incredibly difficult to read and to understand.

See Also   For Each . . . Next Statement

For Each . . . Next Statement

Syntax

```
For Each element In group
[statements]
[Exit For]
[statements]
Next
```

element

> Use: Required   Data Type: Variant

> A variable to which the current element from the group is assigned.

---

group
> Use: Required
>
> A collection or an array.

statements
> Use: Optional
>
> A line or lines of program code to execute within the loop.

Description   Loops through the items of a collection or the elements of an array.

Rules at a Glance

- The For...Each code block is executed only if *group* contains at least one element.

- All *statements* are executed for each *element* in *group* in turn until either there are no more elements in *group*, or the loop is exited prematurely using the Exit For statement. Program execution then continues with the line of code following Next.

- For Each...Next loops can be nested, but each *element* must be unique. For example:

```
For Each myObj In anObject
    For Each subObject In myObject
        sName(ctr) = subObject.NameProperty
        ctr = ctr + 1
    Next
Next
```

  uses a nested For Each...Next loop, but two different variables, *myObj* and *subObject*, represent *element*.

- Any number of Exit For statements can be placed with the For Each...Next loop to allow for conditional exit of the loop prematurely. On exiting the loop, execution of the program continues with the line immediately following the Next statement. For example, the following loop terminates once the program finds a name in the *myObj* collection that has fewer than 10 characters:

```
For Each subObject In myObj
    SName = subObject.NameProperty
    If Len(Sname) < 10 then
        Exit For
    End if
Next
```

Programming Tips and Gotchas

- Each time the loop executes when iterating the objects in a collection, an implicit Set statement is executed. The following code reflects the "longhand" method that is useful for explaining what is actually happening during each iteration of the For Each...Next loop:

```
For i = 1 to MyObject.Count
    Set myObjVar = MyObject.Item(i)
    MsgBox myObjVar.Name
Next
```

- Because the elements of an array are assigned to *element* by value, *element* is a local copy of the array element and not a reference to the array element itself. This means that you can't make changes to the array element using For Each...Next and expect them to be reflected in the array once the For Each...Next loop terminates, as demonstrated in the example shown next.

```
Dim strNameArray(1)
Dim intCtr

strNameArray(0) = "Paul"
strNameArray(1) = "Bill"

intCtr = 0

For Each varName In strNameArray
    varName = "Changed"
  Msgbox strNameArray(intCtr)
intCtr = intCtr + 1
Next
```

For example, on the first iteration of the loop, although *varName* has been changed from "Paul" to "Changed," the underlying array element, *strNameArray(0)*, still reports a value of "Paul." This proves that a referential link between the underlying array and object variable isn't present; instead, the value of the array element is passed to *element* by value.

See Also   Exit Statement, For . . . Next Statement

FormatCurrency, FormatNumber, FormatPercent Functions

Syntax

```
FormatCurrency(number[,DecimalPlaces ][, _
    IncLeadingZero[,UseParenthesis[,GroupDigits]]]])
FormatNumber(number[,DecimalPlaces ][, _
    IncLeadingZero[,UseParenthesis[,GroupDigits]]]])
FormatPercent(number[,DecimalPlaces ][, _
    IncLeadingZero[,UseParenthesis[,GroupDigits]]]])
```

number
>   Use: Required   Data Type: Any numeric expression
>
>   The number to be formatted.

DecimalPlaces
>   Use: Optional   Data Type: Long
>
>   Number of digits the formatted string should contain after the decimal point.

IncLeadingZero
>   Use: Optional   Data Type: Long
>
>   Indicates whether the formatted string is to have a 0 before floating-point numbers between 1 and –1.

UseParenthesis
>   Use: Optional   Data Type: Long
>
>   Specifies whether parentheses should be placed around negative numbers.

GroupDigits
>   Use: Optional   Data Type: Long
>
>   Determines whether digits in the returned string should be grouped using the delimiter specified in the computer's regional settings. For example, on American English systems, the value 1000000 is returned as 1,000,000 if *GroupDigits* is True.

Return Value   String

Description   The three functions are almost identical. They all take identical arguments. The only difference is that *FormatCurrency* returns a formatted number beginning with the currency symbol specified in the computer's regional settings, while *FormatNumber* returns just the formatted number, and *FormatPercent* returns the formatted number followed by a percentage sign (%).

Rules at a Glance

*   If *DecimalPlaces* isn't specified, the value in the computer's regional settings is used.

*   Possible values for the *IncLeadingZero*, *UseParenthesis*, and *GroupDigits* parameters are −1, TristateTrue; 0, TristateFalse; and −2, TriStateUseDefault. You can define the constants in your scripts by using the VBScript Const statement as follows:

    ```
    Const TristateTrue = -1
    Const TristateFalse = 0
    Const TristateUseDefault = -2
    ```

If you're using the constants in a WSH script, you could also include the following line in a Windows Script Host (*.wsf*) file in order to access the constants from the Scripting Runtime type library:

```
<reference GUID="{420B2830-E718-11CF-893D-00A0C9054228}" />
```

To access the constants in the ASP page, you can add the following METADATA tag to the application's *global.asa* file:

```
<!--METADATA TYPE="TypeLib"
      UUID="420B2830-E718-11CF-893D-00A0C9054228"
-->
```

Programming Tips and Gotchas

These three functions first appeared in VBScript Version 2 as "light" alternatives to the VBA *Format* function. They are quick and easy to use, and make your code more self-documenting; you can instantly see what format is being applied to a number without having to decipher the format string.

FormatDateTime Function

Syntax

```
FormatDateTime(date[,format])
```

date
    Use: Required   Data Type: Date or String

    Any expression that can be evaluated as a date.

format
    Use: Optional   Data Type: Long

    Defines the format; see the list of values in "Rules at a Glance."

Return Value   String

Description   Formats a date or time expression based on the computer's regional settings.

Rules at a Glance

- The intrinsic constants to use for the format argument are:

vbGeneralDate
> Value: 0
>
> Displays a date and/or time. If there is a date part, displays it as a short date. If there is a time part, displays it as a long time. If present, both parts are displayed. For example:
>
> ```
> MsgBox FormatDate Time(#04/10/03#, vbGeneralDate)
> ```
>
> displays 4/10/2003.

VbLongDate
> Value: 1
>
> Uses the long date format specified in the client computer's regional settings. For example:
>
> ```
> MsgBox FormatDate Time(#04/10/03#, vbLongDate)
> ```
>
> displays Thursday, April 10, 2003.

VbShortDate
> Value: 2
>
> Uses the short date format specified in the client computer's regional settings. For example:
>
> ```
> MsgBox FormatDate Time(#04/10/03#, vbShortDate)
> ```
>
> displays 4/102003.

VbLongTime
> Value: 3
>
> Uses the time format specified in the computer's regional settings. For example:
>
> ```
> MsgBox FormatDate Time(#1:03:00 PM#, vbLong Time)
> ```
>
> displays 1:03:00 PM.

VbShortTime
> Value: 4
>
> Uses a 24-hour format (hh:mm). For example:
>
> ```
> MsgBox FormatDate Time(#1:03:00 PM#, vbShortTime)
> ```
>
> displays 13:03.

- The default date format is vbGeneralDate(0).
- These constants are all defined in the VBScript library and hence are an intrinsic part of the language.

Programming Tips and Gotchas

Remember that date and time formats obtained from the client computer are based on the client computer's regional settings. It's not uncommon for a single application to be used internationally, so that date formats can vary widely. Not only that, but you can never be sure that a user has not modified the regional settings on a computer. In short, never take a date coming in from a client machine for granted; ideally, you should always insure it's in the format you need prior to using it.

Function Statement

Syntax

```
[Public [Default] | Private] Function name [(arglist)] [( )]
    [statements]
    [name = expression]
    [Exit Function]
    [statements]
    [name = expression]
End Function
```

Public

Use: Optional   Type: Keyword

Indicates that the function is accessible in all scripts. If used in a class, indicates that the function is a member of the class's public interface. Public and Private are mutually exclusive; Public is the default.

Default

Use: Optional   Type: Keyword

Defines a method as the default member of a class. It is valid only for a public function defined within a Class...End Class statement. Only one property or method in a class block can be defined as the default member of the class.

Private

Use: Optional   Type: Keyword

Restricts access to the function to other procedures in the script where it is declared. If the function is a member of a class, it makes the function accessible only to other procedures in that class.

name

Use: Required

The name of the function.

arglist uses the following syntax and parts:

Use: Optional

A comma-delimited list of variables to be passed to the function as arguments from the calling procedure.

statements

Use: Optional

Program code to be executed within the function.

expression

Use: Optional

The value to return from the function to the calling procedure.

arglist uses the following syntax and parts:

```
[ByVal | ByRef] varname[( )]
```

ByVal

Use: Optional   Type: Keyword

The argument is passed by value; that is, the local copy of the variable is assigned the value of the argument.

ByRef

Use: Optional   Type: Keyword

The argument is passed by reference; that is, the local variable is simply a reference to the argument being passed. All changes made to the local variable are also reflected in the calling argument. ByRef is the default method of passing variables.

varname

Use: Required

The name of the local variable containing either the reference or value of the argument.

Description   Defines a function procedure.

Rules at a Glance

- If you don't include either Public or Private keywords, a function is Public by default.

- Any number of Exit Function statements can be placed within the function. After an Exit Function statement, execution continues on the line of code from which the function was called. For example, in the code:

  ```
  var = AddOne (AddTwo(x))
  ```

  an Exit Function statement in the *AddTwo* function causes execution to return to the line of code calling the function, so that the *AddOne* function is called next. If a value has not been assigned to the function when the Exit Function statement executes, the function will return Empty.

- The return value of a function is passed back to the calling procedure by assigning a value to the function name. This may be done more than once within the function.

- To return an object reference from a function, the object must be assigned to the function's return value using the Set statement. For example:

  ```
  Set x = GetAnObject ( )

  Function GetAnObject ( )
      Dim oTempObject
      Set    oTempObject = New SomeObject
      oTempObject.Name = "Jane Doe"
      Set  GetAnObject = oTempObject
  End Function
  ```

- VBScript allows you to return arrays of any type from a procedure. Here's a quick example showing this in operation. Here, the *PopulateArray* function is called and is passed a string value. *PopulateArray* takes this value and concatenates the number 0 to 10 to it, assigns each value to an element of an array, then passes this array back to the calling procedure. Note that in the calling procedure, the variable used to accept the array returned from the function is a simple variant that is never explicitly dimensioned as an array:

  ```
  Dim i
  Dim sReturnedArray

  sReturnedArray = PopulateArray("A")

  For i = 0 To UBound(sReturnedArray)
  ```

```
            msgbox sReturnedArray(i)
        Next

        Private Function PopulateArray(sVal)

            Dim sTempArray(10)
            Dim i

            For i = 0 To 10
                sTempArray(i) = sVal & CStr(i)
            Next

            PopulateArray = sTempArray

        End Function
```

Programming Tips and Gotchas

- There is often confusion between the ByRef and ByVal methods of assigning arguments to the function. ByRef assigns a reference to the variable in the calling procedure to the variable in the function; any changes made to the variable from within the function are in reality made to the variable in the calling procedure. On the other hand, ByVal assigns the value of the variable in the calling procedure to the variable in the function. Changes made to the variable in the function have no effect on the variable in the calling procedure.

- Functions can return only one value, or can they? Look at the following code:

```
        Sub testTheReturns( )

            Dim iValOne

            iValOne = 10
            If testValues(iValOne) Then
                Msgbox iValOne
            End If

        End Sub

        Function testValues(ByRef iVal)

            iVal = iVal + 5
            testValues = True

        End Function
```

Because the argument was passed ByRef, the function acted upon the underlying variable *iValOne*. This means you can use ByRef to obtain several "return" values (although they're not strictly return values) from a single function call.

- There are many occasions where you will run into the dreaded (by some!) *recursive* function call. Recursion occurs when you call a function from within itself. Recursion is a legitimate and often essential part of software development; for example, it's an efficient method for enumerating or iterating a hierarchical structure. However, you must be aware that recursion can lead to stack overflow. The extent to which you can get away with recursion really depends upon the complexity of the function concerned, the amount and type of data being passed in, and an infinite number of other variables and unknowns.

See Also   Sub Statement

GetLocale Function

Syntax
```
GetLocale( )
```

Return Value   A Long indicating the current locale ID.

Description   Gets the current locale ID.

Rules at a Glance
- A locale ID represents a language as well as regional conventions. It determines such things as keyboard layout, alphabetic sort order, and date, time, number, and currency formats.
- Appendix D lists valid locale IDs.

Programming Tips and Gotchas
- If you want to temporarily change the locale, there is no need to call *GetLocale* and store its returned value before calling *SetLocale*, since *SetLocale* returns the value of the previous locale ID.
- *GetLocale* returns the locale ID currently in use by the script engine.
- Although you can set the locale using either a decimal, hexadecimal, or string locale ID, the *GetLocale* function returns only a decimal locale ID value.
- The default value of the script engine's locale ID is determined as follows: When the script engine starts up, the host passes it a locale ID. If the host does not do so, the script engine uses the user's default locale ID. If there is no user, then the script engine uses the system's default locale ID.
- Note that the script engine's locale ID is different from the system locale ID, the user locale ID, and the host application's locale ID. The *GetLocale* function reports the locale ID in use by the script engine only.

VBA/VBScript Differences
The *GetLocale* function is not supported by VBA.

See Also   SetLocale Function

GetObject Function

Syntax
```
GetObject([pathname] [, class])
```
pathname
    Use: Optional   Data Type: String

    The full path and filename of a file that stores the state of an automation object, or a moniker (that is, a name that represents an object) along with the information required by the syntax of the moniker to identify a specific object.

Use: Optional   Data Type: String

The object's programmatic identifier (ProgID), as defined in the system registry.

Return Value   A reference to an ActiveX object.

Description   Returns a reference to an automation object. The *GetObject* function has three functions:

- It retrieves references to objects from the Running Object Table.
- It loads persisted state into objects.
- It creates objects based on monikers.

Rules at a Glance

- Although both *pathname* and *class* are optional, at least one argument must be supplied.

- *GetObject* can be used to retrieve a reference to an existing instance of an automation object from the Running Object Table. For this purpose, you supply the object's programmatic identifier as the *class* argument. However, if the object cannot be found in The Running Object Table, *GetObject* is unable to create it and instead returns runtime error 429, "ActiveX component can't create object." To create a new object instance, use the *CreateObject* function.

- If you specify a class argument and specify *pathname* as a zero-length string, *GetObject* returns a new instance of the object—unless the object is registered as single instance, in which case the current instance is returned. For example, the following code launches Excel and creates a new instance of the Excel Application object:

```
Dim  excel
Set   excel = GetObject (" ",   "Excel. Application")
```

In this case, the effect of the function is similar to that of *CreateObject*.

- To assign the reference returned by *GetObject* to your object variable, you must use the Set statement:

```
Dim myObject
Set myObject = GetObject("C:\OtherApp\Library.lib")
```

To load an object's persisted state into an object, supply the filename in which the object is stored as the *pathname* argument and omit the *class* argument.

- The details of how you create different objects and classes are determined by how the server has been written; you need to read the documentation for the server to determine what you need to do to reference a particular part of the object. There are three ways you can access an ActiveX object:

— The overall object library. This is the highest level, and it gives you access to all public sections of the library and all its public classes:

```
GetObject("C:\OtherApp\Library.lib")
```

— A section of the object library. To access a particular section of the library, use an exclamation mark (!) after the filename, followed by the name of the section:

```
GetObject("C:\OtherApp\Library.lib!Section")
```

— A class within the object library. To access a class within the library, use the optional Class parameter:

```
GetObject("C:\OtherApp\Library.lib", "App.Class")
```

- To instantiate an object using a moniker, supply the moniker along with its required arguments. For details, see the discussion of monikers in the Programming Tips and Gotchas section.

Example

The example uses the IIS moniker to retrieve a reference to the IIS metabase. It then iterates the IIS metabase class hierarchy and writes the names of all classes to a file. Its code is:

```
Dim oIIS, oFS, msg, txtStream, filename

fileName = "C: \ IISClasses.txt"

Set oIIS = GetObject ("IIS:// localhost")
IterateClasses oIIS, 0
Set oFS = CreateObject ("Scripting.FileSystemObject")
txtStream.Write  msg
txtStream. Close

MsgBox "IIS Metabse information written to " & filename

Sub IterateClasses (collec, indent)

    Dim oItem

    For  Each oItem In collec
        msg = msg & space(indent) & oItem.Name & vbCrL
            IterateClasses oItem, indent  + 3f
    Next
End  Sub
```

Programming Tips and Gotchas

- Pay special attention to objects registered as single instance. As their type suggests, there can be only one instance of the object created at any one time. Calling *CreateObject* against a single-instance object more than once has no effect; you still return a reference to the same object. The same is true of using *GetObject* with a pathname of " "; rather than returning a reference to a new instance, you obtain a reference to the original instance of the object. In addition, you must use a pathname argument with single-instance objects (even if this is " "); otherwise an error is generated.

- You can't use *GetObject* to obtain a reference to a class created with VBScript; this can only be done using the New keyword.

- The following table shows when to use *GetObject* and *CreateObject*:

Use	Task
CreateObject	Create a new instance of an OLE server
CreateObject	Create a subsequent instance of an already instantiated server (if the server isn't registered as single instance)

Use	Task
GetObject	Obtain a further reference to an already instantiated server without launching a subsequent instance
GetObject	Launch an OLE server application and load an instance of a subobject
CreateObject	Instantiate a class registered on a remote machine
GetObject	Instantiate an object using a moniker

- A *moniker* is simply a name that represents an object without indicating how the object should be instantiated. (It contrasts with a programmatic identifier, for instance, which indicates that information stored in the system registry is used to locate and instantiate an object.) The following are some of the valid monikers recognized by the *GetObject* function, along with their required arguments:

Moniker	Arguments	Description
`IIS:`	*metabasepath*	Retrieves a reference to an IIS metabase object, which allows the programmer to view or modify the configuration of IIS
`JAVA:`	*classname*	Returns a reference to an unregistered Java object stored in the *java\trustlib* folder
`SCRIPT:`	*path*	Returns a reference to an unregistered Windows Script Component
`CLSID:`	*clsid*	Returns a reference to an object based on its class identifier (ClsID) in the system registry
`WINMGMTS:`	*string*	Returns a reference to a WMI object that allows access to core Windows functionality
`QUEUE:`	*clsid* or *progid*	Uses MSMQ to return a reference to a queued COM+ component
`NEW:`	*clsid* or *progid*	Creates a new instance of any COM component that supports the `IClassFactory` interface (that is, of any createable COM component)

See Also   CreateObject Function, Set Statement

GetRef Function

Syntax

```
GetRef(procname)
```

procname
    Use: Required   Data Type: String
    Name of a sub or function

Return Value   A Long containing a reference to *procname*.

Description   Returns a reference to a sub or function. This reference can be used for such purposes as binding to events or defining callback functions.

Rules at a Glance

- *GetRef* can be used whenever a function or procedure reference is expected.
- When using *GetRef* to define event handlers for events, the Set keyword is required. For example, the code required to bind the Window.OnLoad event to a procedure named *ShowGreetingDialog* is:

```
Set Window.OnLoad = GetRef("ShowGreetingDialog")
```

Example

```
<HTML>
<HEAD>
<TITLE>The VBScript GetRef Function</TITLE>
</HEAD>
<BODY>
<SCRIPT LANGUAGE="VBSCRIPT">

Set popWin = Window.CreatePopup( )
Set Window.Onload = GetRef("ShowPopup")

Sub ShowPopup( )
    Set popBody = popWin.Document.Body
    popBody.Style.BackgroundColor = "lightblue"
    popBody.Style.Border = "solid black"
    popBody.innerHTML = "Click outside <B>popup</B> to close."
    popWin.Show 100, 100, 220, 30, Document.body
End Sub

</SCRIPT>
</BODY>
</HTML>
```

Programming Tips and Gotchas

- A common use of *GetRef* is to bind to DHTML events in Internet Explorer. You can use *GetRef* to bind to any of the events in the DHTML object model.
- *GetRef* can be used to pass the address of a procedure to a routine that expects the address of a callback function as an argument.

VBA/VBScript Differences

The *GetRef* function is not supported by VBA. However, similar functionality is provided in VBA by the AddressOf operator, which returns a pointer to (or the address of) a procedure.

See Also   Function Statement, Sub Statement, Set Statement

Hex Function

Syntax

```
Hex(number)
```

number

    Use: Required   Data Type: Numeric or String

    A valid numeric or string expression.

Return Value   String representing the hexadecimal value of *number*.

Description   Returns a string that represents the hexadecimal value of a number.

Rules at a Glance

- If *number* contains a fractional part, it's rounded automatically to the nearest whole number prior to processing. If the number ends in .5, it's rounded to the nearest even whole number.

- *number* must evaluate to a numeric expression that ranges from –2,147,483,648 to 2,147,483,647. If the argument is outside this range, runtime error 6, "Overflow," results.

- The return value of Hex is dependent upon the value and type of *number*:

number	Return value
Null	Null
Empty	Zero (0)
Any other number	Up to eight hexadecimal characters

Programming Tips and Gotchas

If the value of *number* is known beforehand and isn't the result of an expression, you can represent the number as a hexadecimal by simply affixing &H to *number*. Each of the following statements assigns a hexadecimal value to a variable:

```
lngHexValue1 = &HFF                    ' Assigns 255
```

VBA/VBScript Differences

The Hex$ function is not available in VBScript.

See Also   Oct Function

Hour Function

Syntax

```
Hour(time)
```

time
    Use: Required   Data Type: Any expression that can be converted to a date.
    Any valid time expression.

Return Value   A variant of data type Integer representing the hour of the day.

Description   Extracts the hour element from a time expression.

Rules at a Glance

- *Hour* returns a whole number between 0 and 23, representing the hour of a 24-hour clock.

- If *time* contains Null, Null is returned.

See Also   Minute Function, Now Function, Second Function

If . . . Then . . . Else Statement

Syntax

```
If condition Then
    [statements]
[ElseIf condition-n Then
    [elseifstatements] ...
[Else
    [elsestatements]]
End If
```

Or, you can use the single-line syntax:

```
If condition Then [statements] [Else elsestatements]
```

condition

    Use: Required   Data Type: Boolean

    An expression returning either True or False or an object type.

statements

    Use: Optional

    Program code to be executed if *condition* is True.

condition-n

    Use: Optional

    Same as *condition*.

elseifstatements

    Use: Optional

    Program code to be executed if the corresponding *condition-n* is True.

elsestatements

    Use: Optional

    Program code to be executed if the corresponding *condition* or *condition-n* is False.

Description   Executes a statement or block of statements based on the Boolean (True or False) value of an expression.

Rules at a Glance

- If *condition* is True, the statements following the If statement are executed.
- If *condition* is False and no Else or ElseIf statement is present, execution continues with the corresponding End If statement. If *condition* is False and ElseIf statements are present, the condition of the next ElseIf is tested. If *condition* is False, and an Else is present, the statements following the Else are executed.
- In the block form, each If statement must have a corresponding End If statement. ElseIf statements don't have their own End If. For example:

```
If condition Then
    statements
ElseIf condition Then
    statements
End If
```

- ElseIf and Else are optional, and any number of ElseIf and Else statements can appear in the block form. However, no ElseIf statements can appear after an Else.

- *condition* can be any statement that evaluates to True or False.

- If *condition* returns Null, it's treated as False.

- *statements* are optional only in the block form of If. However, *statements* are required when using the single-line form of If in which there is no Else clause.

Programming Tips and Gotchas

- You can use the single-line form of the If statement to execute multiple statements, which you can specify by delimiting the statements using colons; however, single-line form If statements are hard to read and maintain, and should be avoided for all but the simplest of situations.

- In situations where you have many possible values to test, you will find the Select Case statement much more flexible, manageable, and readable than a bunch of nested If statements.

- You will come across situations in which very large blocks of code have to execute based one or more conditions. In these—and in all situations—you should try to make your code as readable as possible, not only for other programmers, but for yourself when you try to maintain the code several months down the line. Take a common scenario in which, at the beginning of a procedure, a check is made to see if the procedure should in fact be executed under the current circumstances. You have the choice of surrounding the whole code with an If...Then...End If construct, like this:

```
If iSuccess Then
    ...
    ...
    ... 'x000 lines of code
End If
```

Or you can switch the result to look for a False, then exit the sub, like this:

```
If Not iSuccess Then
    Exit Sub
End If
.... 'x000 lines of code
```

The difference is that, with the second method, you don't have to scroll down screens worth of code looking for the matching End If.

- Indentation is important for the readability of If, and especially nested If, statements. The recommended indentation is four characters. The set of statements within each new If...Else...End If block should be indented. The following example shows correctly indented code:

```
If x = y Then
    DoSomethingHere
    If y < z Then
        DoSomethingElseToo
    Else
        DoAnotherThing
        If z = 101 Then
            DoAThing
        End If
```

```
        End If
    Else
        DoAlternative
    End If
```

- Use of the If statement requires some understanding of the implicit and explicit use of True in VBScript. The following If statement uses an implicit True:

```
If iSuccess Then
```

Notice that you are allowing VBScript to evaluate the iSuccess variable to True or False. When this implicit form is used, any nonzero value evaluates to True, and conversely, a zero value evaluates to False. The following code evaluates *iSuccess* as True and prints the "OK" message box:

```
Dim iSuccess
iSuccess = 41
If iSuccess Then
    MsgBox "OK"
Else
    MsgBox "False"
End If
```

However, when you compare a variable to an explicit True or False, the value must be –1 to evaluate to True, and 0 for False. If you amend:

```
iSuccess = 41
If iSuccess = True Then
```

iSuccess doesn't evaluate to VB's version of True (–1). As you can imagine, this can lead to some confusion, since a variable can evaluate to True when using an implicit comparison but not when using an explicit comparison. Actually, just to add to the confusion, you could get the explicit comparison to behave the same as the implicit one by converting *iSuccess* to a Boolean:

```
If CBool(iSuccess) = True Then
```

This isn't entirely recommended, but it does show that VBScript's built-in constants of True and False evaluate *only* –1 and 0, respectively.

- Logical comparison operators can be included in the *condition* expression, allowing you to make decisions based on the outcome of more than one individual element. The most common are And and Or. You can create:

```
If x = 1 And y = 3 Then
```

- VBScript always evaluates both sides of a logical comparison, unlike some languages that stop once the value of the expression is known; this is known as *short circuiting*. For example, in the following code, if *x* does equal 1, then the If condition is true. Some languages would stop the evaluation here. But regardless of the value of *x*, VBScript still evaluates the comparison with *y*. This means that the second part of an expression can generate an error even if the result of the expression is already known. This is the case if the second comparison assumes the truth or falsity of the first comparison. For example:

```
If (Not x Is Nothing) And x.SomeProperty = 123   Then    'BAD CODE
```

Here, the first comparison tests whether x is a valid object reference. But the second comparison, which tests the value of the value of x's SomeProperty property, presupposes that x is a valid object reference.

```
If x = 1 Or y = 3 Then
```

- The If statement is also used with objects to determine if an object reference has been successfully assigned to an object variable. (Actually, that's not completely accurate; you check to see whether the object variable is still set to Nothing.) However, you can't use the equality operator (=) for this comparison. Instead, you must use the object comparison operator Is:

```
If Not objectname Is Nothing Then
```

VBA/VBScript Differences

In VBA, you can determine an object type with a statement like:

```
If TypeOf oObj Is CClass Then
```

In VBScript, however, the TypeOf operator is not supported; you must use the *TypeName* function instead.

See Also   Select Case Statement

Initialize Event

Syntax

```
Sub object_Initialize( )
```

Description   Use the Initialize event of a class defined with the Class...End Class construct to prepare the object or class for use, setting any references to subobjects or assigning default values to properties and values to class-level variables.

Rules at a Glance

- The Initialize event is triggered automatically when a class is first instantiated by the Set statement. For example, in the following code, the Set statement generates the Initialize event:

```
Dim MyObject As MyClass
'some code

...
'initialize event called here
Set MyObject = New MyClass
StrName = MyObject.CustName
```

- The Initialize event doesn't take any arguments.
- It is best to declare the Initialize event as Private, although this is not required.

Programming Tips and Gotchas

- While it's possible to explicitly call the Initialize event from within the object at any stage after the object has been created, it isn't recommended, because the code in the Initialize event should be written to be "run once" code.
- Use the Initialize event of a class module to generate references to dependent objects. For example:

```
Option Explicit

Dim custOrder
Set custOrder = New Order
' ...other code
```

```
Class Order
      Private cust, itemsOrdered
      Private Sub Class_Initialize()
         Set cust = New Customer
         Set itemsOrdered = New Items
      End Sub
End Class

Class Customer
      ' Implementation of Customer
End Class

Class Items
      Dim orderItem(10)

      Private Sub Class_Initialize()
         Set orderItem(0) = New Item
      End Sub
      ' Other implementation details of Items collection
End Class

Class Item
      ' Implementation of Item
End Class
```

- The Initialize event is triggered only once, when a new object is created. When an object variable is assigned a reference to an existing object, the Initialize event isn't invoked. For example, in the following code fragment, the Initialize event is invoked only once when the Set objMine1 statement is executed:

```
Dim objMine1, objMine2
Set objMine1 = New MyObj
Set objMine2 = objMine1
```

See Also   Set Statement, Terminate Event

InputBox Function

Syntax

```
InputBox(prompt[, title] [, default] [, xpos] [, ypos] [, helpfile,
context])
```

prompt
    Use: Required   Data Type: String

    The message in the dialog box.

title
    Use: Optional   Data Type: String

    The titlebar of the dialog box.

default
    Use: Optional   Data Type: String

    String to be displayed in the text box on loading.

xpos
Use: Optional   Data Type: Numeric

The distance from the left side of the screen to the left side of the dialog box.

ypos
Use: Optional   Data Type: Numeric

The distance from the top of the screen to the top of the dialog box.

helpfile
Use: Optional   Data Type: String

The Help file to use if the user clicks the Help button on the dialog box.

context
Use: Optional   Data Type: Numeric

The context number to use within the Help file specified in *helpfile*.

Return Value   *InputBox* returns a variant string containing the contents of the text box from the *InputBox* dialog.

Description   Displays a dialog box containing a label, which prompts the user about the data you expect them to input, a text box for entering the data, an OK button, a Cancel button, and optionally, a Help button. When the user clicks OK, the function returns the contents of the text box.

Rules at a Glance

- If the user clicks Cancel, a zero-length string (" ") is returned.
- *prompt* can contain approximately 1,000 characters, including nonprinting characters like the intrinsic vbCrLf constant.
- If the *title* parameter is omitted, "VBScript" is displayed in the titlebar.
- If you don't use the *default* parameter to specify a default entry for the text box, the text box is shown empty; a zero-length string is returned if the user doesn't enter anything in the text box prior to clicking OK.
- *xpos* and *ypos* are specified in twips. A *twip* is a device-independent unit of measurement that equals 1/20 of a point or 1/1440 of an inch.
- If the *xpos* parameter is omitted, the dialog box is centered horizontally.
- If the *ypos* parameter is omitted, the top of the dialog box is positioned approximately one-third of the way down the screen.
- If the *helpfile* parameter is provided, the context parameter must also be provided, and vice versa.
- In VBScript, when both *helpfile* and *context* are passed to the *InputBox* function, a Help button is automatically placed on the *InputBox* dialog, allowing the user to click and obtain context-sensitive help.

Programming Tips and Gotchas

- If you are omitting one or more optional arguments and using subsequent arguments, you must use a comma to signify the missing argument. For example, the following code fragment displays a prompt, a default string in the text box, and the help button, but default values are used for the title and positioning.

```
sString = InputBox("Enter it now", , "Something", , _
    , "help.hlp", 321321)
```

- Because it is a user-interface element that would execute on the server, the *InputBox* function should not be used in Active Server Pages or it will generate runtime error 70, "Permission denied."
- In a client-side web page, it's preferable to rely on HTML intrinsic controls with validation using client-side script, rather than on the *InputBox* function.

VBA/VBScript Differences

In VBA, in an Office-hosted environment, the maximum length of *prompt* is 256 characters. This limitation doesn't exist in VBScript.

See Also   MsgBox Function

InStr, InStrB Functions

Syntax

InStr([*start,*]*stringtosearch, stringtofind*[, *comparemode*])

start
> Use: Optional   Data Type: Numeric

> The starting position for the search.

stringtosearch
> Use: Required   Data Type: String

> The string being searched.

stringtofind
> Use: Required   Data Type: String

> The string being sought.

comparemode
> Use: Optional   Data Type: Integer

> The type of string comparison.

Return Value   A Long.

Description   Finds the starting position of one string within another.

Rules at a Glance

- The return value of *InStr* is influenced by the values of *stringtosearch* and *stringtofind*, as shown in the following table:

Condition	InStr return value
stringtosearch is zero-length	0
stringtosearch is Null	Null
stringtofind is zero-length	*start*
stringtofind is Null	Null
stringtofind is not found	0
stringtofind is found within *stringtosearch*	Position at which the start of *stringtofind* is found
start > len(stringtofind)	0

- If the *start* argument is omitted, *InStr* commences the search with the first character of *stringtosearch*.
- If the *start* argument is Null, an error occurs.
- You must specify a *start* argument if you are specifying a *comparemode* argument.
- VBScript supports intrinsic constants for *comparemode*, as follows:

Comparison mode	Value	Constant
Binary (default)	0	vbBinaryCompare
Text—case- insensitive	1	vbTextCompare

In effect, a binary comparison means that the search for *stringtofind* in *stringtosearch* is case-sensitive. A text comparison means that the search for *stringtofind* in *stringtosearch* is not case-sensitive.

- If the *comparemode* argument contains Null, an error is generated.
- If *comparemode* is omitted, the type of comparison is vbBinaryCompare.

Programming Tips and Gotchas

You can use the *InStrB* function to compare byte data contained within a string. In this case, *InStrB* returns the byte position of *stringtofind*, as opposed to the character position.

VBA/VBScript Differences

In VBA, the default value of the compare parameter is determined by the setting of the Option Compare statement. VBScript, however, does not support the Option Compare statement, and *comparemode* defaults to vbBinaryCompare.

See Also   InstrRev Function, Left, LeftB Functions, Mid, MidB Functions, Right, RightB Functions, StrComp Function

---

InstrRev Function

Syntax

```
InstrRev(sourcestring, soughtstring[, start[, compare]])
```

sourcestring
    Use: Required   Data Type: String

    The string to be searched.

soughtstring
    Use: Required   Data Type: String

    The substring to be found within *sourcestring*.

start
    Use: Optional   Data Type: Numeric

    Starting position of the search. If no value is specified, *start* defaults to 1.

compare
    Use: Optional   Data Type: Integer

    The method that compares *soughtstring* with *sourcestring*; its value can be vbBinaryCompare or vbTextCompare

Return Value   Variant of type Long.

Description   Determines the starting position of a substring within a string by searching from the end of the string to its beginning.

Rules at a Glance

- While *InStr* searches a string from left to right, *InStrRev* searches a string from right to left.
- vbBinaryCompare is case-sensitive; that is, *InstrRev* matches both character and case, whereas vbTextCompare is case-insensitive, matching only character, regardless of case.
- The default value for *compare* is vbBinaryCompare.
- *start* designates the starting point of the search and is the number of characters from the start of the string.
- If *start* is omitted, the search begins from the last character in *sourcestring*.
- *sourcestring* is the complete string in which you want to find the starting position of a substring.
- If *soughtstring* isn't found, *InStrRev* returns 0.
- If *soughtstring* is found within *sourcestring,* the value returned by *InStrRev* is the position of *sourcestring* from the start of the string.

Programming Tips and Gotchas

One of the useful applications of *InstrRev* is to search backward through a path and filename to extract each successive component.

Example

This example uses both *InStr* and *InStrRev* to highlight the different results produced by each. Using a *sourcestring* that states "I like the functionality that *InStrRev* gives," *InStr* finds the first occurrence of "th" at character 8, while *InStrRev* finds the first occurrence of "th" at character 26:

```
Dim myString
Dim sSearch
myString = "I like the functionality that InStrRev gives"
sSearch = "th"

Msgbox InStr(myString, sSearch)
Msgbox InStrRev(myString, sSearch)
```

See Also   InStr, InStrB Functions

Int Function

Syntax

```
Int(number)
```

number

Use: Required   Data Type: Any valid numeric data type

The number to be truncated.

Return Value   Returns a value of the numeric data type passed to it.

Description   Returns the integer portion of a number.

Rules at a Glance

- The fractional part of *number* is removed and the resulting integer value returned. *Int* doesn't round *number* to the nearest whole number; for example, Int(100.9) returns 100.

- If *number* is negative, *Int* returns the first negative integer less than or equal to *number*; for example, Int(-10.1) returns –11.

Programming Tips and Gotchas

- *Int* and *Fix* work identically with positive numbers. However, for negative numbers, *Fix* returns the first negative integer greater than *number*. For example, *Int(-10.1)* returns –10.

- Don't confuse the *Int* function with *CInt*. *CInt* casts the number passed to it as an Integer data type, whereas *Int* returns the same data type that was passed to it.

See Also   Fix Function

Is Operator

Syntax

```
object1 Is object2
```

object1
   Use: Required   Data Type: Object
   An object variable.

object2
   Use: Required   Data Type: Object
   A second object variable.

Return Value   Boolean.

Description   Compares two object variables to determine whether they reference the same object.

Rules at a Glance

- Both *object1* and *object2* must be object references, or runtime error 424, "Object required," results.

- The operation returns a result of True if the object references are identical and False if they are not.

- It is also possible to determine whether an object contains a valid reference by replacing *object2* with the special Nothing keyword. For example:

  ```
  If oDrive Is Nothing Then
  ```

  returns True if *oDrive* does not refer to an object and False if it does. This should be used to test for an uninitialized object reference.

Programming Tips and Gotchas

- Note that objects in VBScript are references—that is, they reference an object in memory. This means that if two variables reference the same object and you make changes to the object's properties using the first object variable, those changes are reflected when you retrieve the object's property settings using the second object variable.

- You may wonder why there is a special Is operator for objects. When you perform a comparison of scalar variables, you want to know whether their values are the same. But in the case of objects, you want to know whether two references point to a single object. (Many objects have identical property values; a test for equal values is meaningless.) This is the reason for the Is operator.

- You can create identical object references in a number of ways. One is by assigning an existing reference to a second object variable:

```
Dim oDrive1, oDrive2
Set oDrive1 = oFS.Drives("C")
Set oDrive2 - oDrive1
```

You can also set two objects equal to a third object reference:

```
Dim oDrive1, oDrive2, oDrive
Set oDrive = oFS.Drives("C")
Set oDrive1 = oDrive
Set oDrive2 = oDrive
```

Finally, you can set both object references equal by retrieving them from the same object in an object model. For example:

```
Dim oDrive1, oDrive2
Set oDrive1 = oFS.Drives("C")
Set oDrive2 - oFS.Drives("C")
```

- Typically, the Is operator is used in an If...Then...Else construct to take some action if objects are the same or if an object reference does not point to a valid object.

IsArray Function

Syntax

```
IsArray(varname)
```

varname

    Use: Required   Data Type: Any

    The name of the variable to be checked.

Return Value   Boolean (True or False).

Description   Tests whether a variable is an array.

Rules at a Glance

If the variable passed to *IsArray* is an array or contains an array, True is returned; otherwise, *IsArray* returns False.

Programming Tips and Gotchas

Due to the nature of variants, it isn't always obvious if a variant variable contains an array, especially if you pass the variant to a function, and the function may or may not attach an array to the variant. Calling any of the array functions—such as *LBound* or *UBound*—or trying to access an element in an array that doesn't exist will obviously generate an error. In these situations, you should first use the *IsArray* function to determine whether you can safely process the array.

IsDate Function

Syntax

    IsDate(*expression*)

expression
    Use: Required   Data Type: Any.

    Variable or expression containing a date or time.

Return Value   Boolean (True or False).

Description   Determines whether a variable's value can be converted to a date.

Rules at a Glance

If the expression passed to *IsDate* is a valid date, True is returned; otherwise, *IsDate* returns False.

Programming Tips and Gotchas

- *IsDate* uses the locale settings of the current Windows system to determine whether the value held within the variable is recognizable as a date. Therefore, what is a legal date format on one machine may fail on another.

- *IsDate* is particularly useful for validating data input.

IsEmpty Function

Syntax

    IsEmpty(*varname*)

varname
    Use: Required   Data Type: Any

    A numeric or string expression.

Return Value   Boolean (True or False).

Description   Determines whether the variable has been initialized by having an initial value (other than Empty) assigned to it.

Rules at a Glance

- If the variant passed to *IsEmpty* has not been initialized, True is returned; otherwise, *IsEmpty* returns False.

- Although *IsEmpty* can take an expression as the value of *varname*, it always returns False if more than one variable is used in the expression. *IsEmpty* is therefore most commonly used with single variables.

Programming Tips and Gotchas

When passed an object variable that has been set equal to Nothing, the *IsEmpty* function returns False. Hence, the function should not be used to test whether a previously initialized object variable now holds a valid object reference.

IsNull Function

Syntax

IsNull(*expression*)

expression

Use: Required   Data Type: Any

An expression containing string or numeric data.

Return Value   Boolean (True or False).

Description   Determines whether *expression* contains is Null.

Rules at a Glance

- If the expression passed to *IsNull* is Null, True is returned; otherwise, *IsNull* returns False.
- All variables in *expression* are checked for null values. If a null value is found in any one part of the expression, True is returned for the entire expression.
- In VBScript, Null is a separate data type that can take on a single value, Null. It is used to indicate that data is missing. Because it represents missing data, all expressions that include a Null value also result in a Null value. This makes perfect sense. For instance, if we have an array containing two valid months of sales data and a Null representing the third month's sales data, the quarter's sales data should also be Null, since accurate data for the quarter is not available.

Programming Tips and Gotchas

- *IsNull* is useful when returning data from a database. You should check field values in columns that allow Nulls against *IsNull* before assigning the value to a collection or other variable. This stops the common "Invalid Use of Null" error from occurring.
- *IsNull* is the only way to evaluate an expression containing a null. For example, the seemingly correct statement:

      If varMyVar = Null Then

  always evaluates to False, even if *varMyVar* is null. This occurs because the value of an expression containing Null is always Null, and therefore False.

IsNumeric Function

Syntax

IsNumeric(*expression*)

expression

Use: Required   Data Type: Any

A numeric or string expression.

Return Value   Boolean (True or False).

Description   Determines whether *expression* can be evaluated as a number.

Rules at a Glance

If the expression passed to *IsNumeric* evaluates to a number, True is returned; otherwise, *IsNumeric* returns False.

Programming Tips and Gotchas

- If *expression* is a date or time, *IsNumeric* evaluates to False.
- If *expression* is a currency value, including a string that includes the currency symbol defined by the Control Panel's Regional Settings applet, *IsNumeric* evaluates to True.

IsObject Function

Syntax

```
IsObject(varname)
```

varname
  Use: Required   Data Type: Any
  Name of the variable to be evaluated.

Return Value   Boolean (True or False).

Description   Indicates whether a variable contains a reference to an object—in other words, if it's an object variable.

Rules at a Glance

If the variable passed to *IsObject* references or has referenced an object, even if its value is Nothing, True is returned; otherwise, *IsObject* returns False.

Programming Tips and Gotchas

- *IsObject* doesn't validate the reference being held by an object variable; it simply determines whether the variable is an object. To ensure that an object reference is valid, you can use the syntax Is Nothing, as shown in this code snippet:

```
If objVar Is Nothing Then
   ...
End if
```

- *IsObject* is simply a "convenience" function that is roughly equivalent to the following user-defined function:

```
Public Function IsObject(varObj)

If VarType(varObj) = vbObject Then
   IsObject = True
Else
   IsObject = False
End If

End Function
```

Join Function

Syntax

```
result = Join(sourcearray, [delimiter])
```

sourcearray
  Use: Required   Data Type: Array

  Array whose elements are to be concatenated.

delimiter
  Use: Optional   Data Type: String

  Character used to delimit the individual values in the string.

Return Value   A type String.

Description   Concatenates an array of values into a delimited string using a specified delimiter.

Rules at a Glance

- If no delimiter is specified, the space character is used as a delimiter.
- The members of *sourcearray* must be convertible to strings. The individual members of *sourcearray* can be any data type except Object. In fact, the individual members of *sourcearray* can be objects as long as the object's default member is not another object. For example, the *Join* function in the code fragment:

  ```
  Set oFS = CreateObject("Scripting.FIleSystemObject")
  Set oDrive1 = oFS.Drives("C")
  Set oDrive2 = oFS.DRives("D")

  Set vArr(0) = oDrive1
  Set vArr(1) = oDrive2

  sJoin = Join(vArr, ",")
  returns the string "C:,D:".
  ```

- When a delimiter is specified, unused *sourcearray* elements are noted in the return string by the use of the delimiter. For example, if you specify a delimiter of "," and a source array with 11 elements, of which only the first two are used, *Join* returns a string similar to the following:

  ```
  "a,b,,,,,,,,,"
  ```

Programming Tips and Gotchas

The *Join* function is ideal for quickly and efficiently writing out a comma-delimited text file from an array of values.

LBound Function

Syntax

LBound(*arrayname*[, *dimension*])

arrayname
Use: Required   Data Type: Array

The name of the array.

dimension
Use: Optional   Data Type: Long

A number specifying the dimension of the array.

Return Value   A Long.

Description   Determines the lower limit of a specified dimension of an array. The lower boundary is the smallest subscript you can access within the specified array.

Rules at a Glance

If *dimension* isn't specified, 1 is assumed. To determine the lower limit of the first dimension of an array, set *dimension* to 1, to 2 for the second, and so on.

Programming Tips and Gotchas

- This function appears to have little use in VBScript, since VBScript does not allow you to control the lower bound of an array. Its value, which is 0, is invariable. However, it is possible for ActiveX components created using Visual Basic to return a array with a lower bound other than 0 to a VBScript script.

- *LBound* is useful when handling arrays passed by ActiveX controls written in VB, since these may have a lower bound other than 0.

VBScript/VB & VBA Differences

Unlike VBA, there is no Option Base available in VBScript, nor does VBScript support the To keyword in the Dim, Private, Public, and ReDim statements. Therefore, all arrays will have a lower bound of 0.

See Also   Array Function, UBound Function

LCase Function

Syntax

LCase(*string*)

string
Use: Required   Data Type: String

A valid string expression.

Return Value   A String.

Description   Converts a string to lowercase.

Rules at a Glance

- *LCase* affects only uppercase letters; all other characters in *string* are unaffected.
- *LCase* returns Null if *string* contains a Null.

VBScript/VB & VBA Differences

There is no *LCase$* function available in VBScript.

See Also   UCase Function

Left, LeftB Functions

Syntax

    Left(string, length)

string
     Use: Required   Data Type: String

     The string to be processed.

length
     Use: Required   Data Type: Long

     The number of characters to return from the left of the string.

Return Value   *Left* and *LeftB* return a String.

Description   Returns a string containing the left-most *length* characters of *string*.

Rules at a Glance

- If *length* is 0, a zero-length string (" ") is returned.
- If *length* is greater than the length of *string*, *string* is returned.
- If *length* is less than 0 or Null, the function generates runtime error 5, "Invalid procedure call or argument," and runtime error 94, "Invalid use of Null," respectively.
- If *string* contains Null, *Left* returns Null.
- *Left* processes strings of characters; *LeftB* is used to process binary data.

Programming Tips and Gotchas

- Use the *Len* function to determine the overall length of *string*.
- When you use the *LeftB* function with byte data, *length* specifies the number of bytes to return.

VBScript/VB & VBA Differences

There are no *Left$* or *LeftB$* functions available in VBScript.

See Also   Len, LenB Functions, Mid, MidB Functions, Right, RightB Functions

Len, LenB Functions

Syntax

```
Len(string | varname)
LenB(string | varname)
```

string
    Use: Required   Data Type: String

    A valid string literal or string expression.

varname
    Use: Required   Data Type: Any except Object

    A valid variable name.

Return Value   Long.

Description   *Len* returns the number of characters in a string or variable. *LenB* returns the number of bytes required to store a string in memory.

Rules at a Glance

- *string* and *varname* are mutually exclusive; that is, you must specify either *string* or *varname*, but not both.
- If either *string* or *varname* is Null, *Len* and *LenB* return Null.
- You can't use *Len* or *LenB* with an object variable.
- If *varname* is an array, you must also specify a valid subscript. In other words, *Len* and *LenB* can't determine the total number of elements in or the total size of an array. To determine the size of an array, use the *LBound* and *UBound* functions.

Programming Tips and Gotchas

- Nonstring data is treated the same as strings when passed to the *Len* and *LenB* functions. For example, in the code:

```
Dim number
number = 100
WScript.Echo Len(number)
```

  the *Len* function returns 3, since that is the number of characters in the value of *number*.

- *LenB* is intended to work with string data, and returns the number of bytes required to store that string. If a nonstring data type is passed to the *LenB* function, its value is first converted to a string before its length is determined.

VBA/VBScript Differences

Although the *Len* and *LenB* functions handle strings identically in VBA and VBScript, they handle non-string data types quite differently. *Len* and *LenB* in VBA reports the number of bytes required to store the non-string data type in memory. In contrast, in VBScript, *Len* reports the number of characters in the string representation of non-character data, and *LenB* reports the number of bytes needed to store the string representation of noncharacter data.

LoadPicture Function

Syntax

```
LoadPicture(picturename)
```

picturename
  Use: Required   Data Type: String

  The path and filename of the picture file.

Return Value   A StdPicture object.

Description   Loads a picture object.

Rules at a Glance

- *picturename* consists of an optional path along with the name of a supported image file. If the path component of *picturename* is omitted, the VBScript runtime engine attempts to find the image in the script's current directory.

- *picturename* can be a bitmap (*.bmp*), enhanced metafile (*.emf*), icon (*.ico*), Graphics Interchange Format (*.gif*), JPEG (*.jpg*), run-length encoded (*.rle*), or Windows metafile (*.wmf*).

Example

The following example loads an image into an Outlook contact form:

```
Function Item_Open( )

Dim oPic

Set oPic = LoadPicture("C:\windows\" & Item.FullName & ".bmp")

Set Item.GetInspector.ModifiedFormPages("General").imgContact.Picture = _
          oPic
End Function
```

Programming Tips and Gotchas

- The StdPicture object is defined by the OLE Automation library *STDOLE2.TLB*. It supports the members shown in the following table:

Name	Type	Description
Handle	Property	Returns a handle to the image.
Height	Property	Indicates the height of the image in HiMetric units.
hPal	Property	Returns a handle to the Picture object's palette.
Render	Method	Draws all or part of the image to a destination object.
Type	Property	Returns the Picture object's graphics format. Possible values are 0 (none), 1 (bitmap), 2 (metafile), 3 (icon), and 4 (enhanced metafile).
Width	Property	Indicates the width of the image in HiMetric units.

Log Function

Syntax

```
Log(number)
```

number

Use: Required   Data Type: Double

A numeric expression greater than zero.

Return Value   A Double.

Description   Returns the natural logarithm of a given number.

Rules at a Glance

- The natural logarithm is based on *e*, a constant whose value is approximately 2.718282. The natural logarithm is expressed by the equation:

$$e^z = x$$

where $z = \text{Log}(x)$. In other words, the natural logarithm is the inverse of the exponential function.

- *number*, the value whose natural logarithm the function is to return, must be a positive real number. If number is negative or zero, the function generates runtime error 5, "Invalid procedure call or argument."

Programming Tips and Gotchas

- You can calculate base-*n* logarithms for any number *x*, by dividing the natural logarithm of *x* by the natural logarithm of *n*, as the following expression illustrates:

```
Logn(x) = Log(x) / Log(n)
```

For example, the *Log10* function shows the source code for a custom function that calculates base-10 logarithms:

```
Function Log10(X)
    Log10 = Log(X) / Log(10)
End Function
```

- A number of other mathematical functions that aren't intrinsic to VBScript can be computed using the value returned by the *Log* function. The functions and their formulas are:

Inverse Hyperbolic Sine
```
HArcsin(X) = Log(X + Sqr(X * X + 1))
```

Inverse Hyperbolic Cosine
```
HArccos(X) = Log(X + Sqr(X * X - 1))
```

Inverse Hyperbolic Tangent
```
HArctan(X) = Log((1 + X) / (1 - X)) / 2
```

Inverse Hyperbolic Secant
```
HArcsec(X) = Log((Sqr(-X * X + 1) + 1) / X)
```

Inverse Hyperbolic Cosecant
```
HArccosec(X) = Log((Sgn(X) * Sqr(X * X + 1) +1) / X)
```

Inverse Hyperbolic Cotangent
```
HArccotan(X) = Log((X + 1) / (X - 1)) / 2
```

LTrim Function

Syntax

```
LTrim(stringexp)
```

stringexp
    Use: Required   Data Type: String

    A string expression.

Return Value   A String.

Description   Removes any leading spaces from *stringexp*.

Rules at a Glance

- *LTrim* returns a String.
- If *stringexp* contains a Null, *LTrim* returns Null.

Programming Tips and Gotchas

- Unless you need to keep trailing spaces, it's best to use the *Trim* function, which is the equivalent of LTrim(RTrim(string)). This allows you to remove both leading and trailing spaces in a single function call.
- Although we have seen it done, it's extremely unwise to create data relationships that rely on leading spaces. Most string-based data types in relational database management systems like SQL Server and Access automatically remove leading spaces.

VB/VBA Differences

VBScript does not support the VBA *LTrim$* function.

See Also   RTrim Function, Trim Function

Match Object

Description   A member of the Matches collection that is returned by a call to the RegExp object's Execute method, the Match object represents a successful regular expression match.

Createable   No.

Returned by

    Matches.Item property.

Properties

The Match object supports the following three properties:

FirstIndex
    Data Type: Long

    Indicates the position in the original search string where the regular expression match occurred. The first character in the search string is at position 1.

Length

Data Type: Long

Indicates the number of characters in the match found in the search string. This is also the number of characters in the Match object's Value property.

Value

Data Type: String

The text of the match found in the search string.

Example

Since the RegExp object's Execute method searches only a string, the example program writes the filename of each file in the Windows directory to a variable named *strNames*. Each filename is preceded by two spaces. The RegExp object's Execute method is then called to search for every filename beginning with the letter "B" (the regular expression searches for two spaces followed by a "B"). The Matches collection is then iterated so that each filename can be extracted from strNames and displayed in a message box:

```
Dim fs, root, dir, fls, fl
Dim rexp
Dim mtchs, mtch
Dim strNames, strMsg
Dim lStartPos

strNames = "  "
Set fs = CreateObject("Scripting.FileSystemObject")
Set root = fs.Drives("C").RootFolder
Set dir = root.SubFolders("Windows")
Set fls = dir.Files

For Each fl In fls
    strNames = strNames & fl.Name & "  "
Next
MsgBox Len(strNames)
Set rexp = New RegExp
rexp.Global = True
rexp.Pattern = "(\s\sB)"
Set mtchs = rexp.Execute(strNames)

For Each mtch In mtchs
    lStartPos = mtch.FirstIndex + 2
    strMsg = strMsg & Mid(strNames, lStartPos, _
            InStr(lStartPos, strNames, "  ") - lStartPos + 1) & vbCrLf
Next

MsgBox strMsg
```

See Also   RegExp Object

Matches Collection Object

Description   The collection of zero or more Match objects returned by the RegExp object's Execute method; each Match object allows you to identify and manipulate one of the strings found by the regular expression.

Createable   No.

Returned by   RegExp.Execute Method.

Properties

The Matches collection object supports the following two properties:

Count

>Data Type: Long

>Indicates the number of objects in the collection. A value of zero indicates that the collection is empty. The property is read-only.

Item

>Syntax: `Matches.Item(index)`

>Data Type: Match object

>Returns a particular Match object based on *index*, its ordinal position in the collection. Matches is a zero-based collection; that is, its first member is at ordinal position 0, while its last member is at ordinal position `Matches.Count - 1`.

Example

See the example for the Match object.

See Also   Match Object, RegExp Object, RegExp.Execute Method

---

Me Keyword

Syntax

>`Me`

Description   The `Me` Keyword represents the current instance of the class in which code is executing.

Rules at a Glance

- `Me` is an implicit reference to the current object as defined by the `Class...End Class` statement.

- `Me` is automatically available to every procedure in a VBScript class.

Example

In this example, a class method in a WSH script passes an instance of itself to a function outside of the class by using the `Me` Keyword:

```
Dim oCtr
Set oCtr = New CCounter
oCtr.Increment
oCtr.Increment
MsgBox "Count: " & oCtr.ShowCount


' definition of CCounter class
Class CCounter

    Private lCtr

    Property Get Value
```

```
        Value = lCtr
End Property

Private Sub Class_Initialize( )
    lCtr = 1
End Sub

Public Sub Increment( )
    lCtr = lCtr + 1
End Sub

Public Function ShowCount( )
    ShowCount = ShowObjectValue(Me)
End Function

End Class

' Show value of an object's Value property
Public Function ShowObjectValue(oObj)
    ShowObjectValue = oObj.Value
End Function
```

Programming Tips and Gotchas

- Values can't be assigned to the Me Keyword.
- The Me Keyword is particularly useful when passing an instance of the current class as a parameter to a routine outside of the class.

See Also   Class Statement

Mid, MidB Functions

Syntax

```
Mid(string, start[, length])
```

string
    Use: Required   Data Type: String

    The expression from which to return a substring.

start
    Use: Required   Data Type: Long

    The starting position of the substring.

length
    Use: Optional   Data Type: Long

    The length of the substring.

Return Value   A String.

Description   Returns a substring of a specified length from within a given string.

Rules at a Glance

- If *string* contains a Null, *Mid* returns Null.
- If *start* is more than the length of *string*, a zero-length string is returned.

- If *start* is less than zero, error 5, "Invalid procedure call or argument," is generated.
- If *length* is omitted or is greater than the length of *string*, all characters from *start* to the end of *string* are returned.
- The *MidB* version of the *Mid* function is used with byte data held within a string. When using *MidB*, both *start* and *length* refer to numbers of bytes as opposed to numbers of characters.

Example

The following example is a function that parses a string passed to it as a parameter and writes each word to a dynamic array. Note the use of the *InStr* function to determine the position of a space, which in this case is the character that can terminate a word:

```
Public Function ParseString(strString)

Dim arr( )
Dim intStart, intEnd, intStrLen, intCtr

intCtr = 0
intStart = 1
intStrLen = Len(strString)
Redim Preserve arr(10)

Do While intStart > 0
    intEnd = InStr(intStart, strString, " ") - 1
    If intEnd <= 0 Then intEnd = intStrLen
    If intCtr > UBound(arr) Then
        Redim Preserve arr(UBound(arr)+10)
    End If
    arr(intCtr) = Mid(strString, intStart, _
                      intEnd - intStart + 1)
    intStart = intEnd + 2
    intCtr = intCtr + 1
    If intStart > intStrLen Then intStart = 0
Loop

ParseString = arr

End Function
```

Programming Tips and Gotchas
- Use the *Len* function to determine the total length of *string*.
- Use *InStr* to determine the starting point of a given substring within another string.

VBA/VBScript Differences
- Because it does not support strong typing, VBScript does not support the *Mid$* and *MidB$* functions, which explicitly return a string, rather than a String.
- VBA supports the Mid statement, which allows a portion of the string to be replaced with another substring. For example:

```
Dim strPhrase As String

strPhrase = "This will be the day."
Mid(strPhrase, 3, 2) = "at"
```

changes the value of *strPhrase* to "That will be day." This usage of *Mid* in statement form is not supported by VBScript.

See Also   Left, LeftB Functions; Len, LenB Functions; Right, RightB Functions

Minute Function

Syntax

```
Minute(time)
```

time

Use: Required   Data Type: Date

Any valid date/time expression, or an expression that can be evaluated as a date/time expression.

Return Value   An Integer.

Description   Returns an integer between 0 and 59 representing the minute of the hour from a given date/time expression.

Rules at a Glance

If *time* is `Null`, the *Minute* function returns `Null`.

Programming Tips and Gotchas

If *time* isn't a valid date/time expression, the function generates runtime error 13, "Type mismatch." To prevent this, use the *IsDate* function to check the argument before calling the *Minute* function.

See Also   Hour Function, Second Function

Month Function

Syntax

```
Month(date)
```

date

Use: Required   Data Type: Date

Any valid date expression.

Return Value   An Integer between 1 and 12.

Description   Returns a variant representing the month of the year of a given date expression.

Rules at a Glance

If *date* contains `Null`, *Month* returns `Null`.

Programming Tips and Gotchas

- The validity of the date expression and the position of the month element within the date expression are initially determined by the locale settings of the current Windows system. However, some intelligence has been built into the *Month* function that surpasses the usual comparison of a date expression to the current locale settings. For example, on a Windows machine set to U.S. date format (mm/dd/yyyy), the date "13/12/2000" is technically illegal. However, the Month function returns 12 when passed this date. The basic rule for the *Month* function is that if the system-defined month element is outside legal bounds (i.e., greater than 12), the system-defined day element is assumed to be the month and is returned by the function.

- Since the *IsDate* function adheres to the same rules and assumptions as *Month*, it determines whether a date is valid before passing it to the *Month* function.

See Also   DatePart Function, Day Function, IsDate Function, MonthName Function, Year Function

MonthName Function

Syntax

```
MonthName monthnumber [, abbreviate]
```

monthnumber
    Use: Required   Data Type: Long

    The ordinal number of the month, from 1 to 12.

abbreviate
    Use: Optional   Data Type: Boolean

    A flag to indicate whether an abbreviated month name should be returned.

Return Value   A String.

Description   Returns the month name of a given month. For example, 1 returns January, or if *abbreviate* is True, Jan.

Rules at a Glance

The default value for *abbreviate* is False.

Programming Tips and Gotchas

monthnumber must be an integer or a long; it can't be a date. Use DatePart("m", *dateval*) to obtain a month number from a date.

See Also   DatePart Function, Month Function, WeekdayName Function

MsgBox Function

Syntax

```
MsgBox(prompt[, buttons][, title][, helpfile, context])
```

prompt
    Use: Required   Data Type: String

    The text of the message to display in the message box dialog.

Use: Optional   Data Type: Numeric

The sum of the Button, Icon, Default Button, and Modality constant values.

title

Use: Optional   Data Type: String

The title displayed in the titlebar of the message box dialog.

helpfile

Use: Optional   Data Type: String

An expression specifying the name of the help file to provide help functionality for the dialog.

context

Use: Optional   Data Type: Numeric

An expression specifying a context ID within *helpfile*.

Return Value   An Integer indicating the button clicked by the user.

Description   Displays a dialog box containing a message, buttons, and optional icon to the user. The action taken by the user is returned by the function as an integer value.

Rules at a Glance

- *prompt* can contain approximately 1,000 characters, including carriage return characters such as the built-in vbCrLf constant.

- In order to divide *prompt* onto multiple lines, you can use any of the vbCr, vbLf, vbCrLf, or vbNewLine constants. For example:

  ```
  SMsg = "This is line 1" & vbCrLf & _
  "This is line 2"
  ```

- If the *title* parameter is omitted, the text of *title* depends on the type of script being executed, as the following table shows:

Script type	Caption
ASP script	not applicable
IE script	"VBScript"
Outlook form	"VBScript"
WSH script	"VBScript"

- If the *helpfile* parameter is provided, the context parameter must also be provided, and vice versa.

- When both *helpfile* and *context* are passed to the *MsgBox* function, a Help button is automatically placed on the *MsgBox* dialog, allowing the user to click and obtain context-sensitive help.

- If you omit the *buttons* argument, the default value is 0; VB opens an application modal dialog containing only an OK button.

- The following intrinsic constants can be added together (or logically Or'ed) to form a complete *buttons* argument:

```
ButtonDisplayConstant + IconDisplayConstant + _
DefaultButtonConstant + ModalityConstant
```

Only one constant from each group can make up the overall *buttons* value.

Button Display Constants

Constant	Value	Buttons to display
vbOKOnly	0	OK only
vbOKCancel	1	OK and Cancel
vbAbortRetryIgnore	2	Abort, Retry, and Ignore
vbYesNoCancel	3	Yes, No, and Cancel
vbYesNo	4	Yes and No
vbRetryCancel	5	Retry and Cancel

Icon Display Constants

Constant	Value	Icon To display
vbCritical	16	Critical Message
vbQuestion	32	Warning Query
vbExclamation	48	Warning Message
vbInformation	64	Information Message

Default Button Constants

Constant	Value	Default button
vbDefaultButton1	0	First button
vbDefaultButton2	256	Second button
vbDefaultButton3	512	Third button
vbDefaultButton4	768	Fourth button

Modality Constants

Constant	Value	modality
vbApplicationModal	0	Application
vbSystemModal	4096	System

- The following intrinsic constants determine the action taken by the user and represent the value returned by the *MsgBox* function:

Return Values

Constant	Value	Button clicked
vbOK	1	OK
vbCancel	2	Cancel (or Esc key pressed)

Constant	Value	Button clicked
vbAbort	3	Abort
vbRetry	4	Retry
vbIgnore	5	Ignore
vbYes	6	Yes
vbNo	7	No

- If the *MsgBox* contains a Cancel button, the user can press the Esc key, and the function's return value is that of the Cancel button.

- The Help button doesn't itself return a value, because it doesn't close the *MsgBox* dialog. If the user clicks the Help button, a Help window is opened. Once the Help window is closed, the user clicks one of the other buttons on the message box to close the dialog; this then returns a value.

Programming Tips and Gotchas

- *Application modality* means that the user can't access other parts of the application until a response to the message box has been given. In other words, the appearance of the message box prevents the application from performing other tasks or from interacting with the user other than through the message box.

- *System modality* used to mean that all applications were suspended until a response to the message box was given. However, with multitasking operating systems such as the Windows family of 32- and 64-bit operating systems, this isn't the case. Basically the message box is defined to be a "Topmost" window that is set to "Stay on Top," which means that the user can switch to another application and use it without responding to the message box; but because the message box is the topmost window, it's positioned on top of all other running applications.

- Unlike its *InputBox* counterpart, *MsgBox* can't be positioned on the screen; it's always displayed in the center of the screen.

- Since it produces a user interface that is displayed on the server rather than on the client, *MsgBox* should not be used within an ASP script that runs on the server. It can, however, be included as script in the text stream that an ASP page sends to the client.

- If WSH scripts are run in batch mode (that is, with the /B switch), calls to the *MsgBox* function are ignored. Note that, if the return value of the *MsgBox* function is used to define the value of variables or to control program flow, the script may no longer function as intended when run in batch mode.

VBA/VBScript Differences

In VBA, if the `title` parameter is omitted, the name of the current application or project is displayed in the title bar. In VBScript, the string that appears on the title bar depends on the type of script that executes.

See Also   InputBox Function

Now Function

Syntax

```
Now
```

Return Value   A Date.

Description   Returns the current date and time based on the system setting.

Example

The following example returns the date 10 days from today:

```
Dim dFutureDate
dFutureDate = DateAdd("d", 10, Now)
```

Programming Tips and Gotchas

- It's often overlooked that workstations in a modern Windows environment are at the mercy of the user! If your application relies on an accurate date and time setting, you should consider including a line in the workstation's logon script to synchronize the time with one of the servers. Many so-called bugs have been traced to a workstation that has had its date or time wrongly altered by the user. The following line of code, when added to the logon script of an NT/Windows 2000 machine, synchronizes the machine's clock with that of a server called NTSERV1:

  ```
  net time \\NTSERV1 /set
  ```

- If you convert the date returned by Now to a string, it takes the Windows General Date format based on the locale settings of the local computer. The U.S. setting for General Date is mm/dd/yy hh:mm:ss.

- The *Now* function is often used to generate timestamps. However, for short-term timing and intra-day timestamps, the *Timer* function, which returns the number of milliseconds elapsed since midnight, affords greater precision.

See Also   Timer Function

Oct Function

Syntax

```
Oct(number)
```

number

  Use: Required   Data Type: Numeric or String

  Number or string representation of a number to convert.

Return Value   A String.

Description   Returns a string containing the octal representation of a given number.

Rules at a Glance

- If *number* isn't already a whole number, it's rounded to the nearest whole number before being evaluated.

- If *number* is Null, *Oct* returns Null.

- If *number* is the special `Empty` variant, *Oct* returns 0 (zero).
- *Oct* returns up to 11 octal characters.

Programming Tips and Gotchas

You can also use literals in your code to represent octal numbers by appending &0 to the relevant octal value. For example, 100 decimal has the octal representation &0144. The following statement assigns an octal value to a variable:

```
lngOctValue1 = &o200                    ' Assigns 128
```

See Also   Hex Function

On Error Statement

Syntax

```
On Error Resume Next
On Error Goto 0
```

Description   Enables or disables error handling within a procedure. If you don't use an `On Error` statement in your procedure, or if you have explicitly switched off error handling, the VBScript runtime engine handles the error automatically. First, it displays a dialog containing the standard text of the error message, something many users are likely to find incomprehensible. Second, it terminates the application, so any error that occurs in the procedure produces a fatal runtime error.

Rules at a Glance

- When a runtime error occurs in the routine in which the `On Error Resume Next` statement occurs, program execution continues with the program line following the line that generated the error. This means that, if you want to handle an error, this line following the line that generated the error should call or include an inline error-handling routine.
- When a runtime error occurs in any routine called by the routine in which the `On Error Resume Next` statement occurs, or by its subroutines, program execution returns to the statement immediately after the subroutine call in the routine containing the `On Error Resume Next` statement.
- When used in an ASP page for IIS 5.0, `On Error Resume Next` disables ASP's own error handling.
- You disable error handling by using the `On Error Goto 0` statement.

Programming Tips and Gotchas

- If you have no error handling in your procedure, the VBScript runtime engine traces back through the call stack until a procedure is reached where error handling is enabled. In this case, the error is handled by that procedure by executing the statement immediately after the call to the subroutine that caused program control to leave the procedure. However, if no error handler can be found in the call stack, a runtime error occurs, and program execution is halted.
- `On Error Resume Next` can be useful in situations where you are certain that errors will occur, or where the errors that could occur are minor. The following example shows how you can quickly cycle through an array with some uninitialized values

to sum its elements. By using the On Error Resume Next statement, you force your program to ignore errors caused by elements with invalid data and carry on with the next element. For example, the following code fragment allows you to ignore errors caused by attempting to add nonnumeric data:

```
On Error Resume Next
Dim arr, element, sum
arr = array(12, "string", 14, 7, 19, 2)

For Each element in arr
      sum = sum + element
Next
```

- The quality of error trapping, error handling, and error reporting within a program often determines the success or failure of the application. Attention to detail in this area can be the difference between a stable, well-behaved, and robust application and one that seems to generate nothing but hassle. Using logs like the application and event logs in Windows NT, Windows 2000, and Windows XP within your error-handling routines can help you track down persistent problems quickly and efficiently. See Chapter 4, which explains creation of robust VBScript error-handling routines.

- It's important to understand the flow of program control in the event an error occurs in a subroutine, and in particular, to understand that in the event of an error in a called routine, program execution returns to the statement after the statement that caused program flow to leave the routine containing the On Error Resume Next statement. In most cases, this behavior is highly undesirable. It can be prevented by including an On Error Resume Next statement in each routine of a script or module.

- You can provide inline error handling after lines of code that are particularly likely to cause errors. Typically, this is done by checking whether the Err object's Number property is nonzero, as in the following code fragment:

```
On Error Resume Next

Dim oDAO

Set oDAO = CreateObject("DAO.DBEngine.30")
If Err.Number <> 0 Then
   MsgBox Err.Number & ": " & Err.Description      'Handle error
Err.Clear
End If
```

Note that it's particularly important to test for a *nonzero* error code rather than a positive error code, since most errors are unsigned long integers that VBScript (which does not support unsigned integers) represents as negative numbers. It's also important, once you've handled the error, to clear the error information by calling the Err object's Clear method.

- You cannot trap syntax errors with the On Error statement. This is because syntax errors do not terminate a program; a program with syntax errors never even begins execution.

VBA/VBScript Differences

Unlike VBA, which also supports the On Error Goto syntax to branch program flow to an error-handling section within a routine or function, VBScript supports only the On

---

Error Resume Next statement. This means that, if you're programming with VBScript, you must use inline error handling.

See Also   Err Object, Chapter 6

Option Explicit Statement

Syntax
```
Option Explicit
```

Description   Use Option Explicit to generate an error whenever a variable that has not been declared is encountered.

Rules at a Glance
- The Option Explicit statement must appear in a script before any other statements; otherwise, a nontrappable error occurs.
- In modules where the Option Explicit statement isn't used, any undeclared variables are declared automatically.
- Where Option Explicit is used, all variables must be declared using the Dim, Private, Public, or ReDim statements.

Programming Tips and Gotchas
- It's considered good programming practice to always use the Option vbCrLfExplicit statement. The following example shows why:
  ```
  Dim iVariable

  iVariable = 100
  iVariable = iVarable + 50
  MsgBox iVariable
  ```
  In this code snippet, a variable, *iVariable*, has been declared. However, because the name of the variable has been mistyped in line 3, the message box shows its value as 50 instead of 150. This is because *iVarable* is assumed to be an undeclared variant whose value is 0. If the Option Explicit statement had been used, the code wouldn't have executed without generating an error, and *iVarable* would have been highlighted as the cause when Error 500, "Variable is undefined," was raised.
- For ASP pages, the Option Explicit statement must appear before the beginning of the HTML stream. For example:
  ```
  <% Option Explicit %>
  <HTML>
  ```
  A single Option Explicit statement applies to all script blocks in an ASP page.

Private Statement

Syntax
```
Private varname[([subscripts])] [, varname[([subscripts])]] . . .
```
varname
  Use: Required   Variant Type: Any
  The name of the variable, following Visual Basic naming conventions.

subscripts

    Use: Optional   Variant Type: Integer or Long

    Denotes *varname* as an array and optionally specifies the number and extent of array dimensions.

Description   Used in a script or in a class to declare a private variable and allocate the relevant storage space in memory.

Rules at a Glance

- A Private variable's visibility is limited to the script in which it's created for global variables and to the class in which it is declared for class-level variables. Elsewhere, the Private keyword generates an error.

- *varname* follows standard VB naming conventions. It must begin with an alphabetic character, can't contain embedded periods or spaces, can't be the same as a VBScript reserved word, must be shorter than 255 characters, and must be unique within its scope.

- You can override standard variable naming conventions by placing your variable name in brackets. This allows you to use reserved words or illegal characters in variable names. For example:

    ```
    Private [me]
    Private [1Var]
    Private [2-Var]
    ```

- The *subscripts* argument has the following syntax:

    ```
    upperbound [,upperbound]...
    ```

    For example:

    ```
    Private strNames(10)
    ```

    defines an array of 11 elements (an array whose lower bound is 0 and whose upper bound is 10). Similarly:

    ```
    Private lngPrices(10, 10)
    ```

    defines a two-dimensional array of eleven elements in each dimension.

- Using the *subscripts* argument, you can declare up to 60 multiple dimensions for the array.

- If the *subscripts* argument isn't used (i.e., the variable name is followed by empty parentheses), the array is declared dynamic. You can change both the number of dimensions and the number of elements of a dynamic array using the ReDim statement.

- VBScript supports only the variant data type: all variables are variants. The following table shows the values held by each type of variant when it is first initialized:

Variable type	Initial value	Example
Array	Variant( )	Private arrNames(10)
Array Element	Empty	arr(0)
Variant Variable	Empty	Private vCtr

Programming Tips and Gotchas

- The behavior of variables defined using the Private statement outside of a class is determined by the host. In general, there is rarely a good reason to declare a private variable outside of a class.

- Within a class, you should prevent variables from being modified outside of the class by declaring them as private. Instead, public properties should be used to provide a means of accessing and modifying private variables. For example, rather than defining a public variable Age as follows:

```
Class Person
    Dim Age
End Class
```

- You can define it as follows and allow properties to provide access to the private data:

```
Class Person
    Dim iAge

    Public Property Get Age()
        Age = iAge
    End Property

    Public Property Let Age(value)
        iAge = value
    End Property
End Class
```

- One of the uses of private variables is in client-side scripts for IE. If there are multiple script blocks in a single page, a private variable is visible only in the script block in which it is declared; it is not visible in any other script block on that page.

- All variables created at procedure level (that is, in code within a Sub...End Sub, Function...End Function, or Property...End Property construct are local by default. That is, they don't have scope outside the procedure in which they are created. The use of the Private keyword in these cases generates a runtime error.

- You cannot change the dimensions of arrays that were defined to be dynamic arrays while preserving their original data.

- It's good practice to always use Option Explicit at the beginning of a module to prevent misnamed variables from causing hard-to-find errors.

VBA/VBScript Differences

- In VBA, you can explicitly define the lower bound of an array in the *subscripts* argument. In VBScript, this is not permitted; the lower bound of all arrays is always 0.

- VBA supports the WithEvents keyword to allow an object reference to receive notification of the events fired by its corresponding object. VBScript, however, does not support the WithEvents keyword. Note, though, that some scriptable applications (such as Windows Script Host, Internet Explorer, and Active Server Pages) do expose their events to scripts.

- VBA supports the New keyword to create early bound objects. However, since scripting languages necessarily rely on late binding, the New keyword is not supported in a variable declaration statement.

See Also   Dim Statement, Public Statement, ReDim Statement, Set Statement

Property Get Statement

Syntax

```
[Public [Default] | Private Property Get name [(arglist)]
    [statements]
    [name = expression]
    [Exit Property]
    [statements]
    [name = expression]
End Property
```

Public

Use: Optional   Type: Keyword

Makes the property accessible from outside the class, giving it visibility through all procedures in all scripts. Public and Private are mutually exclusive.

Default

Use: Optional   Type: Keyword

Used only with the Public keyword to indicate that a public property is the default property of the class.

Private

Use: Optional   Type: Keyword

Restricts the visibility of the property to those procedures within the same Class.. .End Class code block. Public and Private are mutually exclusive.

name

Use: Required

The name of the property.

arglist

Use: Optional   Data Type: Any

A comma-delimited list of variables to be passed to the property as arguments from the calling procedure.

statements

Use: Optional

Program code to be executed within the property.

expression

Use: Optional   Variant Type: Any

The value to return from the property to the calling procedure.

arglist has the following syntax:
```
[ByVal | ByRef] argname[( )]
```

ByVal

Use: Optional

The argument is passed by value; that is, a local copy of the variable is assigned the value of the argument.

ByRef

Use: Optional

The argument is passed by reference; that is, the local variable is simply a reference to the argument being passed. Changes made to the local variable are reflected in the argument. ByRef is the default way of passing variables.

argname

Use: Required

The name of the local variable representing the argument.

Description   Declares the name, arguments, and code for a procedure that reads the value of a property and returns it to the calling procedure. The Property Get statement is used within a class defined by the Class... End Class construct.

Rules at a Glance

- Property procedures are Public by default.
- The Default keyword indicates that this Property Get procedure is the class's default member. A *default member* is automatically executed in an assignment statement without the need to explicitly reference it. To take a common example, the following two statements are identical:

```
Set oCDrive = FileSystemObject.Drives.Item("C")
Set oCDrive = FileSystemObject.Drives("C")
```

Both return a reference to a *Drive* object representing the local system's C drive. The second statement works because Item is the default member of the Drives collection.

- A class can have only a single default member. This must be a public procedure defined either by the Property Get statement or by the Function statement.
- Unlike other function and procedure names, the name of the Property Get procedure doesn't have to be unique within its class module. Specifically, the Property Let and Property Set procedures can have the same name as the Property Get procedure. For example:

```
Property Let Name(sVal)
    msName = sVal
End Property

Property Get Name( )
    Name = msName
End Property
```

- The number of arguments passed to a Property Get statement must match the corresponding Property Let or Property Set statement. For example:

```
Public Property Let MyProperty(sVal, iVal)
    miMyProperty = iVal
End Property

Public Property Get MyProperty(sVal)
    MyProperty = miMyProperty
End Property
```

Both the `Property Let` and `Property Get` procedures share a common argument, *sVal*. The `Property Let` procedure has one additional argument, *iVal*, which represents the value that is to be assigned to the MyProperty property. (For details, see the next point.)

- In a `Property Let` procedure, the last argument defines the data assigned to the property. The data returned by the `Property Get` procedure must match the last argument of a corresponding `Property Let` or `Property Set` procedure.

- If an `Exit Property` statement is executed, the property procedure exits and program execution immediately continues with the statement from which the property procedure was called. Any number of `Exit Property` statements can appear in a `Property Get` procedure.

- If the value of the `Property Get` procedure has not been explicitly set when the program execution exits the procedure, its value will be empty, the uninitialized value of a variant.

Programming Tips and Gotchas

- You can create a read-only property by defining a `Property Get` procedure without a corresponding `Property Let` or `Property Set` procedure.

- If the value of the property is an object, be sure to use the `Set` keyword when the `Property Get` procedure is called. For example:

```
Property Get Drive
    Set Drive = oDrive
End Property
```

- You should protect the value of properties by defining a `Private` variable to hold the internal property value and control the updating of the property by outside applications through the `Property Let` and `Property Get` statements, as the following template describes:

```
Class Object
    'Class Module Declarations Section
    'private data member only accessible from within
    'this code module
    Private miMyProperty

    Public Property Let MyProperty(iVal)
        'procedure to allow the outside world to
        'change the value of private data member
        miMyProperty = iVal
        '(do not use a Property Let when creating a
        'Read-Only Property)
    End Property

    Public Property Get MyProperty( ) As Integer
        'procedure to allow the outside world to
        'read the value of private data member
        MyProperty = miMyProperty
    End Property
End Class
```

Otherwise, if the variable used to store a property value is public, its value can be modified arbitrarily by any application that accesses the class containing the property.

- Using a `Property Let` procedure rather than allowing the user to access a class variable directly allows you to perform validation on incoming data. For example, the following code insures that the value assigned to the Age property is a number that is between 0 and 110:

```
Class Person
    Private iAge

    Property Get Age
        Age = iAge
    End Property
    Property Let Age(value)
        ' Check that data is numeric
        If Not IsNumeric(value) Then
            Err.Raise 13    ' Type mismatch error
            Exit Property
        ' Check that number is in range
        ElseIf value < 0 Or value > 110 Then
                Err.Raise 1031    ' Invalid number error
        End If

        iAge = value
    End Property
End Class
```

- The default method of passing a parameter is `ByRef`, which means that any modifications made to a variable passed as an argument to the `Property Get` statement are reflected in the variable's value when control returns to the calling routine. If this behavior is undesirable, explicitly pass parameters by value using the `ByVal` keyword in *arglist*.
- You can use only the property defined by the `Property Get` statement on the right side of a property assignment.

VBA/VBScript Differences

- VBScript allows you to designate a particular `Property Get` procedure as the default member of its class. As of Version 6.0, VBA does not.
- VBA supports Friend property procedures as well as public and private ones. VBScript supports only public and private property procedures.
- VBA supports the `Static` keyword in the property declaration, which preserves the value of all local variables between calls to the `Property Get` procedure. VBScript does not have an `Optional` keyword to support optional arguments. "Optional arguments" in VBScript are supported only by omitting arguments to a procedure call. VBScript provides no way of assigning default values to optional arguments.
- VBA supports optional parameters and allows them to be assigned a default value. VBScript does not support optional arguments.

See Also   Property Let Statement, Property Set Statement

Property Let Statement

Syntax

```
[Public | Private Property Let name ([arglist,] value)
    [statements]
    [Exit Property]
    [statements]
End Property
```

`Public`

Use: Optional　　　Type: Keyword

Makes the property visible outside of the class, giving it visibility through all procedures in all scripts. `Public` and `Private` are mutually exclusive.

`Private`

Use: Optional　　　Type: Keyword

Restricts the visibility of the property to those procedures within the same `Class.. .End Class` code block. `Private` and `Public` are mutually exclusive.

name

Use: Required

The name of the property.

arglist

Use: Optional　　　Data Type: Any

A comma-delimited list of variables to be passed to the property as arguments from the calling procedure.

value

Use: Required　　　Data Type: Any

The last (or only) argument in *arglist*; a variable containing the value to be assigned to the property.

statements

Use: Optional

Program code to be executed within the property.

arglist uses the following syntax:

```
[ByVal | ByRef] varname[( )]
```

`ByVal`

Use: Optional　　　Type: Keyword

The argument is passed by value; that is, a local copy of the variable is assigned the value of the argument.

`ByRef`

Use: Optional　　　Type: Keyword

The argument is passed by reference; that is, the local variable is simply a reference to the argument being passed. All changes made to the local variable are reflected in the calling argument when control returns to the calling procedure. `ByRef` is the default method of passing variables.

varname

Use: Required

The name of the local variable containing either the reference or value of the argument.

Description   Declares the name, arguments, and code for a procedure that assigns a value to a property. The Property Let statement is used within a class defined by the Class...End Class construct.

Rules at a Glance

- A Property Let statement must contain at least one argument in *arglist*. If there is more than one argument, the last one contains the value to be assigned to the property. (This is the argument indicated as *value* in the prototype for the Property Let statement.)

- The last argument in *arglist* should correspond to both the private data member (at least, it should be defined as Private; see the first comment in the "Programming Tips and Gotchas" section) used to hold the property value and the return value of the corresponding Property Get procedure, if there is one.

- Property procedures are Public by default.

- Unlike other functions and procedures, the name of the Property Let procedure can be repeated within the same module as the name of the Property Get and Property Set procedures.

- The number of the arguments passed to a Property Let statement must match the corresponding Property Get statement. For details, see the section "Rules at a Glance" in the entry for Property Get.

- If an Exit Property statement is executed, program flow continues with the statement following the call to the property. Any number of Exit Property statements can appear in a *Property Let* procedure.

Programming Tips and Gotchas

- You should protect the values of properties by defining a Private variable to hold the internal property value and control the updating of the property by outside applications via Property Let and Property Get statements, as described in the "Programming Tips and Gotchas" section of the Property Get statement.

- You can create a write-only property by defining a Property Let procedure without a corresponding Property Get procedure. Write-only properties, however, are comparatively rare, and are used primarily to prevent access to sensitive information such as passwords.

- The default method of passing parameters is ByRef, which means that any modifications made to a variable passed as an argument to the Property Let statement are reflected in the variable's value when control returns to the calling routine. If this behavior is undesirable, explicitly pass arguments by value using the ByVal keyword in *arglist*.

- You can use the property defined by the Property Let statement only on the left side of a property assignment.

VBA/VBScript Differences

- VBA supports Friend property procedures as well as public and private ones. VBScript supports only public and private property procedures.

- VBA supports the Static keyword in the property declaration, which preserves the value of all local variables between calls to the Property Let procedure. VBScript does not have an Optional keyword to support optional arguments. "Optional arguments" in VBScript are supported only by omitting arguments to a procedure call. VBScript provides no way of assigning default values to optional arguments.

- VBA supports optional parameters and allows them to be assigned a default value. VBScript does not support optional arguments.

See Also   Property Get Statement

Property Set Statement

Syntax

```
[Public | Private Property Set name ([arglist,] reference)
    [statements]
    [Exit Property]
    [statements]
End Property
```

Public

> Use: Optional   Type: Keyword
>
> Makes the property accessible from outside the class, so that it is visible to all procedures in all scripts. Public and Private are mutually exclusive.

Private

> Use: Optional   Type: Keyword
>
> Restricts the scope of the property to code within the Class...End Class construct in which the property is declared. Public and Private are mutually exclusive.

name

> Use: Required
>
> The name of the property.

arglist

> Use: Optional   Data Type: Any
>
> A comma-delimited list of variables to be passed to the property as arguments from the calling procedure.

reference

> Use: Required   Data Type: Object
>
> The last (or only) argument in *arglist*, it must be a variable containing the object reference to be assigned to the property.

statements

> Use: Optional
>
> Program code to be executed within the property.

arglist uses the following syntax and parts:
```
    [ByVal | ByRef] varname[( )] _
```

ByVal

> Use: Optional   Type: Keyword
>
> The argument is passed by value; that is, a local copy of the variable is assigned the value of the argument.

ByRef

> Use: Optional   Type: Keyword
>
> The argument is passed by reference; that is, the local variable is simply a reference to the argument being passed. All changes made to the local variable are reflected in the calling argument when control returns to the calling procedure. ByRef is the default method of passing variables.

varname

    Use: Required   Data Type: Any

    The name of the local variable containing either the reference or value of the argument.

Description   Declares the name, arguments, and code for a procedure that assigns an object reference to a property. The Property Set statement is used within a class defined by the Class...End Class construct.

Rules at a Glance

- A Property Set statement must contain at least one argument in *arglist*. (This is the argument indicated as *reference* in the statement's prototype.) If there is more than one argument, it's the last one that contains the object reference to be assigned to the property.

- The last argument in *arglist* must match both the private data member used to hold the property value and the data returned by the corresponding Property Get procedure, if there is one.

- Property procedures are Public by default.

- Unlike other variables and procedures, the name of a Property Set procedure can be repeated within the same module as the name of a Property Get procedure.

- The number of arguments passed to a Property Set statement must match the corresponding Property Get statement. For example:

```
Public Property Set MyProperty(iVal, oVal)
    Set miMyProperty(iVal) = oVal
End Property

Public Property Get MyProperty(iVal)
    Set MyProperty = miMyProperty(iVal)
End Property
```

Both the Property Set and the Property Get procedures share a common argument, *iVal*. The Property Set procedure has one additional argument, *oVal*, which represents the object that is to be assigned to the MyProperty property.

- If an Exit Property statement is executed, program execution immediately continues with the statement following the call to the property. Any number of Exit Property statements can appear in a Property Set procedure.

Programming Tips and Gotchas

- You should protect the values of properties by defining a Private variable to hold the internal property value and control the updating of the property by outside applications via Property Set and Property Get statements, as described in the "Programming Tips and Gotchas" section of the entry for the Property Get statement.

- The default method of passing parameters is ByRef, which means that any modifications made to a variable passed as an argument to the Property Set statement are reflected in the variable's value when control returns to the calling routine. If this behavior is undesirable, explicitly pass arguments by value using the ByVal keyword in *arglist*.

- The property defined by the Property Set statement can occur only on the left side of a statement that assigns an object reference.

VBA/VBScript Differences

- VBA supports Friend property procedures as well as public and private ones. VBScript supports only public and private property procedures.

- VBA supports the Static keyword in the property declaration, which preserves the value of all local variables between calls to the Property Set procedure. VBScript does not have an Optional keyword to support optional arguments. "Optional arguments" in VBScript are supported only by omitting arguments to a procedure call. VBScript provides no way of assigning default values to optional arguments.

- VBA supports optional parameters and allows them to be assigned a default value. VBScript does not support optional arguments.

See Also   Property Get Statement, Property Let Statement

Public Statement

Syntax

```
Public varname[([subscripts])] _
    varname[([subscripts])]
```

varname

> Use: Required   Data Type: Any

> The name of the variable, which must follow VBScript naming conventions (see the second bullet in "Rules at a Glance").

subscripts

> Use: Optional   Data Type: Integer or Long

> Denotes *varname* as an array and optionally specifies the dimensions and number of elements of the array.

Description   Used in a script or a Class block to declare a public variable and allocate the relevant storage space in memory. A Public variable has global scope—that is, it can be used by all procedures in a script. When used in a class construct, it is visible outside the class project.

Rules at a Glance

- The behavior of a Public variable depends on where it's declared, as the following table shows:

Variable declared in...	Scope
Any procedure, Function or Property statement	Illegal; generates a syntax error; use the Dim statement instead.
Global code	Variable is available throughout the script.
Class block declarations section	Variable is available as a property of the class to all code within the script.

- You can override standard variable naming conventions by placing your variable name in brackets. This allows you to use reserved words or illegal characters in variable names. For example:

```
Public [me]
Public [1Var]
Public [2-Var]
```

- *varname* follows standard VB naming conventions. It must begin with an alphabetic character, can't contain embedded periods or spaces, can't be the same as a VBScript reserved word, must be shorter than 255 characters, and must be unique within its scope.

- The *subscripts* argument has the following syntax:

    upperbound [, *upperbound*]

- Using the *subscripts* argument, you can declare up to 60 dimensions for the array.

- If the *subscripts* argument isn't used (i.e., the variable name is followed by empty parentheses), the array is declared as dynamic. You can change both the number of dimensions and number of elements of a dynamic array using the ReDim statement.

- All variables are variants. The following table shows the values held by each type of variant when it is first initialized:

Data type	Initial value	Example
Array	Variant( )	Public arrNames(10)
Array Element	Empty	arr(0)
Scalar Variable	Empty	Public vCtr

Programming Tips and Gotchas

- The precise meaning of a public variable is defined by the host environment. In Internet Explorer, a variable defined as public in a script block is visible in all other script blocks on the page, including those written in JScript.

- Instead of declaring a variable as Public within a class construct, you should create Property Let and Property Get procedures that assign and retrieve the value of a private variable, respectively.

- You cannot change the dimensions of arrays that were not defined to be dynamic arrays.

- It's good programming practice to always use Option Explicit at the beginning of a module to prevent misnamed variables causing hard-to-find errors.

VBA/VBScript Differences

- In VBA, you can explicitly define the lower bound of an array in the *subscripts* argument. In VBScript, this is not permitted; the lower bound of all arrays is always 0.

- VBA supports the WithEvents keyword to allow an object variable to receive notification of the events fired by the object to which it refers. VBScript, however, does not support the WithEvents keyword. Note, though, that some scriptable applications (such as Windows Script Host, Internet Explorer, and Active Server Pages) do expose their events to scripts.

- VBA supports the New keyword to create early bound objects. However, since scripting languages necessarily rely on late binding, the New keyword is not supported in a variable declaration statement.

See Also   Private Statement, ReDim Statement, Set Statement

Randomize Sub

Syntax

```
Randomize [number]
```

number

    Use: Optional   Data Type: Numeric

    Any valid numeric expression.

Description

Initializes the random number generator.

Rules at a Glance

- Randomize uses *number* as a new seed value to initialize the random number generator used by the Rnd function. The seed value is an initial value that generates a sequence of pseudorandom numbers.
- If you don't pass *number* to the Randomize statement, the value of the system timer is used as the new seed value.
- Repeatedly passing the same number to Randomize doesn't cause Rnd to repeat the same sequence of random numbers.
- If Randomize is not used and the Rnd function is called either with no argument or with 1 as an argument, the *Rnd* function always uses the same number as the seed value the first time it is called, and subsequently uses the last generated number as a seed value.

Programming Tips and Gotchas

If you need to repeat a sequence of random numbers, you should call the Rnd function with a negative number as an argument immediately prior to using Randomize with any numeric argument. This is illustrated in the example program.

Example

```
RepeatNumbers()

Sub RepeatNumbers()
  Dim arr(9, 3)
  Dim loopCtr, intCtr
  Dim strMsg

  For loopCtr = 0 To 3
      Rnd -1
      Randomize(100)
      For intCtr = 0 To 9
        strMsg = strMsg & Rnd() & " "
      Next
      strMsg = strMsg & vbCrLf
  Next

  MsgBox strMsg
End Sub
```

See Also

Rnd Function

ReDim Statement

Syntax

```
ReDim [Preserve] varname(subscripts)_
                [, varname(subscripts)] ...
```

Preserve

    Use: Optional   Type: Keyword

    Preserves the data within an array when changing its single or its last dimension.

varname

    Use: Required   Data Type: Any

    Name of the variable.

subscripts

    Use: Required

    Number of elements and dimensions of the array, using the following syntax:

        upper [, *upper*] . . .

    where *upper* is the upper bound of a particular array dimension.

Description   Used within a procedure to resize and reallocate storage space for a dynamic array.

Rules at a Glance

- A dynamic array is created using a Private, Public, or Dim statement with empty parentheses. Only dynamic arrays created in this manner can be resized using the ReDim statement. There is no limit to the number of times you can redimension a dynamic array.

- Use of the Preserve keyword allows you to retain the current values within the array, but it also places several limitations on how the Redim statement can be used:

  — Only the last dimension of an array can be resized.

  — The number of dimensions can't be changed.

  — Only the upper bound of the array can be changed.

- If you reduce either the number of elements of the array or the number of dimensions in the array, data in the removed elements is permanently lost, irrespective of the use of the Preserve keyword.

Programming Tips and Gotchas

- You can pass an array by reference to a procedure, redimension it within the procedure, and return the modified array to the calling program. This is illustrated in the following code:

```
CreateArray( )

Private Sub CreateArray( )

    Dim strArray( ), strElement, strMsg
    Dim intCtr

    ReDim strArray(9)
```

```
                    For intCtr = 0 To UBound(strArray)
                        strArray(intCtr) = "Original element"
                    Next

                    ExpandArray strArray

                    For intCtr = 0 To UBound(strArray)
                        strMsg = strMsg & strArray(intCtr) & vbCrLf
                    Next

                    MsgBox strMsg

               End Sub

               Private Sub ExpandArray(ByRef arrDynamic( ))

                    Dim intBound, intCtr

                    intBound = UBound(arrDynamic)

                    ReDim Preserve arrDynamic(UBound(arrDynamic) * 2)

                    For intCtr = intBound + 1 To UBound(arrDynamic)
                        arrDynamic(intCtr) = "New element"
                    Next

               End Sub
```

When you run this example, both the original elements and new elements are listed in a message box, proving that the array was successfully expanded in the ExpandArray procedure.

- It's possible to create a new dynamic array within a procedure using the ReDim statement if the array to which it refers doesn't already exist. Typically, this results from an error of omission; the programmer forgets to explicitly define the array using Dim, Public, or Private. Since this method of creating an array can cause conflicts if a variable or array of the same name is subsequently defined explicitly, ReDim should be used only to redimension an existing array, not to define a new one.

- When a dynamic array is initialized, its individual elements are Empty. You can determine whether a value has been assigned to a particular element by using the *IsEmpty* function.

VBA/VBScript Differences

VBA allows you to define the lower limit of a redimensioned array as well as its upper limit. Arrays in VBScript, on the other hand, are always zero-based.

See Also   Dim Statement, Private Statement, Public Statement

RegExp Object

Description   The RegExp object provides support for regular expression matching—for the ability to search strings for substrings matching general or specific patterns.

In order to conduct a pattern search, you must first instantiate the regular expression object, with code like the following:

```
Dim oRegExp                ' Instance of RegExp object
Set oRegExp = New RegExp
```

To conduct a search using the RegExp object, do the following:

- Determine whether the search should be case-sensitive.
- Determine whether all instances or just the first instance of the substring should be returned.
- Supply the pattern string that you want to find.
- Provide a string that the RegExp object is to search.

The RegExp object allows you to search for a substring that matches your pattern string in any of three ways:

- You can determine whether a pattern match is found in the string.
- You can return one or all of the occurrences of the matching substrings. In this case, results are returned in Match objects within the Matches collection.
- You can replace all substrings matching the pattern string with another string.

Properties

The RegExp object supports the three properties shown in the following table. Each is documented in depth in its own section in the Language Reference.

Property name	Description
Global	Indicates whether to search for all occurrences of the pattern string or just for the first one
IgnoreCase	Indicates whether the pattern search is case-sensitive
Pattern	Indicates the pattern string to search for

Methods

The RegExp object supports the three methods shown in the following table. Each is documented in depth in its own section in the Language Reference.

Method name	Description
Execute	Returns a Matches collection containing information about the substrings in a larger string that match a pattern string
Replace	Replaces all substrings in a larger string that match a pattern string with a second string
Test	Indicates whether the search of a string has succeeded in finding a pattern match

VBA/VBScript Differences

The RegExp object, which was introduced to give VBScript comparable features to JScript, is exclusive to VBScript; it does not exist as a core part of the VBA language. However, the RegExp object is implemented as a member of the *VBScript.dll* library and can be added to any Visual Basic project. It is listed in the References dialog (which is available by selecting the References option from the Visual Basic Project menu) as "Microsoft VBScript Regular Expressions."

See Also   InStr, InStrB Functions, InstrRev Function, Match Object, Matches Collection Object

RegExp.Execute Method

Syntax

```
RegExp.Execute(string)
```

string
    Use: Required   Data Type: String
    The string to be searched.

Return Value   A Matches collection containing one or more Match objects.

Description   Performs a regular expression search against *string* and returns the results in the Matches collection.

Rules at a Glance

- The method searches *string* using the RegExp object's Pattern property.
- The results are returned in the Matches collection, which is a collection of Match objects.
- If the search finds no matches, the Matches collection is empty.

Programming Tips and Gotchas

- Remember to use the Set statement to assign the Matches collection returned by the Execute method to an object variable.
- You can determine whether the Matches collection returned by the Execute method is empty by examining its Count property. It is empty if the value of Count is 0.

Example

See the example for the RegExp.Pattern Property.

See Also   Matches Collection Object, RegExp.Pattern Property, RegExp.Replace Method, RegExp.Test Method

RegExp.Global Property

Data Type   Boolean

Description   Determines whether the search for a pattern string should match all occurrences in the search string or just the first one.

Rules at a Glance

A search will attempt to locate only the first occurrence of the pattern string in a search string; that is, the default value of the Global property is False. If you want to search for all occurrences of the pattern string in the search string, you must set the Global property to True.

Programming Tips and Gotchas
If you're interested only in determining whether the pattern string exists in the search string, there's no point in overriding the Global property's default value of False.

See Also   Matches Collection Object, Match Object, RegExp Object

---

RegExp.IgnoreCase Property

Data Type   Boolean

Description   Determines whether the search for a pattern string is case-sensitive.

Rules at a Glance
By default, regular expression searches are case-sensitive; that is, the default value of the IgnoreCase property is False. If you don't want the search to be case-sensitive, you must set the IgnoreCase property to True.

Programming Tips and Gotchas
If your search string does not attempt to match any alphabetic characters (A–Z and a–z), you can safely ignore the setting of IgnoreCase, since it won't affect the results of your search.

See Also   RegExp Object, RegExp.Pattern Property

RegExp.Pattern Property

Data Type   String

Description   Contains a pattern string that defines the substring to be found in a search string.

Rules at a Glance
The following table defines the meaning of the individual characters that can be included in the pattern string. The table in the "Programming Tips and Gotchas" section lists a pattern string using each symbol and shows the results returned by the Execute method.

Symbol	Description
\	Marks the next character as either a special character (such as \n for the newline character) or as a literal (if that character otherwise has special meaning in a pattern search string). The special characters are:
	\f form feed character
	\n newline character
	\r carriage return character
	\t tab character
	\v vertical tab character
^	Matches the beginning of input.
$	Matches the end of input.
*	Matches the preceding atom zero or more times.

Symbol	Description
+	Matches the preceding atom one or more times.
?	Matches the preceding atom zero or one time.
.	Matches any single character except a newline character.
( )	Defines a subexpression within the larger subexpression. A subexpression: • Overrides the order of precedence used in evaluating pattern strings. • Can be referenced again in the pattern string. To insert the result of the subexpression later in the pattern string, reference it by its one-based ordinal position among subexpressions, preceded by the backslash symbol (e.g., \1). See the example using the \num syntax in the "Programming Tips and Gotchas" section. • Can be referenced again in the replacement string in calls to the RegExp.Replace method. To use the result of the original subexpression as a replacement string, reference its one-based ordinal position among subexpressions, preceded by a dollar sign (e.g., $1). See RegExp.Replace Method for an example.
x|y	Matches either x or y.
{n}	Matches exactly n times, where n is a nonnegative integer.
{n,}	Matches at least n times, where n is a nonnegative integer. o{1,} is the same as o+, and o{0,} is the same as o*.
{n,m}	Matches at least n and at most m times, where m and n are nonnegative integers. o{0,1} is the same as o?.
[abc]	Matches any one of the enclosed characters (represented by abc) in the character set.
[^xyz]	Matches any character (represented by xyz) not enclosed in the character set. For example, [^abc] matches the "p" in "plain."
[a-z]	Matches any character in a range of characters (represented by a-z).
[^m-z]	Matches any character not included in a range of characters (represented by m-z).
\b	Matches a word boundary; that is, the position between a word and a space. The word boundary symbol does not include newline characters or the end of input (see the \s symbol).
\B	Matches a nonword boundary. ea*r\B matches the "ear" in "never early."
\d	Matches a digit character. Equivalent to [0-9].
\D	Matches a nondigit character. Equivalent to [^0-9].
\s	Matches any whitespace, including space, tab, form-feed, etc. Equivalent to [\f\n\r\t\v].
\S	Matches any nonwhitespace character. Equivalent to [^ \f\n\r\t\v].
\w	Matches any word character including underscore. Equivalent to [A-Za-z0-9_].
\W	Matches any nonword character, including whitespace and carriage returns. Equivalent to [^A-Za-z0-9_].
\num	Matches the subexpression (enclosed in parentheses) whose ordinal position in the pattern is num, where num is a positive integer.
\n	Matches n, where n is the octal value of an ASCII code. Octal escape values must be 1, 2, or 3 digits long and must not exceed 256; if they do, only the first two digits are used.
\xn	Matches n, where n is the hexadecimal value of an ASCII code. Hexadecimal escape values must be two digits long.

Programming Tips and Gotchas

The following table shows a search string and the Value property of each Match object returned by the Execute method when the string:

```
"To be or not to be. That is the question." & vbCrLf & _
"Whether 'tis nobler in the mind to endure..."
```

is passed to the Execute method. The RegExp object's Global property is set to True, and its IgnoreCase property is set to True.

Pattern	Matches
\n.....	Wheth
^.....	To be
.....$	re...
no*	no, n, no, n, n, n (6 matches)
no+	no, no (2 matches)
bo*e?	be, be, b (3 matches)
qu...	quest
th(at|e)	That, the, the, the (4 matches)
to|i	To, to, i, i, i, i, i, to (8 matches)
\.{3}	...
\.{2,}	...
\.{1,3)	., ., ... (3 matches)
i[nst]	is, is, in, in (4 matches)
[^bhm]e	ue, le, e, re (4 matches)
[r-z]o	To, to, to (3 matches)
[^o-z]o	o, no, io, no (4 matches)
.o\b	To, to, to (3 matches)
.o\B	o, no, io, no (4 matches)
\d	(0 matches)
\D\.\b	e., n. (2 matches)
...\s	be, not, be., hat, the, on., her, tis, ler, the, ind (11 matches)
\b\S{3}\b	not, the, tis, the (3 matches)
\w{3}\.\s	ion.
\W{3}	. (vbCrLf), ... (2 matches)
(\S+)(\s+)\S+\2\S+\2\S+\2	To be or not, to be. That is, Whether 'tis nobler in (3 matches)
\164\157	To, to, to (3 matches)
\x74\x6f	To, to, to (3 matches)

Searches using regular expressions can be quite complex. If you're interested in a book that deals exclusively with regular expressions and pattern searches, see *Mastering Regular Expressions*, written by Jeffrey E. Friedl (O'Reilly).

Example

The following routine allows you to experiment with searches using regular expressions. When you call it, just pass the string you'd like to search. A dialog appears repeatedly, prompting you for a pattern string, followed by another dialog that displays the results of the search using the regular expression you've entered. When you're finished, simply click the Cancel button to exit the routine:

```
Public Sub SearchExp(strSearch)

Dim oRegExp, colMatches, oMatch
Dim strPattern

Set oRegExp = New RegExp
```

```
oRegExp.Global = True
oRegExp.IgnoreCase = True

Do

    strPattern = InputBox("Enter pattern string: ", "Pattern", "")
    if strPattern = "" then
        Exit Do
    Else
        oRegExp.Pattern = strPattern
    end If
    strMsg = "Pattern: " & oRegExp.Pattern

    Set colMatches = oRegExp.Execute(strSearch)
    strMsg = strMsg & ", Matches: " & colMatches.Count & vbcrlf & vbcrlf
    if colMatches.Count > 0 Then
        for each oMatch in colMatches
            strMsg = strMsg & oMatch.Value & vbCrLf
        next
    Else
        strMsg = strMsg & "No match found"
    End If

    MsgBox strMsg

Loop

End Sub
```

See Also   RegExp Object, RegExp.Execute Method, RegExp.Replace Method, RegExp.Test Method

RegExp.Replace Method

Syntax

```
RegExp.Replace(searchString, replaceString)
```

searchString
   Use: Required   Data Type: String

   The string to be searched.

replaceString
   Use: Required   Data Type: String

   The replacement string.

Return Value   A String containing the entire string that results when matched substrings in *searchString* are replaced with *replaceString*.

Description   Performs a regular expression search against *searchString* and replaces matched substrings with *replaceString*.

Rules at a Glance

- The method searches *searchString* using the RegExp object's Pattern property.
- If no matches are found, the method returns *searchString* unchanged.

Programming Tips and Gotchas

replaceString the replacement string, can contain pattern strings that control how substrings in *searchString* should be replaced.

Example

The following WSH code illustrates the use of subexpressions in the search and replacement strings. The search returns three subexpressions: "to be", "or", and "not to be". The first subexpression is replaced with the third, while the third subexpression is replaced with the first, resulting in the string "not to be or to be":

```
Dim strString, strPattern, strReplace, strResult
Dim oRegExp

strString = "to be or not to be "
strPattern = "(\S+\s+\S+\s+)(\S+\s+)(\S+\s+\S+\s+\S+\s+)"
strReplace = "$3$2$1"

Set oRegExp = New RegExp
oRegExp.Pattern = strPattern

strResult = oRegExp.Replace(strString, strReplace)
If strResult = strString Then
    MsgBox "No replacements were made"
Else
    MsgBox strResult
End If
```

See Also   RegExp.Execute Method, RegExp.Pattern Property, RegExp.Test Method

---

RegExp.Test Method

Syntax

```
RegExp.Test(string)
```

string
    Use: Required   Data Type: String

    The string to be searched.

Return Value   A Boolean indicating whether a match was found.

Description   Performs a regular expression search against *string* and indicates whether a match was found

Rules at a Glance

- Prior to calling the Test method, the search string should be defined by setting the Pattern property.
- The method searches *string* using the RegExp object's Pattern property.
- The method returns True if the search succeeds and False otherwise.

Programming Tips and Gotchas

- Since a search is successful if one match is found, you do not have to set the RegExp object's Global property before calling the Test method.

- You can use the method to determine whether a match exists before calling either the Execute or the Replace methods.

See Also   RegExp.Execute Method, RegExp.Pattern Property, RegExp.Replace Method

---

Rem Statement

Syntax

```
Rem comment
' comment
```

comment

> Use: Optional
>
> A textual comment to place within the code.

Description   Use the Rem statement or an apostrophe (') to place remarks within the code.

Rules at a Glance

Apostrophes held within quotation marks aren't treated as comment markers, as this code snippet shows:

```
myVar = "'Something'"
```

VBA/VBScript Differences

- In VBA, if you use the Rem statement (but not the apostrophe) on the same line as program code, a colon is required after the program code and before the Rem statement. For example:

```
Set objDoc = Server.CreateObject("MyApp.MyObj") : Rem Define the object
                                                  Rem reference
```

  VBScript, on the other hand, successfully recognizes the Rem statement even without the colon.

- In VBA using the VBA editor, if you "comment out" a line, that line and all of its line continuations are affected. In VBScript, the comment keyword or symbol must be added to each line to be "commented out."

Replace Function

Syntax

```
Replace(string, stringToReplace, replacementString [, start[, count[,
compare]]])
```

string

> Use: Required   Data Type: String
>
> The complete string containing the substring to be replaced.

stringToReplace
> Use: Required   Data Type: String

> The substring to be found by the function.

replacementString
> Use: Required   Data Type: String

> The new substring to replace *stringToReplace* in *string*.

start
> Use: Optional   Data Type: Long

> The character position in *string* at which the search for *stringToReplace* begins.

count
> Use: Optional   Data Type: Long

> The number of instances of *stringToReplace* to replace.

compare
> Use: Optional   Data Type: Integer

> The method that compares *stringToReplace* with *string*; its value can be vbBinaryCompare or vbTextCompare.

Return Value   The return value from *Replace* depends on the parameters you specify in the argument list, as the following table shows:

If	Return value
string = ""	Zero-length string ("")
string is Null	An error
StringToReplace = ""	Copy of *string*
replacementString = ""	Copy of *string* with all instances of *stringToReplace* removed
start > Len(string)	Zero-length string ("")
count = 0	Copy of *string*

Description   Replaces a given number of instances of a specified substring in another string.

Rules at a Glance

- If *start* is omitted, the search begins at the start of the string.
- If *count* is omitted, its value defaults to –1, which means that all instances of the substring after *start* are replaced.
- vbBinaryCompare is case-sensitive; that is, *Replace* matches both character and case, whereas vbTextCompare is case-insensitive, matching only character, regardless of case.
- The default value for *compare* is vbBinaryCompare.
- *start* not only specifies where the search for *stringToReplace* begins, but also where the new string returned by the *Replace* function commences.

Programming Tips and Gotchas

- If *count* isn't used, be careful when replacing short strings that may form parts of unrelated words. For example, consider the following:

```
Dim sString
sString = "You have to be careful when you do this " _
            & "or you could ruin your string"
Msgbox Replace(sString, "you", "we")
```

Because we don't specify a value for *count*, the call to *Replace* replaces every occurrence of "you" in the original string with "we." But the fourth occurrence of "you" is part of the word "your," which is modified to become "wer."

The best way to avoid this problem is to use regular expressions. By specifying the word-break pattern in your search criterion, you can insure that only whole words are matched. For example:

```
strSearch = "You have to be careful when you do this " _
            & "or you could ruin your string for you."

oRegExp.Pattern = "you•"
str = oRegExp.Replace(strSearch, "we")

MsgBox str
```

- You must also be aware that if *start* is greater than 1, the returned string starts at that character and not at the first character of the original string, as you might expect. For example, given the statements:

```
sOld = "This string checks the Replace function"
sNew = Replace(sOld, "check", "test", 5, _
            vbTextCompare)
sNew will contain the value:
"string tests the Replace function"
```

See Also   InStr, InStrB Functions, Mid, MidB Functions

RGB Function

Syntax

RGB(*red, green, blue*)

red

    Use: Required   Data Type: Integer

    A number between 0 and 255, inclusive.

green

    Use: Required   Data Type: Integer

    A number between 0 and 255, inclusive.

blue

    Use: Required   Data Type: Integer

    A number between 0 and 255, inclusive.

Return Value   A Long integer representing the RGB color value.

Description   Returns a system color code that can be assigned to object color properties.

Rules at a Glance

- The RGB color value represents the relative intensity of the red, green, and blue components of a pixel that produces a specific color on the display.
- The RGB function assumes any argument greater than 255 is 255.
- The following table demonstrates how the individual color values combine to create certain colors:

Color	Red	Green	Blue
Black	0	0	0
Blue	0	0	255
Green	0	255	0
Red	255	0	0
White	255	255	255

Programming Tips and Gotchas

- The RGB value is derived with the following formula:

    RGB = *red* + (*green* * 256) + (*blue* * 65536)

    In other words, the individual color components are stored in the opposite order one would expect. VBScript stores the red color component in the low-order byte of the long integer's low-order word, the green color in the high-order byte of the low-order word, and the blue color in the low-order byte of the high-order word.
- VBScript has a wide range of intrinsic color constants that can assign color values directly to color properties of objects. For a list of these, see Appendix B.

Right, RightB Functions

Syntax

    Right(*string*, *length*)

string
> Use: Required   Data Type: String
>
> The string to be processed.

length
> Use: Required   Data Type: Long
>
> The number of characters to return from the right of the string.

Return Value   A String.

Description   Returns a string containing the right-most *length* characters of *string*.

Rules at a Glance

- If *length* is 0, a zero-length string (" ") is returned.
- If *length* is greater than the length of *string*, *string* is returned.
- If *length* is less than zero or is Null, an error is generated.
- If *string* contains a Null, *Right* returns Null.

Example

The following function assumes it's passed either a filename or a complete path and filename, and returns the filename from the end of the string:

```
Private Function ParseFileName(strFullPath)

Dim lngPos, lngStart
Dim strFilename

lngStart = 1
Do
    lngPos = InStr(lngStart, strFullPath, "\")
    If lngPos = 0 Then
        strFilename = Right(strFullPath, Len(strFullPath) - lngStart + 1)
    Else
        lngStart = lngPos + 1
    End If
Loop While lngPos > 0

ParseFileName = strFilename

End Function
```

Programming Tips and Gotchas

- Use the *Len* function to determine the total length of *string*.

- When you use the *RightB* function with byte data, *length* specifies the number of bytes to return.

VB/VBA Differences

Because VBScript doesn't support strong typing, it does not support the *Right$* and *RightB$* functions, which explicitly return a data type.

See Also   Len, LenB Functions, Left, LeftB Functions

Rnd Function

Syntax

```
Rnd[(seed)]
```

seed

Use: Optional   Data Type: Single

Any valid numeric expression.

Return Value   A random number of variant type Single.

Description   Returns a random number.

Rules at a Glance

- The behavior of the *Rnd* function is determined by *seed*, as described in this table:

Number	Rnd generates...
< 0	The same number each time, using *seed* as the seed number
> 0	The next random number in the current sequence

Number	Rnd generates...
0	The most recently generated number
Not supplied	The next random number in the current sequence

- The *Rnd* function always returns a value between 0 and 1.
- If number isn't supplied, the *Rnd* function uses the last number generated as the seed for the next generated number. This means that given an initial seed (*seed*), the same sequence is generated if number isn't supplied on subsequent calls.

Example

The following example uses the Randomize statement along with the *Rnd* function to fill 100 cells of an Excel worksheet with random numbers:

```
Public Sub GenerateRandomNumbers( )

Dim objExcel, objBook, objSheet
Dim intRow, intCol

' Start Excel
Set objExcel = CreateObject("Excel.Application")

' Get or create active worksheet
If objExcel.ActiveSheet Is Nothing Then
    Set objBook = objExcel.Workbooks.Add
End If
Set objSheet = objExcel.ActiveWorkbook.ActiveSheet
Randomize

' make Excel visible
objExcel.Visible = True
' Set the color of the input text to blue
objSheet.Cells.Font.ColorIndex = 5
' Loop through first 10 rows & columns,
' filling them with random numbers
For intRow = 1 To 10
    For intCol = 1 To 10
        objSheet.Cells(intRow, intCol).Value = Rnd
    Next
Next
' Resize columns to accommodate random numbers
objSheet.Columns("A:C").AutoFit

End Sub
```

Programming Tips and Gotchas

- Before calling the *Rnd* function, you should use the Randomize statement to initialize the random number generator.
- The standard formula for producing numbers in a given range is as follows:

        Int((*highest* - *lowest* + 1) * Rnd + *lowest*)

    where *lowest* is the lowest required number in the range, and *highest* is the highest.

See Also   Randomize Sub

Round Function

Syntax

Round(*expression*[, *numdecimalplaces*])

expression
　　Use: Required　　Data Type: Numeric

　　Any numeric expression.

numdecimalplaces
　　Use: Optional　　Data Type: Long

　　The number of places to include after the decimal point.

Return Value　　The same data type as *expression*.

Description　　Rounds a given number to a specified number of decimal places.

Rules at a Glance

- *numdecimalplaces* can be any whole number between 0 and 16.
- *Round* follows standard rules for rounding:
  — If the digit in the position to the right of *numdecimalplaces* is greater than 5, the digit in the *numdecimalplaces* position is incremented by one.
  — If the digit in the position to the right of *numdecimalplaces* is less than 5, the digits to the right of *numdecimalplaces* are dropped.
  — If the digit in the position to the right of *numdecimalplaces* is 5 and the digit in the *numdecimalplaces* position is odd, the digit in the *numdecimalplaces* position is incremented by one.
  — If the digit in the position to the right of *numdecimalplaces* is 5 and the digit in the *numdecimalplaces* position is even, the digits to the right of *numdecimalplaces* are dropped.

Programming Tips and Gotchas

If *expression* is a string representation of a numeric value, *Round* converts it to a numeric value before rounding. However, if *expression* isn't a string representation of a number, *Round* generates runtime error 13, "Type mismatch." The *IsNumeric* function insures that *expression* is a proper numeric representation before calling *Round*.

See Also　　Fix Function, Int Function

RTrim Function

Syntax

RTrim(*stringexp*)

stringexp
　　Use: Required　　Data Type: String

　　A valid string expression.

Return Value　　A String.

Description　　Removes any trailing spaces from *stringexp*.

Rules at a Glance

If *stringexp* contains a Null, *RTrim* returns Null.

Programming Tips and Gotchas

Unless you need to keep leading spaces, you should use the *Trim* function, which is the equivalent of RTrim(LTrim(*string*)), thereby clearing both leading and trailing spaces in a single function call.

VB/VBA Differences

Because it does not support strong typing, VBScript does not support the VBA *RTrim$* function, which returns a strongly typed string rather than a string variant.

See Also   LTrim Function, Trim Function

ScriptEngine Function

Syntax

```
ScriptEngine( )
```

Return Value   A String.

Description   Indicates the scripting language currently in use.

Rules at a Glance

According to the documentation, the function returns the values shown in the following table:

Return value	Description
JScript	Microsoft JScript
VBA	Visual Basic for Applications
VBScript	VBScript

Programming Tips and Gotchas

The function is implemented in *VBScript.dll*, as well as in *JScript.dll*. However, it is not implemented in the VB Version 6 runtime libraries. Calls to this function from VBA code will generate an error rather than return the string "VBA".

VBA/VBScript Differences

This function is not supported in VBA.

See Also   ScriptEngineBuildVersion   Function,   ScriptEngineMajorVersion Function

---

ScriptEngineBuildVersion Function

Syntax

```
ScriptEngineBuildVersion( )
```

Return Value   A Long.

Description   Returns the build number of the VBScript script engine.

Programming Tips and Gotchas

The function is also implemented in the JScript script engine.

VBA/VBScript Differences

This function is not supported in VBA.

ScriptEngineMajorVersion Function

Syntax

```
ScriptEngineMajorVersion( )
```

Return Value   A Long.

Description   Indicates the major version (1, 2, etc.) of the scripting language currently in use.

Rules at a Glance

The following table lists the versions of VBScript through 5.0, as well as the year in which they were released and the products with which they were initially released:

Version	Year	Product
1.0	1996	Internet Explorer 3.0
2.0	1997	IIS 2.0
3.0	1998	Internet Explorer 4.0, IIS 4.0, WSH 1.0, Outlook 98
4.0	1998	Visual Studio 6.0
5.0	1999	Internet Explorer 5.0
5.5	2001	Internet Explorer 5.5
5.6	2002	Microsoft Visual Studio .NET

Programming Tips and Gotchas

- The function is also implemented in the JScript script engine.
- If your script requires some functionality available in a baseline version, ordinarily you want to make sure that the script is running on that version or a later version. For instance, if your script requires regular expression support, which became available only in VBScript Version 5, you would test for the version with a code fragment like:

```
If ScriptingEngineMajorVersion >= 5 Then
```

You do not want to test for equality, as in:

```
If ScriptingEngineMajorVersion = 5 Then
```

since that may leave your script unable to run on versions of VBScript later than Version 5.

VBA/VBScript Differences

This function is not supported in VBA.

See Also   ScriptEngineBuildVersion   Function,   ScriptEngineMinorVersion
Function

ScriptEngineMinorVersion Function

Syntax

```
ScriptEngineMinorVersion( )
```

Return Value   A Long.

Description   Indicates the minor version (the number to the right of the decimal
point) of the scripting language engine currently in use.

Programming Tips and Gotchas

- The function is also implemented in the JScript script engine.
- If your script requires some functionality available in a baseline minor version,
  you ordinarily would want to make sure that the script is running on that version
  or a later version. Test for a minor version with a code fragment like:

```
lMajor = ScriptingEngineMajorVersion
lMinor = ScriptingEngineMinorVersion
If (lMajor = 5 And lMinor >= 1) Or (lMajor > 5) Then
```

You should *not* test for equality, and you should never test for a minor version
alone, without considering the major version.

VBA/VBScript Differences

This function is not supported in VBA.

See Also   ScriptEngine   Function,   ScriptEngineBuildVersion   Function,
ScriptEngineMajorVersion Function

Second Function

Syntax

```
Second(time)
```

time
    Use: Required   Data Type: String, numeric, or date/time
    Any valid expression that can represent a time value.

Return Value   An Integer in the range 0 to 59.

Description   Extracts the seconds from a given time expression.

Rules at a Glance

If the time expression time is Null, the *Second* function returns Null.

See Also   Hour Function, Minute Function

Select Case Statement

Syntax

```
Select Case testexpression
    [Case expressionlist
        [statements-n]] ...
    [Case Else
        [elsestatements]]
End Select
```

testexpression
> Use: Required   Data Type: Any
>
> Any numeric or string expression whose value determines which block of code is executed.

expressionlist
> Use: Required   Data Type: Any
>
> Comma-delimited list of expressions to compare values with *testexpression*.

statements-n
> Use: Optional
>
> Program statements to execute if a match is found between any section of *expressionlist* and *testexpression*.

elsestatements
> Use: Optional
>
> Program statements to execute if a match between *testexpression* and any *expressionlist* can't be found.

Description   Allows for conditional execution of a block of code, typically out of three or more code blocks, based on some condition. Use the Select Case statement as an alternative to complex nested If...Then...Else statements.

Rules at a Glance

- Any number of Case clauses can be included in the Select Case statement.
- If a match between *testexpression* and any part of *expressionlist* is found, the program statements following the matched *expressionlist* are executed. When program execution encounters the next Case clause or the End Select clause, execution continues with the statement immediately following the End Select clause.
- Both *expressionlist* and *testexpression* must be a *valid expression* that can consist of one or more of the following: a literal value, a variable, an arithmetic or comparison operator, or the value returned by an intrinsic or user-defined function.
- If used, the Case Else clause must be the last Case clause. Program execution encounters the Case Else clause—and thereby executes, the *elsestatements*—only if all other *expressionlist* comparisons fail.
- Select Case statements can also be nested, resulting in a successful match between *testexpression* and *expressionlist* being another Select Case statement.

Example

The following example uses Select Case to read a variable populated by the user and determine the name of the user's operating system:

```
Dim varOS, varOSDesc

Select Case varOS
   Case 1
      varOSDesc = "Windows NT"
   Case 2
      varOSDesc = "Windows 98"
   Case 3
      varOSDesc = "Windows 95"
   Case 4
      varOSDesc = "Windows 3.11"
   Case 5
      varOSDesc = "Windows 2000"
   Case 6
      varOSDesc = "Windows ME"
   Case 7
      varOSDesc = "Windows XP"
   Case Else
      varOSDesc = "OS is unknown"
End Select
```

Programming Tips and Gotchas

- The Select Case statement is the VBA/VBScript equivalent of the Switch construct found in C and C++.

- The Case Else clause is optional. However, as with If...Then...Else statements, it's often good practice to provide a Case Else to catch the exceptional instance when—perhaps unexpectedly—a match can't be found in any of the *expressionlists* you have provided.

- If *testexpression* satisfies more than one *expressionlist* comparison, only the code in the first is executed.

VBA/VBScript Differences

VBA supports two variations of *expressionlist* that are not supported by VBScript. These are shown in the following table:

Not supported	Examples
To keyword	Case 10 To 20, 110 To 120
Is keyword	Case Is >= 100Case Is <= 10, Is >= 100

See Also   If...Then Statement

SetLocale Function

Syntax

```
SetLocale(lcid)
```

lcid

  Use: Optional   Data Type: Long or String

  A number representing a locale ID.

Return Value   A Long indicating the previous locale ID.

Description   Sets the current locale ID.

Rules at a Glance

- A locale ID represents language as well as regional conventions. It determines such things as keyboard layout, alphabetic sort order, and date, time, number, and currency formats.
- Appendix D lists valid locale IDs.
- If *SetLocale* is called with no arguments, it resets the script locale back to the host default, which is usually the user default.
- If *lcid* is zero or 1024, the locale is set as defined by the user's locale ID.
- If *lcid* is 2048, the local is set as defined by the system's regional settings.

Programming Tips and Gotchas

- There is no need to call *GetLocale* and store its returned value before calling *SetLocale*, since *SetLocale* returns the value of the previous locale ID.
- *SetLocale* sets the locale ID of the script engine only. It does not affect the system, user, or host/application locale IDs.

VBA/Script Differences

The *SetLocale* function is not supported by VBA.

See Also   GetLocale Function

Set Statement

Syntax

    Set objectvar = (objectexpression | New classname Nothing)

objectvar

  Use: Required   Data Type: Object

  The name of the object variable or property.

objectexpression

  Use: Optional   Data Type: Object

  An expression evaluating to an object.

New

  Use: Optional   Type: Keyword

  Creates a new instance of an object defined using the Class...End Class construct, or with the syntax New RegExp instantiates the Regular Expression object.

classname

  Use: Required   Data Type: String literal

  The name of the class defined by the Class...End Class construct to be instantiated.

```
Nothing
```
    Use: Optional   Type: Keyword

    Assigns the special data type `Nothing` to *objectvar*, thereby releasing the reference to the object.

Description   Assigns an object reference to a variable or property.

Rules at a Glance

- *objectvar* doesn't hold a copy of the underlying object; it simply holds a reference to the object.

- If the `New` keyword is used is used to instantiate a VBScript class defined using the `Class...End Class` construct, a new instance of the class is immediately created and its Class Initialize event fires. This applies only to classes defined using the `Class...End Class` construct.

  You can also instantiate a Regular Expression object with the `New` keyword by using a statement like the following:

  ```
  Set oRegExp = New RegExp
  ```

- All classes defined by the `Class...End Class` construct can be created using the `New` keyword. For external objects, the application's object model determines which objects can be created and which cannot.

- If *objectvar* holds a reference to an object when the `Set` statement is executed, the current reference is released and the new one referred to in *objectexpression* is assigned.

- *objectexpression* can be any of the following:

  — The name of an object. This creates a duplicate object reference in which two references point to the same object. For instance:

  ```
  Dim oFS, oRoot, oFolder
  Set oFS = CreateObject("Scripting.FileSystemObject")
  Set oRoot = oFS.Drives("C").RootFolder
  Set oFolder = oRoot
  ```

  — A variable that has been previously declared and instantiated using the `Set` statement and that refers to the same type of object:

  ```
  Dim dSpace
  Dim oFS, oDrive

  dSpace = CDbl(0)
  Set oFS = CreateObject("Scripting.FileSystemObject")
  Set oDrive = oFS.Drives("C")
  dSpace = dSpace + oDrive.FreeSpace
  Set oDrive = oFS.Drives("D")
  dSpace = dSpace + oDrive.FreeSpace

  MsgBox "Total free space: " & dSpace & "  " & typename(dSpace)
  ```

  — A call to a function, method, or property that returns the same type of object.

- By assigning `Nothing` to *objectvar*, the reference held by *objectvar* to the object is released.

Example

The following code creates a simple web page that prompts the user for a name and an email address if she desires to be added to a discussion forum:

```
<HTML>
<HEAD>
<TITLE>Join Discussion Forum</TITLE>
</HEAD>
<BODY>
<H2><CENTER>Join the Discussion Forum</CENTER></H2>
<FORM ACTION="AddContact.asp" NAME=frmAdd METHOD="POST">
    Name:
    <INPUT TYPE="Text" NAME="txtName"><BR>
    Email Address:
    <INPUT TYPE="Text" NAME="txtEmail"><BR><BR>
    <INPUT TYPE="Submit" VALUE="Submit">
</FORM>
</BODY>
</HTML>
```

Following is the source for *AddContact.asp*, the ASP application that instantiates an instance of the CContact class to handle data access using ADO:

```
<HTML>
<HEAD>
<TITLE>Our Discussion Forum</TITLE>
<SCRIPT LANGUAGE="VBSCRIPT" RUNAT="SERVER">

Const adLockOptimistic = 3
Const adOpenDynamic = 2
Const adCmdTable = 2

Class CContact

Private rs
Private sName, sEmail

Public Property Get ShowCount( )
    rs.MoveLast
    ShowCount = rs.RecordCount
End Property

Public Function AddContact
    Dim sRetString

    sName = Server.HTMLEncode(Request.Form("txtName"))
    sEmail = Request.Form("txtEmail")
    If sName = "" Or sEmail = "" Then
        sRetString = "Please press the back button and enter both " & _
                     "your name and your email address."
    Else
        rs.AddNew
        rs.Fields("ContactName") = sName
        rs.Fields("Email") = sEmail
        rs.Update
        sRetString = "<H3><CENTER>" & _
```

```
                    "Thank you for joining our forum!" & _
                    "</H3></CENTER><P>" & _
                    "Your information has been added to the " & _
                    "forum membership list.<P>" & _
                    "The forum now has   " & Me.ShowCount & " members.<P>"
        End If

    AddContact = sRetString
End Function

Private Sub Class_Initialize()
    Dim sConnect
    sConnect = "Provider=Microsoft.Jet.OLEDB.4.0;" & _
               "Data Source=E:\Databases\DiscussionList.mdb"
    Set rs = CreateObject("ADODB.Recordset")
    rs.Open "Contacts", sConnect, adOpenDynamic, adLockOptimistic, _
            adCmdTable
End Sub

Private Sub Class_Terminate()
    rs.Close
    Set rs = Nothing
End Sub

End Class
</SCRIPT>
</HEAD>
<BODY>
<H1>From the Discussion Forum...</H1><P>
<%
    Dim oContact
    Set oContact = New CContact
    Response.Write oContact.AddContact
%>
</BODY>
</HTML>
```

Programming Tips and Gotchas

- You can have more than one object variable referring to the same object. However, bear in mind that a change to the underlying object using one object variable is reflected in all the other object variables that reference that object. For example, consider the following code fragment, in which the *objColorCopy* object reference is set equal to the *objColor* object:

```
Dim objColor, objColorCopy
Set objColor = New CColor      ' CColor class not shown
Set objColorCopy = objColor

objColor.CurrentColor = "Blue"
Msgbox objColorCopy.CurrentColor
```

Since both *objColor* and *objColorCopy* reference a single object, the value of the CurrentColor property is Blue in both cases.

- It is commonly believed that you should release object references as soon as you are finished with them using code like the following:

```
Dim myClass
Set myClass = New SomeObject
' Do something here
Set myClass = Nothing
```

Most of the time, though, releasing object references is unnecessary, since they are released anyway by the garbage collector when the object reference goes out of scope. There are only a couple of situations in which it is necessary to explicitly release object references:

1. When the object encapsulates a scarce resource, such as a database connection. In this case, it often makes sense to release the object reference as soon as you are done with it.

2. When two objects hold references to one another. In this situation, the objects are not destroyed when their references go out of scope. And their references going out of scope means that it is no longer possible to release the objects programmatically. VBScript objects (i.e., objects instantiated from classes declared with the Class... End Class construct will be destroyed when the scripting engine is torn down, which may be before application shutdown. COM objects instantiated with the *CreateObject* or *GetObject* functions, though, may persist until the application terminates. Since terminating a web server or the ASP process, in particular, is highly undesirable, it is far preferable to release object references explicitly by setting them to nothing. The following code illustrates a circular reference:

```
Class MyClass
    Dim Subclass

    Public Property Get MySubclass
        Set MySubclass = Subclass
    End Property

    Public Property Set MySubclass(value)
        Set Subclass = value
    End Property
End Class

Dim myClass1, myClass2

Set myClass1 = New MyClass
Set myClass2 = New MyClass

Set myClass1.MySubclass = myClass2
Set myClass2.MySubclass = myClass1
```

• When trying to discover whether an object reference has been successfully assigned, you should determine if the object variable has been assigned as Nothing. However, you can't use the equality comparison operator (=) for this purpose; you must use the Is operator, as the following code snippet shows:

```
If objectvar Is Nothing Then
    ... 'assignment failed
End If
```

- Any function that returns an object reference requires the use of the Set statement to assign the reference to a variable. This includes the VBScript *CreateObject* and *GetObject* functions, as well as the WSH WScript.CreateObject method and the ASP Server.CreateObject method.

```
Dim oMainObject
Set oMainObject = CreateObject("MainLib.MainObject")
```

VBA/VBScript Differences
- An external createable object can be instantiated using VBA's New when the variable is declared if the VBA project has a reference to its type library:

```
Dim oFS As New Scripting.FileSystemObject
```

In this case, there is no need use the Set statement to instantiate the object, since it will be instantiated when it is next referenced in code. Since this early binding is not supported by VBScript, however, this use of the New keyword is not allowed.

- An external createable object can be instantiated using the VBA New keyword along with the Set statement if the VBA project has a reference to its type library. For example:

```
Dim oFS As Scripting.FileSystemObject
Set oFS = New Scripting.FileSystemObject
```

Since VBScript does not support early binding, however, this usage is not allowed. The Set statement, along with the New keyword, can be used only to instantiate a class declared with the Class...End Class construct.

See Also   CreateObject Function, GetObject Function, GetRef Function

---

Sgn Function

Syntax

```
Sgn(number)
```

number
     Use: Required   Data Type: Any expression capable of conversion into a numeric value

A numeric expression.

Return Value   An Integer.

Description   Determines the sign of a number.

Rules at a Glance
The return value of the *Sgn* function is determined by the sign of *number*:

If number is...	Sgn returns
Positive	1
Zero	0
Negative	−1

Programming Tips and Gotchas

- If you're planning on using the *Sgn* function to evaluate a result to False (0) or True (any nonzero value), you could also use the *CBool* function.
- The major use for *Sgn*—a fairly trivial one—is to determine the sign of an expression. It's equivalent to the following code:

```
Function Sgn(varNumber)
    If varNumber > 0 Then
        Sgn = 1
    ElseIf varNumber = 0 Then
        Sgn = 0
    Else
        Sgn = -1
    End If
End Function
```

- *Sgn* is useful in cases in which the sign of a quantity defines the sign of an expression. For example:

```
lngResult = lngQty * Sgn(lngValue)
```

- Although *Sgn* handles the conversion of strings to numeric data, it's a good idea to make sure that number is valid by calling the *IsNumeric* function before the call to *Sgn*.

See Also   If...Then Statement

Sin Function

Syntax

```
Sin(number)
```

number
  Use: Required   Data Type: Numeric

  An angle expressed in radians.

Return Value   A Double containing the sine of an angle.

Description   Returns the ratio of two sides of a right triangle in the range –1 to 1.

Rules at a Glance

The ratio is determined by dividing the length of the side opposite the angle by the length of the hypotenuse.

Programming Tips and Gotchas

- You can convert radians to degrees using the formula:

```
radians = degrees * (pi/180)
```

- You can convert degrees to radians using the formula:

```
degrees = radians * (180/pi)
```

Space Function

Syntax

```
Space(number)
```

number
> Use: Required   Data Type: Integer
>
> An expression evaluating to the number of spaces required.

Return Value   A String containing *number* spaces.

Description   Creates a string containing *number* spaces.

Rules at a Glance

- While *number* can be zero (in which case the function returns a empty string), runtime error 5, "Invalid procedure call or argument," is generated if *number* is negative.
- *Space* is a "convenience function" that is equivalent to the function call:

```
sString = String(number, 32)
```

VBA/VBScript Differences

VBScript doesn't support the VBA *Space$* function.

Split Function

Syntax

```
Split(expression, [delimiter[, count[, compare]]])
```

expression
> Use: Required   Data Type: String
>
> A string to be broken up into multiple strings.

delimiter
> Use: Optional   Data Type: String
>
> The character used to delimit the substrings in *expression*.

count
> use: Optional   Data Type: Long
>
> The number of strings to return.

compare
> Use: Optional   Data Type: Long
>
> The method of comparison. Possible values are vbBinaryCompare or vbTextCompare. Note that both are intrinsic VBScript constants; you do not have to define them yourself using the Const statement.

Return Value   A variant array consisting of the arguments passed into the function.

Description   Parses a single string containing delimited values into an array.

Rules at a Glance

- If *delimiter* isn't found in *expression*, *Split* returns the entire string in element 0 of the return array.
- If *delimiter* is omitted, a space character is used as the delimiter.
- If *count* is omitted or its value is –1, all strings are returned.
- The default comparison method is vbBinaryCompare. If *delimiter* is an alphabetic character, this setting controls whether the search for it in *expression* is case-sensitive (vbBinaryCompare) or not (vbTextCompare).
- Once *count* has been reached, the remainder of the string is placed, unprocessed, into the next element of the returned array.

Programming Tips and Gotchas

- The variable you declare to assign the return value of Filter must be a simple variant, rather than a variant array. The following code is incorrect:

```
' Incorrect
Dim sArray( )
sArray = Split(sString, ",")
```

This error is corrected in the following code fragment:

```
' Correct
Dim sArray
sArray = Split(sString, ",")
```

- Strings are written to the returned array in the order in which they appear in *expression*.

See Also   Join Function

Sqr Function

Syntax

```
Sqr(number)
```

number
  Use: Required   Data Type: Double
  Any numeric expression greater than or equal to 0.

Return Value   A Double containing the square root of *number*.

Description   Calculates the square root of a given number.

Rules at a Glance

number must be equal to or greater than zero or runtime error 5, "Invalid procedure call or argument," occurs.

StrComp Function

Syntax

```
StrComp(string1, string2[, compare])
```

string1
> Use: Required   Data Type: String
>
> Any string expression.

string2
> Use: Required   Data Type: String
>
> Any string expression.

compare
> Use: Optional   Data Type: Integer constant
>
> The type of string comparison to perform.

Return Value   An Integer.

Description   Determines whether two strings are equal and which of two strings is greater.

Rules at a Glance

- The following intrinsic constants are available as the settings for *compare*:

Constant	Value	Comparison to perform
vbBinaryCompare	0	Binary (default)
vbTextCompare	1	Textual

- If *compare* isn't specified, its value defaults to vbBinaryCompare. In other words, the comparison of *string1* and *string2* is case-sensitive.

- This table describes the possible return values from the *StrComp* function:

Scenario	Return value
string1 < *string2*	−1
string1 = *string2*	0
string1 > *string2*	1
string1 or *string2* is Null	Null

Programming Tips and Gotchas

- If you just need to know whether *string1* is greater than *string2* (or vice versa), couldn't you simply use the < or > comparison operators? When you're dealing with strings of characters, VBScript sees each character as a number. Simply using the comparison operators therefore compares the numerical value of one string with the other. Take this scenario:

```
Dim sString1
Dim sString2

sString1 = "hello world"
sString2 = "HELLO WORLD"
```

Subjectively, because of the significance of uppercase letters in text, we'd probably say that *sString2* is greater than *sString1*. But VBScript sees these strings as a series of Unicode numbers, and because uppercase characters have a lower Unicode number than lowercase numbers, the lowercase string (*sString1*) is greater.

This is similar to how the default StrComp option vbBinaryCompare operates—comparing the Unicode numbers of each string at binary level. The sort order is derived from the international binary representations of the characters. vbCompareText performs a case-insensitive search, which means that it ignores the difference between upper- and lowercase characters. It also means that it will equate different representations of the same character in some Far Eastern character sets. vbCompareText, in other words, indicates a case-insensitive textual sort order as determined by the user's locale.

- Even performing a simple single comparison like:

```
If UCase(sString1) < UCase(sString2) Then
```

shows a performance hit of about 30 percent over the much more elegant and efficient *StrComp* function call:

```
If StrComp(sString1,sString2, vbTextCompare) = -1 Then
```

The former version, though, is easier to read and makes the code self-documenting.

String Function

Syntax

```
String(number, character)
```

number
Use: Required   Data Type: Long

The length of the required string.

character
Use: Required   Data Type: Variant

Character or character code used to create the required string.

Return Value   A string made up of *character*, repeated *number* times.

Description   Creates a string comprising a specified single character repeated a specified number of times.

Rules at a Glance

- If *number* contains Null, Null is returned.
- If *character* contains Null, Null is returned.
- *character* can be specified as a string or as an ANSI character code. For example:

```
strBuffer1 = String(128, "=")    ' Fill with "="
strBuffer2 = String(128, 0)      ' Fill with Chr$(0)
```

- If *character* consists of multiple characters, the first character is used only, and the remainders are discarded.

Programming Tips and Gotchas

- The *String* function is useful for creating long strings of _, -, or = characters to create horizontal lines for delimiting sections of a report.

VB/VBA Differences

VBScript does not support the VBA *String$* function.

See Also   Space Function

StrReverse Function

Syntax

StrReverse(*str_expression*)

str_expression
   Use: Required   Data Type: String

   The string whose characters are to be reversed.

Return Value   A String.

Description   Returns a string that is the reverse of the string passed to it. For example, if the string "and" is passed to it as an argument, *StrReverse* returns the string "dna."

Rules at a Glance

- If *str_expression* is a zero-length string (" "), the function's return value is a zero-length string.

- If *str_expression* is Null, the function generates runtime error 94, "Invalid use of Null."

Sub Statement

Syntax

```
[Public [Default] | Private] Sub name [(arglist)]
   [statements]
   [Exit Sub]
   [statements]
End Sub
```

Public
   Use: Optional   Type: Keyword

   Gives the sub procedure visibility to all scripts. If used in a class definition, the sub procedure is also accessible from outside the class. Public and Private are mutually exclusive.

Default
   Use: Optional   Type: Keyword

   Indicates that a public procedure defined in a VBScript class (that is, defined within a Class...End Class construct) is the default member of the class.

Private
   Use: Optional   Type: Keyword

   Restricts the visibility of the sub procedure to those procedures within the same script. In a class definition, restricts the visibility of the sub procedure to the class itself. Public and Private are mutually exclusive.

name
   Use: Required

   The name of the sub procedure.

arglist

Use: Optional   Data Type: Any

A comma-delimited list of variables to be passed to the sub procedure as arguments from the calling procedure.

statements

Use: Optional

Program code to be executed within the sub procedure.

arglist uses the following syntax and parts:
```
[ByVal | ByRef] varname[( )]
```

ByVal

Use: Optional

The argument is passed by value; that is, a local copy of the variable is assigned the value of the argument.

ByRef

Use: Optional

The argument is passed by reference; that is, the local variable is simply a reference to the argument being passed. All changes made to the local variable are also reflected in the calling argument. ByRef is the default method of passing variables.

varname

Use: Required

The name of the local variable containing the reference or argument value.

Description   Defines a sub procedure.

Rules at a Glance

- If you don't include the Public or Private keywords, a sub procedure is Public by default.

- Unlike a Function procedure, a sub procedure doesn't return a value to the calling procedure. You would think that this means that a sub procedure can't be used as part of an expression, but in fact this isn't the case; subs can be included in expressions are treated as functions that return Empty.

- Any number of Exit Sub statements can be placed within the sub procedure. Execution continues with the line of code immediately following the call to the sub procedure.

- Only one property, procedure, or function in a class can be designated as its default member by assigning it the Default keyword.

- The Default keyword can be used only with public procedures.

- You can invoke a sub procedure using the Call statement, in which parameters are enclosed in parentheses. For example:

  ```
  Call MySub(param1, param2)
  ```

  You can also omit the Call keyword, in which case the parentheses around parameters are also omitted. For example:

  ```
  MySub param1, param2
  ```

Programming Tips and Gotchas

- There is often confusion between the ByRef and ByVal methods of assigning arguments to the sub procedure. ByRef assigns the reference of the variable in the calling procedure to the variable in the sub procedure. As a result, any changes made to the variable from within the sub procedure are, in reality, made to the variable in the calling procedure. On the other hand, ByVal assigns the value of the variable in the calling procedure to the variable in the sub procedure; that is, it makes a separate copy of the variable in a separate memory location. Changes made to the variable in the sub procedure have no effect on the variable in the calling procedure.

- You can override arguments passed to sub procedures by reference and instead pass them by value by enclosing them in parentheses. For instance, in the code:

```
Dim x
x = 10
SubByRef(x)
MsgBox "x after SubByRef: " & x

Sub SubByRef(y)
    y = 20
End Sub
```

x retains its original value of 10 when control returns from the *SubByRef* sub procedure. Note that you can enclose the argument list in parentheses when there is a single argument, but that argument is then passed to the calling sub procedure by value rather than by reference.

If a sub procedure has two or more arguments, you can pass a particular argument by reference by enclosing it in parentheses. For instance:

```
Dim x, x1
x = 10
x1 = 10
SubByRef (x),x1          ' after return, x=10, x1=20
x1 = 10
Call SubByRef((x), x1)   ' after return, x=10, x1=20
Sub SubByRef(y, z)
    y = 20
    z = 20
End Sub
```

- Sub procedures can't return a value, or can they? Look at the following code:

```
Sub testTheReturns( )
    Dim iValOne

    iValOne = 10
    testValues iValOne
    Msgbox iValOne
End Sub

Sub testValues(ByRefiVal)
    iVal = iVal + 5
End Sub
```

Because the argument was passed with ByRef, the sub procedure acted upon the underlying variable *iValOne*. This means that you can use ByRef to obtain a "return" value or values (although they're not strictly return values) from a sub procedure call.

- There are many occasions in which recursively calling a sub procedure can be used to solve a programming problem. Recursion occurs when you call a sub procedure from within itself. Recursion is a legitimate and often essential part of software development; for example, it offers a reliable method of enumerating or iterating a hierarchical structure. However, you must be aware that recursion can lead to stack overflow. The extent to which you can get away with recursion really depends upon the complexity of the sub procedure concerned, the amount and type of data being passed in, and an infinite number of other variables and unknowns.

See Also   Call Statement, Exit Statement, Function Statement

Tan Function

Syntax
Tan*(number)*

number
    Use: Required   Data Type: Numeric expression
    An angle in radians.

Return Value   A Double containing the tangent of an angle.

Description   Returns the ratio of two sides of a right-angle triangle.

Rules at a Glance
The returned ratio is derived by dividing the length of the side opposite the angle by the length of side adjacent to the angle.

Programming Tips and Gotchas
- You can convert degrees to radians using the following formula:

```
radians = degrees * (pi/180)
```
- You can convert radians to degrees using the following formula:

```
degrees = radians * (180/pi)
```

Terminate Event

Syntax
```
Private Sub Class_Terminate( )
```

Description   The Terminate event is fired when an instance of a class is removable from memory.

Rules at a Glance
- The Terminate event applies to classes defined with the Class...End Class construct.
- Instances of a class are removed from memory by explicitly setting the object variable to Nothing or by the object variable going out of scope.
- If a script ends because of a runtime error, a class's Terminate event isn't fired.

Example

The following example shows a typical Terminate event in a class object that decrements a global instance counter used to ensure that only a single instance of a particular utility object is created. When the counter reaches 0, the global object reference to the utility object is destroyed.

```
Private Sub Class_Terminate( )

    glbUtilCount = glbUtilCount - 1
    If glbUtilCount = 0 then
        Set goUtils = Nothing
    End If

End Sub
```

Programming Tips and Gotchas

- Because the Terminate event is fired when an object becomes removable from memory, it is possible, but not recommended, for the Terminate event handler to add references back to itself and thereby prevent its removal. However, in this case, when the object actually is released, the Terminate event handler will not be called again.

- The Terminate event is fired under the following conditions:

  — An object goes out of scope.

  — The last reference to an object is set equal to Nothing.

  — An object variable is assigned a new object reference.

- The Terminate event is fired when an object is about to be removed from memory, not when an object reference is about to be removed. In other words, if two variables reference the same object, the Terminate event will be fired only once, when the second reference is about to be destroyed.

See Also   Initialize Event, Set Statement

TextStream Object

Createable   No

Returned by

File.OpenAsTextStream Method
FileSystemObject.CreateTextFile Method
FileSystemObject.GetStandardStream Method
FileSystemObject.OpenTextFile Method

Library   Microsoft Scripting Runtime

Windows Script Host

Description   Most commonly, the TextStream object represents a text file. As of Windows Script Host 2.0 and VBScript 5.5, however, it also represents any input/output stream, such as standard input, standard output, and the standard error stream. Depending on the precise character of the I/O stream, you can open a TextStream object to read from, append to, or write to the stream. The TextStream object provides methods to read, write, and close the text file or I/O stream.

When dealing with files, note that the TextStream object represents the file's contents or internals; the File object represents the file's externals or the file as an object in the filesystem.

The TextStream object is one of the objects in the File System object model; for an overview of the model, including the library reference needed to access it, see the File System Object Model entry.

Properties

The availability of TextStream object properties depends on the precise character of the TextStream object; some properties are available only when the stream is opened in read mode (indicated by an R in the Availability field); others are available in both read and write modes (indicated by a RW in the Availability field). All of the following TextStream object properties are read-only:

AtEndOfLine

> Data Type: Boolean
>
> Availability: R
>
> A flag denoting whether the end-of-a-line marker has been reached (True) or not (False). Relevant only when reading a file.
>
> When reading a standard input stream from the keyboard, the end of a line is indicated by pressing the Enter key.

AtEndofStream

> Data Type: Boolean
>
> Availability: R
>
> A flag denoting whether the end of the stream has been reached (True) or not (False). Relevant only when reading a file.
>
> When reading from a standard input stream from the keyboard, the end of the input stream is indicated by the Ctrl-Z character.

Column

> Data Type: Long
>
> Availability: RW
>
> Returns the column number position of the file marker. The first column position in the input stream and in each row is 1.
>
> Examining the value of the Column property is most useful in input streams after calls to the TextStream object's Read and Skip methods. Although it is less useful for output streams, it can be used after a call to the TextStream object's Write method.

Line

> Data Type: Long
>
> Availability: RW
>
> Returns the line number position of the file marker. Lines in the text stream are numbered starting at 1.
>
> Unless the end of the text stream has been reached, the value of the Line property is incremented after calls to the ReadAll, ReadLine, and SkipLine methods. Similarly, in output streams, it is incremented after calls to the WriteLine and WriteBlankLines methods.

Methods

Close
Read
ReadAll
ReadLine
Skip
SkipLine
Write
WriteBlankLines
WriteLine

TextStream.Close Method

Syntax

oTextStreamObj.Close

Availability   RW

Description   Closes the current TextStream object.

Rules at a Glance

Although calling the Close method does not invalidate the object reference, you shouldn't try to reference a TextStream object that has been closed.

Programming Tips and Gotchas

- After closing the TextStream object, set oTextStreamObj to Nothing.

- If you are writing to a file-based text stream, text is automatically written to the file. You do not have to call the Save method to commit changes to a disk file before calling the Close method.

TextStream.Read Method

Syntax

oTextStreamObj.Read(*Characters*)

oTextStreamObj
Use: Required   Data Type: TextStream object

Any property or object variable returning a readable TextStream object.

Characters
Use: Required   Data Type: Long

The number of characters you want to read from the input stream.

Return Value   A String.

Availability   R

Description   Reads a given number of characters from a file or the standard input and returns the resulting string.

Rules at a Glance

- Files opened for writing or appending can't be read; you must first close the file and reopen it using the ForReading constant.

- After the read operation, the file pointer advances *Characters* characters, unless the end of the file is encountered.

- If the number of characters available to be read are less than *Characters*, all characters will be read.

- When reading the standard input stream from the keyboard, program execution pauses until an end-of-line or end-of-stream character is encountered. However, only the first *Characters* characters of the stream are read. If at least *Characters* characters are available in the input stream for subsequent read operations, program execution does not pause to wait for further keyboard input. The usual technique is to process keystrokes in a loop until the end-of-stream marker is encountered. For example:

```
Do While Not oIn.AtEndOfStream
    sIn = oIn.Read(10)        ' Read up to 10 characters
    ' process text
Loop
```

See Also   TextStream.ReadAll Method, TextStream.ReadLine Method

---

TextStream.ReadAll Method

Syntax

```
oTextStreamObj.ReadAll
```

Return Value   A String.

Availability   R

Description   Reads the entire file or input stream into memory.

Rules at a Glance

- For large files, use the ReadLine or Read methods to reduce the load on memory resources.

- Files opened for writing or appending can't be read; you must first close the file and reopen it using the ForReading constant.

- When used to read the standard input stream from the keyboard, the ReadAll method pauses program execution and polls the keyboard until the AtEndOfStream symbol is encountered. For this reason, the ReadAll method should not be executed repeatedly in a loop.

See Also   TextStream.Read Method, TextStream.ReadLine Method

---

TextStream.ReadLine Method

Syntax

```
oTextStreamObj.ReadLine
```

Return Value   A String.

Availability   R

Description   Reads a line of the text file or input stream into memory, from the start of the current line up to the character immediately preceding the next end-of-line marker.

Rules at a Glance

- Files opened for writing or appending can't be read; you must first close the file and reopen it using the ForRead constant.
- The ReadLine method causes the file pointer to advance to the beginning of the next line, if there is one.
- When used to retrieve standard input from the keyboard, the ReadLine method pauses program execution and waits until the end-of-line character (i.e., the Enter key) has been pressed. Unless your script expects to retrieve just one line of input, it's best to call the ReadLine method repeatedly in a loop.

See Also   TextStream.Read Method, TextStream.ReadAll Method

TextStream.Skip Method

Syntax

```
oTextStreamObj.Skip (Characters)
```

oTextStreamObj
Use: Required   Data Type: TextStream object

Any property or object variable returning a readable TextStream object.

NoOfChars
Use: Required   Data Type: Long

Number of characters to skip when reading.

Availability   R

Description   Ignores the next *Characters* characters when reading from a text file or input stream.

Rules at a Glance

- As a result of the skip operation, the file pointer is placed at the character immediately following the last skipped character.
- The Skip method is available only for input streams—that is, for files or streams opened in ForReading mode.

See Also   TextStream.SkipLine Method

TextStream.SkipLine Method

Syntax

```
oTextStreamObj.SkipLine
```

Availability   R

Description   Ignores the current line when reading from a text file.

Rules at a Glance

- The SkipLine method is available only for files opened in ForReading mode.
- After the SkipLine method executes, the internal file pointer is placed at the beginning of the line immediately following the skipped line, assuming that one exists.

TextStream.Write Method

Syntax

```
oTextStreamObj.Write(Text)
```

oTextStreamObj

 Use: Required Data Type: TextStream object

 Any property or object variable returning a writable TextStream object.

Text

 Use: Required Data Type: String

 Any string expression to write to the file.

Availability W

Description Writes a string to the text file.

Rules at a Glance

The file marker is set at the end of string. As a result, subsequent writes to the file adjoin each other, with no spaces inserted. To write data to the file in a more structured manner, use the WriteLine method.

See Also TextStream.WriteBlankLines Method, TextStream.WriteLine Method

TextStream.WriteBlankLines Method

Syntax

```
oTextStreamObj.WriteBlankLines(Lines)
```

oTextStreamObj

 Use: Required Data Type: TextStream object

 Any property or object variable returning a writable TextStream object.

Lines

 Use: Required Data Type: Long

 The number of newline characters to insert.

Availability W

Description Inserts one or more newline characters in the file or output stream at the current file marker position.

See Also TextStream.Write Method, TextStream.WriteLine Method

TextStream.WriteLine Method

Syntax

> *oTextStreamObj*.WriteLine *(String)*

oTextStreamObj
> Use: Required   Data Type: TextStream object
>
> Any property or object variable returning a writable TextStream object.

String
> Use: Required   Data Type: String
>
> A string expression to write to the file.

Availability   W

Description   Writes a string immediately followed by a newline character to a text file.

See Also   TextStream.WriteBlankLines Method

Time Function

Syntax

> Time

Return Value   A Date.

Description   Returns the current system time.

Rules at a Glance

The *Time* function returns the time.

Programming Tips and Gotchas

The *Time* function returns but does not allow you to set the system time.

VBA/VBScript Differences

VBA includes a *Time$* function that returns the time as a string rather than a variant. Because VBScript does not support strong typing, the function is not implemented in VBScript.

See Also   Now Function

Timer Function

Syntax

> Timer( )

Return Value   A Single.

Description   Returns the number of seconds since midnight.

Programming Tips and Gotchas

- You can use the *Timer* function as an easy method of passing a seed number to the Randomize statement, as follows:

    ```
    Randomize Timer
    ```

- The *Timer* function is ideal for measuring the time taken to execute a procedure or program statement, as the following ASP snippet shows:

    ```
    <%
    Dim sStartTime
    Dim i, j

    sStartTime = Timer()
    For i = 1 To 100
        Response.Write  "Hello <BR>"
        For j = 0 To 1000
        Next
    Next
    Response.Write "Time Taken = " & _
        FormatDateTime(Timer - sStartTime, vbShortTime) & _
           " Seconds"
    %>
    ```

TimeSerial Function

Syntax

```
TimeSerial(hour, minute, second)
```

hour
    Use: Required   Data Type: Integer

    A number in the range 0 to 23.

minute
    Use: Required   Data Type: Integer

    Any valid integer.

second
    Use: Required   Data Type: Integer

    Any valid integer.

Return Value   A Date.

Description   Constructs a valid time given a number of hours, minutes, and seconds.

Rules at a Glance

- Any of the arguments can be specified as relative values or expressions.

- The *hour* argument requires a 24-hour clock format; however, the return value is always in a 12-hour clock format suffixed with A.M. or P.M.

- If any of the values are greater than the normal range for the time unit to which it relates, the next higher time unit is increased accordingly. For example, a second argument of 125 is evaluated as 2 minutes 5 seconds.

- If any of the values are less than zero, the next higher time unit is decreased accordingly. For example, TimeSerial(2,-1,30) returns 01:59:30.

- If any of the values are outside the range –32,768 to 32,767, an error occurs.
- If the value of any parameter causes the date returned by the function to fall outside the range of valid dates, an error occurs.

Programming Tips and Gotchas

Because *TimeSerial* handles time units outside of their normal limits, it can be used for time calculations. However, because the *DateAdd* function is more flexible and is internationally aware, it should be used instead.

See Also   DateAdd Function

TimeValue Function

Syntax

```
TimeValue(time)
```

time
    Use: Required   Data Type: String

    Any valid string representation of a time.

Return Value   A Date.

Description   Converts a string representation of a time to a Variant Date type.

Rules at a Glance

- If *time* is invalid, a runtime error is generated.
- If *time* is Null, *TimeValue* returns Null.
- Both 12- and 24-hour clock formats are valid.
- Any date information contained within *time* is ignored by the *TimeValue* function.
- If *TimeValue* returns invalid time information, an error occurs.

Programming Tips and Gotchas

- A time literal can also be assigned to a Variant or Date variable by surrounding the date with hash characters (#), as the following snippet demonstrates:

```
Dim dMyTime
dMyTime = #12:30:00 AM#
```

- The *CDate* function can also cast a time expression contained within a string as a Date variable, with the additional advantage of being internationally aware.

See Also   CDate Function, TimeSerial Function

Trim Function

Syntax

```
Trim(string)
```

string
    Use: Required   Data Type: String

    Any string expression.

Return Value   A String.

Description   Returns a string in which any leading and trailing spaces in an original string are removed.

Rules at a Glance
If string is Null, the *Trim* function returns Null.

Programming Tips and Gotchas
Trim combines into a single function call what would otherwise be separate calls to the *RTrim* and *LTrim* functions.

VBA/VBScript Differences
VBA includes a *Trim$* function that returns the a trimmed string rather than a trimmed string variant. Because VBScript does not support strong typing, the function is not implemented in VBScript.

See Also   LTrim Function, RTrim Function

TypeName Function

Syntax
    TypeName(*varname*)

varname
    Use: Required   Data Type: Any
    The name of a variable.

Return Value   A String.

Description   Returns a string containing the name of the data type of a variable.

Rules at a Glance
- *TypeName* returns the variant's data type. If the variant has not been assigned a value, *TypeName* returns Empty. Therefore, *TypeName* never actually returns the string "Variant."
- The following table describes the possible return values and their meaning:

Return value	Underlying data type
Boolean	Boolean
Byte	Byte
classname	An object variable of type *classname*
Currency	Currency
Date	Date
Decimal	Decimal
Double	Double-precision floating-point number
Empty	Uninitialized variable
Error	A missing argument error
Integer	Integer

Return value	Underlying data type
Long	Long integer
Nothing	A variable of type Object that is not set to a valid object
Null	No valid data
Object	A generic object
Single	Single-precision floating-point number
String	String
Unknown	An object whose type is unknown
Variant( )	An array

VBA/VBScript Differences

- In VBA, the data type of a strongly typed variable can be ascertained earlier than the data type of a VBScript variable. For instance, in VBA, the code fragment:

```
Dim lNumber As Long
MsgBox TypeName(lNumber)
```

indicates that *lNumber* is a long. The equivalent VBScript code fragment:

```
Dim lNumber
MsgBox TypeName(lNumber)
```

indicates that *lNumber* is Empty, since it hasn't yet been assigned a value and therefore VBScript cannot determine its data type. (Note that, in VBA, if *lNumber* is defined as a variant, the behavior of the *TypeName* function is identical to its behavior in VBScript.)

- In VBA, the type name of an object variable that has been declared but not yet initialized returns "Nothing." In VBScript, the *TypeName* function returns "Nothing" only for object variables that have been explicitly set equal to Nothing.

- In VBScript, all arrays return the value Variant( ). In VBA, the return value depends on whether the array is strongly typed.

- In part because VBA can be strongly typed, a number of data types are more common than their corresponding VBScript data types. The Decimal data type does not exist in VBScript, since VBScript does not support the *CDec* function, which is the only method available for defining a Decimal. Similarly, the Byte and Currency data types are much rarer in VBScript than in VBA.

See Also   VarType Function

UBound Function

Syntax

```
UBound(arrayname[, dimension])
```

arrayname
    Use: Required
    An array variable or an expression that evaluates to an array.

dimension
    Use: Optional   Data Type: Long
    A number specifying the dimension of the array.

Return Value   A Long.

Description   Indicates the upper limit of a specified dimension of an array. The upper boundary is the largest subscript you can access within the specified array.

Rules at a Glance

- If *dimension* isn't specified, 1 is assumed. To determine the upper limit of the first dimension of an array created by VBScript code, set *dimension* to 1, set it to 2 for the second dimension, and so on.

- The upper bound of an array dimension can be set to any integer value using Dim, Private, Public, and Redim.

Programming Tips and Gotchas

- Note that *UBound* returns the actual subscript of the upper bound of a particular array dimension.

- *UBound* is especially useful for determining the current upper boundary of a dynamic array.

- The *UBound* function works only with conventional arrays. To determine the upper bound of a collection object, retrieve the value of its Count or Length property.

See Also   LBound Function

UCase Function

Syntax

    UCase(string)

string
    Use: Required   Data Type: String

    A valid string expression.

Return Value   A String.

Description   Converts a string to uppercase.

Rules at a Glance

- *UCase* affects only lowercase alphabetical letters; all other characters within *string* remain unaffected.

- *UCase* returns Null if *string* contains a Null.

VBA/VBScript Differences

VBA includes a *UCase$* function that returns an uppercase string rather than a uppercase string variant. Because VBScript does not support strong typing, the function is not implemented in VBScript.

See Also   LCase Function

Unescape function

Syntax

```
Unescape(string)
string
```

Use: Required   Data Type: String

An encoded string

Return Value   A string variant containing the decoded version of *string*.

Description   Decodes a URL-encoded or HTML-encoded string.

Rules at a Glance

Replaces all encoded characters with their corresponding characters. Encoded values in the form of %*xx* are replaced with their corresponding ASCII characters, while values in the form %u*xxxx* are replaced with their corresponding Unicode characters.

Programming Notes

- The *Unescape* function is not documented in the VBScript documentation.
- The function corresponds to the JScript Unescape method.
- If *string* has no encoded characters, the function merely returns *string* unchanged.
- All encoded characters in the form %*xx* are replaced with their equivalent ASCII strings.
- All encoded characters in the form %u*xxxx* are replaced with their equivalent Unicode character strings.

VB/VBA Differences

This function is not supported in VBA.

See Also   Escape Function

VarType Function

Syntax

```
VarType(varname)
```

varname

Use: Required

The name of a variable.

Return Value   An Integer representing the data type of *varname*.

Description   Determines the data type of a specified variable.

Rules at a Glance

- The following intrinsic constants can test the return value of the *VarType* function:

Constant	Value	Data type
vbBoolean	11	Boolean
vbByte	17	Byte
vbCurrency	6	Currency
vbDataObject	13	A data access object variable
vbDate	7	Date
vbDecimal	14	Decimal
vbDouble	5	Double-precision floating-point number
vbEmpty	0	Uninitialized
vbError	10	An error type that indicates a missing argument
vbInteger	2	Integer
vbLong	3	Long integer
vbNull	1	No valid data
vbObject	9	A generic object
vbSingle	4	Single-precision floating-point number
vbString	8	String
vbVariant	12	Variant—returned only with vbArray (8194)

- If *varname* is an array created by VBScript code, the *VarType* function returns 8200 (vbArray) and vbVariant.

- If varname is an array returned to the script by a component, the *VarType* function returns 8200 (vbArray) and the value representing the data type of the array. For instance, a Visual Basic Integer array returned to a VBScript script produces a value of 8196(vbInteger + vbArray).

- To test for an array, you can use the intrinsic constant vbArray. For example:

```
If VarType(myVar) And vbArray Then
    MsgBox "This is an array"
End If
```

Alternatively, you can also use the *IsArray* function.

Programming Tips and Gotchas

- When you use *VarType* with an object variable, you may get what appears to be an incorrect return value. The reason for this is that if the object has a default property, *VarType* returns the data type of the default property.

- There is no such value as vbNothing.

- For most purposes, the *TypeName* function, which returns a string indicating a variable's data type, is much more convenient and easy to use.

VBA/VBScript Differences

- In VBA, the data type of a strongly typed variable can be ascertained earlier than the data type of a VBScript variable. For instance, in VBA, the code fragment:

```
Dim lNumber As Long
MsgBox VarType(lNumber)
```

returns vbLong, indicating that *lNumber* is a Long. The equivalent VBScript code fragment:

```
Dim lNumber
MsgBox VarType(lNumber)
```

returns vbEmpty, indicating that *1Number* is Empty, since it hasn't yet been assigned a value and therefore VBScript cannot determine its data type. (Note that, in VBA, if *1Number* is defined as a variant, the behavior of the *VarType* function is identical to its behavior in VBScript.)

- In VBA, if *varname* is an array, the value returned by the function is 8194 (vbArray) plus the value of the data type of the array. For example, an array of strings will return 8192 + 8 = 8200, or vbArray + vbString. In VBScript, all arrays return 8192 + 10, or vbArray + vbVariant.

- In part because VBA can be strongly typed, a number of data types are more common than their corresponding VBScript data types. The Decimal data type does not exist in VBScript, since VBScript does not support the *CDec* function, which is the only method available for defining a Decimal. Similarly, the Byte and Currency data types are much rarer in VBScript than in VBA.

See Also   TypeName Function

Weekday Function

Syntax
     Weekday(*date*, [*firstdayofweek*])

date
     Use: Required   Data Type: Variant
     Any valid date expression.

firstdayofweek
     Use: Optional   Data Type: Integer
     Integer specifying the first day of the week.

Return Value   An Integer.

Description   Determines the day of the week of a given date.

Rules at a Glance
- The following intrinsic VBScript constants determine the value returned by the *Weekday* function:

Constant	Return value	Day represented
vbSunday	1	Sunday
vbMonday	2	Monday
vbTuesday	3	Tuesday
vbWednesday	4	Wednesday
vbThursday	5	Thursday
vbFriday	6	Friday
vbSaturday	7	Saturday

- If *date* is Null, the *Weekday* function also returns Null.

- The following table describes the settings for the *firstdayofweek* argument:

Constant	Value	Description
vbUseSystem	0	Use the NLS API setting
vbSunday	1	Sunday (default)
vbMonday	2	Monday
vbTuesday	3	Tuesday
vbWednesday	4	Wednesday
vbThursday	5	Thursday
vbFriday	6	Friday
vbSaturday	7	Saturday

Programming Tips and Gotchas

- If you specify a *firstdayofweek* argument, the function returns the day of the week relative to *firstdayofweek*. For instance, if you set the value of *firstdayofweek* to vbMonday (2), indicating that Monday is the first day of the week, and attempt to determine the day of the week on which October 1, 1996, falls, the function returns a 2. That's because October 1, 1996, is a Tuesday, the second day of a week whose first day is Monday.

- Because the function's return value is relative to *firstdayofweek*, using the day of the week constants to interpret the function's return value is confusing, to say the least. If we use our October 1, 1996, example once again, the following expression evaluates to True if the day of the week is Tuesday:

        If vbMonday = WeekDay(CDate("10/1/96"), vbMonday) Then

See Also   DatePart Function, Day Function, Month Function, Year Function

WeekdayName Function

Syntax

    WeekdayName(WeekdayNo, [abbreviate [, FirstDayOfWeek]])

WeekdayNo
   Use: Required   Data Type: Long

   The ordinal number of the required weekday, from 1 to 7.

abbreviate
   Use: Optional   Data Type: Boolean

   Specifies whether to return the full day name or an abbreviation.

FirstDayOfWeek
   Use: Optional   Data Type: Integer

   Specifies which day of the week should be first.

Return Value   A String.

Description   Returns the real name of the day.

Rules at a Glance

- *WeekDayNo* must be a number between 1 and 7, or the function generates runtime error 5, "Invalid procedure call or argument."
- If *FirstDayOfWeek* is omitted, WeekdayName treats Sunday as the first day of the week.
- The default value of *abbreviate* is False.

Programming Tips and Gotchas

- You'd expect that, given a date, *WeekDayName* would return the name of that date's day. But this isn't how the function works. To determine the name of the day of a particular date, combine *WeekDayName* with a call to the *WeekDay* function, as the following code fragment shows:

```
sDay = WeekDayName(Weekday(dDate, iFirstDay), _
                   bFullName, iFirstDay)
```

Note that the value of the *FirstDayOfWeek* argument must be the same in the calls to both functions for *WeekDayName* to return an accurate result.

See Also   Weekday Function

While ... Wend Statement

Syntax

```
While condition
   [statements]
Wend
```

condition
> Use: Required   Data Type: Boolean

> An expression evaluating to True or False.

statements
> Use: Optional

> Program statements to execute while condition remains True.

Description   Repeatedly executes program code while a given condition remains True.

Rules at a Glance

- A Null condition is evaluated as False.
- If *condition* evaluates to True, the program code between the While and Wend statements is executed. After the Wend statement is executed, control is passed back up to the While statement, where *condition* is evaluated again. When *condition* evaluates to False, program execution skips to the first statement following the Wend statement.
- You can nest While...Wend loops within each other.

Programming Tips and Gotchas

The While...Wend statement remains in VBScript for backward compatibility only. It has been superseded by the much more flexible Do...Loop statement.

See Also   Do ... Loop Statement

With Statement

Syntax

```
With object
    [statements]
End With
```

object
> Use: Required   Data Type: Object

> A previously declared object variable.

statements
> Use: Optional

> Program code to execute against object.

Description   Performs a set of property assignments and executes other code against a particular object, thus allowing you to refer to the object only once. Because the object is referred to only once, the "behind the scenes" qualification of that object is also performed only once, leading to improved performance of the code block.

Rules at a Glance

- The single object referred to in the With statement remains the same throughout the code contained within the With...End With block. Therefore, only properties and methods of *object* can be used within the code block without explicitly referencing the object. All other object references within the With...End statement must start with a fully qualified object reference.

- With statements can be nested, as long as the inner With statement refers to a child object or a dependent object of the outer With statement.

See Also   Do . . . Loop Statement, Set Statement

Year Function

Syntax

```
Year(date)
```

date
> Use: Required   Data Type: Date

> Any valid date expression.

Return Value   An Integer.

Description   Returns an integer representing the year in a given date expression.

Rules at a Glance

If *date* contains Null, Year returns Null.

Programming Tips and Gotchas

- The validity of the date expression and position of the year element within the given date expression are initially determined by the locale settings of the Windows system. However, some extra intelligence relating to two-digit year values has been built into the *Year* function that surpasses the usual comparison of a date expression to the current locale settings.

- What happens when you pass a date over to the *Year* function containing a two-digit year? Quite simply, when the *Year* function sees a two-digit year, it assumes that all values equal to or greater than 30 are in the 20th Century (i.e., 30 = 1930, 98 = 1998) and that all values less than 30 are in the 21st century (i.e., 29 = 2029, 5 = 2005). Of course, if you don't want sleepless nights rewriting your programs in the year 2029, you should insist on a four-digit year, which will see your code work perfectly for about the next 8,000 years!

See Also   DatePart Function, Day Function, IsDate Function, Month Function, Weekday Function

Appendixes

Part III contains five appendixes that supplement the core reference material provided in Part II. These include:

- Appendix A, *Language Elements by Category*, which lists each VBScript statement, function, procedure, property, or method in each of a number of categories. You can use it to identify a particular language element so that you can look up its detailed entry in Part II.

- Appendix B, *VBScript Constants*, which lists the constants that are automatically supported by VBScript.

- Appendix C, *Operators*, which lists VBScript operators, including a somewhat more detailed treatment of the logical and bitwise operators.

- Appendix D, *Locale IDs*, which lists valid locale IDs for the *GetLocale* and *SetLocale* functions.

- Appendix E, *The Script Encoder*, which documents the Script Encoder, a tool for creating encoded script.

Language Elements by Category

This appendix lists all the functions and statements, available within the VBScript language by category. The categories are:

- Array Handling
- Assignment
- Comment
- Constants
- Data Conversion
- Date and Time
- Dictionary Object
- Error Handling
- File System Objects
- Information Functions
- Mathematical and Numeric
- Miscellaneous
- Object Programming
- Program Structure and Flow
- String Manipulation
- User Interaction
- Variable Declaration

Where necessary, individual language elements may appear in more than one category. Note that neither constants nor operators are listed here; the former are listed in Appendix B, while the latter appear in Appendix C.

Array Handling

Array Function	Creates and returns an array from a comma-delimited list of values
Dim Statement	Declares a fixed or dynamic array
Erase Statement	Clears the contents of an array
Filter Function	Returns an array of strings matching (or not) a specified value
IsArray Function	Indicates whether a variable is an array
Join Function	Returns a string constructed by concatenating an array of values with a given separator
LBound Function	Returns the lower bound of an array, which is always 0 in VBScript
Preserve Statement	Used with the `ReDim` statement to copy a dynamic array to a resized dynamic array
ReDim Statement	Declares or redimensions a dynamic array
Split Function	Returns an array of values derived from a single string and a specified separator
UBound Function	Returns the upper bound of an array

Assignment

= Operator	Assigns a value to a variable or property
Set Statement	Assigns an object reference to a variable

Comment

' Statement	Declares all text from the apostrophe onward as a comment to be ignored by the language engine
Rem Statement	Declares all text following the `Rem` statement as a comment to be ignored by the language engine

Constants

Const Statement	Defines a constant

Data Type Conversion

Asc Function	Returns the ASCII code for a character
AscW Function	Returns the Unicode code for a character
CBool Function	Converts a value to a Boolean
CByte Function	Converts a value to a Byte
CCur Function	Converts a value to Currency
CDate Function	Returns a Date data type
CDbl Function	Converts a value to a Double
Chr Function	Returns the character corresponding to a numeric ASCII code
ChrW Function	Returns the character corresponding to a particular Unicode value
CInt Function	Converts a value to an Integer
CLng Function	Converts a value to a Long

CSng Function	Converts a value to a Single
CStr Function	Converts a value to a String
DateSerial Function	Returns a date from valid year, month, and day values
DateValue Function	Returns a date from any valid date expression
Fix Function	Returns an integer portion of number
Hex Function	Returns a hexadecimal representation of a number
Int Function	Returns the integer portion of a number
Oct Function	Returns an octal representation of a number
TimeSerial Function	Returns a date from valid hour, minute, and second values
TimeValue Function	Returns a date value from any valid time expression

Date and Time

CDate Fujnction	Converts a value to a date
Date Function	Returns the current system date
DateAdd Function	Returns the result of a data/time addition or subtraction calculation
DateDiff Function	Returns the difference between two dates
DatePart Function	Returns the part of the date requested
DateSerial Function	Returns a date from an expression containing month, day, and year
DateValue Function	Returns a date from a representation of a date
Day Function	Returns a number representing the day of the month
FormatDateTime Function	Returns a string variant formatted using the date settings for the current locale
Hour Function	Returns a number representing the hour of the day
Minute Function	Returns a number representing the minute of the hour
Month Function	Returns a number representing the month of the year
MonthName Function	Returns the name of the month for a given date
Now Function	Returns the current system time
Second Function	Returns a number representing the second of the minute
Time Property	Returns or sets the current system time
Timer Property	Returns the number of seconds elapsed since midnight
TimeSerial Function	Returns a representation of a given hour, minute, and second
TimeValue Function	Returns a time value from a string representation of a time
Weekday Function	Returns a number representing the day of the week
WeekdayName Function	Returns a string indicating the day of the week
Year Function	Returns a number representing the year in a date expression

Dictionary Object

Add Method	Adds an item to the dictionary
CompareMode Property	Returns or sets the comparison mode
Count Property	Returns the number of items in the dictionary
Exists Method	Returns True if the key exists
Item Property	Returns or sets the item associated with a given key
Items Method	Returns an array of all items in the dictionary
Key Property	Renames a given key
Keys Method	Returns an array of all keys in the dictionary
Remove Method	Removes an item associated with a given key
RemoveAll Method	Removes all items from the dictionary

Error Handling

Clear Method	Resets the current Err object
Description Property	Returns or sets the Err object's description of the current error
Err Object	Contains information about the last error
HelpContext Property	Returns or sets the help file ID for the Err object's current error
HelpFile Property	Returns or sets the name and path of the help file relating to the Err object's current error
Number Property	Returns or sets the current error code for an Err object
On Error Resume Next Statement	Indicates that errors will be handled within script and that program execution should continue on the line of code following an error
Raise Method	Generates a user-defined error
Source Property	Returns or sets the name of the object or application which raised an Err object's error

File System Objects

Drive Object

AvailableSpace Property	Returns a number representing the available space on the drive in bytes
DriveLetter Property	Returns a string containing the drive letter
DriveType Property	Returns a DriveTypeConst specifying the type of drive
FileSystem Property	Returns a string containing an abbreviation for the filesystem type (i.e., FAT)
FreeSpace Property	Returns the free space on the drive in bytes
IsReady Property	Returns True if the specified drive is ready
Path Property	Returns a string containing the full path of the drive
RootFolder Property	Returns a Folder object representing the root of the drive
SerialNumber Property	Returns a Long containing the serial number of the disk
ShareName Property	Returns a String containing the share name, if any
TotalSize Property	Returns a variant containing the total size of the disk in bytes
VolumeName Property	Returns a string containing the name of the current volume

Drives Collection Object

Count Property	Returns the number of Drive objects in the collection
Item Property	Returns the Drive object associated with the given key (the drive name)

File Object

Attributes Property	Returns a FileAttributes constant
Copy Method	Copies this file to another location
DateCreated Property	Returns the date the file was created
DateLastAccessed Property	Returns the date the file was last accessed
DateLastModified Property	Returns the date the file was last modified
Delete Method	Removes this file
Drive Property	Returns a Drive object representing the drive on which this file is located
Move Method	Moves this file to another location
Name Property	Returns the name of this file

OpenAsTextStream	Opens this file for text manipulation and returns the open file as a Text-Stream object
ParentFolder Property	Returns a Folder object representing the folder in which this file is contained
Path Property	Returns a string containing the full path of this file
ShortName Property	Returns a string containing the short name of this file
ShortPath Property	Returns a string containing the short path of this file
Size Property	Returns a Variant specifying the size of this file
Type Property	Returns a string detailing the type of this file

Files Collection Object

Count Property	Returns the number of Folder objects in the collection
Item Property	Returns the File object associated with the specified key

FileSystemObject Object

BuildPath Function	Returns a string containing the full path
CopyFile Method	Copies a file
CopyFolder Method	Copies a folder and its contents
CreateFolder Function	Returns a Folder object for the newly created folder
CreateTextFile Function	Returns a TextStream object for the newly created text file
DeleteFile Method	Removes a file from disk
DeleteFolder Method	Removes the folder and its contents from disk
DriveExists Function	Returns True if the specified drive is found
Drives Property	Returns a Drive object
FileExists Function	Returns True if the specified file is found
FolderExists Function	Returns True if the specified folder is found
GetAbsolutePathName Function	Returns the canonical representation of the path
GetBaseName Function	Returns the base name from a path
GetDrive Function	Returns a Drive object for the specified drive
GetDriveName Function	Returns a string representing the name of a drive
GetExtensionName Function	Returns a string containing the extension from a given path
GetFile Function	Returns a File object
GetFileName Function	Returns a string containing the name of a file from a given path
GetFileVersion Function	Returns a string containing the version of a file
GetFolder Function	Returns a Folder object
GetParentFolderName Function	Returns the name of the folder immediately above the folder in a given path
GetSpecialFolder Function	Returns a folder object representing one of the special Windows folders
GetStandardStream	Returns a TextStream object representing the standard input, standard output, or standard error stream
GetTempName Function	Returns a string containing a valid windows temporary filename
MoveFile Method	Moves a file from one location to another
MoveFolder Method	Moves a folder and all its contents from one location to another
OpenTextFile Function	Returns a TextStream object of the opened file

Folder Object

Attributes Property	Returns a FileAttributes constant value
Copy Method	Copies this folder and its contents to another location
CreateTextFile Function	Returns a TextStream object for the newly created text file
DateCreated Property	Returns the date the folder was created

DateLastAccessed Property	Returns the date the folder was last accessed
DateLastModified Property	Returns the date the folder was last modified
Delete Method	Removes the folder and all its contents
Drive Property	Returns a Drive object representing the drive on which the folder is located
Files Property	Returns a Files collection object representing the files in the folder
IsRootFolder Property	Returns True if the folder is the root of the drive
Move Method	Moves the folder and its contents to another location
Name Property	Returns the name of the folder
ParentFolder Property	Returns a Folder object representing the next folder up in hierarchy
Path Property	Returns a string containing the full path of the folder
ShortName Property	Returns a string containing the short name of the folder
ShortPath Property	Returns a string containing the short path of the folder
Size Property	Returns a Variant specifying the total size of all files and all subfolders contained in the folder
SubFolders Property	Returns a Folders collection object representing the subfolders contained in the folder
Type Property	Returns a string detailing the type of folder

Folders Collection Object

Add Function	Returns a Folder object for the newly created folder
Count Property	Returns the number of Folder objects in the collection
Item Property	Returns the Folder object associated with the specified key

TextStreamObject

AtEndOfLine Property	Returns True if the end of the line has been reached
AtEndOfStream Property	Returns True if the end of the text stream has been reached
Close Method	Closes the TextStream object
Column Property	Returns a Long specifying the current column number
Line Property	Returns a Long specifying the current line number
Read Function	Returns a string containing a specified number of characters from the TextStream
ReadAll Function	Returns a string containing the entire contents the TextStream
ReadLine Function	Returns a string containing the current line within the TextStream
Skip Method	Skips a specified number of characters
SkipLine Method	Skips to the next line
Write Method	Writes a specified string to the TextStream
WriteBlankLines Method	Writes a specified number of blank lines to the TextStream
WriteLine Method	Writes a specified string and a line break to the TextStream

Information Functions

GetLocale Function	Returns the ID of the current locale
IsArray Function	Returns True if a variable is an array
IsDate Function	Returns True if an expression can be converted to a date
IsEmpty Function	Returns True if a variant variable has not been initialized
IsNull Function	Returns True if an expression evaluates to Null
IsNumeric Function	Returns True if an expression can be evaluated as a number
IsObject Function	Returns True if a variable contains an object reference

Len Function	Returns the length of a variable
LenB Function	Returns the number of bytes needed to hold a given variable
RGB Function	Returns a number representing an RGB color value
ScriptEngine Function	Returns a string representing the scripting language in use
ScriptEngineBuildVersion Function	Returns VBScript's build number
ScriptEngineMajorVersion Function	Returns VBScript's major version number
ScriptEngineMinorVersion Function	Returns VBScript's minor version number
TypeName Function	Returns the data type name of a variable
VarType Function	Returns a number representing the data type of a variable

Mathematical and Numeric

Abs Function	Returns the absolute value of a given number
Atn Function	Returns the arctangent of a number
Cos Function	Returns the cosine of an angle
Exp Function	Returns the base of a natural logarithm raised to a power
FormatNumber Function	Returns a number formatted according to a specified format
FormatPercent Function	Returns a number formatted using the % symbol
Fix Function	Returns the integer portion of number
Int Function	Returns the integer portion of a number
Log Function	Returns the natural logarithm of a number
Randomize Sub	Initializes the random number generator
Rnd Function	Returns a random number
Round Function	Rounds a number
Sgn Function	Indicates the sign of a number
Sin Function	Returns the sine of an angle
Sqr Function	Returns the square root of a number
Tan Function	Returns the tangent of an angle

Miscellaneous

Eval Function	Evaluates an expression that can be built dynamically at runtime and returns the result
Execute Statement	Executes one or more statements that can be built dynamically at runtime
ExecuteGlobal Statement	Executes one or more statements that can be built dynamically at runtime in the script's global namespace
LoadPicture Function	Returns a Picture object

Object Programming

Class...End Class Statement	Defines a class
CreateObject Function	Returns a reference to a COM component

For Each... Next Statement	Iterates through a collection or array of objects or values, returning a reference to each of the members
Function Statement	Defines a function
GetObject Function	Returns a reference to a COM object
GetRef Function	Returns a reference to a procedure that can be used as an object's event handler
Initialize Event	Fired when a class is first instantiated
Is Operator	Compares two object references to determine whether they are identical
Property Get Statement	Returns the value of a property
Property Let Statement	Sets the value of a property
Property Set Statement	Assigns an object reference to a property
Set Statement	Assigns an object reference to an object variable
Sub Statement	Defines a sub; that is, a procedure that does not return a value
Terminate Event	Fired when the last reference to an instance of a class is destroyed
With... End With Statement	Allows the implicit use of an object reference

Program Structure and Flow

Call Statement	Passes execution to a subroutine or event handler
Do... Loop Statement	Repeats a section of code while or until a condition is met; can take the form of Do Until...Loop (loops until an expression is True), Do...Loop Until (loops at least once until an expression is True), Do While...Loop (loops while an expression is True), and Do...Loop While (loops at least once while the expression is True)
Exit Statement	Branches to the next line of code outside of the currently executing structure; can take the form of Exit Do, Exit For, Exit Function, Exit Property, and Exit Sub
End Statement	Marks the end of a program control structure; can take the form of End Class, End Function, End If, End Property, End Select, End Sub, and End With
For Each... Next Statement	Iterates through a collection or array of objects or values, returning a reference to each of the members
For... Next Statement	Iterates through a section of code a given number of times
Function Statement	Declares a procedure
If..Then..Elseif... Else Statement	Defines a conditional block or blocks of code
Private Statement	Declares the procedure or variable to have scope only within the module in which it is defined
Property Get Statement	Defines a prototype for a property procedure that returns a value
Property Let Statement	Defines a prototype for a property procedure that accepts a value
Property Set Statement	Defines a prototype for a property procedure that sets a reference to an object
Public Statement	Declares a global or public variable or function. In a class, marks the member as part of the class' public interface
Select Case... *End Select Statement*	A series of code blocks of which only one will execute based on a given value
Sub Statement	Declares a procedure that does not return a value
While... Wend Statement	Repeats a section of code while or until a condition is met
With... End With Statement	Allows the implicit use of an object reference

String Manipulation

Asc Function	Returns a number representing the ASCII character of the first character of a string
AscB Function	Returns the value of the first byte in a string
AscW Function	Returns the Unicode character code of the first character in a string
Chr Function	Returns a string containing the character associated with the specified character code
ChrB Function	Returns a string containing the specified single byte
ChrW Function	Returns a string with the character that corresponds to a particular Unicode character code
Escape Function	Returns an encoded version of a string
Execute Method	Performs a regular expression search on a string
Filter Function	Returns an array of strings matching (or not) a specified value
FirstIndex Property	Returns the starting position in a search string where a regular expression match represented by a Match object occurred.
FormatCurrency Function	Returns a string formatted using the currency settings for the current locale
FormatDateTime Function	Returns a string formatted using the date settings for the current locale
FormatNumber Function	Returns a number formatted to a specified format
FormatPercent Function	Returns a number formatted using the % symbol
Global Property	Indicates whether a RegExp object's pattern should match all occurrences in a search string or just one
IgnoreCase Property	Indicates whether a RegExp object's pattern match should be case-insensitive
InStr Function	Returns the position of the first occurrence of one string within another
InStrB Function	Returns the byte position of the first occurrence of one string in another
InStrRev Function	Returns the last occurrence of a string within another string
Join Function	Returns a string constructed by concatenating an array of values with a given separator
LCase Function	Returns a variant string converted to lowercase
Left Function	Returns a variant string containing the leftmost *n* characters of a string
LeftB Function	Returns a variant string containing the leftmost *n* bytes of a string
Len Function	Returns the length of a given string
LenB Function	Returns the number of bytes in a given string
Length Property	Returns the length of a match represented by a Match object in a search string
LTrim Function	Returns a variant string with any leading spaces removed
Match Object	Represents a single match from a regular expression search
Matches Collection	Contains all the Match objects representing the matches found in a regular expression search
Mid Function	Returns a variant substring containing a specified number of characters
MidB Function	Returns a variant string containing a specified number of bytes from a string
Pattern Property	Sets or returns the pattern that the RegExp object attempts to find in its search string
RegExp Object	An object designed to provide regular expression support
Replace Function	Returns a string where a specified value has been replaced with another given value
Replace Method	Replaces substrings found in a regular expression search
Right Function	Returns a variant string containing the rightmost *n* characters of a string
RightB Function	Returns a variant string containing the rightmost *n* bytes of a string
RTrim Function	Returns a variant string with any trailing spaces removed
Space Function	Returns a variant string consisting of the specified number of spaces

Split Function	Returns an array of values derived from a single string and a specified separator
StrComp Function	Returns the result of a comparison of two strings
String Function	Returns a variant string containing a repeated character
StrReverse Function	Returns the reverse of a string
Test Method	Indicates whether a match was found in a RegExp object search
Trim Function	Returns a variant string with both leading and trailing spaces removed
UCase Function	Returns a variant string converted to uppercase
Unescape Function	Decodes a URL- or HTML-encoded string
Value Property	Returns the text of a regular expression match represented by a Match object

User Interaction

InputBox Function	Displays a dialog box to allow user input
MsgBox Function	Displays a dialog box and returns a value indicating the command button selected by the user
SetLocale Function	Sets the current locale and returns the ID of the previous locale

Variable Declaration

Const Statement	Declares a constant
Dim Statement	Declares a variable
Option Explicit Statement	Requires variable declaration
Private Statement	Declares the procedure or variable to have scope only in the module in which it is defined
Public Statement	Declares a global or public variable or function; marks the member as part of the class' public interface in a class
ReDim Statement	Declares a dynamic array variable

B

VBScript Constants

What follows is a series of tables listing the intrinsic constants supported by VBScript and their values. Note that, because the constants are part of the VBScript language, you don't have to define them using the Const statement.

Color Constants

These constants represent the values returned by *RGB* for standard colors:

Constant	Value	Description
vbBlack	0	Black
vbRed	255	Red
vbGreen	65280	Green
vbYellow	65535	Yellow
vbBlue	16,711,680	Blue
vbMagenta	16,711,935	Magenta
vbCyan	16,776,960	Cyan
vbWhite	16,777,215	White

Comparison Constants

The comparison constants are used by a number of functions (*Filter*, *StrComp*, *Split*, and *Replace*), as well as by the CompareMode property of the Dictionary object, to determine whether a string comparison should be case-sensitive or not:

Constant	Value	Description
vbBinaryCompare	0	Binary (case-sensitive comparison)
vbTextCompare	1	Text (case-insensitive comparison)
vbDatabaseCompare	2	Database (unused in VBScript)

Date and Time Constants

A number of functions (*DateDiff*, *DatePart*, *Weekday*, and *WeekdayName*) have a *FirstDayOfWeek* parameter whose value can be one of the day of the week constants (vbSunday through vbSaturday) as well as vbUseSystemDayOfWeek.

The *DateDiff* and *DatePart* functions also have a *FirstWeekOfYear* parameter whose value can be vbUseSystem, vbFirstJan1, vbFirstFourDays, or vbFirstFullWeek.

Constant	Value	Description
vbSunday	1	Sunday
vbMonday	2	Monday
vbTuesday	3	Tuesday
vbWednesday	4	Wednesday
vbThursday	5	Thursday
vbFriday	6	Friday
vbSaturday	7	Saturday
vbUseSystem	0	Use the date format defined by the local computer's regional settings
vbUseSystemDayOfWeek	0	Use the day of the week specified in your system settings for the first day of the week
vbFirstJan1	1	Use the week in which January 1 occurs; this is the default value for both *DateDiff* and *DatePart*
vbFirstFourDays	2	Use the first week that has at least four days in the new year
vbFirstFullWeek	3	Use the first full week of the year

Date Format Constants

The *FormatDateTime* function allows you to specify the format in which a date or time is displayed by choosing one of the date format constants to supply to its *NamedFormat* parameter:

Constant	Value	Description
vbGeneralDate	0	Display a date in short date format and a time in long time format. If present, both parts are displayed.
vbLongDate	1	Use the long date format defined in the local computer's regional settings.
vbLongTime	3	Use the long time format defined in the local computer's regional settings.
vbShortDate	2	Use the short date format defined in the local computer's regional settings.
vbShortTime	4	Use the short time format defined in the local computer's regional settings.

Error Constant

vbObjectError is used as a base error number for user-defined errors:

Constant	Value	Description
vbObjectError	-2,147,221,504	The base error number, to which a specific number is added when a user-defined error is raised. For example: `Err.Raise vbObjectError + 102`

Logical and TriState Constants

In many cases, only the logical constants vbTrue and vbFalse can be used. In other cases, the third constant, vbUseDefault, can be used to indicate a setting that is neither True nor False, or a setting that is defined elsewhere in the system:.

Constant	Value	Description
vbFalse	0	False
vbTrue	−1	True
vbUseDefault	−2	Use the default value defined by the system, or not applicable

Message Box Constants

Except for vbMsgBoxHelpButton, any one of the following constants can be used with the *buttons* parameters of the *MsgBox* function to determine which buttons appear in the dialog. The vbMsgBoxHelpButton constant can be ORed with the button constant to add a Help button to provide context-sensitive help; this, however, also requires that arguments be supplied to the function's *helpfile* and *context* parameters.

Constant	Value	Description
vbAbortRetryIgnore	2	Abort, Retry, and Ignore buttons
vbMsgBoxHelpButton	16384	Help button
vbOKCancel	1	OK and Cancel buttons
vbOKOnly	0	OK button; this is the default value
vbRetryCancel	5	Retry and Cancel buttons
vbYesNo	4	Yes and No buttons
vbYesNoCancel	3	Yes, No, and Cancel buttons

You can determine which of these buttons is the default (that is, it appears selected and will be chosen if the user presses the Enter key) by logically ORing any one of the following constants with any other constants passed to the *buttons* parameter. The selected button is designated by its position on the dialog. By default, the first button appears selected.

Constant	Value	Description
vbDefaultButton1	0	First button is the default
vbDefaultButton2	256	Second button is the default
vbDefaultButton3	512	Third button is the default
vbDefaultButton4	768	Fourth (Help) button is the default

The *MsgBox* function also allows you to designate an icon that appears in the message box to indicate the message type. You can logically OR any one of the message box icon constants with the other values that you pass as arguments to the *buttons* parameter, as in the following code fragment:

```
iResult = MsgBox("Is this OK?", vbYesNo Or vbQuestion Or _
                 vbApplicationModal, "Delete File")
```

Constant	Value	Description
vbCritical	16	Critical (stop sign) icon
vbExclamation	48	Exclamation (caution) icon
vbInformation	64	Information icon
vbQuestion	32	Question mark icon

You can also determine the modality of the message box by ORing one of the following constants with any other constants passed to the *buttons* parameter:

Constant	Value	Description
vbApplicationModal	0	The focus cannot move to another interface object in the application until the dialog is closed.
vbSystemModal	4096	The focus cannot move elsewhere in the system until the dialog is closed.

Three miscellaneous constants can be used to control the behavior of the dialog. Once again, they must be logically ORed with any other constants passed to the *buttons* parameter.

Constant	Value	Description
vbMsgBoxRight	524288	Right aligns text
vbMsgBoxRtlReading	1048576	On Hebrew and Arabic systems, specifies that text should appear from right to left
vbMsgBoxSetForeground	65536	Makes the message box the foreground window

Finally, the value returned by the *MsgBox* function can be compared with the following constants to determine which button was selected. Note that there is no need for a vbHelp constant, since selecting the Help button, if it is displayed, keeps the message box open but opens a help window to display context-sensitive help information.

Constant	Value	Description
vbAbort	3	The Abort button
vbCancel	2	The Cancel button
vbIgnore	5	The Ignore button
vbNo	7	The No button
vbOK	1	The OK button
vbRetry	4	The Retry button
vbYes	6	The Yes button

String Constants

The following constants are replacements for one or more characters. For instance, to add a line break to a string that's not being displayed in a web page, you can use a statement like the following:

```
sMsg = sMsg & vbCrLf
```

Constant	Value	Description
vbCr	Chr(13)	Carriage return
vbCrLf	Chr(10) & Chr(13)	Carriage return and linefeed characters
vbFormFeed	Chr(12)	Form-feed character
vbLf	Chr(10)	Linefeed character
vbNewLine	Platform Specific	New line character
vbNullChar	Chr(0)	Null character
vbNullString	0	Null pointer, used for calling external routines
vbTab	Chr(9)	Tab character
vbVertical Tab	Chr(11)	Vertical tab character

Variable Type Constants

The VarType constant returns one of the following constants to indicate the data subtype of the variable passed to it as a parameter. The exception is an array, which returns a value of 8204, or vbArray Or vbVariant.

Constant	Value	Description
vbArray	8192	Array
vbBoolean	11	Boolean
vbByte	17	Byte
vbCurrency	6	Currency
vbDataObject	13	Data Object
vbDate	7	Date
vbDecimal	14	Decimal (unavailable in VBScript)
vbDouble	5	Double
vbEmpty	0	Empty

Constant	Value	Description
vbError	10	Error
vbInteger	2	Integer
vbLong	3	Long
vbNull	1	Null
vbObject	9	Object
vbSingle	4	Single
vbString	8	String
vbVariant	12	Variant

C

Operators

There are four groups of operators in VBScript: arithmetic, concatenation, comparison, and logical. You'll find some to be instantly recognizable, while others may be unfamiliar. However, if you have the need to use these types of operators, it is likely that you know the mathematics fundamentals behind them. We will look at each group of operators in turn before discussing the order of precedence VBScript uses when it encounters more than one type of operator within an expression.

Arithmetic Operators

+   The addition operator. Used to add numeric expressions, as well as to concatenate (join together) two string variables. However, it's preferable to use the concatenation operator with strings to eliminate ambiguity. For example:

```
result = expression1 + expression2
```

-   The subtraction operator. Used to find the difference between two numeric values or expressions, as well as to denote a negative value. Unlike the addition operator, it cannot be used with string variables. For example:

```
result = expression1 - expression2
```

/   The division operator. Returns a floating-point number.

```
result = expression1 / expression2
```

*   The multiplication operator. Used to multiply two numerical values. For example:

```
result = expression1 * expression2
```

\   The integer division operator. Performs division on two numeric expressions and returns an integer result (no remainder or decimal places). For example:

```
result = expression1 \ expression2
```

Mod

The modulo operator. Performs division on two numeric expressions and returns only the remainder. If either of the two numbers are floating-point numbers, they are rounded to integer values prior to the modulo operation. For example:

```
result = expression1 Mod expression2
```

^

The exponentiation operator. Raises a number to the power of the exponent. For example:

```
result = number ^ exponent
```

String Operator

There is only one operator for strings: the concatenation operator, represented by the ampersand symbol (&). It is used to bind a number of string variables together, creating one string from two or more individual strings. Any nonstring variable or expression is converted to a string prior to concatenation. Its syntax is:

```
result = expression1 & expression2
```

Comparison Operators

There are three main comparison operators: < (less-than), > (greater-than), and = (equal to). They can be used individually, or any two operators can be combined with each other. Their general syntax is:

```
result = expression1 operator expression2
```

The resulting expression is True (–1), False (0), or Null. A Null results only if either *expression1* or *expression2* itself is Null.

What follows is a list of all the comparison operators supported by VBScript, as well as an explanation of the condition required for the comparison to result in True:

>   *expression1* is greater than and not equal to *expression2*

<   *expression1* less than and not equal to *expression2*

<> *or* ><

     expression1 not equal to *expression2* (less than or greater than)

>= *or* =>

     expression1 greater than or equal to *expression2*

<= *or* =<

     expression1 less than or equal to *expression2*

=   *expression1* equal to *expression2*

Comparison operators can be used with both numeric and string variables. Literal numbers and strings are called hard. Variables and other expressions are called soft. When comparing two expressions where one is a string and one is a numeric, the rules are:

1. If both are hard, the string is converted to a number before the comparison is executed.
2. If one is hard and one is soft, then the soft one is converted to the type of the hard one before the comparison.
3. If both are soft, then the number will be considered "smaller" than the string.

The Is Operator

The Is operator determines whether two object reference variables refer to the same object. Thus, it tests for the "equality" of two object references. Its syntax is:

```
result = object1 Is object2
```

If both *object1* and *object2* refer to the same object, the result is True; otherwise, the result is False. You also use the Is operator to determine whether an object variable refers to a valid object. This is done by comparing the object variable to the special Nothing value:

```
If oVar Is Nothing Then
```

The result is True if the object variable does not hold a reference to an object.

Logical and Bitwise Operators

Logical operators allow you to evaluate one or more expressions and return a logical value. VBA supports six logical operators: And, Or, Not, Eqv, Imp, and Xor. These operators also double as bitwise operators. A bitwise comparison examines each bit position in both expressions and sets or clears the corresponding bit in the result depending upon the operator used. The result of a bitwise operation is a numeric value.

And

Performs logical conjunction; that is, it returns True only if both *expression1* and *expression2* evaluate to True. If either expression is False, then the result is False. If either expression is Null, then the result is Null. Its syntax is:

```
result = expression1 And expression2
```

For example:

```
If x = 5 And y < 7 Then
```

In this case, the code after the If statement will be executed only if the value of *x* is five and the value of *y* is less than seven.

As a bitwise operator, And returns 1 if the compared bits in both expressions are 1, and returns 0 in all other cases, as shown in the following table:

Bit in expression1	Bit in expression2	Result
0	0	0
0	1	0
1	0	0
1	1	1

For example, the result of 15 And 179 is 3, as the following binary representation shows:

```
00000011 = 00001111 And 10110011
```

Or

Performs logical disjunction; that is, if either *expression1* or *expression2* evaluates to True, or if both *expression1* and *expression2* evaluate to True, the result is True. Only if neither expression is True does the Or operation return False. If either expression is Null, then the result is also Null. The syntax for the Or operator is:

```
result = expression1 Or expression2
```

For example:

```
If x = 5 Or y < 7 Then
```

In this case, the code after the If statement will be executed if the value of *x* is five or if the value of *y* is less than seven.

As a bitwise operator, Or returns 0 if the compared bits in both expressions are 0, and returns 1 in all other cases, as shown in the following table:

Bit in expression1	Bit in expression2	Result
0	0	0
0	1	1
1	0	1
1	1	1

For example, the result of 15 Or 179 is 191, as the following binary representation shows:

```
10111111 = 00001111 Or 10110011
```

Not

Performs logical negation on a single expression; that is, if the expression is True, the Not operator causes it to become False, while if it is False, the operator causes its value to become True. If the expression is Null, though, the result of using the Not operator is still a Null. Its syntax is:

```
result = Not expression1
```

For example:

```
If Not IsNumeric(x) Then
```

In this example, the code following the If statement will be executed if IsNumeric returns False, indicating that *x* is not a value capable of being represented by a number.

As a bitwise operator, Not simply reverses the value of the bit, as shown in the following table:

expression1	Result
0	1
1	0

For example, the result of Not 16 is 239 (or −17, depending on how the high-order bit is interpreted), as the following binary representation shows:

```
Not 00010000 = 11101111
```

Eqv

Performs logical equivalence; that is, it determines whether the value of two expressions is the same. Eqv returns True when both expressions evaluate to True or both expressions evaluate to False, but it returns False if either expression evaluates to True while the other evaluates to False. Its syntax is:

```
result = expression1 Eqv expression2
```

As a bitwise operator, Eqv returns 1 if the compared bits in both expressions are the same, and it returns 0 if they are different, as shown in the following table:

Bit in expression1	Bit in expression2	Result
0	0	1
0	1	0
1	0	0
1	1	1

For example, the result of 15 Eqv 179 is 67 (or −189), as the following binary representation shows:

```
01000011 = 00001111 Eqv 10110011
```

Imp

Performs logical implication, as shown in the following table:

expression1	expression2	Result
True	True	True
True	False	False
True	Null	Null
False	True	True
False	False	True
False	Null	True
Null	True	True
Null	False	Null
Null	Null	Null

Its syntax is:

```
result = expression1 Imp expression2
```

As a bitwise operator, Imp returns 1 if the compared bits in both expressions are the same or if *expression1* is 1; it returns 0 if the two bits are different and the bit in *expression1* is 1, as shown in the following table:

Bit in expression1	Bit in expression2	Result
0	0	1
0	1	1

Bit in expression1	Bit in expression2	Result
1	0	0
1	1	1

For example, the result of 15 Imp 179 is 243 (or −13), as the following binary representation shows:

```
11110011 = 00001111 Imp 10110011
```

Xor

Perform logical exclusion, which is the opposite of Eqv; that is, Xor (an abbreviation for eXclusive OR) determines whether two expressions are different. When both expressions are either True or False, then the result is False. If only one expression is True, the result is True. If either expression is Null, the result is also Null. Its syntax is:

```
result = expression1 Xor expression2
```

As a bitwise operator, Xor returns 1 if the bits being compared are different, and returns 0 if they are the same, as shown in the following table:

Bit in expression1	Bit in expression2	Result
0	0	0
0	1	1
1	0	1
1	1	0

For example, the result of 15 Xor 179 is 188, as the following binary representation shows:

```
10111100 = 00001111 Xor 10110011
```

Operator Precedence

If you include more than one operator in a single line of code, you need to know the order in which VBScript will evaluate them. Otherwise, the results may be completely different than you intend. The rules that define the order in which a language handles operators is known as the *order of precedence*. If the order of precedence results in operations being evaluated in an order other than the one you intend—and therefore if the value that results from these operations is "wrong" from your point of view—you can explicitly override the order of precedence through the use of parentheses. However, the order of precedence still applies to multiple operators within parentheses.

When a single line of code includes operators from more than one category, they are evaluated in the following order:

1. Arithmetic operators
2. Concatenation operators
3. Comparison operators
4. Logical operators

Within each category of operators except for the single concatenation operator, there is also an order of precedence. If multiple comparison operators appear in a single line of code, they are simply evaluated from left to right. The order of precedence of arithmetic operators is as follows:

1. Exponentiation (^)
2. Division and multiplication (/,*) (No order of precedence between the two)
3. Integer division (\)
4. Modulo arithmetic (Mod)
5. Addition and subtraction (+,-) (No order of precedence between the two)

If the same arithmetic operator is used multiple times in a single line of code, the operators are evaluated from left to right.

The order of precedence of logical operators is:

1. Not
2. And
3. Or
4. Xor
5. Eqv
6. Imp

If the same arithmetic or logical operator is used multiple times in a single line of code, the operators are evaluated from left to right.

D

Locale IDs

The following table lists the locale IDs used by the *GetLocale* and *SetLocale* functions. The *GetLocale* function returns a Long containing the decimal locale ID. In most cases, the *SetLocale* function accepts a locale ID in the form of a decimal, a hexadecimal, or a string value.

Locale	Decimal ID	Hex ID	String ID
Afrikaans	1078	&h0436	af
Albanian	1052	&h041C	sq
Arabic (No location)	1	&h0001	ar
Arabic (United Arab Emirates)	14337	&h3801	ar-ae
Arabic (Bahrain)	15361	&h3C01	ar-bh
Arabic (Algeria)	5121	&h1401	ar-dz
Arabic (Egypt)	3073	&h0C01	ar-eg
Arabic (Iraq)	2049	&h0801	ar-iq
Arabic (Jordan)	11265	&h2C01	ar-jo
Arabic (Kuwait)	13313	&h3401	ar-kw
Arabic (Lebanon)	12289	&h3001	ar-lb
Arabic (Libya)	4097	&h1001	ar-ly
Arabic (Morocco)	6145	&h1801	ar-ma
Arabic (Oman)	8193	&h2001	ar-om
Arabic (Qatar)	16385	&h4001	ar-qa
Arabic (Saudi Arabia)	1025	&h0401	ar-sa
Arabic (Syria)	10241	&h2801	ar-sy
Arabic (Tunisia)	7169	&h1C01	ar-tn
Arabic (Yemen)	9217	&h2401	ar-ye
Azeri (Latin)	1068	&h042C	az-az
Basque	1069	&h042D	eu

Locale	Decimal ID	Hex ID	String ID
Belarusian	1059	&h0423	be
Bulgarian	1026	&h0402	bg
Catalan	1027	&h0403	ca
Chinese (No location)	4	&h0004	zh
Chinese (China)	2052	&h0804	zh-cn
Chinese (Hong Kong S.A.R.)	3076	&h0C04	zh-hk
Chinese (Singapore)	4100	&h1004	zh-sg
Chinese (Taiwan)	1028	&h0404	zh-tw
Croatian	1050	&h041A	hr
Czech	1029	&h0405	cs
Danish	1030	&h0406	da
Dutch (The Netherlands)	1043	&h0413	nl
Dutch (Belgium)	2067	&h0813	nl-be
English (No location)	9	&h0009	en
English (Australia)	3081	&h0C09	en-au
English (Belize)	10249	&h2809	en-bz
English (Canada)	4105	&h1009	en-ca
English (Caribbean)	9225	&h2409	
English (Ireland)	6153	&h1809	en-ie
English (Jamaica)	8201	&h2009	en-jm
English (New Zealand)	5129	&h1409	en-nz
English (Philippines)	13321	&h3409	en-ph
English (South Africa)	7177	&h1C09	en-za
English (Trinidad)	11273	&h2C09	en-tt
English (United Kingdom)	2057	&h0809	en-gb
English (United States)	1033	&h0409	en-us
Estonian	1061	&h0425	et
Farsi	1065	&h0429	fa
Finnish	1035	&h040B	fi
Faroese	1080	&h0438	fo
French (France)	1036	&h040C	fr
French (Belgium)	2060	&h080C	fr-be
French (Canada)	3084	&h0C0C	fr-ca
French (Luxembourg)	5132	&h140C	fr-lu
French (Switzerland)	4108	&h100C	fr-ch
Gaelic (Ireland)	2108	&h083C	
Gaelic (Scotland)	1084	&h043C	gd
German (Germany)	1031	&h0407	de
German (Austria)	3079	&h0C07	de-at
German (Liechtenstein)	5127	&h1407	de-li
German (Luxembourg)	4103	&h1007	de-lu
German (Switzerland)	2055	&h0807	de-ch

Locale	Decimal ID	Hex ID	String ID
Greek	1032	&h0408	el
Hebrew	1037	&h040D	he
Hindi	1081	&h0439	hi
Hungarian	1038	&h040E	hu
Icelandic	1039	&h040F	is
Indonesian	1057	&h0421	in
Italian (Italy)	1040	&h0410	it
Italian (Switzerland)	2064	&h0810	it-ch
Japanese	1041	&h0411	ja
Korean	1042	&h0412	ko
Latvian	1062	&h0426	lv
Lithuanian	1063	&h0427	lt
FYRO Macedonian	1071	&h042F	mk
Malay (Malaysia)	1086	&h043E	ms
Maltese	1082	&h043A	mt
Marathi	1102	&h044E	mr
Norwegian (Bokmål)	1044	&h0414	no
Norwegian (Nynorsk)	2068	&h0814	
Polish	1045	&h0415	pl
Portuguese (Portugal)	2070	&h0816	pt
Portuguese (Brazil)	1046	&h0416	pt-br
Raeto-Romance	1047	&h0417	rm
Romanian (Romania)	1048	&h0418	ro
Romanian (Moldova)	2072	&h0818	ro-mo
Russian	1049	&h0419	ru
Russian (Moldova)	2073	&h0819	ru-mo
Sanskrit	1103	&h044F	
Serbian (Cyrillic)	3098	&h0C1A	sr
Serbian (Latin)	2074	&h081A	
Setsuana	1074	&h0432	tn
Slovenian	1060	&h0424	sl
Slovak	1051	&h041B	sk
Sorbian	1070	&h042E	sb
Spanish (Spain)	1034	&h0C0A	es
Spanish (Argentina)	11274	&h2C0A	es-ar
Spanish (Bolivia)	16394	&h400A	es-bo
Spanish (Chile)	13322	&h340A	es-cl
Spanish (Colombia)	9226	&h240A	es-co
Spanish (Costa Rica)	5130	&h140A	es-cr
Spanish (Dominican Republic)	7178	&h1C0A	es-do
Spanish (Ecuador)	12298	&h300A	es-ec
Spanish (Guatemala)	4106	&h100A	es-gt

Locale	Decimal ID	Hex ID	String ID
Spanish (Honduras)	18442	&h480A	es-hn
Spanish (Mexico)	2058	&h080A	es-mx
Spanish (Nicaragua)	19466	&h4C0A	es-ni
Spanish (Panama)	6154	&h180A	es-pa
Spanish (Peru)	10250	&h280A	es-pe
Spanish (Puerto Rico)	20490	&h500A	es-pr
Spanish (Paraguay)	15370	&h3C0A	es-py
Spanish (El Salvador)	17418	&h440A	es-sv
Spanish (Uruguay)	14346	&h380A	es-uy
Spanish (Venezuela)	8202	&h200A	es-ve
Sutu	1072	&h0430	sx
Swahili	1089	&h0441	
Swedish (Sweden)	1053	&h041D	sv
Swedish (Finland)	2077	&h081D	sv-fi
Tamil	1097	&h0449	
Tatar	1092	0X0444	
Thai	1054	&h041E	th
Turkish	1055	&h041F	tr
Tsonga	1073	&h0431	ts
Ukrainian	1058	&h0422	uk
Urdu	1056	&h0420	ur
Uzbek (Cyrillic)	2115	&h0843	uz-uz
Uzbek (Latin)	1091	&h0443	uz-uz
Vietnamese	1066	&h042A	vi
Xhosa	1076	&h0434	xh
Yiddish	1085	&h043D	
Zulu	1077	&h0435	zu

Locale IDs

E

The Script Encoder

The Script Encoder, *screnc.exe*, is a command-line utility that encodes script, including the script embedded in HTML page, ASP pages (including incline ASP script), and *.wsf* scripts for the Windows Script Host. The encoded script, rather than the original source code, is then decoded and executed when the script is run. Using the Script Encoder to encode script offers two advantages:

Source code protection
>Ordinarily, script is plainly visible to prying eyes. Client-side script in particular can be inspected by anyone who requests a web page. Although both ASP and WSH scripts are accessible to a smaller number of users, they nevertheless can be read by anyone with access to the system on which they reside. By encrypting the code, the Script Component renders it illegible.

Security
>Not only can scripts be viewed, but in some cases they can even be modified. Once a script is encoded, however, any further modification renders it inoperable. By permitting scripts to be encoded, the Script Encoder has two objectives:
>
>- Stop casual inspection and modification of a script.
>- Provide a legal recourse, should inspection or modification take place.

At the same time, it is important to recognize that the script encoder is *not* cryptographically strong; encoded scripts can be unencoded very easily (and unencoders are readily downloadable from the Internet). The Script Encoder ultimately offers the same level of minimal protection as locking a car provides to its contents. It mitigates casual inspection of code, but should not be used to protect valuable or sensitive information like passwords.

The Script Encoder can successfully encode most scripts written in VBScript. An exception, however, is script written for Outlook forms, in part because their script is not stored in standalone script files, and in part because Outlook forms support only one language, VBScript, whereas from the viewpoint of the host, encoded script is a separate language: VBScript.Encode.

In addition, problems arise when using encoded script on Far East operating systems. In particular, it is possible for collisions with DBCS characters to occur, causing the encoded script to be incorrectly decoded. As a result, the Script Encoder should not be used if a script is ever going to be run on a Far East operating system.

How Encoding and Decoding Works

The command-line Script Encoder utility (*screnc.exe*) is responsible for encoding scripts. To determine what to encode, the Script Encoder looks for a start encode marker, which takes the following form for VBScript code:

```
'**Start Encode**
```

The Script Encoder encodes the file from the point at which the start encode marker is encountered until the closing </SCRIPT> or %> tag, or until the end of the file is found. If there is no start encode marker, the Script Encoder encodes the entire script block indicated by the <SCRIPT>...</SCRIPT>, <%...%>, or <%=...%> tags, or it will encode the entire file if no tags are encountered.

In addition to encoding the script, the Script Encoder changes the LANGUAGE attribute of the <SCRIPT> tag from VBScript to VBScript.Encode. For an ASP page, it also adds the following attribute to the beginning of the page:

```
<%@ LANGUAGE = VBScript.Encode %>
```

When the page is loaded and the script is executed, VBScript.Encode serves as the programmatic identifier that specifies not only the language in use, but also the COM component responsible for parsing and handling the script. The hosting environment, such as ASP or the MSIE browser, uses the programmatic identifier to look up the class identifier, which, in this case, corresponds to COM components in *vbscript.dll*. So *vbscript.dll* is responsible for not only interpreting and executing the codes, but also for decoding it.

Script Encoder Syntax

The Script Encoder has the following simplified syntax:

```
screnc inputfile outputfile
```

where *inputfile* is the target file containing script to be decoded, along with its optional path, and *outputfile* is the file containing encoded script that the Script Encoder is to create, along with its optional path. Note that *inputfile* and *outputfile* can include the standard wildcard characters.

The Script Encoder also accepts the following optional command-line switches:

/?

    Display help information for the Script Encoder.

/f

    The output file is to overwrite the source file, which means that the original decoded source file is lost. With the /f switch, *outputfile* need not be specified. By default, the Script Encoder will not overwrite *inputfile*.

/s

    The Script Encoder is to work in silent mode, without producing screen output. By default, the Script Encoder produces verbose output.

/xl

    Specifies that the Script Encoder should not add the @LANGUAGE directive to the top of ASP files. (The @LANGUAGE directive determines the scripting language used by ASP to process the page; VBScript is the default.) By default, the Script Encoder adds an @LANGUAGE directive whenever it encodes an ASP page.

/l *defLanguage*

    Defines the default scripting language for the Script Encoder to use. Script blocks lacking a LANGUAGE attribute are assumed to be written in this language. If no language is specified, the Script Encoder otherwise assumes that JScript is the default language for HTML pages and *.js* files, and that VBScript is the default language for ASP and *.vbs* files. The Script Encoder does not recognize a default language for Windows Script Component (*.wsc*) files. Either the LANGUAGE attribute must be specified in the file's <SCRIPT> tag, or the /l switch must be used; otherwise, no script will be encoded.

/e *defExtension*

    Associates *inputfile*, whose file extension does not correspond to a scriptable file type, with a recognizable file type. Recognized extensions are *.asa*, *.asp*, *.cdx*, *.htm*, *.html*, *.js*, *.sct*, and *.vbs*.

Encoding Examples

Encoding most file types containing VBScript (such as *.asp* files without client-side script or *.htm* or *.html* files with client-side script) is quite intuitive. Consequently, in this section, we'll examine how to use the Script Encoder's command-line parameters to encode some of the scripted files that are otherwise difficult to encode. In each case, the conventional syntax of:

```
screnc inputfile outputfile
```

either generates an error or does not achieve the desired results.

Encoding .vbs Files

Although the documentation notes that the Script Encoder encodes VBScript (*.vbs*) files "out of the box," it does not indicate how to do this. The usual syntax, such as the following:

```
screnc OriginalScript.vbs EncodedScript.vbs
```

creates an encoded file, but attempting to execute it generates a runtime error.

The reason for this is that VBScript files lack any equivalent to the @ LANGUAGE directive or the <SCRIPT> tag, which tell the VBScript interpreter what type of code (VBScript or VBScript.Encode) the file contains. Instead, when the VBScript interpreter is invoked and is passed a filename, it determines the file type from the file's extension. The *.vbs* extension indicates a file of type VBScript—that is, an unencoded VBScript file. The VBScript interpreter detects encoded files (files of type VBScript.Encode) by their *.vbe* file extension.

Example E-1 shows the contents of a *.vbs* file that lists free space on available drives. This script can be encoded using the following command-line syntax:

```
screnc freespace.vbs freespace.vbe
```

The result (with line breaks added) is shown in Example E-2. Note that there is no need to add the /xl switch, since the encoder recognizes a VBScript file and automatically suppresses its default @ LANGUAGE directive.

Example E-1. An unencoded .vbs file

```
' FreeSpace Script
' Calculates the amount of free space on available drives
' (c) 2003 O'Reilly & Associates
'**Start Encode**

Const FIXED = 2

Dim oFS, oDrive, oDrives
Dim sMsg

Set oFS = CreateObject("Scripting.FileSystemObject")

Set oDrives = oFS.Drives
sMsg = "Drive Space Information:" & vbCrLf
For Each oDrive in oDrives
    If oDrive.DriveType = FIXED Or oDrive.IsReady Then
        sMsg = sMsg & vbCrLf
        sMsg = sMsg & "     " & oDrive.DriveLetter & " " _
                & FormatNumber(oDrive.Freespace, 0, True, False, True)
    Else
        sMsg = sMsg & vbCrLf
        sMsg = sMsg & "     " & oDrive.DriveLetter & " Unavailable"
    End If
Next
WScript.Echo sMsg
```

Example E-2. An encoded .vbs file

```
' FreeSpace Script
' Calculates the amount of free space on available drives
' (c) 2003 O'Reilly & Associates
'**Start Encode**#@~^YgIAAA==@#@&@#@&;W/Y,s&p2GPxPy@#@&@#@&fks~Ww?~,
G9Db\ ~~W9.b\n/@#@&fb:~dt/o@#@&@#@&j+D~Ksj,',ZD lDnr(LnmD`Ej1DkaOkoRwrs
+UXkYn:68N+^Yrb@#@&@#@&j YPG9Mk-+k~{PGw?cfDb\ d@#@&/\/TPx~rfDb-+,?wm^nP&x6W.:
CObWU)r~[,\8/MSO@#@&wW.PAC1t~KfMk\ PbUPKf.k7+d@#@&PP,(O,WfMr-+cfMk-+Pza+~',
oqo29~}DPG9Mk-+c(kInmNHPK4+@#@&,P~P,Pd\koP{~/t/o,'~\(ZMSW@#@&~,P~P,dHko~x,
```

The Script Encoder

Example E-2. An encoded .vbs file (continued)

```
/HdL,[~J,~,P~rPLPWGDb-+cf.k7+JnDY+M~[,JPr~m@#@&P,P~P~~,P~P,~P,P~~LPsG.sl01!h(+
.vWGDk7+coD +dwmmnS,!~,PD!+~,oCVk+BPPD;n*@#@&P,~2^/n@#@&PP~~,PdHkL,
'~kHkoPLP78ZMSW@#@&P~~,PPk\/TP',d\/TPLPEP~~,
PEPL~WGDr- Rf.r7+J+DO D~LPrPjl7Ck^18V J@#@&,PPAUN,qO@#@&H+XY@#@&?^.
bwORA^tKPd\koVKMAAA==^#~@
```

Encoding .wsf Files

The Script Encoder does not appear to be able to encode Windows Script Host's *.wsf* files. This seems curious, since Windows Script Files contain <SCRIPT>... </SCRIPT> tags that should make the encoding and decoding processes easy. Nevertheless, there are two reasons that *.wsf* files cannot be encoded using the most simple Script Encoder syntax:

- *.wsf* is not a file extension recognized by the Script Encoder.
- The Script Encoder automatically inserts an @ LANGUAGE directive at the top of the page, which causes WSH to generate an error.

Both of these problems can be addressed using command-line switches. In particular, we can use the /xl switch to suppress the @ LANGUAGE directive. And we can indicate a file type, such as an *.htm* file, that's similar to a *.wsf* file and that the Script Encoder does know how to handle. (We can't the *.asp* file type, since because the <SCRIPT> tag lacks the RUNAT attribute, Script Encoder won't encode the script.)

Example E-3 shows the unencoded contents of a *.wsf* file that includes a routine to list free space on available drives. This script can be encoded using the following command-line syntax:

```
screnc filesystemutil.wsf filesystemutilenc.wsf /e htm /xl
```

The result (with line breaks added) is shown in Example E-4.

Example E-3. An unencoded .wsf file

```
<package>
<job id="ShowDiskSpace">
<?job error="true"?>
  <script language="vbscript">
  ' ShowDiskSpace script
  '
  ' Calculates the amount of free space on available drives
  ' (c) 2003 O'Reilly & Associates
  '**Start Encode**
  Dim oFS, oDrive, oDrives
  Dim sMsg
  Set oFS = CreateObject("Scripting.FileSystemObject")
  Set oDrives = oFS.Drives
  sMsg = "Drive Space Information:" & vbCrLf
  For Each oDrive In oDrives
     If oDrive.DriveType = Fixed Or oDrive.IsReady Then
        sMsg = sMsg & vbCrLf
        sMsg = sMsg & "      " & oDrive.DriveLetter & " " _
```

```
                        & oDrive.FreeSpace
    Else
        sMsg = sMsg & vbCrLf
        sMsg = sMsg & "       " & oDrive.DriveLetter & " Unavailable"
    End If
  Next
  WScript.Echo sMsg
  </script>
</job>
</package>
```

Example E-4. An encoded .wsf file

```
<package>
<job id="ShowDiskSpace">
<?job error="true"?>
  <script language="VBScript.Encode">
  ' ShowDiskSpace script
  '
  ' Calculates the amount of free space on available drives
  ' (c) 2003 O'Reilly & Associates
  '**Start Encode**#@~^VgIAAA==~,@#@&,P,fksPKo?BPGfMk-
nBPWG.k7+/@#@&~P,fb:~/\dT@#@&P,~? Y~Gw?Px~;DnlDn}4% mD`JUmMrw
DkUocsrs ?XkO+sr4Nn^Yr#@#@&~P~j Y~WG.k7+d~{PWojcf.k7nk@#@&,P,
/Hko,xP,J9Db\n~Uwl1nP&xoK.hlDkKxlJ~',\8ZMJo@#@&~~,sW.~Al^t,
GGDr7+,qx,WG.k7+d@#@&P~~,PP&WPKfDb-nRGDb\nKz2 PxPwr6 N~6MPW9.b\
nR&d"+C9X,Kt x@#@&P,P~P,P~~kH/T~',
/HkL~[,\(Z.SW@#@&P~P,~P,P~dt/o~x,/\/T~LPE,P,PPrPL~WGDr\ R9.b
\+dnYD+D,'~J,J,{@#@&~~,P~P,~P,P~~,PP~~,P~PL~Kf.b\ RsM+ jwmmn
@#@&P~~,PPAs/ @#@&,~~P,P,P~/\dTPxPk\/TP'~74Z.J6@#@&P,~,P~,P,
/Hko,xPkHdo,[~E,PP,~J,[PK9.k7+cf.k-nd+OY .PLPE~`xl-CbVC4^nr
@#@&,P,PP,2[P&o@#@&,P~H 6Y@#@&P,P U^.kaYc2^tG~kHdo@#@&P,PJJo
AAA==^#~@
  </script>
</job>
</package>
```

Encoding ASP Files with Client-Side Script

Encoding ASP files is simple enough, as is encoding HTML files with client-side script. But encoding all script in an ASP file that contains embedded (rather than dynamically generated) client-side script is not straightforward. Using the simple version of the Script Encoder's syntax to encode an ASP file leaves client-side script unencoded. Encoding an ASP file as if it were an HTML file, as with the following syntax:

```
screnc form2.asp form2enc.asp /e htm
```

encodes both client-side script and ASP <SCRIPT> blocks, but it does not encode script in the <%...%> and <%=...%> tags found within the HTML stream.

The solution is to double-encode an ASP file. For example, Example E-5 shows a very simple ASP page that contains embedded client-side script. It can first be encoded using the conventional syntax:

```
screnc form2.asp form2enc.asp
```

This encodes the ASP script only. The next step is to encode the client-side script using the following syntax:

```
screnc form2enc.asp /f /e htm
```

These command-line switches treat the ASP file as if it were an HTML file and overwrite the source *form2enc.asp file*. The result, which is shown (with added line breaks) in Example E-6, is encoded ASP script and client-side script

Example E-5. An unencoded ASP file with client-side script

```
<HTML>
<HEAD>
<TITLE>A Sample Form</TITLE>
</HEAD>
<BODY>
<SCRIPT LANGUAGE="VBSCRIPT">
    '
    ' Event handler fired when window loads
    ' Displays dialog to user
    Sub Window_OnLoad()
        Alert "Thank you for filling out the form!"
    End Sub
</SCRIPT>
You provided us with the following information: <P>
<% ShowInformation %>
<P>
Thank you for submitting this information.

<SCRIPT LANGUAGE="VBSCRIPT" RUNAT="SERVER">

Sub ShowInformation()
    If Not Request("txtName") = "" Then
        Response.Write "Name: " & Server.HTMLEncode(Request("txtName")) & "<BR>"
        Response.Write "Country: " & Server.HTMLEncode(Request("txtCountry")) &
"<P>"
    Else
        Response.Write "None"
    End If
End Sub
</SCRIPT>
</BODY>
</HTML>
```

Example E-6. An ASP page with both ASP and client-side script encoded

```
<%@ LANGUAGE = VBScript.Encode %>
<HTML>
<HEAD>
<TITLE>A Sample Form</TITLE>
```

Example E-6. An ASP page with both ASP and client-side script encoded (continued)

```
</HEAD>
<BODY>
<SCRIPT LANGUAGE="VBScript.Encode">#@~^twAAAA==@#@&P~,B@#@&P,PE~27+UY,
tCU9V+M~ObD+9~At x,hrx[GSPsWm[/@#@&~~,BP9rkwslHd,NrmVKoPDW,;/ D@#@&,
P~j!4Pqrx9Wh|6USKl9`b@#@&~,P~P,)V DO~rKtCUOPzW!~6W.,ObVVbxT~W!Y~Y4+~WKD:
eE@#@&PP,3UN,?!4@#@&sTIAAA==^#~@</SCRIPT>
You provided us with the following information: <P>
<%#@~^EQAAAA==~UtGSqOWM:mOkKx~ZwYAAA==^#~@%>
<P>
Thank you for submitting this information.

<SCRIPT LANGUAGE="VBScript.Encode" RUNAT="SERVER">
#@~^OgEAAA==@#@&@#@&UE(P?4WS(x6W.:mYrG`#@#@&P,Pq6~HWDP"+5EndD`EYXO1m:
nE*P'~ErPPt U@#@&~,P,PP"+k2W/nRqDrO PJgC: )Pr~'PU+M
\nD u:HJ2^W9+c] ;EndD`EYXOglh J*#PLPr@!A"@*E@#@&P~~,
PP"n/aWxkn  MkD+~J/G!xODHlPrP'~U+D-nMRuKtJAx^KN `I ;!n/D`EYXY
/G!xYMzJ*#PL~E@!h@*r@#@&P~~AVd+@#@&P,P~~,
I+d2Kxd+cMkO Pr1W+r@#@&,P~2N~(6@#@&AUN,
?E(@#@&X1QAAA==^#~@</SCRIPT>
</BODY>
</HTML>
```

Index

Symbols

+ addition operator, 451
<!-- --> comment tags, 158
& concatenation (string) operator, 452
<%= %> delimiter, 94
<%...%> delimiter, 94
/ division operator, 451
. dot delimiter, 85
= equal to operator, 452
^ exponentiation operator, 452
> greater-than operator, 452
\ integer division operator, 451
< less-than operator, 452
* multiplication operator, 451
<> not equal operator, 452
. period, 85
- subtraction operator, 451

A

Abandon method, Session object
    (ASP), 100
Abs function, 202
absolute pathnames, 288
absolute values, 202
accessing file data, 415–417
accessing other object models
    from Outlook forms, 123
    from WSH, 152

Actions property, current item
    (Outlook), 116
Activate method, Inspector object
    (Outlook), 118
Active Directory Service Interface
    (ADSI), WSH and, 152
Active Server Pages object
    model, 95–101
    resources for further reading, 101
Active Server Pages (see entries at ASP)
activeElement property, Document
    object (IE), 168
ActiveX Data Objects (ADO objects)
    Outlook and, 124
    WSH and, 152
ActiveX objects
    creating, 220–223
    references to, 325
Add method
    Dictionary object, 235
    Folders collection object, 314
    Pages collection (Outlook), 119
AddHeader method, Response object
    (ASP), 98
addition operator (+), 451
AddPrinter Connection method,
    WshNetwork object, 137
AddressLists property, NameSpace
    object (Outlook), 121

We'd like to hear your suggestions for improving our indexes. Send email to *index@oreilly.com*.

BinaryRead method, Request object
(ASP), 97
BinaryWrite method, Response object
(ASP), 98
bitwise operators, 453–456
blur method, Window object (IE), 168
Body property, current item
(Outlook), 116
body property, Document object
(IE), 168
Boolean type, 39
converting expressions to, 208
bounds/boundaries, 51
lower, determining for arrays, 345
upper, determining for arrays, 423
Break at Next Statement option (Script
Debugger), 78
breakpoint, setting, 78
browsers, commenting out scripts for
older, 158
Buffer property, Response object
(ASP), 98
bugs (see debugging; errors; error
handling)
BuildPath method, FileSystemObject
object, 277
built-in constants, 48, 445–450
built-in conversion functions, 45
button property, Event object (IE), 175
buttons
adding to web pages, 161
radio, 164
Byte type, 40
converting expressions to, 209

C

CacheControl property, Response object
(ASP), 98
Call Stack window (Script
Debugger), 77
Call statement, 14, 207
CallByName function, not supported in
VBScript, 208
calling
functions, 17
subroutines, 14
Caption property, Inspector object
(Outlook), 118

case sensitivity
HTML attributes/elements and, 155
strings and
comparison constants for, 445
converting, 345, 424
variable names and, 47
Categories property, current item
(Outlook), 116
Category property, FormDescription
object (Outlook), 119
CategorySub property, FormDescription
object (Outlook), 119
CBool function, 208
CByte function, 45, 209
CCur function, 46, 210
CDate function, 45, 210–212
CDbl function, 46, 212
CDO objects, WSH and, 152
CGI (Common Gateway Interface), 91
characters
character codes, converting to, 213
ignoring when reading, 417
lowercase, converting to, 345
repeating into strings, 408
uppercase, converting to, 424
(see also strings)
Characters property, WshRemoteError
object, 142
Charset property, Response object
(ASP), 98
Checkbox control (HTML), 170
checked property
Checkbox control (HTML), 170
radio button control (HTML), 172
Chr, ChrB, ChrW functions, 213
CInt function, 46, 214
class events, 27
class methods, 26
class properties, 25
Class property
current item (Outlook), 116
FormDescription object
(Outlook), 120
Inspector object (Outlook), 118
MAPIFolder object (Outlook), 122
NameSpace object (Outlook), 121
Pages collection (Outlook), 119
Class statement, 215–217
Class...End Class construct and, 24

CustomAction event (Outlook), 109
CustomPropertyChange event
    (Outlook), 109

D

Data Access Objects (DAO objects)
    Outlook and, 124
    WSH and, 152
data formatting, 318
data types
    converting from one to another, 45
        list of functions for, 436
    supported by WshShell registry
        methods, 145
    variant (see variant data type)
data validation, 163–166
date and time, 224–233
    constants for, 446
    converting expressions and, 210–212
    FormatDateTime function for, 319
    list of functions for, 437
Date function, 224
Date type, 40
    converting expressions to, 210–212
DateAdd function, 225
DateDiff function, 226–228
DatePart function, 229
DateSerial function, 231
DateValue function, 232
Day function, 233
debugging, 68–83
    common problems and how to avoid
        them, 89
    RUNAT attribute omitted and, 94
    script components and, 180
    (see also errors; error handling)
declaring/defining
    constants, 48, 50, 218
    functions, 14–18, 321–324
    storage space for variables, 243
    subprocedures, 409–412
    subroutines, 11–14
    variables, 50
        errors when undeclared, 363
        list of statements for, 444
Default ASP Language property, 94
DefaultItemType property, MAPIFolder
    object (Outlook), 122
DefaultMessageClass property,
    MAPIFolder object
    (Outlook), 122

defaultValue property, textbox control
    (HTML), 170
Delete method
    current item (Outlook), 117
    File object, 271
    Folder object, 311
    MAPIFolder object (Outlook), 123
DeleteFile method, FileSystemObject
    object, 283
DeleteFolder method, FileSystemObject
    object, 284
deleting (clearing)
    Dictionary keys and data, 242
    Err object, resetting and, 254
    files, 271, 283
    folders, 284, 311
    whitespace from strings, 350, 392,
        421
Description property
    Err object, 86, 255
    MAPIFolder object (Outlook), 122
    WshRemoteError object, 142
    WshShortcut object, 147
<description> tag, 150
design mode for Outlook forms, 105
DHTML (Dynamic HTML), 177
DHTML interface handler, 180
dialog boxes, 334, 356–359
Dictionary object, 201, 234
    list of methods/properties for, 437
    Outlook and, 124
    WSH and, 152
Dim statement, 243
    arrays and, 51
    constants/variables and, 50
    replaced with public visibility, 66
dimensioning arrays, 51
DisconnectObject method, WScript
    object (WSH), 132
Display method
    current item (Outlook), 117
    Inspector object (Outlook), 118
    MAPIFolder object (Outlook), 123
DisplayName property,
        FormDescription object
        (Outlook), 120
division by zero error, 90
division operator (/), 451
.doc files, 124
Document Object Model (DOM), 166
Do...Loop statement, 245–247

GetObject method, WScript object
(WSH), 133
  accessing object models and, 152
GetParentFolderName method,
  FileSystemObject object, 295
GetRecipientFromID method,
  NameSpace object
  (Outlook), 121
GetRef function, 327
GetSharedDefaultFolder method,
  NameSpace object
  (Outlook), 122
  MAPIFolder object and, 122
GetSpecialFolder method,
  FileSystemObject object, 296
GetStandardStream method,
  FileSystemObject object, 297
GetTempName method,
  FileSystemObject object, 298
global code, 27–31, 113
global.asa file, 92
"glue" languages, 6
go method, History object (IE), 174
greater-than operator (>), 452

H

Height property, Inspector object
  (Outlook), 118
HelpContext property, Err object, 256
HelpFile property, Err object, 257
Hex function, 329
hexadecimal numbers, 329
Hidden property, FormDescription
  object (Outlook), 120
HideFormPage method, Inspector object
  (Outlook), 118
History object (IE), 174
history property, Window object
  (IE), 167
Hotkey property, WshShortcut
  object, 147
hotkey strings (WSH), 147
Hour function, 329
HTML, 154–177
  Script Encoder for, 462–469
  using resources and (sample
    code), 194
HTMLEditor property, Inspector object
  (Outlook), 118
HTMLEncode method, Server object
  (ASP), 100

I

Icon property, FormDescription object
  (Outlook), 120
IconLocation property, WshShortcut
  object, 147
IDE (integrated development
  environment), 10
IE (see Internet Explorer)
If...Then...Else statement, 330–333
IIS (Internet Information Server), 4, 91
  IIS components, ASP implemented
    as, 92
  snap-in for, 94
images, LoadPicture function for, 348
Immediate window, 79
Imp operator, 455
<implements> element, 190
Importance property, current item
  (Outlook), 116
#include directive, 32
include files
  in ASP, 33
  in Internet Explorer, 36
  in Windows Script Host (WSH), 34
index, 51
  finding upper/lower, 56
index property, Individual Option object
  (HTML list box control), 173
information functions, list of, 440
Initialize event, 333
InputBox function, 334
  WSH support for, 125
Insert Event Handler dialog (VBScript
  editor), 108
Inspector object (Outlook), 104, 117
Inspector pane (Outlook), 104
installation scripts, WSH and, 126
instantiating objects, 23
InStr, InStrB functions, 336
InStrRev function, 337
Int function, 339
integer division operator (\), 451
integer type, 40, 214
integrated development environment
  (IDE), 10
interface handlers, 178, 180
  for script components, 190–193
Internet, shortcuts for, 149
Internet Explorer Document Object
  Model, 166–177
  using, 175

name property
  Checkbox control (HTML), 170
  command button controls
    (HTML), 174
  list box control (HTML), 173
  radio button control (HTML), 172
  textbox control (HTML), 170
  Window object (IE), 167
Name text box (Script Component
    Wizard), 178, 179
named arguments vs. positional
    arguments, 10
Named property, WshArguments
    object, 134, 136
<named> tag, 150
names
  of data types, 422
  of drives, 291
  of filename extensions, 291
  of files, determining, 293
  of folders, 295
    temporary, 298
  of pathnames, 288, 289
  of weekdays, 428
NameSpace object (Outlook), 104, 121
naming script components, 178
natural logarithms, 349
navigate method, Window object
    (IE), 168
negativity of numbers, 403
Netscape Navigator, ECMAScript
    and, 154
network resources
  accessing via WSH, 126
  WshNetwork object and, 136
New keyword, not supported in
    VBScript when used with Dim
    statement, 244
NoAging property, current item
    (Outlook), 116
nonalphanumeric hotkey strings
    (WSH), 147
not equal operator (<>), 452
Not operator, 454
Now function, 360
null data, IsNull function for, 342
Null type, 39
Number property
  Err object, 85, 258
  FormDescription object
    (Outlook), 120
  WshRemoteError object, 142

numbers
  formatting, 318
  list of numeric functions for, 441
  random, 376, 390
  rounding, 392
  signs/negativity of, 403
  truncating, 305, 339

O

object browsers, 107
Object data type, 41
object models, 6, 201
  accessing other
    from Outlook forms, 123
    from WSH, 151–153
  ASP, 95–101
  building, 195–198
  COM, 91
  Document, 166
  Excel, 124, 152
  File System, 274
  IE, 166–177
  Outlook, 114–123
  Word, 124, 152
  WSH, 130–150
object property assignment
    procedures, 25
object references, 24
<OBJECT> tag, 92
<object> tag, 151
ObjectContext object (ASP), 96
objects, 24
  creating, 220–223
  GetObject function for, 325
  IsObject function for, 343
  programming, list of events/
    functions/statements for, 441
Oct function, 360
octal numbers, 360
On Error Resume Next statement, 83
On Error statement, 361–363
onChange event
  list box control (HTML), 173
  textbox control (HTML), 170
onClick event
  Checkbox control (HTML), 171
  command button controls
    (HTML), 174
  list box control (HTML), 173
  radio button control (HTML), 172

RegWrite method, WshShell
    object, 144
Rem statement, 386
remarks in program code, 386
remote scripting, WSH and, 138
Remove method
    Contents collection
        Application object (ASP), 96
        Session object (ASP), 101
    Dictionary object, 242
    Pages collection (Outlook), 119
    StaticObjects collection (Session
        object, ASP), 101
    WshEnvironment object, 135
RemoveAll method
    Contents collection
        Application object (ASP), 96
        Session object (ASP), 101
    Dictionary object, 243
    StaticObjects collection (Session
        object, ASP), 101
RemoveNetworkDrive method,
    WshNetwork object, 138
RemovePrinterConnection method,
    WshNetwork object, 138
Replace function, 386
    comparison constants for, 445
Reply event (Outlook), 110
ReplyAll event (Outlook), 110
Request object (ASP), 97
reserved words, 47
Reset button (HTML), 173
resetting
    array element values, 252
    Err object properties, 254
<resource id=id> tag, 151
resources for further reading
    ASP components, 92
    ASP object model, 101
    DHTML, 177
    Document Object Model, 166
    HTML controls, 162
    Outlook forms, 102
resources, using, 193
Response object (ASP), 98
return values, functions and, 15
reusable code libraries, 32–37
reversing strings, 409
RGB function, 388
    color constants and, 445
Right, RightB functions, 389

Rnd function, 390
Round function, 392
rounding numbers, 392
routines, Exit statement for, 22
.rtf files, 124
RTrim function, 392
Run method, WshShell object, 144
    intWindowsStyle parameter values
        and, 145
RUNAT attribute, 94
Running Documents window (Script
    Debugger), 77
running WSH scripts, 126
runtime engines, 125
runtime errors, 69, 72–74
    common, list of, 88
    generating, 259
    string describing, 255
<runtime> tag, 151

S

sample code
    arrays, 52–55
        multidimensional, 60
        two-dimensional, 62
    ASP, 95
    ASP components, 191
    class methods, 26
    client-side scripting, 159, 176
    custom subroutines, 14
    data validation, 163–164
    Document Object Model
        hierarchy, 175
    encoding scripts, 464–469
    error handling/debugging, 70–88
    form submission, cancelling, 165
    functions, calling, 17
    global code, 28–31
    global.asa file, 93
    include files, 33–37
    object models, building, 195–198
    private variables, wrapping, 25
    remote scripting, 139–141
    resources, using, 194
    scope, 64, 66
    script components, 184, 187, 189
    <SCRIPT FOR> tag, 156
    <SCRIPT> tag, 157
    TypeName function, 45
    UBound function, 56
    variable name, typo in, 51

X

Y

Z

About the Authors

Paul Lomax is Technical Director of Mentorweb (*http://www.mentorweb.net/*), a leading web design and hosting company. Over the past two years, Paul has created and maintained over 60 commercial web sites for Mentorweb's clients. He is also the driving force behind ShopAssistant, a new NT/ASP-based high-end shopping cart/web commerce server (*http://www.shopassistant.com/*). He has been a programmer for over 12 years and has been a dedicated fan of Visual Basic since Version 1. Paul has written systems for financial derivatives forecasting, satellite TV broadcasting, and the life insurance industry, and he's written a major materials tracking system for the oil and gas industry. He is also responsible for the concept, design, and programming of the successful "Contact" series of national business databases. In addition, Paul has created a web resource dedicated to VBScript at *http://www.vbscripts.com/*. When not sitting in front of a keyboard, Paul can usually be found behind the wheel of a racing car competing in events around the U.K. Paul and his family—wife Deborah and children Russel and Victoria—have recently returned to their home in England after several years spent living in the Arabian Gulf.

Matt Childs is currently a Senior Systems Analyst with GCI, Alaska's leading telecommunications company, which is based in Anchorage, Alaska. Matt has over a decade of experience in the information technology field, and has worked with transportation, energy, and consulting firms during that time. Presently Matt is also working on a master's degree in History from Alaska Pacific University. He holds an undergraduate degree from the University of Alaska, Anchorage. Matt spends his free time with his wife LeAndra and their daughter Meghan, enjoying hockey games and long summer days. Born into a military family, Matt has lived in many different places, but considers Alaska to be his home.

Ron Petrusha began working with computers in the mid 1970s, programming in SPSS (a programmable statistical package) and FORTRAN on the IBM 370 family. Since then, he has been a computer book buyer, editor of a number of books on Windows and Unix, and consultant on projects written in dBASE, Clipper, and Visual Basic. Ron also has a background in quantitative labor history, specializing in Russian labor history, and holds degrees from the University of Michigan and Columbia University.

Colophon

Our look is the result of reader comments, our own experimentation, and feedback from distribution channels. Distinctive covers complement our distinctive approach to technical topics, breathing personality and life into potentially dry subjects.

The animal on the cover of *VBScript in a Nutshell*, Second Edition is a miniature pinscher. Known only to have existed in Germany up until about 100 years ago, the miniature pinscher is said to have descended from the German pinscher or is possibly a cross between the Italian greyhound and the dachshund. He is not a small Doberman pinscher, as some may think. He was bred to be a ratter and a good barking watchdog.

The miniature pinscher is considered the smallest breed of guard dog. It is classified in Group 2, which also includes the Doberman pinscher, rottweiler, mastiff, boxer, and Great Dane.

The miniature pinscher has been characterized as having a heroic demeanor and a striking personality. Pinscher owners commonly affirm that the dog is small and fragile only in appearance, not in temperament.

Mary Brady was the production editor and proofreader for *VBScript in a Nutshell*, Second Edition. Emily Quill and Claire Cloutier provided quality control. Jamie Peppard and Derek Di Matteo provided production support. Brenda Miller wrote the index.

Ellie Volckhausen designed the cover of this book, based on a series design by Edie Freedman. The cover image is a 19th-century engraving from the Dover Pictorial Archive. Emma Colby produced the cover layout with QuarkXPress 4.1 using Adobe's ITC Garamond font.

Bret Kerr designed the interior layout, based on a series design by David Futato. This book was converted by Mike Sierra to FrameMaker 5.5.6 with a format conversion tool created by Erik Ray, Jason McIntosh, Neil Walls, and Mike Sierra that uses Perl and XML technologies. The text font is Linotype Birka; the heading font is Adobe Myriad Condensed; and the code font is LucasFont's TheSans Mono Condensed. The illustrations that appear in the book were produced by Robert Romano and Jessamyn Read using Macromedia FreeHand 9 and Adobe Photoshop 6. The tip and warning icons were drawn by Christopher Bing. This colophon was written by Maureen Dempsey.

CPSIA information can be obtained
at www.ICGtesting.com
Printed in the USA
BVOW10s1450140617

486912BV00017B/301/P